RSF: The Russell Sage Foundation Journal of the Social Sciences

Undocumented Immigrants and Their Experience with Illegality

VOLUME 3 • NUMBER 4 • JULY 2017

RSF: The Russell Sage Foundation Journal of the Social Sciences ISSN 2377-8261

The Russell Sage Foundation

The Russell Sage Foundation, one of the oldest of America's general purpose foundations, was established in 1907 by Mrs. Margaret Olivia Sage for "the improvement of social and living conditions in the United States." The foundation seeks to fulfill this mandate by fostering the development and dissemination of knowledge about the country's political, social, and economic problems. While the foundation endeavors to assure the accuracy and objectivity of each book it publishes, the conclusions and interpretations in Russell Sage Foundation publications are those of the authors and not of the foundation, its trustees, or its staff. Publication by Russell Sage, therefore, does not imply foundation endorsement.

Board of Trustees

Sara S. McLanahan, *Chair*
Larry M. Bartels
Karen S. Cook
W. Bowman Cutter III
Sheldon H. Danziger
Kathryn Edin
Michael Jones-Correa
Lawrence F. Katz
David Laibson
Nicholas Lemann
Martha Minow
Peter R. Orszag
Claude M. Steele
Shelley E. Taylor
Hirokazu Yoshikawa

Mission Statement

RSF: The Russell Sage Foundation Journal of the Social Sciences is a peer-reviewed, open-access journal of original empirical research articles by both established and emerging scholars. It is designed to promote cross-disciplinary collaborations on timely issues of interest to academics, policymakers, and the public at large. Each issue is thematic in nature and focuses on a specific research question or area of interest. The introduction to each issue will include an accessible, broad, and synthetic overview of the research question under consideration and the current thinking from the various social sciences.

RSF Journal Editorial Board

Elizabeth O. Ananat, Duke University
Karen S. Cook, Stanford University
Sheldon H. Danziger, Russell Sage Foundation
Mesmin Destin, Northwestern University
Janet C. Gornick, The CUNY Graduate Center
Jennifer Hochschild, Harvard University
Mary E. Pattillo, Northwestern University
Becky Pettit, University of Texas at Austin
James Sidanius, Harvard University
Miguel S. Urquiola, Columbia University
Mary C. Waters, Harvard University

Copyright © 2017 by Russell Sage Foundation. All rights reserved. Printed in the United States of America. No part of this publication may be reproduced, stored in a retrieval system, or transmitted in any form or by any means, electronic, mechanical, photocopying, recording, or otherwise, without the prior written permission of the publisher. Reproduction by the United States Government in whole or in part is permitted for any purpose.

Opinions expressed in this journal are not necessarily those of the editors, editorial board, trustees, or the Russell Sage Foundation.

We invite scholars to submit proposals for potential issues through the *RSF* application portal: https://rsfjournal.onlineapplicationportal.com/. Submissions should be addressed to Suzanne Nichols, Director of Publications.

To view the complete text and additional features online please go to **www.rsfjournal.org**.

Russell Sage Foundation
112 East 64th Street
New York, NY 10065

ISSN (print): 2377-8253
ISSN (electronic): 2377-8261
ISBN: 978-0-87154-740-8

RSF: The Russell Sage Foundation
Journal of the Social Sciences

Undocumented Immigrants and Their Experience with Illegality

ISSUE EDITORS
Roberto G. Gonzales, Harvard University
Steven Raphael, University of California, Berkeley

CONTENTS

Illegality: A Contemporary Portrait of Immigration 1
Roberto G. Gonzales and Steven Raphael

Patterns of Family Visitation During Immigration Detention 18
Caitlin Patler and Nicholas Branic

Assessing Parental Fitness and Care for Unaccompanied Children 37
Lauren Heidbrink

Exploring the Effects of U.S. Immigration Enforcement on the Well-being of Citizen Children in Mexican Immigrant Families 53
Lauren E. Gulbas and Luis H. Zayas

Employer Sanctions and the Wages of Mexican Immigrants 70
Peter Brownell

Revisiting Ethnic Niches: A Comparative Analysis of the Labor Market Experiences of Asian and Latino Undocumented Young Adults 97
Esther Yoona Cho

Crossing the Mexico-U.S. Border: Illegality and Children's Migration to the United States 116
Katharine M. Donato and Samantha L. Perez

Parental Legal Status and the Political Engagement of Second-Generation Mexican Americans 136
Susan K. Brown and Alejandra Jazmin Sanchez

"Don't Let the Illegals Vote!": The Myths of Illegal Latino Voters and Voter Fraud in Contested Local Immigrant Integration 148
Robert Courtney Smith

Illegality: A Contemporary Portrait of Immigration

ROBERTO G. GONZALES AND STEVEN RAPHAEL

On June 23, 2016, the Supreme Court decided, by a 4-4 vote, to uphold the decisions of the lower courts, blocking President Obama's administrative actions on immigration. After years of congressional gridlock, the Obama plan would have bypassed Congress by expanding the 2012 Deferred Action for Childhood Arrivals (DACA) program to parents. The administrative action, known as Deferred Action for Parents of Americans (DAPA), would have extended deportation relief and work authorization to undocumented immigrants with citizen or lawful permanent resident children and to those who migrated at young ages but who did not meet the cutoffs for DACA. The action was challenged by Texas and twenty-five other states on the grounds that it overstepped the bounds of executive power and violated the Constitution. A Texas judge, Andrew Hanen, issued an injunction preventing the action from going into effect, which was upheld by the 5th U.S. Circuit Court of Appeals.

All told, the planned administrative actions would have provided relief to nearly five million undocumented immigrants (Capps et al. 2016). The decision was a mere nine words long, but its consequences would be felt widely because it placed the future of immigration reform and that of millions of undocumented immigrants and their families on hold.[1] That's how Isabel Reyes felt.[2] The mother of two U.S.-born children and a laundry attendant at a hotel in a Chicago suburb, Isabel had been struggling to pay her bills and take care of her children after her husband's deportation. Since February 2015, after being stopped by the police in the United States for a broken taillight, Isabel's husband and father to her children had been living in his home state of Michoacán. The incident landed him in the custody of Immigration and Customs Enforcement (ICE) and he was ultimately deported. Isabel, who had lived in Chicago for almost fifteen years, had a lot riding on the Supreme Court decision. "I was hoping things could change for me and my family. I don't know how much longer I can do this on my own. It's not

Roberto G. Gonzales is assistant professor of education at the Harvard Graduate School of Education. **Steven Raphael** is James D. Marver Professor of Public Policy at the Goldman School of Public Policy, University of California, Berkeley.

© 2017 Russell Sage Foundation. Gonzales, Roberto G., and Steven Raphael. 2017. "Illegality: A Contemporary Portrait of Immigration." *RSF: The Russell Sage Foundation Journal of the Social Sciences* 3(4): 1–17. DOI: 10.7758/RSF.2017.3.4.01. Direct correspondence to: Roberto G. Gonzales at roberto_gonzales@gse.harvard.edu, Harvard Graduate School of Education, 6 Appian Way, Cambridge, MA 02138; and Steven Raphael at stevenraphael@berkeley.edu, Goldman School of Public Policy, University of California, Berkeley, 2607 Hearst Avenue, Berkeley, CA 94720.

1. "The judgment is affirmed by an equally divided court" (Liptak and Shear 2016).

2. Isabel is a pseudonym used to preserve anonymity.

only the financial. I feel like we are living in a cage."[3]

By 2016 in communities across the United States, families like Isabel's were reeling from more than a decade of massive immigration enforcement and policies that had sown fear and distrust of law enforcement and had narrowly circumscribed their worlds. Undocumented immigrants make up about one-fourth of all immigrants living in the United States. However, the focus on undocumented migration takes on a central role in the U.S. policy agenda—often at the expense of other immigration issues (Jones-Correa and de Graauw 2013). Although President Obama's immigration actions sought to shield immigrants from deportation, his administration's enforcement policies had widened fear and distrust. In 2013, the United States removed a record 438,421 undocumented immigrants (Gonzalez-Barrera and Krogstad 2014). By 2016, the tally under Obama alone had exceeded 2.5 million, 23 percent more than during the Bush years and more than the sum total of all recorded removals prior to 1997 (Golash-Boza 2015). Cooperation between ICE and local law enforcement under 287(g) agreements and Secure Communities had created an immigration dragnet, snaring immigrants for improper lane changes and countless other noncriminal offenses. In fact, of those removed in 2013 more than half (240,000) did not have a criminal conviction.

Meanwhile, Congress's failure to enact wide-scale immigration reform has kept a large segment of settled immigrants in the shadows, cut off from the very institutions and services that have historically benefited immigrant families. Their poverty and exclusion from the formal polity are disadvantages that are also passed down to their children (Bean, Brown, and Bachmeier 2015; Yoshikawa 2011). Today, an estimated 11.3 million undocumented immigrants live with uncertain futures. However, unlike any time before in history, this population is firmly ensconced in U.S. society. Like Isabel, most have lived in the United States for a considerable time—more than half of all undocumented adults have been in the United States for at least thirteen years and about one in five for twenty years or longer (Passel et al. 2014; Gonzalez-Barrera 2015).

The longer average duration of residence in the United States translates into large numbers of undocumented immigrants married to legal permanent residents or the parents of U.S.-born children. In fact, most undocumented immigrants live in households with citizen or lawful permanent resident family members. More than 16.6 million people live in a mixed-status family with at least one undocumented immigrant (Taylor et al. 2011), and nearly half of undocumented immigrants are parents of minors. Within these families, 4.5 million are citizen children, and more than 2.1 million are undocumented but have lived in the United States since childhood (Dreby 2015; Batalova and McHugh 2010). Nearly 7 percent of all K–12 students had at least one undocumented parent in 2012. Among these students, about eight in ten were born in the United States. Deportations of these immigrants is particularly traumatizing for such families.

What's more, the overall number of undocumented immigrants has stabilized since the Great Recession. Driving much of this trend is the decrease in net migration from Mexico. In fact, since 2009 more Mexicans have departed the United States than have entered. Nonetheless, Mexicans remain the largest group among the unauthorized, making up about half of the population (Gonzalez-Barrera 2015). As a result, those living in the United States today are most likely to be long-term residents and to live in mixed-status families with American-born members.

Six states account for 60 percent of all undocumented immigrants: California, Texas, Florida, New York, New Jersey, and Illinois. However, the composition is changing. Whereas prior to the 1990s the unauthorized immigrant population was concentrated in a handful of states, today undocumented immigrants live, work, and go to school in both traditional immigrant gateways and new destination areas in the Midwest and Southeast.

Although congressional action on immigration has stalled, states and municipalities across the country have attempted to take im-

---

3. Personal interview by Roberto G. Gonzales, June 25, 2016.

migration matters into their own hands. This current political context has resulted in a mixed landscape of state and municipal policies and practices, making geographic location and local context increasingly influential in determining the treatment of immigrants and the opportunities available to them. Some states have opened up access to broader participation and integration—offering undocumented immigrants the ability to apply for driver's licenses, vote in local elections, and receive critical services. Others have adopted a more restrictive stance—for example, by attempting to criminalize unauthorized presence and exclude immigrants from public universities. This uneven geography of local law enforcement and immigration policy demonstrates that today, perhaps more so than ever before, where one resides within the United States shapes a multitude of experiences based on local impediments and opportunities.

In this issue of *RSF*, an interdisciplinary team of scholars presents stark and candid portraits of how various policy changes have impacted the welfare of undocumented immigrants, their families, and their communities. Through empirical research, qualitative analysis, and mixed-method study, the papers in this volume document and explore the consequences, intended and otherwise, of the drastic shifts in policy pertaining to the unauthorized that have occurred in the past few decades. These papers also discuss how policymakers have responded to challenges created by forces beyond the United States that have generated new waves of undocumented immigrants.

THE ENDURING LEGACY OF HART-CELLER

On October 3, 1965, at a ceremony beneath the Statue of Liberty, President Lyndon Johnson signed a landmark immigration reform bill into law. The 1965 Immigration and Nationality Act (INA), often referred to as the Hart-Celler Act, named for its principal sponsors in the Senate and House of Representatives, removed barriers against immigration from Asia and Africa and abolished the much-criticized quota system. The INA followed on the heels of the Civil Rights Act, barring discrimination on the grounds of race, color, religion, sex, or national origin. The United States could no longer maintain a system considered contradictory to its fundamental values.

In addition, 1964 saw the end of the twenty-two-year-old Bracero Program, a guest-worker initiative that supplied low-cost and flexible Mexican labor to America's farms, eliminating a primary legal avenue for temporary migration between Mexico and the United States. At the height of the program, more than five hundred thousand temporary work visas were given to agricultural workers annually. But, like the restrictive quotas of the U.S. immigration system, the program was viewed as out of balance with American ideals. By this time, however, growers in the Southwest had become heavily dependent on their flexible Mexican labor force and were unable and unwilling to find other sources of workers. Growers still demanded the labor of Mexican workers and continued to hire them despite the end of the Bracero Program. However, most were now coming through illegal channels. Moreover, the decades-long patterns of seasonal migration created strong informational links between certain Mexican sending communities and receiving communities and employers in the United States, giving rise to chain migration that survived Bracero. Although labor demand did not subside for many decades, the auspices under which labor migrants came to the United States to work—without legal authorization—changed dramatically.

President Johnson argued that the INA would not dramatically alter the demographic composition of the United States. Prior to 1965, U.S.-bound immigrants were mostly European. They were also largely white. The INA eliminated restrictive immigration policies instituted in the 1920s and created new family and skilled-worker preference categories for entry. By liberalizing the rules for immigration, prioritizing family reunification, and opening migration from Asia, Africa, the Middle East, and southern and eastern Europe, Hart-Celler stimulated a rapid growth in the numbers of new Americans and a change in the ethnic makeup of these newcomers. New ethnic enclaves emerged in several U.S. cities and existing enclaves expanded. These demographic changes refueled debates about immigration, membership, and belonging.

Meanwhile, migration from Mexico surged. However, as the sociologists Douglas Massey and Karen Pren argue, this increase occurred despite, rather than because of, the new system (2012). Before 1965, no numerical limits on immigration from the Western Hemisphere were in place. But the 1965 amendments marked an end to open borders, set limits to annual immigration from the Western Hemisphere of 120,000, and established country quotas of twenty thousand. These changes, which came shortly after the Bracero Program ended, led many employers to view undocumented migration as their only source of cheap labor.

Between 1965 and 1986, twenty-eight million Mexicans entered the United States as undocumented migrants, most for a relatively short stay, and unauthorized immigration from Mexico became a hot political issue in the United States. This ultimately resulted in the passage of the Immigration Control and Reform Act (IRCA) in 1986: the legalization of more than three million undocumented migrants, the introduction of employer sanctions, and the fortification of the border.

LEGALIZATION AND UNINTENDED CONSEQUENCES

The mid-1980s was a pivotal time for U.S. immigration policy. The resident population of unauthorized immigrants had grown to unprecedented levels, most arriving in the United States by either entering without inspection along the U.S.-Mexico border or overstaying a visa. Many had established lives in the United States, were married to lawful permanent residents or naturalized or native-born U.S. citizens, had children, and were gainfully employed with U.S. employers in various sectors. Advocates for these immigrants stressed the impossibility and inhumanity of large-scale deportation of such an established population and the direct and indirect costs such a policy would impose on U.S. society and immigrant communities in particular. Employers who relied heavily on the labor of unauthorized immigrants also stressed the importance of immigrants for their business operations and worried that mass deportations coupled with severe border restrictions would harm business and the economy.

On the other hand, latent demand among the public was to limit unauthorized immigration, to gain control of the nation's borders, and to ensure that immigration followed established legal procedure for entry and residence. Advocates for tougher enforcement stressed the need to strengthen the border, to limit the ability of unauthorized immigrants to find work in the United States and to establish consequences for both unauthorized immigrants as well as employers who knowingly hired them.

The passage of the IRCA represented a grand compromise intended to address the concerns of both sides of this debate. First, IRCA created two legalization programs, the General Amnesty and the Special Agricultural Workers provision, that together lead to the legalization through adjustment to permanent resident status of more than three million people. Second, the act made it illegal for the first time in U.S. history to knowingly hire an undocumented immigrant, and created a series of employer sanctions that graduated with more severe and repeat violations. Third, the act provided for additional enforcement resources to strengthen the border with an eye on preventing limiting future immigration flows.

The logic of IRCA was clear. The policy wiped the slate clean for those unauthorized immigrants with established lives in the United States, and made a major concession to a key class of employers (growers in particular) via a legalization for seasonal agricultural workers. At the same time, by creating a sanction system for employers and prohibiting the hiring of the unauthorized, IRCA attempted to eliminate the major pull factor that had long attracted many undocumented immigrants to the United States, namely, the prospects of higher and perhaps more stable earnings.

Despite the large numbers legalized through IRCA's two legalization programs and consequent declines in the resident number of unauthorized, the undocumented population proceeded to grow over the subsequent three decades (see figures 1 and 2). Several factors contributed to this growth. The employer

Figure 1. Undocumented Immigrant Population in the United States

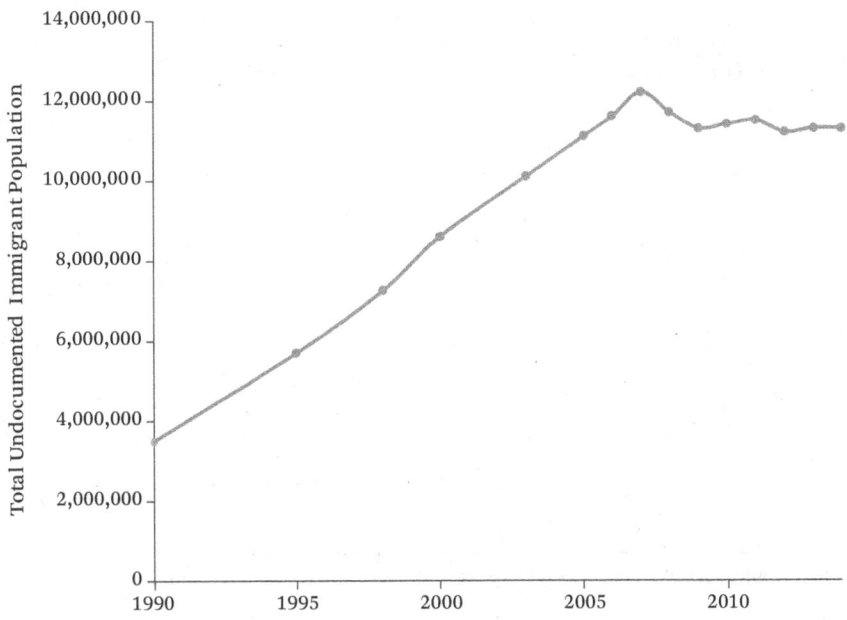

Source: Passel and Cohn 2015.

sanctions system did little to deter the hiring of undocumented migrants, effectively nullifying a key component of the IRCA enforcement strategy. The fortification of the U.S.-Mexico border certainly raised the likelihood of being apprehended. Also, subsequent changes to federal policy—increasing the sanctions for being apprehended and enhancing the volume of geographically interior enforcement (discussed in the following section)—likely deterred new entrants and return entrants to some degree. However, this latter factor coupled with the availability of employment fundamentally shifted the nature of undocumented migration in the post-IRCA period.

THE DISRUPTION OF CIRCULAR MIGRATION

In the pre-IRCA era, undocumented Mexicans were mostly seasonal labor migrants whose families remained at home. The IRCA was the first in a series of laws that fortified the nearly two-thousand-mile U.S.-Mexico border through physical barriers, higher border-enforcement staffing levels, and increased use of technology to detect migrant crossings. The greater militarization of the border made the act of crossing much more difficult, costly, and dangerous. Migrants started bringing their spouses and children to the United States to live with them and were reluctant to return home given the increased costs and risks of the trip back to the United States (Massey, Durand, and Malone 2002). In addition, the Illegal Immigration Reform and Immigrant Responsibility Act (IIRAIRA) of 1996 established bars to reentry for persons unlawfully present in the United States. The effect of these reentry bars was amplified by the expiration of 245(i), a provision that had allowed migrants to adjust their status while still within the United States. Undocumented residents were now required to return to their countries of origin to apply for legal status. However, the reentry bars are triggered on departure, creating the unintended consequence of keeping a large, settled population of unauthorized immigrants in the United States (figure 2).

Throughout the 1990s and into the twenty-first century, the number of undocumented immigrants residing in the United States grew substantially, as did efforts to address their presence and participation in U.S. society. With greater overall time in the United States, mi-

Figure 2. Proportion of Undocumented Immigrants in the United States

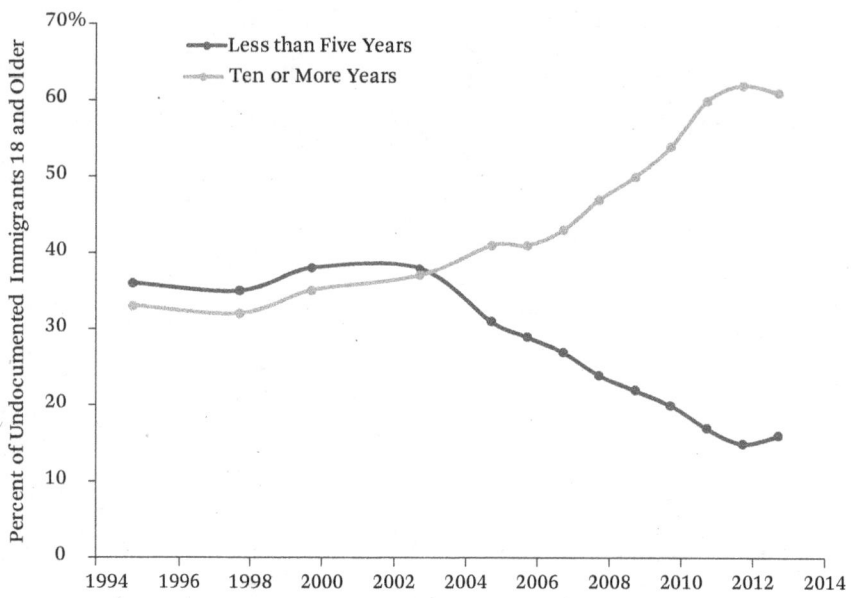

Source: Passel et al. 2014.

grant families developed deeper ties to U.S. communities. They did so through marriage, by bearing U.S.-born children who are by law U.S. citizens, and by deepening connections to employers, schools, and other institutions. All the while, the policy context made life in the United States increasingly difficult.

THE RISE OF THE "FORMIDABLE DEPORTATION MACHINE"

Over the last two decades, immigration laws and enforcement practices have narrowed the rights of noncitizens and have made neighborhoods and public spaces unsafe. Coinciding with the rise in the size of the unauthorized population residing in the United States has been the creation of a more extensive and punitive enforcement apparatus. This new infrastructure has been aimed at deporting unauthorized immigrants apprehended at the border as well from the country's interior and deterring future return migrations through accelerated deportation or severe sanctions for subsequent unlawful entry. The emergence of the "formidable deportation machine" meticulously documented by Doris Meissner and her colleagues (2013) and by Marc Rosenblum and Meissner (2014) dates to the mid-1990s.

In 1996 Congress passed the Antiterrorism and Effective Death Penalty Act (AEDPA) and the Illegal Immigration Reform and Immigrant Responsibility Act (IIRAIRA).[4] These two laws significantly expanded the number of crimes considered deportable offenses and made deportation mandatory for all immigrants sentenced to a year or more. In addition, the 1996 laws eliminated the "suspension of deportation" practice, which had protected immigrants without a criminal history deportation.[5] In consequence, the 1996 laws increased the

---

4. Public Law No. 104-132, 110 Statute 1214 (1996) and Public Law No. 104-208, 110 Statute 3009-546 (1996), respectively.

5. Prior to the passage of AEDPA and IIRIRA, § 212(c) of the Immigration and Nationality Act had provided discretionary relief from exclusion and deportation for certain noncitizens ("§ 212(c) relief"). Under § 212(c), lawful permanent residents who had lived in the United States for seven continuous years were eligible for the relief. Even permanent residents who had been convicted of an aggravated felony were eligible, as long as the term of imprisonment served was less than five years. AEDPA rendered noncitizens convicted of aggravated

number of noncitizens eligible for removal and decreased their eligibility for relief from removal proceedings, thus subjecting both noncitizens convicted of crimes and those with past criminal convictions to mandatory detention and deportation without previously available avenues of relief. Of equal consequence, the removal provisions of these laws were applied retroactively to immigrants who would not have been deported under the laws in place at the time of their original convictions. Immigrants are now left with no recourse to judicial review or appeal. And because immigration courts are civil rather than criminal, the right to counsel does not apply.

During the pre-IRCA era and through the first half of the 1990s, deportations usually involved the voluntary returns of immigrants apprehended at the border or within the border region apprehended at internal checkpoints. Formal removal proceedings from the interior of the nation were relatively rare, were subject to judicial review, and for the most part resulted when what was then the Immigration and Naturalization Service (INS) received an anonymous tip or when an undocumented immigrant committed a serious felony resulting in a fairly lengthy prison term.

Since 1996, this infrastructure has been strengthened by increased staffing levels for the U.S. Customs and Border Protection (CPB) (which is responsible for border enforcement and monitoring) and the ICE (which is responsible for interior enforcement of immigration law), both key operational components of the Department of Homeland Security (DHS). In addition, new modes of cooperation between local enforcement and ICE (at first voluntary and then mandatory) have greatly facilitated identifying deportable immigrants, among both the unauthorized and legal permanent residents with documented criminal histories.

Several major qualitative changes since 1996 have also changed the deportation landscape. To begin, the process of formally removing someone from the United States has been greatly streamlined. Prior to 1996, formal deportations—referred to as *removals*—required judicial review by an immigration judge. Since 1996, the removal process has been expedited for individuals apprehended at the border or individuals with a prior removal order (via reinstatement of a removal order). The alternative to a formal removal is a voluntary return, a less punitive avenue. A formal removal carries heavy consequences, including a ban on reentry for a fixed period depending on the number of prior removals and the rendering of any subsequent attempt to enter the United States a felony punishable by a federal prison sentence. In recent years, the CPB as well as ICE have deliberately processed more individuals as formal removals rather than returns in an effort to deter future return migration through raising the potential sanctions if apprehended. As a consequence, immigration-related felonies and admissions to federal prisons for immigration related offenses have been the fastest growing components of court dockets and federal prison admissions flows since the turn of the century (Sklansky 2012; Rosenblum et al. 2014).

Second, the scope of the definition of who is deportable for an *aggravated felony* expanded greatly. Prior to 1996, formal removals for criminal conduct was limited to unauthorized immigrants and legal permanent residents who had committed and been convicted of relatively serious crimes receiving fairly lengthy prison sentences. The 1996 legislation created a more inclusive definition of who is a deportable criminal alien, with provisions for retrospective application to the unauthorized and to legal permanent residents alike.

Third, following the September 11 terrorist attacks and the consolidation of border enforcement and immigration services under the umbrella of DHS, interior enforcement activity greatly increased. Apprehensions made in the interior of the country nearly always result in formal removals, either expedited for those with prior removal orders or subject to judicial

---

felonies ineligible for discretionary relief from deportation under § 212(c). Effective April 1, 1997, IIRAIRA § 304(b) repealed INA § 212(c) altogether and eliminated all possibility of relief under the old rule. IIRAIRA provided for a form of discretionary relief available to a small group of noncitizens that did not include noncitizens convicted of an aggravated felony, regardless of the length of sentence served.

review. Moreover, staffing levels for CPB and ICE have grown considerably, increasing both the risk of apprehension at the border and the risk of detection and removal from the interior.

Fourth, enforcement actions have increasingly resulted from information gathered in the process of local criminal justice enforcement. This began with the creation of 287(g) agreements, named for the section of the amended INA that authorized such memoranda of agreement, that provided training to local law enforcement and delegates authority to local law enforcement to enforce immigration law within its jurisdiction. This was enhanced by the introduction and complete roll out across U.S. correctional institutions of the Secure Communities program between 2008 and 2014. Secure Communities forwards fingerprints normally collected in the process of booking criminal defendants following an arrest or admission of those convicted of a crime to prison or jail to the Department of Homeland Security. Such information is typically sent to state attorneys general to be entered into state criminal history repositories and forwarded onto the Federal Bureau of Investigation as part of the Interstate Identification Index program. Hence, Secure Communities does not require additional information or the cooperation of local authorities in identifying deportable aliens who pass through the nation's jails and prisons. The program simply dipped into an existing information flow between localities and the federal government. When DHS identifies a deportable alien, they issue a forty-eight-hour hold notice to the local authorities to facilitate detention and the commencement of formal removal proceedings. Participation is not voluntary and local agencies cannot opt out of participating. Furthermore, in 2009, Senator Robert Byrd (D-WV), then chairman of the Appropriations Subcommittee on Homeland Security, added language to the federal budget tying federal funding for ICE's detention budget to a requirement to "maintain a level of not less than 33,400 detention beds on a daily basis" (increased in 2013 to thirty-four thousand).[6] This directive became known as the immigrant detention quota

or bed mandate, and is thought to have driven up immigration enforcement. Secure Communities was discontinued in 2014 and replaced with the Priority Enforcements Program (PEP), which defined a narrower scope of individuals with more serious criminal histories for targeted deportation efforts. Nevertheless, similarities remain, particularly the integration between local law enforcement and ICE.

Collectively, these changes have increased the number of formal removals from the country, increased deportations resulting from interior enforcement, and greatly increased the costs and potential sanctions associated with reentry. The cumulative effects of these changes on enforcement aggregates is evident in figure 3. The figure displays apprehensions of undocumented immigrants, aggregate returns without a removal order, and formal removals from the country from 1980 to 2013. Apprehensions and returns closely chart one another, apprehensions declining by large amounts in recent years as there have been fewer attempts to cross the border without inspection. Formal removals increased notably in 1996 and accelerated after the turn of the century.

All told, these developments radically transformed U.S. enforcement practices and thus life in the United States for undocumented immigrants. Over the last decade, hundreds of thousands of immigrants have been placed in removal proceedings after being arrested or cited for minor traffic violations such as right turns on red lights, U-turns, and failing to use a turn signal when changing lanes or turning (Alonzo et al. 2011). These practices have had the effect of ratcheting up fear and anxiety in communities across the United States that include immigrants, but also their spouses, neighbors, employers, and teachers.

THE LIVED EXPERIENCES OF ILLEGALITY TODAY

Today, the United States finds itself in the same position it did prior to the passage of IRCA, though with some key and very salient differences.

First, the population of undocumented immigrants is large. Although the population

---

6. Department of Homeland Security Appropriations Act, 2010.

Figure 3. Immigrant Apprehensions, Returns, and Removals

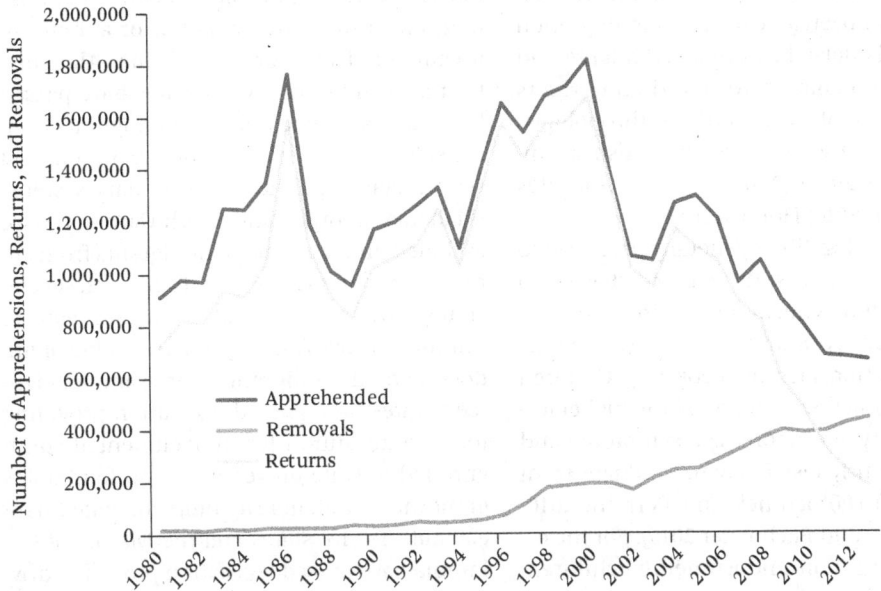

Source: U.S. Department of Homeland Security 2014.

now is much larger, more settled, more integrated into U.S. society, and through births and marriage, more likely to be tied to U.S. citizens and legal residents, then and now a large resident foreign-born population hangs in the balance of U.S. policy decisions.

Second, many employers (if not entire industries) remain that rely heavily on the labor of undocumented immigrants despite the provisions of IRCA. By most accounts, the employer sanctions provisions and the attempt to limit employment opportunities for undocumented workers have been utter failures. Complying with IRCA requires that employers make a good faith effort to establish the identity and work eligibility of a job applicant by reviewing one of several forms of identification listed in the I-9 form (such as passport, birth certificate, social security card, or green card). Complying with these requirements does not involve verifying the authenticity of these documents, and thus the use of fraudulent documents became widespread in the immediate aftermath of IRCA's passage. Moreover, few resources have been devoted to enforcing the prohibition against hiring the unauthorized, naturally resulting in very low deterrence. Employer sanctions have had one important effect on U.S. labor market outcomes. Namely, in the pre-IRCA period, empirical evidence was scant of a wage penalty for being unauthorized once the effects of observable characteristics such as age, education, and English language ability were controlled for. In the post-IRCA period, however, a sizable wage penalty has emerged, suggesting either that employers are passing on the expected costs of sanctions to undocumented workers or that employers have somehow gained the upper hand on undocumented workers as a result of the law and are therefore paying such workers relatively less.

Third, we again observe strong demand among sizable portions of the U.S. public to address undocumented immigration and quite vocal support at least among Republican primary voters for presidential candidates emphasizing a nativist agenda.

As mentioned, policies and enforcement practices that have disrupted circular migration patterns have dramatically increased the number of settled migrants who are long-term stayers with families. These contours makes the unprecedented and wide-scale enforcement practices all the more anxiety inducing, as today's migrants have a greater stake in staying in the United States. All the while, Congress has not been able to act on immigration reform. This delay has produced a large and vulnerable population with shrinking rights and high levels of stress. As the anthropologist Sarah Willen observes, illegality is also an embodied experience (2007; see also Gonzales 2016; Horton 2016; Holmes 2013).

Although illegality is generally perceived to affect adult migrants, these trends have also had deleterious effects on children growing up in the United States (Yoshikawa, Suárez-Orozco, and Gonzales, forthcoming). Children with undocumented parents exhibit higher levels of anxiety and depressive symptoms and are significantly less likely to graduate from high school (Potochnick and Perreira 2010; Bean, Brown, and Bachmeier 2015). For the estimated 2.1 million undocumented children, legal barriers multiply as they begin to make critical developmental transitions (Batalova and McHugh 2010; Abrego 2006; Gonzales 2011; Smith 2008; Suárez-Orozco, Suárez-Orozco, and Todorova 2009). And, because political discourse around immigration has focused almost exclusively on undocumented immigrants, dawning adolescence also brings a growing awareness of the stigma associated with undocumented status (Abrego 2008; Abrego and Gonzales 2010; Castro-Salazar and Bagley 2010). For many young people, this can be discomforting, causing them to withdraw from school and to constrict their social networks (Gonzales 2016; Gonzales and Chavez 2012; Perez et al. 2009). Taken together, growing up under such circumstances can lead to feelings of frustration and increased worry about the future (Gonzales, Suárez-Orozco, and Dedios 2013).

In the absence of comprehensive immigration reform from the federal government, several states have taken it upon themselves to pass legislation that targets the hiring of undocumented immigrants (such as Arizona's 2007 Legal Arizona Workers Act), enhances the ability of law enforcement to identify undocumented immigrants and turn them over to the federal government (Arizona's SB1070), or makes it a crime to be an undocumented immigrant in the state or harbor or aid an undocumented immigrant (Arizona, Alabama, Utah). In addition, several states have passed bills that bar undocumented immigrants from consideration for in-state college tuition, and several states' public postsecondary systems (Alabama, Georgia, and South Carolina) have excluded undocumented immigrants from enrolling in their institutions. To be sure, several states have taken legislative action meant to improve the lives and expand the rights of undocumented immigrants. For example, eighteen states have passed legislation providing for in-state tuition for undocumented youth enrolled in state universities, and four states grant these students eligibility for state financial aid.[7] Twelve states and the District of Columbia have passed legislation providing drivers' licenses to undocumented immigrants. Today, more so than ever before, where one lives dramatically shapes experiences of illegality and integration (Coleman 2012; Olivas 2007).

More recently, the Obama administration has used its executive authority to provide relief from deportation and temporary work authorization to undocumented youth who arrived as children via the Deferred Action for Childhood Arrivals (DACA) program. In the short term, this program has provided a significant boost to its beneficiaries (Gonzales, Terriquez, and Ruszczyk 2014). The administration has also attempted to extend comparable relief and temporary privileges to the unauthorized parents of U.S.-born children through the DAPA program, though, as already discussed, the recent Supreme Court 4-4 decision has effectively shelved this effort. Hence, in the legislative vacuum left by federal government inaction, state level legislation and executive actions on the part of the part of President Obama reflecting the heterogeneity in political sentiment regarding undocumented immigration are filling the void.

In 2014, nearly sixty-nine thousand children from El Salvador, Guatemala, and Honduras, many of whom were under the age of twelve,

---

7. See National Conference of State Legislatures, http://www.ncsl.org/research/immigration/in-state-tuition-and-unauthorized-immigrants.aspx (accessed November 8, 2015).

made their way to the U.S.-Mexico border, traveling without adults and at great risk (USICE 2015). Some fled their countries to escape gang violence; others were trying to join family members already in the United States (Hipsman and Meissner 2015). This surge strained detention facilities and overwhelmed state and municipal governments. Although a small number of these children have been granted asylum and some communities have welcomed them, many others have closed their doors and their presence has reignited debates about border security. The numbers of those arriving at the U.S. border declined the following year, but the immigration status of many of these children remains in limbo and local governments and institutions are struggling to adequately address a wide range of needs (Dryden-Peterson 2015).

STUDYING EXPERIENCES OF ILLEGALITY

Over the last two to three decades, an interdisciplinary group of social scientists, sociologists, demographers, and anthropologists have examined border enforcement, the social and economic costs of migration, labor market effects, gender and other forms of stratification, and health and welfare (Donato and Armenta 2011). Early studies in this area focused on the role of undocumented labor and the experiences of undocumented workers in specific labor sectors or settings (Portes 1978; Bustamonte 1977; Burawoy 1976). As scholars began to conduct binational community studies, much of the scholarship focused on the relationship between rural sending communities in Mexico and (mostly undocumented) migrants' experiences of settlement in the United States (Massey et al. 1990). Soon after, demographers began carrying out quantitative analyses to assess the labor market effects of undocumented workers (Bean, Telles, and Lowell 1987; Warren and Passel 1987). Then, throughout the late 1980s and 1990s, ethnographic research began to explore the everyday experiences of undocumented immigrants as they made lives in U.S. communities (Hagan 1994; Delgado 1993; Chavez 1992; Rodriguez 1987).

Several perspectives have shaped this scholarship. Earlier research viewed illegality as a *process*, beginning when migrants crossed an invisible yet deeply political border, and continuing as they navigate life in the shadows (Eschbach et al. 1999; Chavez 1992). A second perspective has viewed illegality as a *juridical status* assigned to migrants who arrive outside formal or authorized channels or who become unauthorized through an expired visa or through a change in the law. A more recent perspective has shifted the analytic focus away from studying undocumented people as "bearers of illegality" (Menjívar and Kanstroom 2013). This approach instead examines the mechanisms that produce and sustain illegality (Goldring, Berenstein, and Bernhard 2009; Menjívar 2006; Ngai 2004; De Genova 2002; Coutin 1999). Contemporary ethnographic accounts have delved into the experiences of deportation (Boehm 2016; Golash-Boza 2015), low-wage work (Holmes 2013; Gomberg-Muñoz 2011; Zlolniski 2006), and experiences in new immigrant destinations (Stuesse 2016; Ribas 2015; Marrow 2011). Finally, much attention has been paid to the circumstances of children and youth, particularly their coming of age experiences in education and the workforce (Gonzales 2011, 2016; Enriquez 2011, 2014; Terriquez 2015; Abrego 2006, 2008).

Indeed, the growth of large, settled populations lacking legal status has raised many questions of how different segments of these populations are being incorporated into host societies, what factors determine different pathways and outcomes, and how the condition of illegality shapes their everyday lives.

THE CURRENT EXPERIENCE OF ILLEGALITY IN THE UNITED STATES

The lived experience of illegality in the United States today is dramatically different than in the pre-IRCA days. The likelihood of apprehension at both the border and the interior has increased, as has the severity of the consequences of apprehension. Nevertheless, the current undocumented population has stronger social ties to the United States and longer tenures in the country. The numbers affected by this experience are at historical highs. Moreover, the numbers indirectly affected via the illegality of a parent, a sibling, or a member of one's extended family are even larger.

The articles in this issue address the current experience of illegality in the United States, as lived directly by undocumented immigrants and indirectly by their families. The papers are organized around three broad themes: the direct and indirect experiences of being on the receiving end of immigration enforcement, how undocumented immigrants adapt to their illegality or their quasi-legality, and the impact of illegality and immigrant identity on political incorporation and civic participation.

Caitlin Patler and Nicholas Branic present one of the first analyses of a troubling by-product of the rise in deportation: namely, the increase in the population of detainees in formal removal proceedings and the effects on family members and family connections. The authors analyze an original survey of individuals in an immigration detention facility in California who have been detained for at least six months as a result of a deportation removal process. The authors focus on the contact these individuals have with their families, specifically on contact with children. The paper builds on a growing body of literature studying the determinants of visitation of the detained and the effects of visitation and various behavioral outcomes.

A major recent development in immigration trends in the United States is the surge in unaccompanied minors migrating primarily from the Central American countries of Guatemala, Honduras, and El Salvador. These minors present particular challenges to U.S. immigration policy because many have distant relatives in the United States and are fleeing violence and poverty in their home countries. Nonetheless, the United States faces the challenge of processing these children, screening the suitability of family members that step forward to serve as temporary guardians, and adjudicating their petitions to remain in the country. Lauren Heidbrink draws on interviews with unaccompanied minors in the custody of the Office of Refugee Resettlement (ORR) in the U.S. Department of Health and Human Services, individuals that apply sometimes (successfully and sometimes not) to sponsor such minors with the aim of freeing them from ORR custody, and officials in ORR detention centers to study the process that governs ORR release from detention. The paper highlights the manner in which ORR often negates the agency of unaccompanied minors and fails to recognize conventional kinship networks and social roles that are common in the cultures of sending countries yet often inconsistent with western notions of the appropriate social roles of legal minors. The paper presents detailed analysis of how the prescribed activities by ORR for these youth (attending school, engaging in after school activities, socializing) often conflict with the child's sense of responsibility to members of the households, and the extreme barriers that ORR places in attempting to ensure that youth will not come to harm in the homes of sponsors. The discussion of home visits is particularly revealing, because the ORR is imposing standards on family and kin in determining suitability that are beyond what would be imposed by child protective services across the country

Of course, the experience of illegality effects the children of the undocumented, both those who are undocumented as well as those who are U.S.-born citizens. Lauren Gulbas and Luis Zayas analyze the effects of having undocumented parents on the welfare of U.S. citizen children through a series of open-ended interviews with children in the United States and Mexico. The authors focus on three groups of children: U.S. citizen children who follow a deported parent to Mexico, citizen children of deported parents who remain in the United States, and citizen children with undocumented parents who have not had a parent deported as of the date of the interview. Through a systematic analysis of interview transcripts, the authors discuss common themes regarding the hardships and challenges created by the deportation of an undocumented parent (or the threat of deportation), how this affects the child's role within the household, and the factors particular to these population that foster resiliency.

The new reality of being undocumented in the United States has required that undocumented immigrants adapt accordingly. These adaptions may involve settling for lower wages, limiting ambitions about educational attainment and occupational mobility, and for the lucky few who have achieved partial adjustment through DACA, adapting to these new privileges within the context of being the member of a family where others are still constrained by their legal status.

Peter Brownell tests for an effect of employer sanctions risk (operationalized as fines per employee year and the likelihood of an audit by year, industry and state) on the wages of Mexican workers as measured in Mexican Migration Project (MPP) data. Theoretically, the expected value of a fine acts as a tax, the incidence of which should partly be born on the supply side of the labor market. In addition, the author is interested in the extent to which this tax explains the widening gap in earnings between legal and unauthorized workers post-IRCA. The findings suggest that employer sanctions play at most a minor role, with a small significant effect of the fines on wages. These effects do not differ for undocumented and documented Mexican workers, suggesting that the fines may be affecting wages through statistical discrimination against foreign-born Mexican workers more generally. The author does some back-of-the-envelope calculations showing the aggregate magnitude of the post-IRCA unauthorized wage penalty and how this overwhelms the total employer-paid fines. Hence, even if the fines were totally passed off onto the supply side of the market, they could not possibly explain the wage disadvantage that undocumented workers in the post-IRCA period experience. The analysis suggests that the balance of power has shifted to employers, and that employers take advantage of this change to pay the undocumented less than they otherwise would.

Esther Yoona Cho provides an analysis of the experience of college-educated 1.5-generation undocumented youth in California, focusing on how these individuals negotiate the transition from college to the job market and adapt to the limited opportunity structure they face as a direct result of their undocumented status. The paper presents a comparative analysis of undocumented youth from South Korea and Mexico, and provides a rich portrayal of the difference ethnic occupation networks that they can access after college. The South Korean entrepreneurial community is more varied and offers a richer set of informal (in the sense that they pay cash) opportunities that better matches the skills sets of undocumented college graduates. By contrast, the Latino youth are able to access service-sector, very low-paying jobs through their social networks with a great gulf between the skills they acquire in college and what is demanded of them in the workplace. The exception is for those youth who are involved in the pan-ethnic nonprofits serving the Latino communities, where it is often possible to work as an independent contractor.

Katharine Donato and Samantha Perez analyze data from the MPP to document differences in the migration arrangements of Mexican children and how they vary across broad time periods separable by policy events. The authors look at three broad periods (pre-IRCA, or before 1986; pre-IIRAIRA, or before 1996; and post-IIRAIRA, or after 1996) and assess how the migration experience of authorized and unauthorized children vary. The focus here is whether the children migrate alone, with siblings only, or with parents and siblings and the sensitivity of this choice to the enforcement policy environment.

Clearly, undocumented immigrants cannot formally participate in the political process. To the extent that the U.S.-born children of undocumented immigrants do not observe their parents voting, attending public forum, and engaging in other less formal forms of civic participation, they may also participate less as adults despite their citizenship. Moreover, citizens may act to prevent political participation of immigrants, perhaps due to suspicions regarding legal status, or perhaps due to differential priorities regarding local state and federal government spending levels and services. Susan Brown and Alejandra Jazmin Sanchez analyze data from the Immigration and Intergeneration Mobility in Metropolitan Los Angeles Survey to study the effects of having an unauthorized mother on a measure of political integration and political knowledge. The authors present a theoretical discussion of the avenues through which parental immigration status may impact political participation and then test for an impact in a series of multivariate model estimates. The principal findings of this study are that children of unauthorized mothers are less likely to be politically integrated and knowledgeable as young adults. However, this effect appears to be entirely mediated through the educational attainment of the 1.5- or second-generation youth. This paper highlights an important dimension of civic assimilation that has received relatively little serious research attention.

Finally, Robert Courtney Smith provides a detailed case study of a voting rights dispute in Port Chester, New York. Although the town is characterized as generally progressive and welcoming of immigration, a sizable minority of its population believes that undocumented immigrants who are ineligible to vote may seek to do so fraudulently in an effort to steer local policy in a direction more favorably to the relatively new Latino community. The paper presents a detailed discussion of several town meetings, the process and outcomes associated with a federal lawsuit brought against the town by the justice department alleging violation of the Voting Rights Act, detailed analysis of local politics and the role of race and ethnicity in mobilizing blocks of voters and efforts to suppress votes, and the broader narratives that frame the public debate. The paper also details some of the complexities of the key individuals involved in these dispute: politicians at once castigating hecklers harassing speakers of Hispanic origin at a public forum and then anonymously distributing racially inflammatory material, friendships among individuals on both sides of the political divide, and complex sometimes inconsistent views pertaining to immigration and politics in their community. The paper is rich in detail and illustrates many of the direct avenues by which small actions can disenfranchise and marginalize a group. The author situates these conflicts in terms of both racial-ethnic animus as well as simple ethnic politics and power brokering.

CONCLUSION

The large population of undocumented immigrants in the United States poses one of the most pressing, and politically difficult policy problems of the new century. Since the failure of the bipartisan effort at immigration reform in the senate in 2013, undocumented immigration and immigration policy more generally has become a highly salient and polarizing topic. Lost in the intensity of current political conflict is the experience of undocumented immigrants themselves and a measured discussion of the impact policy has on the experience of being undocumented and the impact the undocumented have on the nation.

REFERENCES

Abrego, Leisy J. 2006. "'I Can't Go to College Because I Don't Have Papers': Incorporation Patterns of Latino Undocumented Youth." *Latino Studies* 4(3): 212–31.

———. 2008. "Legitimacy, Social Identity, and the Mobilization of Law: The Effects of Assembly Bill 540 on Undocumented Students in California." *Law & Social Inquiry* 33(3): 709–34.

Abrego, Leisy J., and Roberto G. Gonzales. 2010. "Blocked Paths, Uncertain Futures: The Postsecondary Education and Labor Market Prospects of Undocumented Latino Youth." *Journal of Education for Students Placed at Risk* 15(1–2): 144–57.

Alonzo, Alexsa, Kristin Macleod-Ball, Greg Chen, and Su Kim. 2011. "Immigration Enforcement Off Target: Minor Offenses with Major Consequences." AILA Doc. no. 11081609. Washington, D.C.: American Immigration Lawyers Association.

Batalova, Jeanne, and Margie McHugh. 2010. "DREAM vs. Reality: An Analysis of Potential DREAM Act Beneficiaries." Washington, D.C.: Migration Policy Institute, National Center on Immigrant Integration Policy.

Bean, Frank D., Susan K. Brown, and James D. Bachmeier. 2015. *Parents Without Papers: The Progress and Pitfalls of Mexican American Integration*. New York: Russell Sage Foundation.

Bean, Frank D., Edward E. Telles, and B. Lindsay Lowell. 1987. "Undocumented Migration to the United States: Perceptions and Evidence." *Population and Development Review* 13(4): 671–90.

Boehm, Deborah. 2016. *Returned: Going and Coming in an Age of Deportation*. Oakland: University of California Press.

Brown, Susan K., and Alejandra Jazmin Sanchez. 2017. "Parental Legal Status and the Political Engagement of Second-Generation Mexican Americans." *RSF: The Russell Sage Foundation Journal of the Social Sciences* 3(4): 136–47. DOI: 10.7758/RSF.2017.3.4.08.

Brownell, Peter. 2017. "Employer Sanctions and the Wages of Mexican Immigrants." *RSF: The Russell*

Sage Foundation Journal of the Social Sciences 3(4): 70–96. DOI: 10.7758/RSF.2017.3.4.05.

Burawoy, Michael. 1976. "The Functions and Reproduction of Migrant Labor: Comparative Material from Southern Africa and the United States." *American Journal of Sociology* 81(5): 1050–87.

Bustamante, Jorge A. 1977. "Undocumented Immigration from Mexico: Research Report." *International Migration Review* 11(2): 149–77.

Capps, Randy, Heather Koball, James D. Bachmeier, Ariel G. Ruiz Soto, Jie Zong, and Julia Gelatt. 2016. "Deferred Action for Unauthorized Immigrant Parents: Analysis of DAPA's Potential Effects on Families and Children." Washington, D.C.: Migration Policy Institute.

Castro-Salazar, Ricardo, and Carl Bagley. 2010. "'Ni de aquí ni from there': Navigating Between Contexts: Counter-Narratives of Undocumented Mexican Students in the United States." *Race Ethnicity and Education* 13(1): 23–40.

Chavez, Leo. R. 1992. *Shadowed Lives: Undocumented Immigrants in American Society*. San Antonio, Tex.: Harcourt Brace Jovanovich.

Cho, Esther Yoona. 2017. "Revisiting Ethnic Niches: A Comparative Analysis of the Labor Market Experiences of Asian and Latino Undocumented Young Adults." *RSF: The Russell Sage Foundation Journal of the Social Sciences* 3(4): 97–115. DOI: 10.7758/RSF.2017.3.4.06.

Coleman, Matthew 2012. "The 'Local' Migration State: The Site-Specific Devolution of Immigration Enforcement in the U.S. South." *Law & Policy* 34(2): 159–90.

Coutin, S. B. 1999. "Citizenship and Clandestiny Among Salvadoran Immigrants." *PoLAR: Political and Legal Anthropology Review* 22(2): 53–63.

De Genova, Nicholas P. 2002. "'Migrant Illegality' and Deportability in Everyday Life." *Annual Review of Anthropology* 31 (October): 419–47.

Delgado, Héctor L. 1993. *New Immigrants, Old Unions: Organizing Undocumented Workers in Los Angeles*. Philadelphia, Pa.: Temple University Press.

Donato, Katharine M., and Amada Armenta. 2011. "What We Know About Unauthorized Migration." *Annual Review of Sociology* 37: 529–43.

Donato, Katharine M., and Samantha L. Perez. 2017. "Crossing the Mexico-U.S. Border: Illegality and Children's Migration to the United States." *RSF: The Russell Sage Foundation Journal of the Social Sciences* 3(4): 116–35. DOI: 10.7758/RSF.2017.3.4.07.

Dreby, Joanna. 2015. *Everyday Illegal: When Policies Undermine Immigrant Families*. Oakland: University of California Press.

Dryden-Peterson, Sarah. 2015. "The Educational Experiences of Refugee Children in Countries of First Asylum." Washington, D.C.: Migration Policy Institute.

Enriquez, Laura E., 2011. "'Because We Feel the Pressure and We Also Feel the Support": Examining the Educational Success of Undocumented Immigrant Latina/o Students." *Harvard Educational Review* 81(3): 476–500.

——. 2014. "'Undocumented and Citizen Students Unite': Building a Cross-Status Coalition Through Shared Ideology." *Social Problems* 61(2): 155–74.

Eschbach, Karl, Jacqueline Hagan, Nestor Rodriguez, Ruben Hernandez-Leon, and Stanley Bailey. 1999. "Death at the Border." *International Migration Review* 33(2): 430–54.

Golash-Boza, Tanya. 2015. *Deported: Immigrant Policing, Disposable Labor and Global Capitalism*. New York: NYU Press.

Goldring, Luin, Carolina Berinstein, and Judith K. Bernhard. 2009. "Institutionalizing Precarious Migratory Status in Canada." *Citizenship Studies* 13(3): 239–65.

Gomberg-Muñoz, Ruth. 2011. *Labor and Legality: An Ethnography of a Mexican Immigrant Network*. New York: Oxford University Press.

Gonzales, Roberto G. 2011. "Learning to be Illegal: Undocumented Youth and Shifting Legal Contexts in the Transition to Adulthood." *American Sociological Review* 76(4): 602–19.

——.2016. *Lives in Limbo: Undocumented and Coming of Age in America*. Oakland: University of California Press.

Gonzales, Roberto G., and Leo R. Chavez. 2012. "Awakening to a Nightmare: Abjectivity and Illegality in the Lives of Undocumented 1.5-Generation Latino Immigrants in the United States." *Current Anthropology* 53(3): 255–81.

Gonzales, Roberto G., Carola Suárez-Orozco, and Maria Cecilia Dedios. 2013. "No Place to Belong: Contextualizing Concepts of Mental Health among Undocumented Immigrant Youth in the United States." *American Behavioral Scientist* 57(8): 1173–98.

Gonzales, Roberto G., Veronica Terriquez, and Stephen P. Ruszczyk. 2014. "Becoming DACAmented Assessing the Short-Term Benefits of Deferred Action for Childhood Arrivals (DACA)." *American Behavioral Scientist* 58(14): 1852–72.

Gonzalez-Barrera, Ana. 2015. "More Mexicans Leaving than Coming to the U.S." Washington, D.C.: Pew Research Center.

Gonzalez-Barrera, Ana, and J. M. Krogstad. 2014. "U.S. Deportations of Immigrants Reach Record High in 2013." Washington, D.C.: Pew Research Center.

Gulbas, Lauren E., and Luis H. Zayas. 2017. "Exploring the Effects of U.S. Immigration Enforcement on the Well-being of Citizen Children in Mexican Immigrant Families." *RSF: The Russell Sage Foundation Journal of the Social Sciences* 3(4): 53–69. DOI: 10.7758/RSF.2017.3.4.04.

Hagan, Jacqueline Maria. 1994. *Deciding to be Legal: A Maya Community in Houston*. Philadelphia, Pa.: Temple University Press.

Heidbrink, Lauren. 2017. "Assessing Parental Fitness and Care for Unaccompanied Children." *RSF: The Russell Sage Foundation Journal of the Social Sciences* 3(4): 37–52. DOI: 10.7758/RSF.2017.3.4.03.

Hipsman, Faye, and Doris Meissner, 2015. "In-Country Processing in Central America: A Piece of the Puzzle." Washington, D.C.: Migration Policy Institute.

Holmes, Seth. 2013. *Fresh Fruit, Broken Bodies: Migrant Farmworkers in the United States*. Berkeley: University of California Press.

Horton, Sarah Bronwen. 2016. *They Leave Their Kidneys in the Fields: Illness, Injury, and Illegality Among U.S. Farmworkers*. Berkeley: University of California Press.

Jones-Correa, Michael, and Els de Graauw. 2013. "The Illegality Trap: The Politics of Immigration & the Lens of Illegality." *Daedalus* 142(3): 185–98.

Liptak, Adam, and Michael D. Shear. 2016. "Supreme Court Tie Blocks Obama's Plan." *New York Times*, June 23.

Marrow, Helen. 2011. *New Destination Dreaming: Immigration, Race, and Legal Status in the Rural American South*. Palo Alto, Calif.: Stanford University Press.

Massey, Douglas S., Rafael Alarcón, Jorge Durand, and Humberto Gonzalez. 1990. *Return to Aztlan: The Social Process of International Migration from Western Mexico*. Berkeley: University of California Press.

Massey, Douglas S., Jorge Durand, and Nolan J. Malone. 2002. *Beyond Smoke and Mirrors: Mexican Immigration in an Era of Economic Integration*. New York: Russell Sage Foundation.

Massey, Douglas S., and Karen A. Pren. 2012. "Unintended Consequences of US Immigration Policy: Explaining the Post-1965 Surge from Latin America." *Population and Development Review* 38(1): 1–29.

Meissner, Doris, Donald M. Kerwin, Muzaffar Chishti, and Claire Bergeron. 2013. "Immigration Enforcement in the United States: The Rise of a Formidable Machinery." Washington, D.C.: Migration Policy Institute.

Menjívar, Cecilia. 2006. "Liminal Legality: Salvadoran and Guatemalan Immigrants' Lives in the United States." *American Journal of Sociology* 111(4): 999–1037.

Menjívar, Cecilia, and Daniel Kanstroom, eds. 2013. *Constructing Immigrant 'Illegality': Critiques, Experiences, and Responses*. Cambridge: Cambridge University Press.

Ngai, Mae. 2004. *Impossible Subjects: Illegal Immigrants and the Making of Modern America*. Princeton, N.J.: Princeton University Press.

Olivas, Michael A. 2007. "Immigration-Related State and Local Ordinances: Preemption, Prejudice, and the Proper Role for Enforcement." *University of Chicago Legal Forum* 2007(1): 27–56.

Passel, Jeffrey S., and D'Vera Cohn. 2015. "Unauthorized Immigrant Population Stable for Half a Decade." Washington, D.C.: Pew Research Center.

Passel, Jeffrey S., D'Vera Cohn, Jens Manuel Krogstad, and Ana Gonzalez-Barrera. 2014. "As Growth Stalls, Unauthorized Immigrant Population Becomes More Settled." Washington, D.C.: Pew Research Center's Hispanic Trends Project.

Patler, Caitlin, and Nicholas Branic. 2017. "Patterns of Family Visitation During Immigration Detention." *RSF: The Russell Sage Foundation Journal of the Social Sciences* 3(4): 18–36. DOI: 10.7758/RSF.2017.3.4.02.

Perez, William, Roberta Espinoza, Karina Ramos, Heidi M. Coronado, and Richard Cortes. 2009. "Academic Resilience Among Undocumented Latino Students." *Hispanic Journal of Behavioral Sciences* 31(2): 149–81.

Portes, Alejandro. 1978. "Introduction: Toward a Structural Analysis of Illegal (Undocumented) Immigration." *International Migration Review* 12(4): 469–84.

Potochnick, Stephanie R., and Krista M. Perreira,

2010. "Depression and Anxiety Among First-Generation Immigrant Latino Youth: Key Correlates and Implications for Future Research." *Journal of Nervous and Mental Disease* 198(7): 470–77.

Ribas, Vanesa. 2015. *On the Line: Slaughterhouse Lives and the Making of the New South*. Oakland: University of California Press.

Rodriguez, Nestor P. 1987. "Undocumented Central Americans in Houston: Diverse Populations." *International Migration Review* 21(1): 4–26.

Rosenblum, Marc R., and Doris Meissner, with Claire Bergeron and Faye Hipsman. 2014. "The Deportation Dilemma: Reconciling Tough and Human Enforcement." Washington, D.C.: Migration Policy Institute.

Sklansky, David Alan. 2012. "Crime, Immigration, and Ad Hoc Instrumentalism." *New Criminal Law Review* 15(2): 157–223.

Smith, Robert Courtney. 2008. "Horatio Alger Lives in Brooklyn: Extrafamily Support, Intrafamily Dynamics, and Socially Neutral Operating Identities in Exceptional Mobility among Children of Mexican Immigrants." *Annals of the American Academy of Political and Social Science* 620(1): 270–90.

———. 2017. "'Don't Let the Illegals Vote!': The Myths of Illegal Latino Voters and Voter Fraud in Contested Local Immigrant Integration." *RSF: The Russell Sage Foundation Journal of the Social Sciences* 3(4): 148–74. DOI: 10.7758/RSF.2017.3.4.09.

Stuesse, Angela. 2016. *Scratching Out a Living: Latinos, Race, and Work in the Deep South*. Oakland: University of California Press.

Suárez-Orozco, Carola, Marcelo M. Suárez-Orozco, and Irina Todorova. 2009. *Learning a New Land: Immigrant Students in American Society*. Cambridge, Mass.: Harvard University Press.

Taylor, Paul, Mark Hugo Lopez, Jeffrey S. Passel, and Seth Motel. 2011. "Unauthorized Immigrants: Length of Residency, Patterns of Parenthood." Washington, D.C.: Pew Hispanic Center.

Terriquez, Veronica. 2015. "Dreams Delayed: Barriers to Degree Completion Among Undocumented Community College Students." *Journal of Ethnic and Migration Studies* 41(8): 1302–23.

U.S. Department of Homeland Security. 2014. *2013 Yearbook of Immigration Statistics*. U.S. Department of Homeland Security. Washington: Office of Immigration Statistics.

U.S. Immigration and Customs Enforcement (USICE). 2015. "FYI 2015 ICE Immigration Removals." *Department of Homeland Security*. Accessed November 4, 2016. http://www.ice.gov/removal-statistics.

Warren, Robert, and Jeffrey S. Passel. 1987. "A Count of the Uncountable: Estimates of Undocumented Aliens Counted in the 1980 United States Census." *Demography* 24(3): 375–93.

Willen, Sarah S. 2007. "Toward a Critical Phenomenology of 'Illegality': State Power, Criminalization, and Abjectivity Among Undocumented Migrant Workers in Tel Aviv, Israel." *International Migration* 45(3): 8–38.

Yoshikawa, Hirokazu. 2011. *Immigrants Raising Citizens: Undocumented Parents and Their Children*. New York: Russell Sage Foundation.

Yoshikawa, Hirokazu, Carola S. Suárez-Orozco, and Roberto G. Gonzales. Forthcoming. "Unauthorized Status and Youth Development in the United States: Consensus Statement of the Society for Research in Adolescence." *Journal of Research on Adolescence*. DOI: 10.1111/jora.12272.

Zlolniski, Christian. 2006. *Janitors, Street Vendors, and Activists: The Lives of Mexican Immigrants in Silicon Valley*. Berkeley: University of California Press.

Patterns of Family Visitation During Immigration Detention

CAITLIN PATLER AND NICHOLAS BRANIC

The population detained by Immigration and Customs Enforcement more than doubled between 2001 and 2013, swelling to over 477,000 individuals. Despite this growth, few studies analyze the experiences of detained immigrants. We draw from one of the first studies of detention in the United States, analyzing survey data from 565 noncitizens detained for six months or longer in California. Criminal incarceration literature finds that family visitation helps maintain social ties but is not evenly distributed. We analyze the predictors of contact and visitation with children during immigration detention. Results indicate that demographic background, the type of detention facility, and children's legal status substantially affect contact and visitation experiences. Findings suggest that immigration detention replicates experiences of criminal incarceration and is perpetuating inequality in immigrant communities.

Keywords: immigration detention, visitation, immigration, incarceration, undocumented immigration

A large body of social science research analyzes the causes and consequences of the rise of mass incarceration, yet very few studies document the growth and consequences of a parallel system: mass immigration detention.[1] Indeed, the last three decades have brought about an unprecedented convergence in immigration and criminal laws, leading to an influx of noncitizens into the federal criminal justice system as well as an explosion in the United States' detention and deportation systems. For instance, around half of the individuals sentenced in federal courts are noncitizens (Light, Massoglia, and King 2014) and 9.1 percent of federal prisoners (approximately seventeen thousand inmates) are incarcerated for immigration-related offenses as of October 2015 (Federal Bureau of Prisons 2015). Noncitizens in general and undocumented immigrants in particular are more likely to be incarcerated pre-trial and receive longer criminal sentences than U.S. citizens (Light, Massoglia, and King 2014).

At the same time, the growth of the U.S. immigration detention system has skyrocketed. In 2013, 477,000 immigrants were detained by

Caitlin Patler is assistant professor of sociology at the University of California, Davis. **Nicholas Branic** is a PhD student in the Department of Criminology, Law and Society at the University of California, Irvine.

© 2017 Russell Sage Foundation. Patler, Caitlin, and Nicholas Branic. 2017. "Patterns of Family Visitation During Immigration Detention." *RSF: The Russell Sage Foundation Journal of the Social Sciences* 3(4): 18–36. DOI: 10.7758/RSF.2017.3.4.02. The authors are grateful to Roberto Gonzales, Steven Raphael, and the participants of the Undocumented Immigration and the Experience of Illegality conference, hosted by the Russell Sage Foundation, for their helpful comments and suggestions on earlier drafts of this paper. Data used in this study were collected by Caitlin Patler and Emily Ryo. Direct correspondence to: Caitlin Patler at patler@ucdavis.edu, 1283 Social Sciences & Humanities, One Shields Ave., University of California, Davis, CA 95616; and Nicholas Branic at nbranic@uci.edu, 2301 Social Ecology II, Irvine, CA 92697.

1. Throughout this paper, we refer to immigration detention and immigration imprisonment interchangeably.

Immigration and Customs Enforcement (ICE), representing a nearly 2.5-fold increase in the detainee population since 2001, at a cost of more than $2 billion—or $161 per detainee per day (Simanski 2014; National Immigration Forum 2014). Despite recent efforts to reduce the populations of jails and prisons, immigration detention remains a growth area. Since 2009, Congress has mandated that ICE continue to fill thirty-four thousand detention beds daily, thereby allocating more funding for detention than was requested by the White House in 2014 (National Immigration Forum 2014). Though the scope and cost of immigration detention in the United States has rapidly expanded in recent decades, largely due to issues of access, social science literature on this phenomenon remains scant.

U.S. immigration law is civil rather than criminal and is therefore legally considered nonpunitive. Because few constitutional limits are set on the length of detention, however, noncitizens who commit triggering offenses under U.S. immigration law are often held mandatorily for the entirety of their removal proceedings, in local jails or in facilities run by private prison corporations. In 2013, ICE detained more than thirty thousand immigrants for three months or longer and ten thousand for six months or longer (Transactional Records Access Clearinghouse 2013). A recent study found that more than 15 percent of Mexicans deported from the interior of the United States had been held in ICE custody for more than one year prior to deportation—and half of those were held for more than three years (Bermudez, n.d.). These figures suggest that immigration detention, though legally nonpunitive, has become much more akin to incarceration than ever before. The literature on the experiences of the incarcerated thus provides an important jumping-off point for the present study.

We seek to understand the impact of long-term detention on detained immigrants and their families.[2] One component of this inquiry is how immigrant families experience the long-term detention of a parent, particularly through access to regular communication and visitation. We therefore seek to answer the following research questions: What factors influence whether detained parents have any contact at all (such as letters, phone calls, or visits) with their children? What factors influence whether detained parents have face-to-face visitation with their children? Does the legal status of a detained parent's spouse or child predict visitation?

These questions are particularly important for at least three reasons. First, research on incarceration in the criminal context finds that family visitation is an important predictor of recidivism and can help families stay connected during the separation period (Bales and Mears 2008). However, although existing research has examined variation across inmate visitation in jails and prisons (see, for example, Cochran, Mears, and Bales 2014), no studies have considered the experiences of those held under the jurisdiction of immigration authorities.

Second, the existing assumptions about the importance and value of visitation are based on accessibility of visitation—from both a logistical and a legal standpoint. The extent to which visitation is differentially accessible for immigrant families from certain backgrounds, or when visiting certain facilities, could indicate inequalities within the system of immigration detention. We therefore examine, for the first time, whether experiences of visitation during immigration detention vary depending on the characteristics of detainees, their family members, or the facilities in which they are housed. Third, and relatedly, we pay particular attention to whether spouse and children's immigration statuses predict visitation patterns. If these family members are unable or less able to visit, we might conclude that immigration detention is especially punitive for families containing undocumented family members.

The paper draws empirically from one of the first studies of immigration detention and release in the United States. We analyze data collected in 2013 and 2014 from 565 immigrants who had been detained for six months or lon-

---

2. We conceptualize long-term detention as lasting approximately six months or longer for several reasons discussed in the methods section.

ger in California. The four facilities in which study detainees were held—three jails and one privately operated facility, each subcontracted by ICE to house immigrant detainees—represent the universe of facilities housing long-term detainees in the federal judicial district in California where the study took place. Findings suggest that detainees' ethnicity and sex predict the likelihood of any contact with children (such as phone calls or letters) as well as whether detainees received any face-to-face visits from children. In addition, both the type of facility where detained immigrants are held and the undocumented legal status of detainees' children substantially affect contact and visitation experiences with children. Detainees held in private immigration detention facilities rather than county or city jails experienced lower likelihoods of receiving any in-person visitation with their children as well as fewer total visits. Finally, having undocumented children exhibited mixed effects in our analyses. Although having undocumented children marginally increased the likelihood of receiving any contact from children (such as letters or phone calls), detained parents with undocumented children received comparatively fewer visits, on average, from their children.

This study contributes to several bodies of literature. First, although the magnitude and costs of immigration detention have continued to increase, empirical studies of detention and its impacts on individuals, households, and communities are scarce. Advocacy organizations have released reports documenting punitive conditions within detention facilities as well as difficulties with reentry following release (Chaudry et al. 2010; Amnesty International 2009). However, given the challenges to accessing the detained population, studies of the experiences of immigration detainees are few and far between.

Second, this study provides an important comparative context to research on criminal incarceration and reentry. In contrast to the lack of empirical studies on detention, a broad history of research on incarceration helps situate the current study. Social scientists have explored the impacts of visitation on family relationships (Poehlmann 2005) and the extent to which visitation may be stratified across certain groups of prisoners (Cochran, Mears, and Bales 2014). This body of research has greatly enhanced our understanding about the complex ways in which mass incarceration is perpetuating cycles of poverty and marginalization in communities experiencing high rates of incarceration. By applying the insights from research on incarceration and reentry, this study fills significant gaps in our understanding of the social and economic consequences of prolonged immigrant detention on families. As the criminologist Joshua Cochran and his colleagues point out, an inquiry into visitation is critical because if visitation is differentially accessible, it can indicate inequality in the collateral consequences of imprisonment (2014). Finally, this study allows us to explore whether family members' immigration statuses compound with detention policies to enforce and reinforce family separation.

This study is also relevant to current political and social debates. The first of its kind, it sheds light on some of the experiences and consequences of immigration detention for mixed-immigration-status families at a time when detention is becoming an increasingly common reality for many families and is a source of national discussion. Second, it illustrates some of the implications of the increased criminalization of immigrant communities and the extent to which enforcement measures may be experienced across these communities, which are made up of citizens and noncitizens alike. Relatedly, it is sociologically important for its implications in understanding immigrant integration and immigrant identity formation. Many detained immigrants go on to win their cases and need to reintegrate into their communities afterward. Maintaining family cohesion during the lengthy detention process may be critical to this transition.

THE EXPANSION OF MASS IMMIGRATION DETENTION

The imprisonment of noncitizens for violating U.S. immigration law is not a new phenomenon, though the recent and prodigious expansion in the size and scope of the detention system is unparalleled. Scholars have documented such an unprecedented convergence of immigration and criminal law in recent decades that they have begun to refer to the phenomenon as *crimmigration* (Stumpf 2006). Changes to immigration and criminal laws since the 1980s—especially during the War on Drugs—have vastly inflated the immigration detention system by, for example, drastically lowering the bar for deportable offenses and expanding the categories of individuals who can be held mandatorily pending a judicial decision on their removal proceedings (Stumpf 2006; Sayed 2011; García Hernández 2014; Coutin 2011). The legal scholar César Cuauhtémoc García Hernández argues that Congress has used immigration detention "as a central tool in the nation's burgeoning war on drugs" (2014, 1349).

The vast expansion of deportable offenses and detention authority has led to a boom in immigration detention, with the detained population expanding from just over 200,000 in 2001 to nearly 480,000 in 2013 (Simanski 2014), at a cost of around $161 per detainee per day (National Immigration Forum 2014). This incredible growth has also led to significant delays in the adjudication process in removal proceedings, resulting in longer stays within detention facilities. As mentioned, in 2013, more than thirty thousand individuals were held for three months or longer and more than ten thousand for six months or longer.

U.S. immigration law is civil rather than criminal in nature; therefore, the Supreme Court has held time and time again that immigration detention is legally considered nonpunitive (García Hernández 2014). Given this definition, detained immigrants are not subject to the same constitutional protections available in a criminal context—for example, the Sixth Amendment right-to-counsel provisions or other due process guarantees under the Fifth Amendment (Kaufman 2008; García Hernández 2014). Such constitutional concerns, combined with the vast growth of crimmigration, have led legal scholars to argue that immigration detention has become so akin to criminal incarceration that it should be considered punitive:

> Individuals in immigration confinement are frequently perceived to be no different than individuals in penal confinement.... They are represented as a threat to public safety, locked behind barbed wire, often in remote facilities, and subjected to the detailed control emblematic of all secure environments. Often they are held alongside their criminal counterparts.... By so intertwining immigration detention and penal incarceration, Congress created an immigration detention legal architecture that, in contrast with the prevailing legal characterization, is formally punitive. (García Hernández 2014, 1349)

Scholars and advocates have also raised concerns about the expansion and scope of mandatory immigration detention. Noncitizens who are subject to mandatory detention are required to be held by ICE for the entire length of their removal proceedings, which can last months or even years in some cases (Transactional Records Access Clearinghouse 2013; Bermudez, n.d.). The Immigration and Nationality Act specifies that individuals subject to mandatory detention include, for example, those convicted of most felony offenses and multiple misdemeanors, including minor drug offenses and some traffic offenses.[3] To be clear, mandatory detainees are not being held on criminal charges, but are instead imprisoned while awaiting adjudication in their removal proceedings. The average length of detention for respondents in our sample at the time of the survey was 271 days (approximately nine months).

In summary, changes to immigration and criminal law over the past several decades have led to a prodigious expansion of immigration detention alongside the growth of mass incarceration. The size of the detained population has ballooned in unprecedented fashion, with few constitutional limits on the length of detention. Although detention is legally considered nonpunitive, detained noncitizens are often perceived as criminals, held in the same jails as criminal offenders, and for similar periods as many criminal inmates in local jails. Nearly half a million individuals are held in immigration detention facilities each year, yet few studies have been able to investigate the

---

3. Mandatory detention is specified in the Immigration and Nationality Act, §236 (8 U.S.C.A. §1226).

experiences of immigrant detainees. We know relatively little about how detainees and their families experience immigration imprisonment, and with what consequences. Given the similarities between the systems of mass incarceration and mass detention, it makes theoretical as well as empirical sense to draw from literature on incarceration as a helpful starting point in understanding the experiences of immigrants detained for long periods of time. This paper proceeds with an inquiry into one important aspect of the experience of imprisonment: contact and visitation with family.

FAMILY CONTACT AND VISITATION DURING IMPRISONMENT

For incarcerated parents, imprisonment represents a removal from the family unit. Even for those who strive to remain close with their families during incarceration, contact does not come easily. Phone calls are expensive and limited, letters are read by guards before delivery, and visitation is both limited to certain hours and often logistically difficult for families. In some facilities, no contact visits are allowed, so all in-person communication must be done through glass shields or—more recently—video conferencing. Despite these challenges, studies confirm the importance of visitation during incarceration. Indeed, visitation is one of the only opportunities for communication with the outside world and for maintaining social ties. Contact with family has been found to reduce stress among inmates, in turn reducing negative behaviors within prison settings (Cochran 2012). Visitation also allows imprisoned individuals to continue to access social resources and social capital that can support positive reentry and reduce recidivism (Bales and Mears 2008). Increased visitation has also been linked to health outcomes among the incarcerated, such as by reducing depressive symptoms among mothers (Poehlmann 2005).

Visitation can be a positive experience for incarcerated individuals but it is not equally distributed. In one of the only studies of the predictors of inmate visitation, Joshua Cochran, Daniel Mears, and William Bales find that African Americans, the elderly, and those more frequently incarcerated receive fewer visits (2014). Such results suggest troubling barriers for certain inmates to the benefits of visitation. However, to our knowledge, no studies examine whether the family members' legal status has any impact on visitation.

The Bureau of Justice Statistics reports that 60 percent of mothers and fathers in jails and prisons never receive a visit from their children (Glaze and Maruschak 2008). Understanding the factors that predict such disparities in visitation is important for several reasons. First, visitation rules, however stringent, are generally consistent across imprisoned individuals within the same facilities, with some exceptions. That visitation is more difficult and less frequent for certain groups may constitute an added form of punishment for imprisoned individuals from those groups (Cochran, Mears, and Bales 2014). Second, differential access to visitation may represent a group-specific collateral consequence for family members of the imprisoned (Travis 2005). Finally, as Cochran and his colleagues argue, "to the extent that such punishment [differential visitation] is patterned along social and demographic lines, it raises questions about the social inequality in punishment in America" (2014, 5).

Even if visitation rules were consistent for all inmates, the accessibility of visitation between different types of facilities varies. A recent study analyzed the types of contact allowed at jails, state prisons, and federal prisons and found discrepancies in inmates' access to different types of contact (letter writing and phone calls) and face-to-face visitation by facility type (Shlafer, Loper, and Schillmoeller 2015). For example, local jails often allow only noncontact visits, but state prisons almost always allow contact visits. The authors conclude that the type of facility has important implications for families and children: "The type of facility can impact the inmates' proximity to their families, the probable frequency of contact, as well as the format and rules for contact and visitation" (Shlafer, Loper, and Schillmoeller 2015, 2).

Given such discrepancies, we might expect to see differences, especially in access to face-to-face visitation, across the facilities in which immigrant detainees are held. However, although many immigrant detainees are held in local and county jails alongside criminal offenders, approximately 62 percent of detention beds are subcontracted to private, for-profit prison corporations (Carson and Diaz 2015). Although similar to government-operated facilities in their custodial role, research suggests important differences between private facilities and local or county jails. For example, Alissa Ackerman and Rich Furman provide a review of literature on private prisons, arguing that the reduction of operating costs, a key selling point for private prison contracting, often "comes at the expense of quality" (2013, 258). In particular, the authors note that the conditions in private facilities, such as personnel training and inmate health care, are often of lower quality than their government-operated counterparts. Moreover, it is unclear whether private facilities offer visitation privileges similar to those offered in public facilities. To our knowledge, no research has assessed families' access to these privately operated facilities. However, recent media coverage of U.S. immigration detention facilities housing Central American children and families has demonstrated extensive barriers to accessing such facilities. For example, a related *New York Times Magazine* feature reported some of the logistical challenges attorneys faced in accessing privately operated facilities in Arizona and Texas (see Hylton 2015). Moreover, private facilities are often built far outside metropolitan areas that offer few options for public transportation, which can create additional barriers for potential visitors.

Even when imprisoned individuals can receive visits, many factors could influence the frequency of visits. First, visitation (and contact in general) can be logistically challenging and expensive. In a study of women who visited family members in a large state prison, the clinical psychologist Olga Grinstead and her colleagues documented emotional, social, and financial challenges (2001). Women reported that the economic burden of having an incarcerated family member was worsened by the financial costs of visitation, phone calls, and sending packages. Women reported spending an average of $292 per month on these items, representing more than a quarter of monthly income for those in the lowest economic brackets in the study. To make matters worse, jails and prisons are often located far outside city centers, requiring long drives or bus rides that often take up entire days (Christian 2005). Coupled with challenges of distance and transportation, visitation schedules within facilities may make visitation difficult for working spouses and children.

An additional challenge to family visitation is the negative psychological experience of visitation for family members. In a study of women with partners incarcerated at San Quentin State Prison in California, the sociologist Megan Comfort describes the "secondary prisonization" experienced by the families of the detained (2003). Legally innocent people come to experience the effects of incarceration indirectly due to their sustained contact with the correctional institution, characterized, for example, by dealing with guards and being subject to invasive searches (Comfort 2003, 2007, 2009). Comfort also demonstrates that partners and spouses feel emotionally strained with worry about their incarcerated partner (2009). Children also experience secondary prisonization experiences. In response, some families may decide that it is better for the child not to visit the incarcerated parent (Martin 2001; Poehlmann 2005). Other parents may decide that they don't want children to visit, either because of the nature of the incarcerated parent's criminal record or the deterioration of parents' relationship (Edin, Nelson, and Paranal 2004). In noncitizen families, additional barriers may include language, fear of authorities, and immigration status, an issue we address in the following section.

IMMIGRANT FAMILIES AND VISITATION

Despite the vast similarities between criminal incarceration and immigration detention, it is plausible that immigrant families experience immigration imprisonment differently than families of U.S. citizens do criminal incarceration. In particular, the precarious legal status of family members may impose a barrier to regular visitation.

An emerging body of literature on the impacts of unauthorized status has emerged over the past decade. It has exposed how immigration laws can structure the everyday experiences of undocumented immigrants and their families, with great consequences for their economic, social, and health outcomes (Menjívar and Abrego 2012; Dreby 2012; Coutin 2011; Dreby 2015). Scholars are increasingly concerned with how laws and policies produce and sustain the inequality of individuals, families, and communities (Ngai 2004; De Genova 2002; Coutin 2000; Willen 2007). The geographer Nicholas De Genova argues that the threat of deportability engenders persistent feelings of the "revocability of the promise of the future" among undocumented immigrants (2002, 427). The anthropologists Guillermina Gina Nuñez and Josiah Heyman find that increased immigration enforcement affects undocumented immigrants to such an extent that some will structure their daily decisions to avoid discovery, for example, by selectively choosing which streets to drive on (2007). The fear of exposure may deter undocumented immigrant family members from visiting detained loved ones. This is similar to the concept of *system avoidance* (Brayne 2014), whereby individuals who have had criminal justice contact steer clear of "surveilling institutions" that keep formal records. For undocumented individuals, whose statuses already make them vulnerable, an immigration detention facility may be the most directly threatening form of surveilling institutions. We therefore expect that undocumented families may view visitation as effectively entering the belly of the beast and may feel they have no choice but to avoid it.

An additional challenge to undocumented family members' visitation is logistical. The anthropologist Susan Coutin demonstrates how illegality turns the mundane into the illicit—for example, undocumented immigrants are faced with the daily predicament of unlicensed driving and lack of official government documents (2000). Many undocumented immigrants are barred from getting valid drivers' licenses, which may be a particular impediment in the context of family visitation for two reasons. First, at least one facility in this study requires visitors to show a driver's license and proof of insurance to enter the facility grounds by vehicle. Second, most facilities require visitors to provide photo-identification before visiting family members. These logistical challenges could present barriers to visitation for many low-income families, but are especially problematic for undocumented families. In particular, we might expect undocumented children (or those with undocumented parents who are not imprisoned) not to visit, or to visit with less frequency than documented children.

Even in families that can overcome the logistical and legal challenges discussed, visitation might still be a traumatic event, for reasons that may be particular to immigrant families. To be sure, the ever-present fear of enforcement makes its way through entire families regardless of citizenship status. The sociologist Joana Dreby interviewed the young children of immigrants and finds that they equate police with ICE and exhibit observable fear of family separation and deportation even when no one they know is detained (2012, 2015). Dreby also finds that the children's mothers worried so much about detention and deportation of their spouses that they developed severe symptoms of stress and other mental health concerns (2015). It is possible, therefore, that the children of detained immigrants will visit their detained parents less frequently because the experience could trigger not just the negative emotions associated with having an incarcerated parent, but also increased worry about the potential for parents' deportation and prolonged family separation. It seems likely that undocumented immigration status will only compound the disadvantages that children with detained parents face.

DATA AND METHODS

This study draws from original survey data collected in 2013 and 2014 from 565 detainees in California. The list of participants was drawn from the universe of individuals who had been held for at least six months in the federal judicial district in California where the study took place, and had been scheduled a hearing under *Rodriguez v. Robbins*, ongoing class action litigation requiring custody redetermination hearings (bond hearings) before an immigration judge for individuals who have been detained for 180 days or longer. We focus on detention lasting six months or longer for three reasons. First, in *Rodriguez v. Robbins*, the Ninth Circuit Court of Appeals held that a detention of this length is a profound deprivation of liberty and raises serious constitutional concerns. The court's decision rested on a body of law recognizing that detentions longer than six months require heightened protections, suggesting that long-term detention is particularly punitive. Second, a large portion of jail and prison inmates in the state of California serve less than one year, making this population an important comparison group. Third, in other Western countries, reentry outcomes such as employment are significantly affected by time served lasting six months or longer (see Ramakers et al. 2014). Given these reasons, it makes empirical sense to consider that by the six-month mark much of immigrant detainees' experiences of imprisonment—and the implications of those experiences—will have come to mirror those of the criminally incarcerated.

The 565 detainees in our sample were held at four detention facilities in California subcontracted by ICE to house immigrant detainees. Three facilities are county or city jails; a private, for-profit correctional corporation operates the fourth. Surveys were conducted in person, in English or Spanish, and all participants were at least eighteen years old. Surveys lasted between 90 to 120 minutes and respondents did not receive any incentive for participating. Of detainees who received information about the survey from the interviewers, 92 percent completed the survey. There were no significant differences in refusal rates by gender or country of origin.

To our knowledge, this study is the first to access such a large sample of long-term detainees during their detention. As explained, the sample was drawn from a list of all respondents who had been held for six months or longer and had been scheduled a bond hearing under *Rodriguez v. Robbins*. Because the Department of Homeland Security (DHS) does not release detailed demographic or case-specific information about immigrant detainees, it is not possible to determine how well this sample represents the detained population in the United States. However, it is important to note that the sample may have different characteristics than other detainees held throughout the United States. First, the average respondent in the sample had been detained for 271 days at the time of the survey, which may differentiate them from shorter-term detainees.[4] For example, long-term detainees (many of whom are held mandatorily) may be more likely to have some kind of criminal record that triggered a removal proceeding under immigration law. In our sample, 96 percent of respondents had at least one misdemeanor or felony conviction.[5] The two most common convictions in our sample are traffic and drug-related (both 44 percent). Unfortunately, we are unable to determine whether any particular conviction may have triggered deportation proceedings. Finally, on average, respondents in our sample had lived in the United States for nearly two decades, which may differentiate them from detainees held in other locations—for example, in facilities along the U.S.-Mexico border. Though this sample may not represent the universe of detained individuals in the United States, it is the first of its kind to allow individual-level analysis of the experiences of individuals detained for long periods.

Measures and Method

The survey gathers data on the demographic, family, employment, health, immigration, and criminal background of each detainee. It also explores detainees' experiences in detention, including information about family visitation. We draw on visitation literature from the criminal context, as well as literature on the broader impacts of immigration law enforcement, to construct a series of measures to capture the

---

4. According to one estimate, the average immigrant detainee in the United States is released or deported in thirty-one days, often because he or she chooses not to contest a deportation order (Transactional Records Access Clearinghouse 2013). However, because DHS does not release individual-level information on detainees, it is impossible to compare how our sample aligns with this "average" detainee or even with an average long-term detainee who has been detained for six months or longer.

5. Compare this with data from September 22, 2012 (one day for which data are available on aggregate criminal histories via a Freedom of Information Act request) finding that 61 percent of detainees in ICE custody on that day had a criminal record (Kerwin, Alulema, and Tu 2015).

contact and visitation experiences of detained immigrants and the factors predicting these experiences.

Dependent Variables
We created three dependent variables to measure detainees' contact and visitation with their children. We excluded 107 respondents from the sample who reported having no children, bringing our sample size to 462. First, we generated a binary variable indicating whether respondents received any contact from their children while detained (visits, letters, phone calls, or news from others). Detainees reporting any of these forms of contact during detention were coded as 1; no contact was coded as 0.

A second binary variable measured whether respondents experienced any face-to-face visitation with their children during detention. The visitation variable provided a more specific examination than the overall contact variable because in-person visitation may carry different meaning than other forms of contact. Moreover, direct visitation experiences have a greater impact for both detainees and their children than other types of contact (Shlafer, Loper, and Schillmoeller 2015). Detainees who reported at least one visit with their children during detention were coded as 1; those who reported no visitation were coded as 0.

We generated a separate count variable capturing the extent of visitation experiences among the sample by measuring the total number of visits detainees received from their children. Respondents were asked whether they received visitation from each of their children and subsequently asked the number of times that they were visited by each child. Aggregating the number of reported visits from each child produced a single count measure measuring respondents' total exposure to their children during detention.[6] To account for positive skewness in the variable distribution, and for consistency with prior research on visitation (Cochran, Mears, and Bales 2014), we recoded the count variable to a maximum of forty visits.[7]

Independent Variables
We constructed a series of demographic, detention facility, family, and legal status variables to predict detainees' contact and visitation experiences. Demographic measures included respondents' gender (male = 1, female = 0), self-identified ethnicity (1 = Hispanic-Latino, 0 = not Hispanic-Latino), and age at the time of the survey. To capture detainees' previous socioeconomic status, we included a measure of detainees' self-reported average income through the six months prior to detention by computing average weekly earnings in hundreds of dollars.

Existing literature on criminal incarceration shows that inmates' criminal records significantly predict visitation and that inmates with more frequent experiences of incarceration are less likely to receive visits (Cochran, Mears, and Bales 2014). In addition, inmates with certain types of violent or serious crimes may have less or no contact with children given that family members may deem visitation unsafe or unhealthy for children (Shlafer, Loper, and Schillmoeller 2015). Finally, inmates who have been incarcerated for long periods may have fewer or weakened ties to their families and may therefore receive fewer visits (Cochran, Mears, and Bales 2014; Christian 2005). In our models, three variables measured respondents' self-reported criminal history. First, a count measure captured the total number of prior criminal convictions for each respondent. Next, two binary measures indicated any felony and violent convictions, respectively. We also controlled for the total months detained for each

---

6. This aggregated count variable approximates the total number of visits that respondents experienced during detention. The detention facilities in the study stipulate limitations on the number of family members allowed to visit at one time (for example, two adults and one child, one adult and two children) and permit a maximum of one visit per day. Thus, even detainees with multiple children would only be able to see one or two children per scheduled visit.

7. Imposing a maximum threshold for visitation counts resulted in thirty-six cases recoded at forty visits.

respondent at the time of interviewing to account for potential spuriousness in our models, because longer detention periods may correspond with more visits. Time spent in detention varied from just under six months to over four and a half years at the time of surveying. To account for positive skewness in detention length, we computed a new variable by taking the natural log of total months detained.

The locations where individuals are detained can have important implications for contact and visitation because detention facilities feature their own rules and regulations surrounding visitation with family and are located in different geographic areas (Shlafer, Loper, and Schillmoeller 2015). In light of these potential influences, we created two variables to account for immigrant detainees' locations. First, we generated a dummy variable indicating the type of facility housing each respondent. Detainees in a privately operated detention facility were coded as 1; those in a county or city jail were coded as 0. We also computed the spatial distance between detainees' current detention facility and the city where each individual reported entering ICE custody prior to detention.[8] This distance measure served two purposes in our analyses. First, greater distances between detention facilities and detainees' families may increase the difficulty of visitation, particularly for lower-income families, and therefore are a salient predictor of overall visitation experiences (Shlafer, Loper, and Schillmoeller 2015; Christian 2005).[9] Second, this measure allowed us to examine the unique effects of privately operated detention facilities while controlling for facilities' geographic locations. To account for positive skewness in the distance measure, we calculated the natural log of computed distances.

Last, we created four variables to account for respondents' family structures and family members' legal statuses. We created a binary variable for whether respondents reported being married or having a domestic partner. Similarly, a binary measure indicated whether detainees had any dependent children. We defined dependent children as those age seventeen or younger; related biologically, through adoption, or as a stepchild; and currently residing in the United States. Additionally, two binary variables indicated whether the respondent reported having an undocumented spouse-partner or child, respectively.

ANALYTIC STRATEGY

We examined detained immigrants' contact and visitation experiences with their children across three dependent variables, using logistic regression (any contact, any visits) and negative binomial regression (number of visits) models.[10] Prior to model estimation, we investigated missing data patterns within the dataset. Nearly all variables featured 1 percent or fewer missing observations except for marital status and spouse legal status, each missing

---

8. Using ArcGIS version 10.2, we obtained the *XY* coordinates for city centroids and detention facilities' address-level coordinates. We then computed distance in miles between the coordinates using the economist Austin Nichols's vincenty program in Stata 14. City coordinates approximate detainees' predetention residence and are a proxy for where families are likely to reside. We acknowledge the imprecision of using city coordinates to draw these assumptions, which proves a limitation of the data and warrants consideration when interpreting results. Given the theoretical relevance of distance as a predictor of visitation, however, we elected to include the variable in our analyses.

9. Although families with personal vehicles may take advantage of freeways and comparatively lower travel times, families reliant on public transportation face greater hardships when planning to visit with a detained parent.

10. Using Stata 14, we tested for multicollinearity by estimating ordinary least squares regression models for each dependent variable while including all covariates and obtaining variance inflation factor scores. Results indicated that multicollinearity was not a concern in the models. We then tested for outliers using the Hadi statistic and identified twelve outlier cases that we subsequently omitted from the sample.

approximately 43 to 45 percent of observations.[11] We preserved cases with missing data by generating multiply imputed datasets (Rubin 1987) using chained equations (the multivariate imputation by chained equations, or MICE, method). MICE allows users to specify each variable by type (such as count, dichotomous) for all variables and relaxes the assumption of normal distribution. We estimated fifty multiply imputed datasets to account for the high percentage of missing data on the spouse variables (Graham, Olchowski, and Gilreath 2007).[12] After multiple imputation, we ran diagnostic tests to determine the proper modeling strategy for our count-based visitation measure and verified the test results across all fifty imputed datasets. Initial tests demonstrated significant overdispersion in the visitation count distribution, which indicated the appropriateness of negative binomial models rather than a Poisson regression approach.

FINDINGS

Table 1 provides a descriptive overview of the study respondents. Respondents were typically male (92 percent), and were approximately thirty-eight years old on average. The majority (85 percent) reported Latino-Hispanic ethno-racial identification. The most common countries of origin were Mexico (50 percent), El Salvador (21 percent), Guatemala (12 percent), and Honduras (4 percent). Altogether, respondents indicated forty-three originating nations. Just over half (52 percent) reported being married, and 29 percent indicated having an undocumented spouse. Moreover, 72 percent of respondents indicated having at least one dependent child (biological, step, or adopted child, living in the United States, and under eighteen years old) and 8 percent reported having at least one child with undocumented legal status. In the six months prior to detention, these individuals earned on average about $750 per week. Respondents had an average of about three prior criminal convictions, with approximately 26 percent reporting at least one felony conviction and 40 percent reporting at least one violent conviction. At the time of interviewing, respondents had been detained around nine months and 44 percent were housed in a privately operated detention facility. The average distance between the city of arrest and current detention facility was sixty-two miles. During detention, 83 percent of respondents reported receiving at least some form of contact with their children; more than half (53 percent) reported receiving at least one in-person visit. Moreover, detainees reported an average of approximately eight visits while held in detention, but nearly half (47 percent) indicated no visitation.

We analyzed each of the three dependent variables for contact and visitation experiences by estimating models in a two-step approach.[13] First, we regressed the dependent variable on all independent variables except for the legal

---

11. The original version of the survey did not include questions about respondents' marital status or the legal status of the partner, resulting in high frequencies of missing data. Given the high percentage of missing data on the spouse variables, we reestimated the multiple imputation and regression analyses after excluding the spouse measures; model results did not change significantly from models, including the spouse variables.

12. Because of the later addition of the number of visits questions in a revised version of the survey instrument, missing values on the number of visits with children were perfectly predicted by measures of any contact and any visitation. To prevent model convergence issues during multiple imputation, we estimated three sets of fifty imputations—one for each dependent variable. Comparing descriptive statistics between the three sets of imputations revealed essentially identical means and standard errors. The social psychologist John Graham and his colleagues show that greater proportions of missing data require greater numbers of imputations in order to reduce statistical power loss (2007). The authors recommend forty imputations for models with approximately 50 percent missing data; we estimated fifty imputations as a more conservative approach.

13. Scholars debate whether to include or omit imputed values for dependent variables. Because our imputation models include the presence of auxiliary variables that are not included in the regression models, we opted to retain the imputed Y values after multiple imputation. Comparing the model estimates from both approaches yielded essentially identical results.

Table 1. Descriptive Statistics for Multiply Imputed Sample (N = 462)

	Mean	SD
Any contact	0.83	0.38
Any visits	0.53	0.50
Number of visits[a]	8.13	14.07
Male	0.92	0.28
Hispanic-Latino	0.85	0.36
Age (years)	38.22	9.24
Months detained[b]	8.90	5.17
Predetention weekly earnings ($100s)	7.46	17.41
Prior convictions	3.19	2.43
Prior felony conviction	0.26	0.45
Prior violent conviction	0.40	0.49
Distance to facility[c]	61.53	117.95
Private detention facility	0.44	0.50
Married	0.52	0.67
Dependent children	0.72	0.45
Undocumented spouse	0.29	0.59
Undocumented child	0.08	0.27

Source: Authors' tabulations.
Note: Sample includes parents only.
[a]Number of visits capped at forty.
[b]As of the survey date.
[c]Distance between city of arrest and location of immigration detention facility.

Table 2. Odds Ratios from Logistic Regression Analysis of Detainees Receiving Any Contact from Children

	Without Legal Status Variables	With Legal Status Variables
Male	2.27+	2.31+
	(1.11)	(1.16)
Hispanic-Latino	2.14*	2.19+
	(0.82)	(0.91)
Age	1.01	1.01
	(0.02)	(0.02)
Months detained (ln)[a]	1.13	1.05
	(0.43)	(0.41)
Predetention weekly earnings	1.00	1.00
	(0.01)	(0.01)
Number of prior convictions	1.10	1.10
	(0.07)	(0.08)
Felony conviction	1.53	1.47
	(0.54)	(0.54)
Violent conviction	0.62	0.61
	(0.19)	(0.19)
Distance to facility (ln)[b]	0.98	0.98
	(0.15)	(0.14)
Private facility	0.82	0.84
	(0.27)	(0.28)
Married	2.04	1.82
	(1.07)	(0.99)
Dependent child	7.99***	9.24***
	(2.42)	(3.30)
Undocumented spouse		0.58
		(0.39)
Undocumented child		5.15+
		(4.34)
Constant	0.12+	0.15
	(0.14)	(0.18)
Observations	462	462

Source: Authors' tabulations.
Notes: Sample includes parents only. Standard errors in parentheses.
[a]As of the survey date.
[b]Distance between city of arrest and location of immigration detention facility.
+*p* < .1; **p* < .05; ***p* < .01; ****p* < .001

statuses of spouses and children. Next, we added the legal status measures into the model to identify their unique effects on contact and visitation after controlling for other model covariates.

Table 2 presents odds ratios from logistic regression estimates of whether, during detention, detainees received any form of contact from their children. An odds ratio higher than 1 indicates an increase in the odds associated with a one-unit increase in a given independent variable. A ratio between 0 and 1 indicates a corresponding decrease in the odds associated with a one-unit increase in a given independent variable. Without including legal status measures, the model indicated that Latino detainees had an approximately 114 percent increase in the odds of receiving contact over their non-Latino counterparts (*p* < .05), and having any dependent children increased the odds by nearly 700 percent (*p* < .001), controlling for other variables in the model. Although marginally significant, male detainees also had greater odds of contact with their children than female detainees.

After adding legal status measures for spouses and children, the observed effects for Latino detainees became marginally significant and the effects of having any dependent children became stronger, increasing the odds of receiving any contact by approximately 824 percent ($p < .001$). Moreover, the legal status of detainees' children demonstrated a marginally significant relationship in the model, where detained parents with any undocumented children had higher odds of receiving any contact from their children.

Next, we estimated logistic regression models predicting the likelihood of respondents receiving any direct visitation with their children (table 3). These analyses yielded results similar to those of the general contact models but also some divergent findings. Before accounting for the legal statuses of spouses and children, the model indicated that male detainees had an approximate 162 percent increase in their odds of visitation relative to female detainees ($p < .05$) and Latino detainees had approximately 84 percent higher odds than non-Latinos ($p < .05$), controlling for other variables. Similar to previous findings, detained parents with dependent children showed an approximate 443 percent increase in their odds of visitation ($p < .001$). Unlike in the previous models, however, the facility where respondents were detained showed a significant relationship with visitation. Compared with detainees in city- and county-operated facilities, individuals held in a private detention facility experienced a nearly 60 percent decrease in the odds of any child visitation ($p < .001$). The model also indicated a marginally significant and negative effect for respondents convicted of violent crimes in the past relative to detainees without a violent criminal history.

Adding legal status measures to the binary visitation analyses produced almost no change in covariates' relationships with the predicted odds of visitation. The odds of visitation with their children increased for both male and Latino detainees. Moreover, having dependent

Table 3. Odds Ratios from Logistic Regression Analysis of Detainees Receiving Any Visitation from Children

	Without Legal Status Variables	With Legal Status Variables
Male	2.62*	2.60*
	(1.00)	(1.00)
Hispanic-Latino	1.84*	1.93*
	(0.55)	(0.59)
Age	1.02	1.02
	(0.01)	(0.01)
Months detained (ln)[a]	0.96	0.95
	(0.25)	(0.26)
Predetention weekly earnings	1.00	1.00
	(0.01)	(0.01)
Number of prior convictions	1.00	0.99
	(0.04)	(0.04)
Felony conviction	1.16	1.13
	(0.29)	(0.28)
Violent conviction	0.70+	0.71
	(0.15)	(0.16)
Distance to facility (ln)[b]	0.86	0.85
	(0.10)	(0.10)
Private facility	0.41***	0.41***
	(0.10)	(0.10)
Married	0.97	0.97
	(0.29)	(0.30)
Dependent child	5.43***	5.63***
	(1.37)	(1.48)
Undocumented spouse		0.88
		(0.33)
Undocumented child		0.72
		(0.31)
Constant	0.13*	0.13*
	(0.12)	(0.12)
Observations	462	462

Source: Authors' tabulations.
Notes: Sample includes parents only. Standard errors in parentheses.
[a] As of the survey date.
[b] Distance between city of arrest and location of immigration detention facility.
+$p < .1$; *$p < .05$; **$p < .01$; ***$p < .001$

children significantly increased the odds of visitation but being detained in a private facility decreased them. Neither spouses' nor children's undocumented legal statuses significantly predicted the likelihood of visitation.

The final set of analyses, presented in table 4, examined the relationships between model covariates and the total number of visits that detained individuals had with their children. Before accounting for spouses' and children's legal statuses, model results indicated that respondents' age was significantly associated with visitation, where each year of age corresponded with an approximately 3 percent increase in the expected number of visits ($p < .05$), controlling for other variables. In addition, having a dependent child increased the estimated number of visits by approximately 208 percent ($p < .001$). The type of facility housing respondents was significantly related to the number of visits with children: respondents in a private facility saw an approximately 59 percent decrease in the expected number of visits while in detention ($p < .01$), after controlling for other variables.

Adding legal status measures to the analysis changed several of the model's estimated effects. Detention in a private facility remained statistically significant but its coefficient grew in magnitude, suggesting a 64 percent decrease in the expected number of visits ($p < .001$). The legal status of detainees' children showed a significant and negative relationship with the number of received visits. Respondents with undocumented children showed a 64 percent decrease in the predicted number of visits ($p < .05$), controlling for other variables. Thus, although legal status did not appear to influence the likelihood of having any visitation with children, having undocumented children did suggest a reduction in the overall number of visits for individuals held in immigration detention facilities. Respondents' age remained a salient predictor, with each year of age predicting an approximate 4 percent increase in the expected number of visits ($p < .01$), and having any dependent children increased the expected number of visits by approximately 241 percent ($p < .001$).

Table 4. Incidence Rate Ratios from Negative Binomial Regression Analysis of Detainee's Number of Visits with Children

	Without Legal Status Variables	With Legal Status Variables
Male	1.29	1.39
	(0.56)	(0.61)
Hispanic-Latino	1.21	1.28
	(0.40)	(0.43)
Age	1.03*	1.04**
	(0.01)	(0.01)
Months detained (ln)[a]	0.73	0.65
	(0.22)	(0.20)
Predetention weekly earnings	1.00	1.00
	(0.01)	(0.01)
Number of prior convictions	0.93	0.92
	(0.05)	(0.05)
Felony conviction	1.25	1.26
	(0.34)	(0.35)
Violent conviction	0.70	0.74
	(0.18)	(0.19)
Distance to facility (ln)[b]	0.88	0.88
	(0.12)	(0.12)
Private facility	0.41**	0.36***
	(0.12)	(0.11)
Married	0.99	0.96
	(0.30)	(0.29)
Dependent child	3.08***	3.41***
	(0.85)	(0.97)
Undocumented spouse		0.81
		(0.29)
Undocumented child		0.36*
		(0.17)
Constant	3.85	4.03
	(3.60)	(3.81)
Observations	462	462

Source: Authors' tabulations.
Notes: Sample includes parents only. Standard errors in parentheses.
[a] As of the survey date.
[b] Distance between city of arrest and location of immigration detention facility.
†$p < .1$; *$p < .05$; **$p < .01$; ***$p < .001$

DISCUSSION

Although research on the causes and consequences of mass incarceration is extensive, few studies empirically examine the impacts of a parallel system: mass immigration detention. Legal scholars argue that immigration detention has become increasingly punitive, bringing up several constitutional concerns despite detention's nature as administrative law (García Hernández 2014; Kaufman 2008). This study aimed to examine, for the first time, patterns of family visitation among immigrant detainees imprisoned approximately six months or longer. Differences across family visitation experiences could suggest unequal collateral consequences from the detention system, which could perpetuate inequality and stratification in immigrant communities.

Several findings emerge from our analysis. Overall, being held in private detention facilities reduces the likelihood of face-to-face visitation with children but not general contact, whereas the demographic characteristics of the detainee (sex, ethnicity, and dependent children) increase the likelihood of contact and visitation. Legal status is also a salient predictor: undocumented children are more likely to be in contact with their detained parents but to make comparatively fewer visits to see them.

Controlling for other relevant characteristics, males and Latinos are more likely to have contact with children and to receive a visit from them. Scholars argue that deportation (and detention, as its frequent precursor) is a gendered and racialized process that disproportionately affects Latino males and will therefore have gendered and racialized effects in immigration communities (Golash-Boza and Hondagneu-Sotelo 2013). Our results support this hypothesis. Females may have differential access to the family and community support systems necessary to maintain child visitation during detention. Females may also be more stigmatized for their imprisonment because they are less likely to be policed in the first place (Rios 2011). Further research could explore the mechanisms explaining why Latinos and men are more likely to remain in contact with children during their detention.

A key finding from this study is that being detained in a privately operated facility (compared to a county or city jail) reduces the likelihood of receiving any face-to-face visits from children, as well as the total number of visitors. Although research on criminal incarceration documents discrepancies across local, state, and federal jails and prisons, to our knowledge, ours is the first on facilities run by private corporations (see Shlafer, Loper, and Schillmoeller 2015). Several factors may contribute to our finding that visitation is curtailed in privately operated facilities. Although the private facility in our study is much farther from major cities in the study region than other facilities, distance is not a significant predictor after controlling for the facility.

At first glance, this finding may seem to contradict prior research suggesting the impact of distance on the likelihood of visitation among criminally incarcerated individuals (see, for example, Tahamont 2013). When we reestimate our models and exclude the private facility variable, distance significantly predicts visitation. Yet this effect disappears when the private facility variable is included. Thus, the private immigration detention facility continued to exhibit a separate and distinct influence on the likelihood of visitation and the number of visits. An alternative explanation, therefore, could be that logistical access is more important than physical distance. For example, Google Maps estimates that it will take more than five hours on public transportation, each way, to make the approximately hundred-mile commute from a city where many families reside to the private facility (including four buses, one train, and a two-mile walk). Families who cannot access reliable transportation may be less likely to visit (Christian 2005). Second, the ways that private facilities operate relative to county or city jails may differ. Private facilities may have different rules and regulations for visitation, staff may be trained differently, and facilities may have a different ambiance and style of operations. For example, the private facility in this study allows visitation on only one weekend day, whereas the other facilities have access to visitation throughout the weekend. Additional studies that can address these qualitative differences across facilities would be timely and relevant. Indeed, privatized detention facilities are now the norm rather than the exception: 62 percent of detention beds are subcontracted to private facilities, up from 49 percent in 2009, during which period the quota for detention beds increased by 46 percent (Carson and Diaz 2015).

The legal status of detained immigrants' children exhibits differential effects in our analyses, where undocumented children are more likely to be in contact with their detained parents but make comparatively fewer total face-to-face visits. These results suggest that although undocumented families make efforts to stay in touch during detention, they may face systematic barriers from visitation that might otherwise yield positive effects for both parents and children (Poehlmann 2005; Shlafer, Loper, and Schillmoeller 2015). As a result, undocumented children may be more strongly penalized by a parent's detention than their counterparts with legal status, suggesting unequal collateral consequences across families.

Our analysis contributes to several theoretical, empirical, and political debates. First, it provides one of the first empirical analyses of the experiences and consequences of immigration detention. Applying what we know about criminal incarceration to the immigration detention context enables us to examine the unique aspects of immigration detention and its impacts on detainees and their families. Our findings reinforce the notion that the immigration detention experience mirrors criminal incarceration in many ways, yet remains distinct in others.

Second, we know that family relationships are affected by imprisonment. Visitation provides opportunities for maintaining social ties that can support positive reentry and reduce recidivism (Bales and Mears 2008). Visitation can also reduce negative behavior, stress, and other detrimental health outcomes among the incarcerated (Cochran 2012; Poehlmann 2005). Therefore, "disparities in visitation constitute a form of potentially unequal punishment, a collateral consequence, concentrated more among some groups . . . than others" (Cochran, Mears, and Bales 2014, 2; see also Bales and Mears 2008; Western 2006). That detainees with different demographic backgrounds and across types of facilities experience detention differently suggests that they may also experience the collateral consequences of the detention experience differently, which could lead to further stratification and marginalization.

Third, differential access to visitation may cause an additional hardship to immigrant detainees that incarcerated individuals do not experience. As the criminologist Mary Bosworth has written of immigration detention in the United Kingdom, detention is a process defined by uncertainty (2014). For example, one way that detention is unlike incarceration is that detained individuals are not serving a sentence, simply awaiting adjudication on their removal proceedings. They have no way to gauge how long they may be held, must fight their legal cases while imprisoned, and do not enjoy the privilege of cost-free access to public defenders (Kaufman 2008). This becomes critical because adjustment of status cases can revolve around the participation of family members and others; for example, by providing affidavits of support or confirmation that they will house released detainees (Morando Lakhani 2013). To the extent that families are vital to the legal process, visitation may be a critical way to communicate about legal cases. Unequal access to visitation may indicate a troubling form of legal inequality that could have severe repercussions.

Fourth, this study provides additional evidence of how immigration enforcement actions are experienced across immigrant communities and of varying legal statuses. We observed that detainees with undocumented children receive fewer face-to-face visits. Although a body of research has documented the detrimental effects of "illegality" and of the threats of enforcement mechanisms, to our knowledge, this study is the first to hone in on the experiences of detained immigrants and their families while detention is ongoing (Menjívar and Abrego 2012; Dreby 2015; Núñez and Heyman 2007; De Genova 2002; Brabeck and Xu 2010). It is possible that decreased access to face-to-face visitation could lead to increased despair and reduce family cohesion in immigrant families (Dreby 2015).

Finally, this study is important for its implications in understanding immigrant integration and immigrant identity formation. Future research could explore the ways that the children of detained immigrants, across legal statuses, experience and understand their parent's detention. As these children interact with the legal system, how do they come to understand their identities and their place in American society? In an era characterized by ever-expanding criteria for detention and deportation, these questions may be more important than ever before.

REFERENCES

Ackerman, Alissa R., and Rich Furman. 2013. "The Criminalization of Immigration and the Privatization of the Immigration Detention: Implications for Justice." *Contemporary Justice Review* 16(2): 251–63.

Amnesty International. 2009. *Jailed Without Justice: Immigration Detention in the USA*. New York: Amnesty International.

Bales, William D., and Daniel P. Mears. 2008. "Inmate Social Ties and the Transition to Society: Does Visitation Reduce Recidivism?" *Journal of Research in Crime and Delinquency* 45(3): 287–321.

Bermudez, Juan. n.d. "The Impact of US Immigration Policy in Deported Mexicans Based on the Survey on Migration in the Northern Border of Mexico (EMIF NORTE)." México: Consejo Nacional de Población.

Bosworth, Mary. 2014. *Inside Immigration Detention*. New York: Oxford University Press.

Brabeck, Kalina, and Qingwen Xu. 2010. "The Impact of Detention and Deportation on Latino Immigrant Children and Families: A Quantitative Exploration." *Hispanic Journal of Behavioral Sciences* 32(3): 341–61.

Brayne, Sarah. 2014. "Surveillance and System Avoidance: Criminal Justice Contact and Institutional Attachment." *American Sociological Review* 79(3): 367–91.

Carson, Bethany, and Eleana Diaz. 2015. "Payoff: How Congress Ensures Private Prison Profit with an Immigrant Detention Quota." Austin, Tex.: Grassroots Leadership. Accessed February 1, 2016. http://grassrootsleadership.org/reports/payoff-how-congress-ensures-private-prison-profit-immigrant-detention-quota#1.

Chaudry, Ajay, Randy Capps, Juan Manuel Pedroza, Rosa Maria Castaneda, Robert Santos, and Molly M. Scott. 2010. "Facing Our Future: Children in the Aftermath of Immigration Enforcement." Washington, D.C.: The Urban Institute.

Christian, Johnna. 2005. "Riding the Bus: Barriers to Prison Visitation and Family Management Strategies." *Journal of Contemporary Criminal Justice* 21(1): 31–48.

Cochran, Joshua C. 2012. "The Ties that Bond or the Ties that Break: Examining the Relationship Between Visitation and Prisoner Misconduct." *Journal of Criminal Justice* 40(5): 433–40.

Cochran, Joshua C., Daniel P. Mears, and William D. Bales. 2014. "Who Gets Visited in Prison? Individual- and Community-Level Disparities in Inmate Visitation Experiences." *Crime and Delinquency* 57(4): 572–99. DOI: 10.1177/0011128714542503.

Comfort, Megan. 2003. "In the Tube at San Quentin: The 'Secondary Prisonization' of Women Visiting Inmates." *Journal of Contemporary Ethnography* 32(1): 77–107. DOI: 10.1177/0891241602238939.

———. 2007. "Punishment Beyond the Legal Offender." *Annual Review of Law and Social Science* 3(1): 271–96. DOI: 10.1146/annurev.lawsoc-sci.3.081806.112829.

———. 2009. *Doing Time Together: Love and Family in the Shadow of the Prison*. Chicago: University of Chicago Press.

Coutin, Susan Bibler. 2000. *Legalizing Moves: Salvadoran Immigrants' Struggle for U.S. Residency*. Ann Arbor: University of Michigan Press.

———. 2011. "The Rights of Noncitizens in the United States." *Annual Review of Law & Social Science* 7 (December): 289–308.

De Genova, Nicholas P. 2002. "Migrant 'Illegality' and Deportability in Everyday Life." *Annual Review of Anthropology* 31 (October): 419–47.

Dreby, Joanna. 2012. "The Burden of Deportation on Children in Mexican Immigrant Families." *Journal of Marriage and Family* 74(4): 829–45.

———. 2015. *Everyday Illegal: When Policies Undermine Immigrant Families*. Oakland: University of California Press.

Edin, Kathryn, Timothy J. Nelson, and Rachelle Paranal. 2004. "Fatherhood and Incarceration as Potential Turning Points in the Criminal Careers of Unskilled Men." In *Imprisoning America: The Social Effects of Mass Incarceration*, edited by Mary Pattillo, Bruce Western and David Weiman. New York: Russell Sage Foundation.

Federal Bureau of Prisons. 2015. "Offenses: Statistics Based on Prior Month's Data." *Inmate Statis-*

tics, October 24, 2015. Accessed November 3, 2016. https://www.bop.gov/about/statistics/statistics_inmate_offenses.jsp.

García Hernández, César Cuauhtémoc. 2014. "Immigration Detention as Punishment." *UCLA Law Review* 61(5): 1346–414.

Glaze, Lauren E., and Laura M. Maruschak. 2008. "Parents in Prison and Their Minor Children." Bureau of Justice Statistics special report. Washington: Department of Justice. Accessed November 3, 2016. https://www.bjs.gov/content/pub/pdf/pptmc.pdf.

Golash-Boza, Tanya, and Pierrette Hondagneu-Sotelo. 2013. "Latino Immigrant Men and the Deportation Crisis: A Gendered Racial Removal Program." *Latino Studies* 11(3): 271–92. DOI: 10.1057/lst.2013.14.

Graham, John W., Allison E. Olchowski, and Tamika D. Gilreath. 2007. "How Many Imputations Are Really Needed? Some Practical Clarifications of Multiple Imputation Theory." *Prevention Science* 8(3): 206–13.

Grinstead, Olga, Bonnie Faigeles, Carrie Bancroft, and Barry Zack. 2001. "The Financial Cost of Maintaining Relationships with Incarcerated African American Men: A Survey of Women Prison Visitors." *Journal of African American Studies* 6(1): 59–69.

Hylton, Wil S. 2015. "The Shame of America's Family Detention Camps." *New York Times Magazine*, February 4. Accessed November 3, 2016. http://www.nytimes.com/2015/02/08/magazine/the-shame-of-americas-family-detention-camps.html.

Kaufman, Michael. 2008. "Detention, Due Process, and the Right to Counsel in Removal Proceedings." *Stanford Journal of Civil Rights and Civil Liberties* 4 (April): 113–49.

Kerwin, Donald, Daniela Alulema, and Siqi Tu. 2015. "Piecing Together the U.S. Immigrant Detention Puzzle One Night at a Time: An Analysis of All Persons in D.H.S.-I.C.E. Custody on September 22, 2012." *Journal on Migration and Human Security* 3(4): 330–76.

Light, Michael T., Michael Massoglia, and Ryan D. King. 2014. "Citizenship and Punishment: The Salience of National Membership in U.S. Criminal Courts." *American Sociological Review* 79(5): 825–47.

Martin, James S. 2001. *Inside Looking Out: Jailed Fathers' Perceptions About Separation from Their Children*. New York: LFB Scholarly Publishing.

Menjívar, Cecilia, and Leisy J. Abrego. 2012. "Legal Violence: Immigration Law and the Lives of Central American Immigrants." *American Journal of Sociology* 117(5): 1380–421.

Morando Lakhani, Sarah. 2013. "Producing Immigrant Victims' 'Right' to Legal Status and the Management of Legal Uncertainty." *Law and Social Inquiry* 38(2): 442–73.

National Immigration Forum. 2014. "Detention Costs Still Don't Add Up to Good Policy." Blog, September 24. Accessed November 3, 2016. https://immigrationforum.org/blog/detention-costs-still-dont-add-up-to-good-policy/.

Ngai, Mae M. 2004. *Impossible Subjects: Illegal Aliens and the Making of Modern America*. Princeton, N.J.: Princeton University Press.

Núñez, Guillermina Gina, and Josiah Mc.C. Heyman. 2007. "Entrapment Processes and Immigrant Communities in a Time of Heightened Border Vigilance." *Human Organization* 66(4): 354–65.

Poehlmann, Julie. 2005. "Representations of Attachment Relationships in Children of Incarcerated Mothers." *Child Development* 76(3): 679–96.

Ramakers, Anke, Robert Apel, Paul Nieuwbeerta, Anja Dirkzwager, and Johan Van Wilsem. 2014. "Imprisonment Length and Post-Prison Employment Prospects." *Criminology* 52(3): 399–427. DOI: 10.1111/1745-9125.12042.

Rios, Victor M. 2011. *Punished: Policing the Lives of Black and Latino Boys*. New York: NYU Press.

Rubin, Donald B. 1987. *Multiple Imputation for Nonresponse in Surveys*. New York: John Wiley & Sons.

Sayed, Faiza W. 2011. "Challenging Detention: Why Immigrant Detainees Receive Less Process than 'Enemy Combatants' and Why They Deserve More." *Columbia Law Review* 111(8): 1833–77.

Shlafer, Rebeccca J., Ann Booker Loper, and Leah Schillmoeller. 2015. "Introduction and Literature Review: Is Parent-Child Contact During Parental Incarceration Beneficial?" In *Children's Contact with Incarcerated Parents: Implications for Policy and Intervention*, edited by Julie Poehlmann-Tynan. Cham, SW: Springer.

Simanski, John F. 2014. "Immigration Enforcement Actions: 2013." *Annual Report 2014*. Washington: U.S. Department of Homeland Security Office of

Immigration Statistics. Accessed November 3, 2016. https://www.dhs.gov/sites/default/files/publications/ois_enforcement_ar_2013.pdf.

Stumpf, Juliet P. 2006. "The Crimmigration Crisis: Immigrants, Crime, and Sovereign Power." *American University Law Review* 56(2): 367–419.

Tahamont, Sarah 2013. "Essays on the Effects of Correctional Policies on Prison Misconduct." PhD diss., University of California, Berkeley.

Transactional Records Access Clearinghouse. 2013. "Legal Noncitizens Receive Longest ICE Detention." Syracuse, N.Y.: TRAC Reports. Accessed March 9, 2015. http://trac.syr.edu/immigration/reports/321/.

Travis, Jeremy. 2005. *But They All Come Back: Facing the Challenges of Prisoner Reentry*. Washington, D.C.: Urban Institute Press.

Western, Bruce. 2006. *Punishment and Inequality in America*. New York: Russell Sage Foundation.

Willen, Sarah S. 2007. "Toward a Critical Phenomenology of 'Illegality': State Power, Criminalization, and Abjectivity Among Undocumented Migrant Workers in Tel Aviv, Israel." *International Migration* 45(3): 8–38.

Assessing Parental Fitness and Care for Unaccompanied Children

LAUREN HEIDBRINK

Despite an increasing visibility of unaccompanied children in the media and among policymakers, little is known about the experiences of unaccompanied children within and beyond immigration detention. Based on a three-year, multi-sited ethnography with migrant children and their families, this paper traces the impact of U.S. institutional sponsorship policies and practices on unaccompanied children and their families. The article delineates several intersecting institutional logics—the universalization of childhood, the pathologization of mobility, and the criminalization of transnational parents—that underpin federal policies and practices for the care and custody of unaccompanied children. The article argues that these policies overflow from the spaces of detention and shape young people's help-seeking behaviors and sentiments of belonging following release from detention.

Keywords: unaccompanied children, detention and deportation, migration

Since 2010, the number of unaccompanied migrant children in federal custody has increased from approximately eight thousand annually to more than sixty-eight thousand in 2014. The influx of unaccompanied children has created a humanitarian crisis on the U.S.-Mexico border, generating an expansive network of institutions and organizations designed to "care for" children in immigration detention while the state attempts to remove them via deportation.[1] Reports by the United Nations High Commissioner for Refugees (UNHCR) and nongovernmental organizations (NGOs) largely attribute the influx of migrant children to gang violence, child abuse, and deepening poverty in El Salvador, Honduras, and Guatemala (Bookey 2014; UNHCR 2014). This line of thought frames the child as pathologically vulnerable, susceptible to adult malfeasance, be it parental abuse or neglect or criminal networks. Such explanations often presume that parents are either abusive or neglectful and un-

Lauren Heidbrink is an anthropologist and assistant professor in human development at California State University, Long Beach.

© 2017 Russell Sage Foundation. Heidbrink, Lauren. 2017. "Assessing Parental Fitness and Care for Unaccompanied Children." *RSF: The Russell Sage Foundation Journal of the Social Sciences* 3(4): 37–52. DOI: 10.7758 /RSF.2017.3.4.03. Research was generously funded by the National Science Foundation and the Wenner Gren Foundation. The author is profoundly grateful to the young people and their families who welcomed her into their lives. Direct correspondence to: Lauren Heidbrink at lauren.heidbrink@csulb.edu, 1250 Bellflower Boulevard, Long Beach, CA 90840.

1. An unaccompanied child is an individual under the age of eighteen without a parent or legal guardian able or willing to provide care and custody. Although the term *separated children* more accurately reflects the contingent and temporary nature of separation, the juridical category of the *unaccompanied child* used in the United States is a useful point of analysis because it alludes to children who are alone or unattached to kin or community, a claim that is the basis of legal and institutional interventions (for further discussion, see Heidbrink 2014, 34–36).

able or unwilling to protect and to care for their children. It further assumes that children are not involved contributors to their own migration decisions. Research with migrant children and their families reveals a compelling need to consider alternative narratives of unaccompanied child migration.

Although the past decade has brought increasing visibility to unaccompanied children in the media and among policymakers, little is known about the experiences of unaccompanied children beyond immigration detention.[2] Elsewhere I document the experiences of unaccompanied children in immigration detention in the United States and the ways they navigate immigration and family court (Heidbrink 2013, 2014, 2015). The question here is what happens to young people and their families following their release from detention. How do detention practices and institutional policies shape young people's everyday experiences as they adjust to life in a new country? How do young people understand these policies? And, what are the intended and unintended consequences of institutional policies on young people and their families?

In response to these questions, this article examines the institutional practices of sponsorship, colloquially termed family reunification, within Office of Refugee Resettlement (ORR) detention facilities for unaccompanied children. Under the Flores Settlement Agreement of 1997, unaccompanied children must be placed in the least restrictive environment, allowing them to be released to a parent or sponsor while removal proceedings are contested in immigration court.[3] ORR has designed a sponsorship process in which a parent or qualifying sponsor can complete a series of paperwork with the corresponding supporting documentation to secure an unaccompanied minor from federal custody. For those families able to secure the requisite documents and forms necessary to substantiate a parent's or sponsor's relationship to the child, ORR evaluates the suitability of the care provider and the caregiving environment following a series of institutional logics, logics that, I argue, are based on a series of flawed assumptions. Although these policies are designed to assess the safety and well-being of custodial relationships, tensions emerge between institutionalized notions of children's best interests and the complex sociocultural realities that may spur transnational migration of young people. In particular, I detail a coercive logic behind the ORR's policies and practices that simultaneously universalizes the space of childhood, ignores global inequality spurring migration, and pathologizes the mobility of young people. Such thinking is rooted in a heteronormative notion of the family, which implicates both kin and culture, and in its unattainable standards, ORR risks marginalizing young people and their families.

The confluence of cultural, legal, and institutional assumptions that undergird ORR's family reunification policies are predicated on a presumption that parents of unaccompanied children are unfit, in contrast to the presumption of suitability, absent an accusation of abuse, abandonment, or neglect, customary in the domestic child welfare system (see, for example, Thronson 2005, 2006). To overcome this presumptive deficit, ORR has bureaucratized assessments of parental fitness in a series of institutional processes that are at once disorienting for children and parents and at times insurmountable. Although much of the communication involved in the family reunification process is conducted by telephone and mail,

---

2. For a curated visual exhibit of the public discourses among the news media and nongovernmental organizations surrounding unaccompanied children in the United States, see http://www.youthcirculations.com (accessed March 8, 2017).

3. The 1997 Flores Agreement stipulates that the INS must ensure the prompt release of children from immigration detention; place children with a pending release from detention in the "least restrictive setting appropriate to the minor's age and special needs"; and implement basic standards of care and treatment of children in immigration detention, including a range of requirements for mental health services, health care, education, recreation, religious services, access to legal representation, telephones, and transportation arrangements. The Flores Settlement Agreement continues to set the minimum standards for the care of unaccompanied children in federal custody.

suitability assessments involve a home visit by subcontracted caseworkers to evaluate the caregiver and the caregiving environment and to issue a recommendation to ORR in a written report. Through an analysis of suitability reports and through the observation of home visits, this article examines the ways ORR enters the domestic sphere to assess care and the tension that emerge between assessment criterion and the meanings young people and their families assign to these institutional evaluations.

From long-term ethnographic research with young people within and beyond detention, we learn that the family reunification process has rippling effects on young people and their families long after children are released from detention. Children must contend with competing demands—at once encouraged to assimilate into American life through school attendance, participation in recreational activities, and securing social and health services, yet imminently deportable, needing to secure often costly legal representation to contest their removal in immigration court. These contradictory messages also have an impact on sponsors. ORR requires that family members or sponsors provide a nurturing and supportive environment, yet sponsors must sign agreements to surveil children's actions and movements at great consequence to both young people and their families. In these and other ways, the state shapes the everyday lives of young people beyond the confines of detention. At the same time, young people and their families navigate and contest the imposition of these contradictory demands in ways that attempt to preserve family integrity. By bringing together policies and practice with the everyday experiences of unaccompanied children and their families, I aim to highlight the complex ways young people experience the policies intended to ensure their best interests.

RESEARCH METHODS

This paper emerges from a three-year, multisited ethnography (from 2007 to 2010) that focuses on a largely invisible population of unaccompanied migrant children in highly restrictive and largely inaccessible spaces, such as border patrol stations, immigration detention, immigration and family courts, and in communities. In the larger study, from which this article emerges, I conducted multiple, one-on-one interviews with eighty-two detained and nondetained children from nineteen countries in five facilities in Illinois, Texas, and Indiana, and supplemented that information with participant observation for ten months within additional ORR facilities in New York, Arizona, and Virginia. I interviewed more than 250 stakeholders—individuals engaged in the apprehension and detention of migrant children, including government bureaucrats, NGO facility staff, follow-up service providers, attorneys, guardians ad litem, state court and immigration judges, border patrol and Immigration and Customs Enforcement (ICE) agents, consular officials, foster families, teachers, and policymakers across multiple sites in the United States, Mexico and El Salvador. In addition, I analyzed the files of eighteen unaccompanied children who underwent suitability assessments, accompanied caseworkers in home visits, and conducted semi-formal interviews and participant observation with another twenty young people who received follow-up services provided by ORR subcontractors. I draw on this larger study to provide context for the following ethnographic research with a sample of twenty-six youth and their families or sponsors living in the United States. I focus on their experiences of release from immigration detention, the integration of young people into families, and the force of institutional and legal processes on everyday experiences and help-seeking behaviors of young people.

The majority of young people with whom I conducted longitudinal, ethnographic research are from Mexico (n = 4) and Central America (Guatemala, n = 8; El Salvador, n = 5; Honduras, n = 3; and Nicaragua, n = 1). Four additional countries are represented in this sample: Somalia (n = 2), China (n = 1), India (n = 1), and Brazil (n = 1). In addition to participant observation, archival research, and surveys, I conducted multiple informal or semistructured interviews lasting one to three hours in English, Spanish, or Portuguese; all translations are my own. The majority of interviews with young people were conducted in person, both while detained and at various points after their release. The remaining interviews, primarily with those who moved multiple times, were conducted by telephone. When possible, interviews were recorded and transcribed. In compliance with the policies of ORR and individual facilities, interviews conducted within detention centers were not recorded. For these, I relied on handwritten notes taken during interviews and transcribed immediately afterward. This longitudinal ethnographic approach allows me to track change over time and to critically examine the consequences of policies and institutional practices on young people and their families.

After the research was completed, I served as guardian ad litem (GAL) for unaccompanied children, visiting them in immigration detention and accompanying them following release as they enroll in school, seek employment, access services, and attend immigration court. Although this ongoing GAL work is excluded from this paper for both confidentiality and ethical considerations, it informs my analysis of ongoing patterns and trends.

In contrast to media accounts, which depict unaccompanied child migrants as alone or abandoned by their families, I use the household as the primary unit of analysis because migrant children and youth are members of rich social and kinship networks. Anthropologists have long recognized that migrants are members of transnational, multigenerational households and that children contribute to familial migration decisions (Brettell 2003; Fass 2005). By focusing on households affected by child detention, I attend to how young people reintegrate into their families, peer groups, and communities, paying close attention to the ways institutional policies and practices shape intimate, familial relationships. This methodological approach allows for an analysis of the unintended consequences of policies and practices on children and their families when state-sanctioned care is considered complete.

INSTITUTIONAL ASSUMPTIONS OF CARE

One of the few benevolent provisions for children under U.S. immigration law is that unaccompanied children can be released from immigration detention to the custody of a parent or sponsor without posting a bond as they contest removal proceedings in immigration court. Within seventy-two hours of apprehension, whether by ICE within the interior of the United States or by Customs and Border Protection along the U.S.-Mexico or U.S.-Canada border, unaccompanied children are transferred to the care and custody of the Department of Health and Human Services' Office of Refugee Resettlement. Through a series of subcontracts with nongovernmental organizations, ORR detains unaccompanied children in one of approximately one hundred detention facilities throughout the United States. While the children are detained, ICE initiates deportation proceedings. Simultaneously, children pursue one of the following custodial arrangements: release to a parent or sponsor, placement in federal foster care or group home, transfer between ORR facilities, transfer to adult detention on their eighteenth birthday, or deportation. The complexity and variation of children's custodial and legal cases informs each trajectory: factors taken into consideration include the availability and suitability of care providers, assessments of children's eligibility for legal immigration relief, trauma and delinquency histories, age at the time of detention, and the availability of federal resources. I focus on the processes of family reunification, the most common trajectory for nearly 65 percent of unaccompanied children (Byrne and Miller 2012). In 2012, of those released to a sponsor, 48 percent of children were released to a parent, 23 percent to another adult relative, 15 percent to a sibling, 14 percent to a nonrelative, and 1 percent to a grandparent (ORR 2012).

Despite the significant variation of children's life experiences and origins, the institution's policies and practices are predicated on a series of "child-saving" assumptions, and—as I show in the sections that follow—these assumptions often clash with the socioeconomic realities and cultural beliefs and practices of many migrant communities. Namely, I argue that the cultural construction of childhood and the pathologization of mobility bind children and their families to unattainable expectations. Parental fitness is scrutinized, behaviors criminalized, and cultures implicated as institutional actors evaluate their caregiving. Although delineated discretely for analytical clarity, in practice these expectations intertwine, and are thus experienced in varied ways.

UNIVERSALIZED CHILDHOOD

Now in his third month of detention in a New York facility for unaccompanied children, fifteen-year-old Ricardo grew increasingly anxious about remitting money to his family in Tacaná, a Guatemalan town bordering Mexico, who had mortgaged their home for $6,500 to finance his migration.[4] Ricardo described the consequences of his failure to remit, including verbal threats, physical violence, and expulsion from their land as the local *prestamista* (moneylender) had vowed. Struggling to explain his detention to his parents in a telephone call, Ricardo said, "I am here [in the United States] but this place [detention] is not America. I can't leave. I am losing time here."

The caseworker, known as a family reunification specialist, counseled him to remain calm: "Focus on your education. That is not your responsibility to work. Let your parents worry about paying. This [migration] was their decision, not yours, so it is not your debt." The contrast between the caseworker's advice to ignore his financial debt and Ricardo's anxiety about fulfilling his social obligation to his family reveals an important gap between the assumptions about childhood made the institution and its actors and the expectations held by the population they serve.

Emerging in the early 1900s among European and American middle classes, childhood continues to be understood as the period when a person is younger than eighteen years old that is marked by a series of developmental stages leading to maturation (Bucholtz 2002; Cunningham 2012). Initially institutionalized through psychological assessments of children as "nonsocial" or "presocial," childhood has evolved into assessments of "normal" or "abnormal" children (Fleer, Heregaard, and Tudge 2009). This normative framing views children—understood as naturally innocent, vulnerable, and dependent on adults—as being in the process of becoming rather than being, exclusively reduced to factors of biology and divested from the varied historic, sociocultural, sociopolitical, and socioeconomic contexts that shape differing constructions of childhood. "Children are learners not earners" has gained increasing traction as childhood worldwide has become a period of compulsory schooling and play, insulated from the vagaries of the economic market (Mayall and Morrow 2011). Left uninterrogated, the universalization of childhood not only ignores the vast diversity of childhoods but also pathologizes those not conforming to the hegemonic norm. Although similar values and professional practices are used in the U.S. domestic child welfare system, the consequences of holding global youth and their families to a cultural-constructed understanding of childhood, one historically rooted in white, middle-class norms, has particularly profound consequences on family integrity and young people's sense of belonging.

In recent decades, the anthropology of youth has centered on children and youth as social actors, giving voice to a social group often ignored and marginalized and recognizing their legitimacy and importance as subjects of research (on giving voice, James and Prout 1997; Honwana and Boeck 2005; Bluebond-Langner and Korbin 2007; on recognizing, Mayall 2002). Researchers have documented their social agency in the ways young people create, sustain, and repair their social worlds amid the unequal distributions of power and resources that characterize their social lives (Hutchby and Moran-Ellis 1998). Diverging from existing adult languages and meanings for understanding children and youth, scholars argue that youth employ personal agency to construct their worlds through their own competencies and through their relationships to adults and institutions (Christensen and James 2008). In other words, considering only the structural forces in children's lives and reducing childhood and youth to periods of transition or molding threaten to negate their contributions as social actors.

Although scholars have shown the legal and social categories of a child and childhood to be highly problematic, U.S. immigration law and ORR policies continue to define childhood narrowly and ethnocentrically (see Stephens

---

4. Following disciplinary custom, all names are pseudonyms.

1995; Lancy 2014; Cunningham 2005). For example, caseworkers describe the attributes of a child as dependent on the actions and relationships with his or her parents; whereas in the country of origin, the same child may maintain his or her own household, work independently, at times even be a parent—attributes often associated with adults in the U.S. context. A universalized childhood is institutionalized in the efforts of ORR and NGO subcontractors in the ways children's days are structured around schooling, recreation, and socialization programs, all which belie the fact that children have no freedom of movement and are continually surveilled by staff and cameras throughout facilities (Heidbrink 2014). Within the spaces of detention, ORR seeks to socialize children into American childhood through behavioral modification programs, education, hygiene practices, and incentivized trips to stores like Walmart and Target.

The contradictory messages—that is, the tension between this notion of American childhood as the natural, and best, model for development and their status as detained illegal immigrants—are not lost on young people:

> My mom is sick. She needs me to pay for her medicine. How is coloring inside the lines going to help me? — Manjgit, age sixteen, India

> I just want a cup of hot coffee; the only coffee in this place is on the wall [pointing to a poster hanging on the basement cafeteria wall]. They say it will stunt my growth but I've been drinking it every day of my life. It's too late. —Faviola, age fourteen, Brazil

> The walls here are bright yellow and there are posters all over saying we have human rights; but we have no rights here. They bring people here and show them, look how wonderful this place is and how they are taking care of us, but it isn't that way. We are stuck here and we can't get out. It's like I am caught in this big joke but there is no punchline. —Isaias, age sixteen, Mexico

Some young people describe feeling infantilized by educational and recreational activities that simultaneously ignore their lack of freedom within detention. Others internalize messages of "appropriate" and "proper" childhoods. The ways ORR, NGOs and attorneys reframe childhood provides a new cultural script rooted in a romanticized childhood that clashes with young people's culturally and socially mediated experiences in their countries of origin. Young people are left struggling to reconcile the two, and at times, holding their parents culpable for failing to provide them with the markers of a "good" childhood.

PATHOLOGIZED MOBILITY

Developmental models of childhood are particularly problematic for migrant children and youth, bolstering the fear that a displaced child with fractured social ties and a lack of attachment to community results in solitary, detrimental behavior carried into adulthood (Eckenrode et al. 1995). Children who remain highly mobile are seen as missing the opportunity to learn the skills necessary to live a productive life (Sampson 1988). Spatial fixity, then, becomes the naturalized assumption for the proper place of the child and a requirement for social connectivity (Fass 2005, 938). Although the norm of stability may be an ideal for childhood, a satisfactory or fulfilling childhood is not necessarily forfeited by the child's mobility. For many children, migration may be a rational resource within a context of global inequities. Migration may allow for greater access to educational and employment opportunities and may facilitate consumption practices that otherwise are restricted to those more "privileged" (Hannerz 1996). Young people may circulate between households or geographical territories in an effort to satisfy basic needs, ensure their physical and psychic integrity, or expand educational, professional, or marriage opportunities—and, importantly, this mobility is often undertaken with the explicit or tacit support of their extended kinship networks.

Indeed, although children make up nearly 20 percent of the world's migratory flows (Dobson and Stillwell 2000, 395), their movement is typically viewed as an indication of rupture, be it natural or man-made disasters, violence or abuse, divorce or parental death, leading to the increased vulnerability of children who as a result are exposed to harsh labor or living conditions (Hashim 2006, 4), or to abuse or abandonment (Suárez-Orozco and Suárez-Orozco 2009; Vericker, Kuehn, and Capps 2007). Each reduces childhood mobility outside the family structure to pathological terms, particularly the specialized literatures of child soldiers, street children, and trafficking victims (Huijsmans and Baker 2012; Panter-Brick 2002), and a growing literature on "unaccompanied children" (Bhabha and Schmidt 2008; Byrne and Miller 2012; Terrio 2015). Such discourses respond to child migration as a symptom of trauma and rupture rather than asking why young people migrate, focusing problematically on the presence of the individual child migrant rather than the diverse sociocultural, sociopolitical, and socioeconomic circumstances that spur mobility and the varying meanings young people assign to their (dis)placement. The pathologization of mobility thus ignores histories of colonialism, foreign intervention, civil war, and neoliberal reforms that result in extreme social inequality globally.

For example, in undertaking the unaccompanied journey to the United States, Ricardo and his family sought survival and advancement. His parents' insistence on his remitting of money and repayment of the migration debt documented by the caseworker during his weekly monitored phone calls, however, became a source of concern in his potential placement with an uncle in rural Georgia. The caseworker explained in a weekly staffing meeting: "I am worried that he is just going to work and not go to school. This is an uncle he doesn't know well, who doesn't have kids and who is ill-equipped to provide [Ricardo] with the structure and stability he requires to realize his potential." Citing factors such as the uncle's precarious employment status seasonally harvesting peaches, his limited financial income to support Ricardo, an ambiguous potential for viable child-care arrangements (in spite of Ricardo's upcoming sixteenth birthday), and the household composition of several unrelated men renting a single home, the specialist concluded, "This placement is an unhealthy living arrangement for a young boy coming of age in a new country." These criterion—residential fixity, stable and well-paying employment, supervision, and heteronormative household composition—are rooted in middle-class, Western social norms that reflect a romantic ideal of childhood that conflicts with the social, cultural, and economic realities of many migrant children and their families (for further discussion on the history of the Child Savers movement and its impact on the care of unaccompanied children under ORR custody, see Heidbrink 2014, 63–83). Trapped between these intersecting assumptions of the natural state of childhood and the pathologization of migration, Ricardo's release to his uncle was denied. Ricardo was later deported to Guatemala.

CRIMINALIZATION OF TRANSNATIONAL PARENTS

Implicit in such assumptions about childhood is a condemnation of parents for not providing the requisite conditions for "natural development." Certain epithets are commonly used to describe parents of unaccompanied children—neglectful, abusive, or ignorant—for forcing their children implicitly or explicitly to undertake desperate, clandestine journeys in pursuit of economic opportunity. These assumptions not only decontextualize the complex decision-making processes of young people and their families but also homogenize the multiplicity of young people's experiences of migration, at the same time underwriting the public policies and institutional practices that evaluate parental fitness and determine custody arrangements (Heidbrink and Statz 2017).

At once frightening and onerous to potential guardians and children, the sponsor of an unaccompanied child must complete a complex paperwork process that includes providing proof of the sponsor's identity (birth certificate, passport, national identity document, or driver's license), the child's identity (birth certificate), relationship to the child (such as court records, guardianship records, marriage certificates, or birth certificates), and address if the sponsor is not a biological parent of the child (such as current lease, mortgage statement, utility bills). In addition, sponsors must consent to background and biometric checks, which includes disclosing aliases, current and former residences, and household members. In the case of nonparental sponsors, all household members must also submit biometric data, which are processed through the Federal Bureau of Investigations National Crime Information Center, the Central Index System, and the Deportable Alien Control System. As a caseworker in Texas explained, "The sponsorship process is designed to ensure that we are not releasing children to abusive sponsors or to parents who just want their kids to support them, or worse, criminal networks of traffickers or human smugglers who have a vested financial interest in children working."

As a sponsor of his son, who was detained on arrival from Honduras, Santiago described the logistical, financial, and emotional toll of the family reunification process:

> It is all so overwhelming. *Cédula* [national identity document], birth certificates, death certificates, pay-stubs, leases, so many forms to complete and sign. . . . I want to do right by [my son] but this is too much. I have done nothing wrong. I have tried to be the best father I can, sending money each month, calling regularly, sending gifts at Christmas, asking about their grades. I have tried my best, but this [pointing to a stack of forms] makes me feel like a criminal.

In the interview, Santiago describes his efforts to maintain contact through Facebook, Skype, and phone calls with his wife and children, remitting $500 monthly from his meager income, and cutting costs through sharing a two-bedroom apartment with eight people and "eating only rice and beans my first two years here." Rather than recognizing these as expressions of care, parental responsibility, and self-sacrifice, Santiago's limited access to material and financial resources is held in the institutional process of determining "parental fitness" as condemnatory evidence of his deficiency as a parental provider. In effect, he is criminalized for being a transnational parent.

Simply securing the necessary documents from his native Honduras presented a series of bureaucratic vortexes: paying a notary to secure the requisite documents in Honduras regarding his wife's untimely death, taking several days off work to travel to the embassy in Chicago, and in so doing risking his employment as a stock clerk at a local Aldi. More than 70 percent of sponsors and parents in this study expressed similar concerns regarding the time and cost associated with securing required documentation, at times risking tenuous employment, and most often with no support from ORR or its NGO subcontractors.

Explicitly, the bureaucratic process is intended to ensure the safety and well-being of post-release placements. Implicitly, however, the institutional presumption is that parents of unaccompanied migrant children are unfit by virtue of their child's "unaccompanied" status (6 U.S.C. § 279(g)(2)). The juridical category of the "unaccompanied alien child" points to, and is constructed from, a perceived rupture in the social unit of the nuclear family and calls into question a parent's capacity to attend to the child's "care, custody, and discipline." Rather than a presumption of innocence, as is customary in the domestic child welfare system absent an accusation of abuse, abandonment, or neglect, compliance with a convoluted bureaucratic process becomes the metric of fitness for parents of unaccompanied children. The sacrifices of parents and families to facilitate an often expensive and dangerous journey are ignored, holding a young person's mobility, marked by their status as an "unaccompanied alien minor," as irrevocable evidence of parental malfeasance or neglect. Placing the parent alongside the smuggler or trafficker as actors from whom children need protection, as the caseworker explained, emboldens the criminalization of parents. Because of this situation, only through completing a rigorous series of institutional paperwork and enduring scrutiny by NGO subcontractors may parents regain custody of their children from the federal government.

For undocumented parents who sponsor their children, the risks are compounded. Beyond the obstacles of engaging with multiple state actors to secure documents, and to fluently navigate complex institutional processes required of all sponsors, undocumented parents must divulge their identities (both real and assumed), address, unlawful employment (and employer), as well as identifying information such as date and point of unlawful entry into the United States, information that regularly appears on a Notice to Appear, the charging document issued in deportation proceedings. No presumption or claim of confidentiality exists despite the caseworkers' attempts to allay the fears that ICE will use this information to apprehend unauthorized parents. In 2012, advocates reported that ICE had begun using information disclosed by sponsors in raids on workplaces and households—a fact, several attorneys contended, that ORR seeks to conceal from potential sponsors.

Parents are thus confronted with the stark realities of their deportability in the sponsorship process forced to weigh a multiplicity of factors, emotions, and fates. Ana grappled with this reality in sponsoring her fifteen-year-old daughter Haydee from ORR custody, weighing the multiple demands on her as a single parent of a transnational family:

> What happens if immigration comes after me? I become just a statistic like so many other people that just disappear from here and months later reappear in a different place. And, you know, it isn't just about me or about [Haydee]. I have two children born here [in the United States] and send money each month to my mother who is watching [my son and daughter] in Honduras. They depend on me to eat, to go to school . . . to survive. Look, it isn't just about me; it's about them.

Despite assurances from a caseworker that deportation would not result from sponsorship, Ana did not complete the required paperwork in three months following Haydee's apprehension.

Because she had only limited information about the reunification process, even with regular assurances from her mother that she was working on the paperwork, Haydee grew hopeless in a Texas facility:

> I don't understand. I came this whole way, risked so much so that we could finally be together but now she doesn't want me. She says she loves me and wants me to be with her but maybe she doesn't love me anymore. I am stuck here in this place, losing time. Why doesn't she just turn in the papers? Maybe it is all just words; maybe she wants a new life with her new kids without me. I can't wait anymore . . . enough . . . I don't want to go back [to Honduras] but what option do I have?

Citing the confidentiality of the sponsor's details and the protection of children from "unnecessary worry and anxiety" as an ORR federal field specialist explained, children often struggle to understand the bureaucratic intricacies of the sponsorship process and the social realities of their sponsor or family members. In an absence of information, children decipher the sponsorship process from their peers in the facility and from family members during their weekly phone calls. The absence of communication with children leaves young people to make assumptions about their parent's willingness and ability to provide care, and even love. Haydee was left to interpret her mother's inaction as a lack of emotional investment or care, an interpretation that shaped her willingness to accept voluntary departure rather than to pursue an asylum claim.

ASSESSING SUITABILITY

In a small but growing number of sponsorship applications, ORR subcontractors conduct home studies, known as suitability assessments. Suitability assessments are evaluations to determine the safety and appropriateness of the caregiving environment and caregiver prior to the release of an unaccompanied children from federal custody. Under the William Wilberforce Trafficking Victims Protection Reauthorization Act of 2008,

> A home study shall be conducted for a child who is a victim of a severe form of trafficking in persons, a special needs child with a disability (as defined in section 12102 of title 42), a child who has been a victim of physical or sexual abuse under circumstances that indicate that the child's health or welfare has been significantly harmed or threatened, or a child whose proposed sponsor clearly presents a risk of abuse, maltreatment, exploitation, or trafficking to the child based on all available objective evidence. (U.S. Code § 1232 (c)(3)(B), Public Law 110–457)

Among the criteria determining suitability, both in initial assessments by facility staff and in suitability assessments by subcontracted caseworkers, are factors such as the consistency between the family reunification application and interviews with the child and sponsor, income and employment verification, family relationship, and household composition. More subjective elements include the gender composition of the household, authenticity of family ties, child-care arrangements, sleeping quarters, attitudes of household members, number of family members in the home, poverty level, and the ability of the sponsor or family member to care for the child. Some criteria, such as a criminal record or a pending deportation order, de facto disqualify a sponsor, in which case a suitability assessment would not be conducted.

Among the eighteen suitability assessments I examined and the seven home visits I observed, assessments were required of a father due to a conviction for driving under the influence (DUI) (n = 3), a mother whose HIV status was considered a potential "hazard for the health and safety of the child" (n = 1), a twenty-three-year-old sibling seeking sponsorship of his sixteen-year-old sister (n = 1), parents of children with mental health diagnoses (n = 5) or physical disabilities (n = 3), a nonabusive parent of a child who suffered child abuse (n = 2), and a family who lived in a "dangerous" neighborhood (n = 3).

Imely, a sixteen-year-old born in Mexico and raised since the age of five in the United States, explained: "I haven't always seen eye-to-eye with my mother, but she is a good woman. She has worked lots of jobs, cleaning homes, cooking for people, caring for an old woman at night, all to take care of us kids. I haven't always appreciated her, but she isn't a bad person." Imely was transferred to an ORR facility in Chicago following a six-month stint in domestic residential treatment center in Florida. After nine months in three ORR facilities, she was "stepped up" to increasingly restrictive detention centers due to behavioral issues. Imely was frustrated at the inability to reunify with her mother, because, as the suitability report indicated,

Her mother struggles to provide for her seven children as a single-mother [sic] working under the table. She is unable to provide the financial and emotional structure that [Imely] requires to reintegrate into school and social and familial life. Because her mother is always working, [Imely] is largely left unattended and this lack of supervision is precisely what led to her involvement with the juvenile justice system.

Because of her tenuous employment as a domestic worker and elder-care provider, Imely's mother was unable to monitor her children's behaviors, and so unable to provide the discipline and structure deemed critical for Imely. Compounded by her meager income, her mother was seen as, the report read, "unable to provide the appropriate care and conditions [Imely] requires for healthy growth and development."

Instead, Imely was released to a maternal uncle in Indiana, a legal permanent resident, who was also a single parent with two children, but who maintained a stable job as a medical aide in an assisted living complex. Although better equipped to deliver the material markers of an American childhood, he proved unable to provide the emotional support Imely desired. "He doesn't know how to talk to me. I need to talk and he is afraid of me or something. He has sons so maybe he just doesn't know how to talk to daughters, but you know what I think? I think he just doesn't want to be bothered by me and what I need right now in my life."

At fifteen, José was apprehended with a friend by the Los Angeles police for loitering at 11:00 p.m. at his high school's football stadium. José's friend was found with two ounces of marijuana, and both teenagers were taken into police custody. Before charges were filed, José was transferred to ICE and, because of his status as a minor, was then transferred to an ORR staff secure facility in Chicago. His mother, with whom he had lived for the previous ten years, since they immigrated from El Salvador, completed the required sponsorship paperwork within two weeks. In a phone conversation, his mother disclosed to the caseworker that she had difficulty controlling her son's activities and that he was increasing falling in with "the wrong crowd." After further scrutiny of his police file and lagging school attendance, the caseworker requested a suitability assessment.

Caseworkers are at times wary of requesting a suitability assessment because home studies can delay a child's placement with a sponsor and require that a child remain detained for the duration of the study. During my research, the average length of time for a suitability assessment was ninety days, with a minimum of seventy-five days and a maximum of five months. A suitability assessment often is not immediately requested on the child's apprehension, but instead, as more information is gathered from young people and their sponsors, may be requested several months later.[5] Ultimately, the evaluator recommended that José not be reunified with his mother because she could not protect him from the risks presented by their "gang-infested neighborhood." The caseworker recommended in her report that his mother "seek alternative housing in a safe neighborhood, removed from the risks of gangs and drugs which threaten [José's] physical safety and emotional well-being, discourage his regular school attendance, and limit his future potential." When presented with this recommendation, according to the caseworker, José's mother said that she could not afford to move and currently lived close to both her current employment and her church, which she attended regularly. "These are not unrealistic requests for a mother who loves and desires to reunify with her son," the caseworker remarked. Institutional conceptions of family assume that expressions of care often are met with a prescribed emotive response; his mother's reluctance did not coincide with the caseworker's expectations for a loving mother. José's involvement with the criminal justice system (though never formally charged) was cited as evidence that his mother was unable to parent adequately. After five months in detention, José grew increasingly frustrated and threatened to request voluntary departure to El Salvador, a country he hardly remembered.

When I met Isabella, she was entering her seventh month in a west Texas facility. For two months, her mother struggled to complete the requisite sponsorship paperwork, only to find that on submission, the caseworker requested a suitability assessment. At fourteen years old, Isabella was eager to return to school in Michigan, where she was with an uncle when he was apprehended at a routine traffic stop: "A taillight landed me here and now I don't know what will happen to me. I don't think they will let me live with my mom but they don't say why." The caseworker's home study described Isabella's father as "a domineering head-of-household." In her report, she surmised the possibility of "domestic violence in the household." However, the report indicated that interviews with a neighbor and a teacher did not reveal evidence of this accusation and the father's criminal record was clean, with the exception of a ten-year-old DUI. Describing Isabella's mother as "timid and subservient," the caseworker elaborated: "due to Ms. [Rodriguez's] undocumented status in the United States, she is likely disinclined to contact the authorities if she is threatened or experiences abuse. In addition, it is unlikely she will access the necessary medical and social services for [Isabella]." Caseworkers routinely recognize the unique risks that unauthorized parents face, particularly in states with harsh anti-immigrant policies. Fourteen of the eighteen suitability reports examined indicate that these risks impede a sponsor's ability to navigate state bureaucracies necessary for securing needed services. Yet per the Flores Settlement Agreement, an undocumented parent may sponsor his or her child from federal custody. Ultimately, ORR agreed with the home study and declined to release Isabella to her mother's custody.

Although, ORR routinely assesses parental fitness and makes custody determinations, as an administrative body it has no legal author-

---

5. ORR has recently made efforts to reduce the time to complete home studies; however, the process may still take several months from the time the study is ordered until the final ORR decision.

ity to limit or to terminate parental rights. However, in practice, ORR's refusal to release Isabella to her mother de facto prohibits Isabella from reunifying with her parents. Neither Isabella nor her parents had attorneys to file a writ of habeas corpus to contest ORR's ongoing custody of Isabella. Isabella's parents had few options to reunify with their daughter. Unable to remain in federal custody and found to not qualify for legal relief (a prerequisite to enter federal foster care), Isabella lingered in detention.

Although no single factor universally determines denied placement, the confluence of institutional assumptions that idealize childhood, pathologize mobility, and criminalize impoverished and transnational parents shape the caseworker's assessment of a child's risk of harm and delinquency. Western social norms inculcated in the personal beliefs and professional training of caseworkers are transmitted though assessments of caregiving and caregivers. When working cross-culturally, the judgments documented in suitability assessments become particularly problematic for migrant children. As a result, family members were routinely denied custody of their children because the sponsor was presumed ill-equipped to meet the needs of the child. Held to a living standard, encapsulated by the type of neighborhood, home, and income, families struggle to regain custody of their children.

REVERBERATING EFFECTS

Families and children are not immune to these bureaucratic processes: state policies and practices overflow from the spaces of detention. In its most immediate sense, the bureaucratization of care frequently reconfigures households, most directly by denying release of children to their families. Sponsorship policies also impact household members, who themselves were never detained. At twenty-six, Jorge left his elder brother Juan's home where he had lived since his arrival in the United States; Juan's arrest for robbery a year earlier was preventing a third, younger brother from being released to Juan's custody. Family reunification specialists may advise household members to relocate, or, as with Jorge, family members may preemptively move as a strategy to ensure a young person's reunification with particular attention to ORR's expectations for household composition. ORR policies also reconfigure spatial arrangements within households. A caseworker for Clara, a sixteen-year-old from Mexico, informed Clara's father that she could not be released until the sleeping arrangements in their two-bedroom apartment were segregated by gender. Leaving Clara's father to sleep with his two young stepsons, Clara would sleep with her stepmother, whom she had yet to meet.

Prior to release, a sponsor must sign a written agreement vowing to ensure that a child attends all immigration proceedings, that the child remains in the United States while his or her immigration case is adjudicated, and that a child report for removal if he or she is ordered to be deported. The sponsor must agree to notify the Department of Homeland Security (DHS) within seventy-two hours if a child flees the placement or is threatened by smugglers or traffickers. Furthermore, the sponsor agrees that if he or she does not comply with the agreement, DHS may take custody of the child again. In other words, in signing this agreement, the sponsor must assume the surveillance and discipline of the unaccompanied child from ORR and DHS. This surveillance weighs heavily on children and their sponsors alike.

Young people describe feeling "trapped," "stuck," or "like I'm still in jail" following their release from detention. Over coffee at a diner in Indiana, Esmeralda spoke of her relationship with her aunt who serves as her sponsor:

> She is on edge. Everything I do, she reminds me that they can send me back to jail: "Don't be late to school. Come straight home. Don't get into trouble. Don't, don't, don't or else they will take me to jail." My mom says the same: "Don't do anything wrong or they will deport me and your brother and sisters." My aunt watches me all the time. I feel like I am back in jail with all those cameras watching every move but now it's my aunt and my mom. They say I'll get everyone deported if I mess up. It's too much pressure. I just can't handle it anymore.

When a sponsor assumes custody of a child from ORR, he or she must sign a Sponsor's Agreement to Conditions of Release form, in which the sponsor assumes responsibility for the child's physical, mental, and financial well-being, including medical, dental, and mental health; school enrollment; legal services; and physical needs (food, shelter, and clothing). Children, and by extension their sponsors, are encouraged to establish the markers of middle-class childhood through compulsory school, participation in recreational activities, and basic standards of health and housing. Because children remain in immigration removal proceedings, families are also compelled to secure legal representation, often at great cost. Despite these expectations, no financial support is provided to the sponsor; no health care is provided to children; and no assistance is given in locating an attorney to represent the child in removal proceedings. At the time of my research, 1.5 percent of children released from ORR custody received post-release services. Primarily through telephone conversations, a caseworker assists young people with referrals to school, health, and legal services for up to six months following release.[6] For the 98.5 percent of children without post-release services, young people and their families must navigate a myriad of bureaucracies to meet ORR's conditions of release.

Julio, a fourteen-year-old from Guatemala now residing with his parents in rural Georgia, told me over the telephone, "I tried to enroll in school but they said I couldn't because I don't have the right papers. My mom didn't go to work so she could come with me but they sent us away. Besides, I need to work. I can't spend all day in school when we have to pay a lawyer. They say it is expensive." The barriers to school enrollment are considerable. As a native Mam speaker, Julio and his mother struggled to communicate with the English-speaking administrators. Despite a legal right to enroll in public school regardless of his legal status, without an advocate to assist him he was deterred. Having accompanied dozens of young people to enroll in public schools from Maryland to New Jersey to Illinois to Texas, I have observed that these barriers are not easily overcome, even with a cultural interlocutor or advocate. An additional pressure is to contribute financially to the household through unauthorized employment, at times at the expense of school attendance.

Young people and their families must thus navigate competing narratives that at once encourage them to assimilate and prepare them for removal from the United States (see, for example, Grace and Roth 2015). In court proceedings, affidavits from teachers, pastors, neighbors, and therapists attest to judges that a young person is an asset to his or her community, of good moral character, and worthy of immigration relief. Yet young people are hyperaware of their tentative status in the United States, unsure of the desire to develop social relationships that may be severed should they be removed. Guillermo, a sixteen-year-old from Chiapas, Mexico, struggled with this contradiction:

> Do they want me to stay or go? I mean, they say I should do well in school and make friends and volunteer at church, but the lawyer wants another $5,000 before court. I already paid $2,500. Where am I going to get $5,000? I already borrowed from my aunt and cousin and a couple of friends. I need to work but then I have to be in school and play on the soccer team and then volunteer? I don't have time for all of this.

Rather than enroll in the local high school, Guillermo enlisted in English classes on the weekend and worked in construction, a job his cousin had secured for him. As his court date neared, Guillermo was unable to earn the needed $5,000 for his attorney. In the interim, his mother still residing in Chiapas, had become ill and Guillermo remitted his available income to his mother for dialysis. "I want to stay and do the right thing, but it's my mother. There is no choice here." Children are coun-

---

6. Per the Trafficking Victims Protection Reauthorization Act of 2008, post-release services are provided to children who underwent a home study and who have "mental health or other needs who could benefit from ongoing assistance from a social welfare agency" (8 U.S. Code § 1232 (c)(3)B).

seled and sponsors obliged to seek markers of a middle-class childhood while ignoring the innumerable structural obstacles that impede their efforts.

Young people describe multiple complex emotions, from elation and euphoria at the moment of reunification to distress at not recognizing parents after prolonged periods to despondence on meeting new siblings to anxiety around language acquisition and adaptation to schooling. For detained and nondetained young people, these sentiments are not uncommon when reuniting with family members after a prolonged separation. However, I suggest that institutional policies and practices designed to ensure children's best interests not only intensify an otherwise difficult transition but also inflict significant harm to children's sentiments of self-worth and belonging.

Feelings of anxiety, confusion, disappointment, and resentment that young people describe experiencing during the sponsorship process do not resolve on their release from immigration detention, but rather continue to shape their sentiments of belonging to kin and community following release. After six months in detention, Christina, a fifteen-year-old from Honduras, was released to a family friend who reluctantly served as her sponsor. Christina reflected on the impact of her mother's failure to successfully sponsor her from detention, "We aren't the same, me and my mom. She has her new family. I'm doing my best here. I miss her even though I see her every so often. I wouldn't say that coming here [to the United States] was a mistake but I did not plan on being alone." Christina described a tense relationship, at times feeling lost, and emotionally disconnected from her mother and family. "We fight for no real reason about everything. . . . If I really think about it, I'm sad and angry and disappointed and lonely all at the same time." For Christina, and others, the social and cultural adaptation to a new life in the United States is compounded by the emotional challenges accompanying a failed reunification after prolonged periods of separation. The irony remains that the very institutions claiming to ensure a child's best interests inflict harm through detention (absence of freedom), through valuing or negating kinship relationships, and through the setting of implausible expectations often with no support in reaching them.

CONCLUSION

While detained in ORR facilities, children and youth are subsumed by experiences of deportability, ranging from behavioral modification programs to eating practices to educational curriculum to forms of acceptable communication (Heidbrink 2014). Even after they are released, ORR policies and practices seep into the everyday lives of children who remain in the United States and those who are deported (Heidbrink and Statz 2017). The experiences of children in ORR custody reveal the ways the state devalues and refuses to recognize some kinship relations and how these state policies and practices shape children's notions of relatedness and belonging. In other words, state practices are so pervasive that there are few ways in which youths' lives are not constrained or informed by these institutional modes of being. Families are forced to make difficult calculations to ensure family integrity, sustain transnational families, and care for their children despite residing in multiple localities or maintaining mixed legal statuses (Coe et al. 2011; De Genova and Peutz 2010; Gardner 2012; Zatz and Rodriguez 2015).

Although the state structures kinship in a particular way, young people and their families do resist and at times circumvent the state's assessments of fitness and caregiving in an effort to ensure their collective well-being. In my larger research study, nearly a third of the children who received follow-up services left their initial sponsors' homes, often seeking out parents ORR had denied as suitable guardians during the sponsorship process. Once a child departs from an approved sponsor's custody, ORR advises the voluntary agency to close the case in order to terminate ORR responsibility to and liability for the child. However, caseworkers often scavenge for local services in the child's new locale. Lily, a fifteen-year-old from Ecuador, left her aunt's home in Pennsylvania to live in Tennessee with her mother, who, based on a pending order of deportation, had not been approved for reunification. Her caseworker remarked, "Lily came here to be with her mom. She said she didn't want to live with her aunt but with her mom. She said this throughout the suitability assessment, but ORR didn't listen. So, why are they surprised she left? I could have told you this even before her aunt picked her up from [the facility]." In the same ways that transnational migrants employ "autonomous family reunification" to preserve family integrity, unaccompanied children may defy ORR placements in an effort to reunite with trusted caregivers the state does not recognize as such (Boehm 2008, 798).

As I have argued, despite best intentions, the very policies intended to ensure the best interests of unaccompanied children may inflict harm on young people and their families. The institutional practices of nongovernmental organizations who administer these federal policies are firmly embedded within culturally normative frames that universalize the space of childhood and that, importantly, conflict with the complex lives of the global population of young people they serve. In recognizing the power-filled reflections and experiences of young people like Ricardo, Haydee, Imely, Julio, and Lily, both in and beyond ORR detention, we might recognize the social agency of young people who remain intimately and intricately embedded within communities of origin and destination in spite of claims that pathologize their mobility and criminalize their parents. If these portrayals are not confronted and enhanced with a more nuanced consideration of migration, age and obligation, young people will remain reified on a trajectory that imperils rather than ensures their safety and well-being.

REFERENCES

Bhabha, Jacqueline, and Susan Schmidt. 2008. "Seeking Asylum Alone: Unaccompanied and Separated Children and Refugee Protection in the US." *Journal of the History of Childhood and Youth* 1(1): 126–38.

Bluebond-Langner, Myra, and Jill E. Korbin. 2007. "Challenges and Opportunities in the Anthropology of Childhoods: An Introduction to 'Children, Childhoods, and Childhood Studies'." *American Anthropologist* 109(2): 241–46.

Boehm, Deborah. 2008. "'For My Children': Constructing Family and Navigating the State in the US-Mexico Transnation." *Anthropological Quarterly* 81(4): 777–802.

Bookey, Blaine. 2014. "A Treacherous Journey: Child Migrants Navigating the U.S. Immigration System." Research Paper no. 181. Hastings: University of California. Accessed November 22, 2016. http://www.uchastings.edu/centers/cgrs-docs/treacherous_journey_cgrs_kind_report.pdf.

Brettell, Caroline B. 2003. *Anthropology of Migration*. Oxford: Blackwell Publishing.

Bucholtz, Mary. 2002. "Youth and Cultural Practice." *Annual Review of Anthropology* 31 (October): 525–52.

Byrne, Olga, and Elissa Miller. 2012. *The Flow of Unaccompanied Children Through the Immigration System: A Resource for Practitioners, Policy Makers, and Researchers*. New York: Vera Institute of Justice.

Christensen, Pia, and Allison James, eds. 2008. *Research with Children: Perspectives and Practices*. London: Routledge.

Coe, Cati, Rachel R. Reynolds, Deborah A. Boehm, Julia Meredith Hess, and Heather Rae-Espinoza, eds. 2011. *Everyday Ruptures: Children, Youth, and Migration in Global Perspective*. Nashville, Tenn.: Vanderbilt University Press.

Cunningham, Hugh. 2005. *Children and Childhood in Western Society Since 1500*. Upper Saddle River, N.J.: Pearson Education.

———. 2012. *The Invention of Childhood*. New York: Random House.

De Genova, Nicholas, and Nathalie Peutz, eds. 2010. *The Deportation Regime: Sovereignty, Space, and the Freedom of Movement*. Durham, N.C.: Duke University Press.

Dobson, Janet, and John Stillwell. 2000. "Changing Home, Changing School: Towards a Research Agenda on Child Migration." *Area* 32(4): 395–401.

Eckenrode, John, Elizabeth Rowe, Molly Laird, and Jacqueline Brathwaite. 1995. "Mobility as a Mediator of the Effects of Child Maltreatment on Academic Performance." *Child Development* 66(4): 1130–42.

Fass, Paula 2005. "Children in Global Migrations." *Journal of Social History* 38(4): 937–53.

Fleer, Marilyn, Mariane Heregaard, and Jonathan Tudge. 2009. "Constructing Childhood." In *World Yearbook of Education 2009: Childhood Studies and the Impact of Globalization: Policies and*

Practices at Global and Local Levels, edited by Mariane Hedegaard, Jonathan Tudge, and Marilyn Fleer. London: Routledge.

Gardner, Katy. 2012. "Transnational Migration and the Study of Children: An Introduction." *Journal of Ethnic and Migration Studies* 38(6): 889–912.

Grace, Breann, and Benjamin Roth. 2015. "Post-release: Linking Unaccompanied Immigrant Children to Family and Community." Columbia: University of South Carolina.

Hannerz, Ulf. 1996. *Transnational Connections: Culture, People, Places*. London: Routledge.

Hashim, Iman. 2006. "The Positives and Negatives of Children's Independent Migration: Assessing the Evidence and the Debates." Working Paper no. T16. Sussex, UK: Development Research Centre on Migration, Globalisation and Poverty, University of Sussex.

Heidbrink, Lauren. 2013. "Criminal Alien or Humanitarian Refugee: The Social Agency of Migrant Youth." *Children's Legal Rights Journal* 33(1): 133–90.

———. 2014. *Migrant Youth, Transnational Families, and the State: Care and Contested Interests*. Philadelphia: University of Pennsylvania Press.

———. 2015. "Unintended Consequences: Reverberations of Special Immigrant Juvenile Status." *Journal of Applied Research on Children: Informing Policy for Children at Risk* 5(2): 1–29.

Heidbrink, Lauren, and Michele Statz. 2017. "Parenting Global Youth: Contestations of Debt and Belonging." *Children's Geographies*. DOI: 10.1080/14733285.2017.1284645.

Honwana, Alcinda, and Filip De Boeck. 2005. *Makers & Breakers: Children and Youth in Postcolonial Africa*. Oxford: James Currey.

Huijsmans, Roy, and Simon Baker. 2012. "Child Trafficking: 'Worst Form' of Child Labour, or Worst Approach to Young Migrants?" *Development and Change* 43(4): 919–46.

Hutchby, Ian, and Jo Moran-Ellis. 1998. *Children and Social Competence: Arenas of Action*. London: Psychology Press.

James, Allison, and Alan Prout, eds. 1997. *Constructing and Reconstructing Childhood: Contemporary Issues in the Sociological Study of Childhood*. London: Routledge.

Lancy, David F. 2014. *The Anthropology of Childhood: Cherubs, Chattel, Changelings*. Cambridge: Cambridge University Press.

Mayall, Berry. 2002. *Towards a Sociology for Childhood: Thinking from Children's Lives*. Buckingham, UK: Open University Press.

Mayall, Berry, and Virginia Morrow. 2011. *You Can Help Your Country: English Children's Work During the Second World War*. Herndon, Va.: Stylus Publishing.

Office of Refugee Resettlement (ORR). 2012. *Report to Congress: Fiscal Year 2012*. Washington: Department of Health and Human Services. Accessed September 9, 2015. https://www.acf.hhs.gov/sites/default/files/orr/fy_2012_orr_report_to_congress_final_041014.pdf.

Panter-Brick, Catherine. 2002. "Street Children, Human Rights, and Public Health: A Critique and Future Directions." *Annual Review of Anthropology* 31(1): 147–71.

Sampson, Robert. 1988. "Local Friendship Ties and Community Attachment in Mass Society: A Multilevel Systematic Model." *American Sociological Review* 53(5): 766–79.

Stephens, Sharon, ed. 1995. *Children and the Politics of Culture*. Princeton, N.J.: Princeton University Press.

Suárez-Orozco, Carola, and Marcelo M. Suárez-Orozco. 2009. *Children of Immigration*. Cambridge, Mass.: Harvard University Press.

Terrio, Susan. 2015. *Whose Child Am I?: Unaccompanied, Undocumented Children in US Immigration Custody*. Berkeley: University of California Press.

Thronson, David. 2005. "Of Borders and Best Interests: Examining the Experiences of Undocumented Immigrants in US Family Courts." *Texas Hispanic Journal of Law and Policy* 11(1): 45–73.

———. 2006. "Choiceless Choices: Deportation and the Parent-Child Relationship." *Nevada Law Review* 6(3): 1165–214.

United Nations High Commissioner for Refugees (UNHCR). 2014. *Children on the Run: Unaccompanied Children Leaving Central America and Mexico and the Need for International Protection*. Washington, D.C.: UNHCR.

Vericker, Tracy, Daniel Kuehn, and Randy Capps. 2007. "Latino Children of Immigrants in the Texas Child Welfare System." *Intersection of Migration and Child Welfare: Emerging Issues and Implications* 22(2): 20–40.

Zatz, Marjorie, and Nancy Rodriguez. 2015. *Dreams and Nightmares: Immigration Policy, Youth, and Families*. Berkeley: University of California Press.

Exploring the Effects of U.S. Immigration Enforcement on the Well-being of Citizen Children in Mexican Immigrant Families

LAUREN E. GULBAS AND LUIS H. ZAYAS

In this article, we draw on ecocultural theories of risk and resilience to examine qualitatively the experiences of U.S. citizen children living with their undocumented Mexican parents. Our purpose is to render visible the various ways in which citizen children confront and navigate the possibilities—and realities—of parental deportation. We develop a framework to conceptualize the complex multidimensional, and often multidirectional, factors experienced by citizen children vulnerable to or directly facing parental deportation. We situate youth well-being against a backdrop of multiple factors to understand how indirect and direct encounters with immigration enforcement, the mixed-status family niche, and access to resources shape differential child outcomes. In doing so, we offer insights into how different factors potentially contribute to resilience in the face of adversity.

Keywords: children, citizenship, deportation, undocumented, well-being

An estimated 4.5 million U.S. citizen children live in families in which one or both parents are undocumented (Pew Hispanic Research Center 2013). Researchers are just beginning to understand the ripple effects of immigration enforcement policies on immigrant families, and particularly on those families whose members have different authorizations, or mixed-status families (Dreby 2013). Given escalations in punitive measures that target undocumented individuals in the United States (Peutz and De Genova 2010), a growing number of citizen children face the harsh realities associated with parental deportation: forced family separations, material deprivation, anxiety, and depression (Gonzales and Chavez 2012; Zayas 2015). Citizen children living in Mexican immigrant families experience a disproportionate burden of risk because the sociopolitical practices aimed at policing migrant illegality increasingly target those of Mexican origin (Dreby 2012).

Lauren E. Gulbas is an anthropologist and assistant professor in the School of Social Work at the University of Texas, Austin. **Luis H. Zayas** is professor, endowed chair, and dean of the School of Social Work at the University of Texas, Austin.

© 2017 Russell Sage Foundation. Gulbas, Lauren E., and Luis H. Zayas. 2017. "Exploring the Effects of U.S. Immigration Enforcement on the Well-being of Citizen Children in Mexican Immigrant Families." *RSF: The Russell Sage Foundation Journal of the Social Sciences* 3(4): 53–69. DOI: 10.7758/RSF.2017.3.4.04. Support for this research was provided by National Institute for Child Health and Human Development grant HD068874 to Luis H. Zayas. We express our gratitude to the families who participated in this study. Direct correspondence to: Lauren E. Gulbas at laurengulbas@austin.utexas.edu, School of Social Work, University of Texas, 1925 San Jacinto Blvd., D3500, Austin, TX 78712; and Luis H. Zayas at lzayas@austin.utexas.edu, School of Social Work, University of Texas, 1925 San Jacinto Blvd., D3500, Austin, TX 78712.

To date, research has highlighted the various ways in which immigration enforcement practices increase the likelihood that citizen children will experience academic challenges, physical and mental health problems, and cognitive and developmental delays (Cavazos-Rehg, Zayas, and Spitznagel 2007; Kersey, Geppert, and Cutts 2007; Perreira and Ornelas 2011; Potochnik and Perreira 2010; Suárez-Orozco and Yoshikawa 2013; Yoshikawa 2011; Zayas and Bradlee 2015). Although this research has drawn much-needed attention to the multilevel risk profiles of citizen children, the predominant focus on risk has led to generalized assumptions about the vulnerability of this population and overshadowed the evaluation of citizen children's strengths, agency, and capacity (Panter-Brick 2014). This speaks, in part, to the political nature of research on undocumented individuals and their families. Most research, for good reason, advocates for changes to current immigration laws because studies have been able to demonstrate the negative effects such laws have on citizen children in immigrant families. However, research that focuses attention solely on issues of risk obscures the ways in which citizen children actively navigate stressful situations. Attention to processes of resilience would offer a valuable complement to the literature.

In this article, we draw on ecocultural theories of risk and resilience to examine qualitatively the experiences of citizen children living with their undocumented Mexican parents (Unger et al. 2013; Weisner 2010). We focus attention on how citizen children cope within the context of current immigration enforcement and deportation policies. In doing so, we identify factors that shape the well-being of citizen children and highlight the contextual circumstances that have the potential to produce variable individual outcomes. Our paper is framed to address the following research questions: What are the effects of immigration enforcement on the well-being of citizen children? How do citizen children cope with the fears associated with having an undocumented parent? What strengths do citizen children draw on as they face the realities—and consequences—of parental deportation?

AN ECOCULTURAL PERSPECTIVE ON RESILIENCE IN MIXED-STATUS FAMILIES

Over the past decade, social scientists have turned their attention to resilience-based research to counter the dominant focus on vulnerability, victimization, and suffering. Whereas studies of risk attend to circumstances and behaviors that increase the likelihood of negative outcomes, resiliency approaches emphasize elements and processes that sustain or promote well-being. As the anthropologist Catherine Panter-Brick notes, studies of resilience "uncover how people manage to live their lives and make the best of dire circumstances" (2014, 439). In such efforts, resiliency-oriented research can identify crucial *leverage points* that facilitate successful coping and shape well-being.

Studies of resilience draw on a range of theoretical approaches that emphasize, to different degrees, the salience of individual factors and the broader context. Many social scientists consider Urie Bronfenbrenner's ecological model to be foundational for understanding how interactions between individuals and their contextual environment shape childhood development (Bronfenbrenner 1979; Ungar, Ghazinour, and Richter 2013). Bronfenbrenner posits that proximal processes—those direct interactions between children and their immediate social and material environments (microlevel)—are the basic elements shaping development (Bronfenbrenner and Morris 1998). Broader ecological systems, such as the mesosystem (interaction between microsystems) and macrosystem (broader cultural and structural context) were understood as both shaping and being shaped by interactions in the microsystems (Bronfenbrenner 1993). In this way, change within one system could reverberate across systems.

Bronfenbrenner's ecological approach has influenced studies of risk and resilience by focusing attention to micro-, meso-, and macro-level factors that inhibit or facilitate well-being (Ungar, Ghazinour, and Richter 2013).

Building on Bronfenbrenner's model, anthropologists and sociologists have reconceptualized the role of culture within his eco-developmental framework, critiquing the distal role that he presumed culture to play in the lives of children and their families. As the sociologist Jonathan Tudge argues, "what is missing is that there is no sense . . . that cultural groups with values, beliefs, lifestyles, and patterns of social interchange different from those found in North American middle-class communities would necessarily value different types of proximal processes" (2008, 72–73). Eco-developmental approaches have drawn little attention to the significant ways in which cultural processes *directly* shape childhood experiences and outcomes. Such a limitation is particularly relevant for studies of citizen children, whose experiences are invariably affected by macro-level contexts that mandate discrepant treatment and access to resources based on ethnicity and citizenship status.

In light of this, our paper adopts an ecocultural approach that prioritizes attention to culture, or the everyday activities, routines, and behaviors that children enact within their surrounding environment (Super and Harkness 1986; Trudge 2008; Weisner 2010; Worthman 2010). Ecocultural theory emphasizes the importance of family practices and strategies that families pursue to facilitate child development and well-being (Weisner 2002). As the anthropologist Thomas Weisner notes, families everywhere need to construct and sustain family practices that foster survival, create meaning, and ensure positive outcomes for their children (2010). Yet not all family practices are equally effective or achievable. Even though families actively construct practices, features in the surrounding environment are also an influence. These influences include material and institutional resources, health and safety characteristics of the home and community environment, expectations about the division of household and economic labor, informal and formal systems of support, and sources of cultural influence. Accordingly, family practices reflect a negotiation between opportunities and constraints in the surrounding environment and the *cultural scripts* that families draw on to organize and give meaning to everyday life and promote childhood well-being. The nexus of culture, environmental factors, and everyday family life is constituted in the family niche (Weisner 2002, 2010). We extend an ecocultural conceptualization of the family niche to highlight the unique circumstances facing mixed-status families. A mixed-status family niche reflects both the micro-environment families create as they balance their needs and the daily challenges associated with having an undocumented family member.

Crucial to understanding the mixed-status family niche is what we call a "cultural script of silence." As Genevieve Negrón-Gonzales notes, "silence is a fundamental part of the undocumented experience in this country . . . [because] the potential consequences of discovery are so severe" (2014, 271). Drawing on the notion of a cultural script of silence, we analyze the ways in which citizen children interpret, manage, and navigate everyday life. Citizen children's daily lives are organized around the very real possibility that their undocumented parents could one day be detained and deported. In this context, developmental tasks take on new meaning when a knock on the family's door has the potential to signal a shift in the safety and integrity of the family and the beginning of a terrifying ordeal of parental detention and deportation. Our purpose is to render visible the various ways in which citizen children confront and navigate the possibilities—and realities—of parental deportation, in order to identify factors that potentially contribute to resilience in the face of adversity. In doing so, we highlight those factors that potentially distinguish citizen children from their peers in citizen families.

METHODS

Data analyzed were drawn from a mixed-method, multisited binational study that examined the psychosocial functioning of citizen children with undocumented Mexican parents. Study sites included Austin, Texas; Sacramento, California; and several locations

Table 1. Demographic Characteristics of Citizen Children in Study Sample

Characteristic	Accompanied Parent to Mexico (n = 31)		Remained in United States (n = 18)		Living in United States with Undocumented Parent (n = 34)		Total (n = 83)	
	M (SD)	n (percent)	M (SD)	n (percent)	M (SD)	n (percent)	M (SD)	n (percent)
Age	11.1 (1.9)		11.7 (1.8)		11.6 (1.9)		11.4 (1.9)	
Gender (girl)		19 (61.3)		11 (61.1)		20 (58.8)		50 (60.2)
School enrollment (yes)		30 (96.8)		18 (100)		34 (100)		82 (98.8)
Living arrangement								
Both parents		20 (64.5)		10 (55.6)		26 (76.5)		56 (67.5)
One parent		10 (32.3)		8 (44.4)		7 (20.6)		25 (30.1)
No parent		1 (3.2)		0 (0.0)		1 (2.9)		2 (2.4)

Source: Authors' compilation.

throughout Mexico (Distrito Federal, Hidalgo, Michoacán, Oaxaca, and Sinaloa). The sampling strategy entailed recruitment of three groups of U.S. citizen children between eight and fourteen years old with at least one undocumented Mexican parent: those who had accompanied their deported parents to Mexico; who stayed in the United States with a parent or guardian after one or both parents underwent deportation proceedings, had been deported to Mexico, or returned to the United States following deportation to Mexico; and whose undocumented parents had never been detained by immigration enforcement. Potential participants were excluded if they did not fall within the targeted age range or were living in foster care or child welfare at the time of the study. Additional exclusionary criteria included a diagnosis of psychiatric disorder or cognitive or developmental disability because these present unique challenges that might shape the well-being of citizen children.

Recruitment was carried out with the help of staff at local community agencies at each site. After identifying potential participants who met criteria for participation, agency staff discussed the study with parents. Parents who expressed interest were referred to the research team. All parents and children provided consent and assent for their participation, and institutional review board approval was granted at each of the institutions and sites where research activities took place.

Participants

Table 1 presents the demographic characteristics of citizen children recruited for participation. Of the total eighty-three participants, thirty-one accompanied their deported parent or parents to Mexico, eighteen remained in the United States after their parent or parents were deported, and thirty-four were not directly affected by deportation at the time of the interview. Across participant subgroups, the majority were girls (60.2 percent). Nearly all participants were enrolled in school and living with both parents at the time interview.

Data Collection

In-depth interviews were conducted with citizen children to elicit their narratives about living with parents who were undocumented, and, when applicable, to gather detailed accounts of their perceptions and experiences with immigration enforcement and parental deportation. All interviewers were bilingual, and the majority were Mexican or Mexican American women pursuing graduate degrees in the social sciences and trained to conduct qualitative interviews with children. Each interviewer conducted the interview in the language the participant preferred; approximately 42 percent of the interviews were in Spanish.

To help reduce interviewer bias across multiple research sites, the research team constructed a semistructured interview guide to provide a series of probes and prompts to facilitate deeper exploration of topics. Questions were open-ended to capture how citizen children communicated, gave meaning to, and constructed their experiences and perceptions (Ochs and Capps 1996). The interview was conducted in a way that simulated a casual and everyday conversation; to faciliate rapport, interviewers encouraged children to ask questions and provide feedback about the interview process. Interviews began with a "grand tour" question to explore participants' perceptions about home and family life, including descriptions of family activities and relationships, the child's roles and responsibilities within the family, and social life outside the home (Spradley 1979). These questions set the stage for a discussion about direct and indirect experiences with immigration enforcement or parental deportation. Interviewers focused on eliciting what the child remembered as meaningful, placing particular emphasis on having children describe their perceptions, thoughts, emotions, feelings, reflections, and interpretations to ascertain the psychosocial impact of parental removal or having an undocumented parent. If applicable, children were asked to reflect on how their life had changed as a result of the deportation.

Throughout qualitative data collection, several procedures were followed to monitor and enhance the data quality. All interviews were digitally recorded, transcribed, and analyzed in the language of the interview to enhance validity (Guest and MacQueen 2008). Interview transcripts and notes were systematically reviewed, and a series of debriefing meetings were held with research team members to discuss the rigors of the data collection process (Mack, Bunce, and Akumatey 2008).

Data Analysis

Transcripts were analyzed using a thematic approach to identify and describe participant perspectives (Guest, MacQueen, and Namey 2012).

To develop the coding framework, the first author and a graduate research assistant independently read two interviews, recording their initial interpretations of text. Emergent themes were discussed in a team meeting, and a draft of a codebook was developed from this discussion. Additional interviews were read to test the utility of preliminary themes, with attention directed toward the emergence of new themes. After eight interviews had been read, themes in the codebook appeared to be well established and a final draft of the codebook was produced. To test the utility of the codebook and establish intercoder reliability, four interviews were uploaded into NVivo9, independently coded by the first author and the research assistant, and percent agreement was calculated using the coding comparison module. Text that fell below a 75 percent threshold was discussed during a team meeting, and the codebook was revised as necessary (Miles and Huberman 1994). Interviews were subsequently coded using NVivo9, first by the research assistant, and then by the first author. This approach facilitated the transparency of the coders' interpretations of the data by reviewing and monitoring all coded text.

After data coding was completed, a framework matrix was generated in NVivo9. A framework matrix organizes data by themes (columns) and participants (rows). Each cell of the matrix contained reduced data in the form of direct quotes and summarized information about the manifestation of a given theme in a particular case. The matrix was then exported and converted to a text document that contained the reduced and summarized information pertaining to each specific participant, or case.

To protect against bias in the interpretation of the cases, a panel of thirteen experts reviewed the data to compare the experiences of citizen children across cognitive, emotional, psychological, cultural, and socioeconomic dimensions. The panel included clinical psychologists and social workers in Mexico and the United States, each of whom had expertise in the mental health and cultural issues that Latino youth and their families experience. Each panelist evaluated a random selection of twenty cases to ensure that each case was re-

Figure 1. Framework for Understanding Effects of Immigration Enforcement on Citizen Child Outcomes

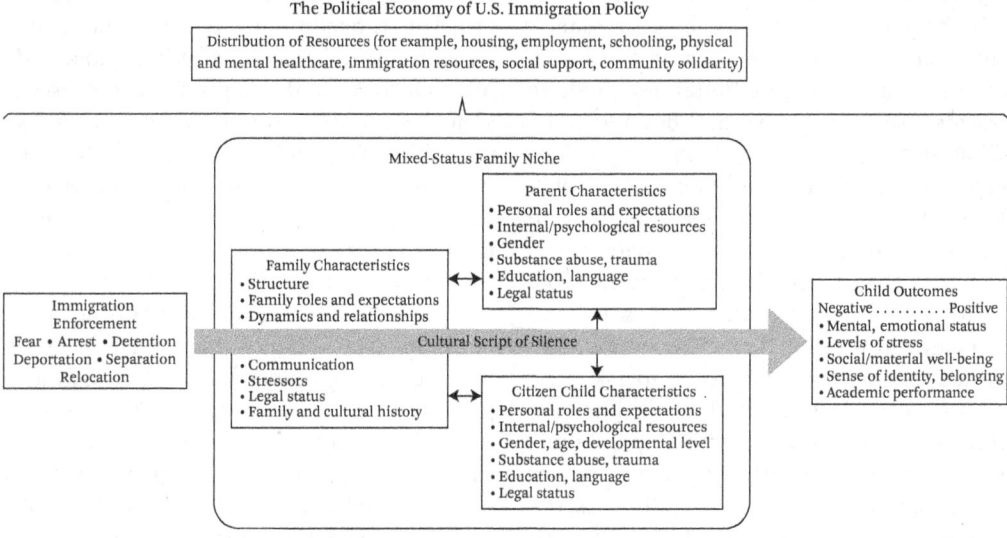

Source: Authors' compilation.

viewed by multiple panelists. The panelists were brought together, by telephone in Mexico and in person in the United States, to discuss the results of their analysis. Their discussions were recorded, transcribed, and analyzed to develop a list of all the issues that citizen children face and the contextual factors that exacerbated or ameliorated their direct and indirect experiences with immigration enforcement. The list originally contained 339 items, which were organized into sixty-one categories, each of which was linked to the interview data by annotating which cases corresponded to a given category. The research team then reviewed and discussed the arrangement of items and specification of categories and revised them accordingly. The list of categories was finalized by consensus and a framework developed to capture the differential effects of immigration enforcement on the well-being of citizen children. The framework was revised and finalized through an iterative team process (see Sobo 2009).

RESULTS

In figure 1, we offer a framework to describe the varied circumstances facing citizen children to conceptualize the range of effects immigration policies have on the well-being of U.S. citizen children. Figure 1 illustrates the interrelationships among five categories that emerged as salient to the perspectives of citizen children: immigration enforcement, the cultural script of silence, the distribution of resources, the mixed-status family niche, and child outcomes. Variations in child outcomes, as experienced and narrated by citizen children, depended strongly on the particular processes and characteristics in place within specific contexts. We begin with a description of the script of silence, followed by an exploration of the ways in which citizen children drew on the cultural script of silence to navigate the various personal, social, and material ecologies that characterized their lives in their efforts to cope with and adapt to situations beyond their control. To contextualize the framework, we present accounts of U.S. citizen children, in their own words. All names are pseudonyms.

THE CULTURAL SCRIPT OF SILENCE

As illustrated in figure 1, the cultural script of silence emerges within a specific context: the enforcement of U.S. immigration policies. Given the potential for an act of immigration enforcement to rupture family ties, most children perceived encounters with immigration enforcement as the worst event that could befall a family. Encounters could be indirect—through the potential threat of parental deportation or knowing others who had been deported—or direct—through the arrest, detention, and deportation of a parent. The condition of illegality, which rendered a parent's deportation possible, created and maintained a context ripe for the development of a cultural script of silence. Nearly every citizen child in our study described the salience of silence within their families. We call this phenomenon the *cultural script of silence*, referencing a shared script, or code, held among family members that prohibited the discussion of legal status both within and outside the household. The script of silence shaped parents' interactions with their children and what they told their children about immigration, citizenship, and undocumented status. The script not only guided the ways in which parents and children interacted, but also informed how parents taught or modeled behaviors, and the ways in which parents communicated and provided support.

The importance of silence was first learned indirectly. As fiftteen-year-old Tommy, whose father had been detained, explained, "I guess it wasn't really that I found out [about my parents' status]. It was more like, like an idea you settle into, and that you think is normal. And like all the fears they have, you start to have, too." Like Tommy, most participants in our sample stated that their parents rarely discussed the realities associated with being undocumented, though many children referenced an embodied comprehension of their parents' undocumented status as a result of the various ways in which illegality organized dynamics within the mixed-status family. Children came to know definitively about their parents' status only through a specific event that forced parents to explain. For example, when one participant, Marianela, was eight years old, she learned that both her parents were undocumented when her father became severely ill. As she recalled the moment, "I told my mom that we should take him to the hospital to see what is going on with him. . . . And that's when my mom told me that we can't take him to the hospital. And that's when I said, 'He's sick. We need to take him to the hospital.' And my mom told me that my dad didn't have any papers."

Once citizen children learned that their parents were undocumented, they became keenly aware of the ways in which a cultural script of silence delineated family expectations for children's interactions outside of the home. For example, Tommy explained that his parents provided him with explicit instructions to monitor his behavior in public: "Whenever we were around important people, you know like, those people who deport other people, I have to behave very well."

In other families, citizen children were strongly encouraged to remain silent about their parents' undocumented status. As nine-year-old Catarina explained, "Because my mom doesn't want me to tell anyone she says that she could get in trouble if I talk to people about it." To be sure, participants were aware of the pragmatic necessity for silence to protect their parents from detection by immigration enforcement agencies. For example, fourteen-year-old Jessica recounted a time when her friend's mother had been deported after being reported to legal authorities: "It happened to my friend. That's the only reason why her mom went to Mexico. Because her neighbors snitched them out that her mom didn't have papers. I worry if I tell someone, the same thing is gonna happen as it happened to her." Despite the pragmatic need for discretion, the script of silence contributed to experiences of powerlessness among citizen children. As Tommy explained, "we can't really say our mind or protest because we might get taken. We have to, like, stay to the laws a lot more than other people. Because they'll judge us on our skin and say, 'Oh, you're Mexican. Go to your side.'"

In its most extreme manifestation, the cultural script of silence could set into motion a series of emotional or family dynamics that negatively affected the well-being of citizen children. The cultural script of silence shaped children's cognitive and emotional expression, and some participants described conscious efforts to "not think" about their parents' situation. Maya, nine years old, put it this way: "I really don't think about that. I just think fun things." For many participants, the potential for a direct encounter with law enforcement produced considerable fear, worry, and stress.

For example, Maria, a ten-year-old who lived with her undocumented parents and younger citizen brother, explained, "I have papers, and they don't. They can't really go places. They could go to prison." This awareness led to extreme fear of police officers. When Maria saw a police car near her house, she would run inside, close the curtains, and cry profusely. It was not until the police left the vicinity that Maria would realize her parents were safe, and only then would she come out of hiding. Her fear of law enforcement stemmed from the very real possibility that "maybe one day, they can just take them. And then, me and my little brother would have to go to foster homes. I really don't want that."

Deliberate efforts to silence thoughts and emotions prevented children from having a space, either with family or friends, to process their fears, anxieties, and worries. The importance of silence within families sometimes acted to weaken supportive bonds between parents and children, and participants reported becoming distrustful of their parents as a result. As eleven-year-old Anthony noted, "They're lying and all that. Like they knew they did not have papers, but they didn't tell me."

Surprisingly, silence often continued even after families experienced the worst possible circumstance: the arrest, detention, and deportation of a parent. Children who experienced parental detention or deportation explained that they knew very little about the immigration proceedings that led to the deportation of their parents. For example, Anthony did not understand why his father "went" to Mexico. Although his father had been deported eight months prior to the interview, he reported that he knew "only that my dad was going to Mexico. [My mom] didn't want to talk about it." Similarly, for eleven-year-old Ernesto, the events resulting in his father's deportation were unclear. Ernesto explained that he woke up one day to learn that his father had been "taken" to Mexico. As he described it, "I just woke up and asked mom what happened. And she said they took him back to Mexico. He was somewhere, and they sent him to Mexico. I think he did something bad . . . I don't know."

Some participants could vividly recall the circumstances surrounding parental deportation because they witnessed directly the arrest and detention of their undocumented parent. For example, Christina was twelve years old when her mother was arrested. According to Christina, who was fourteen at the time of the interview, Immigration and Customs Enforcement (ICE) agents arrived at Christina's house early one morning:

Like five in the morning. They just came . . . knocking on the door. And like, my mom, she was really scared. And my dad was like, "pack your stuff! And let's leave." And [my mom] looked outside the window, and the house was surrounded. It was surrounded by like ICE people. And I heard, like, loud knocking. And like, I just got up . . . and I was like, "what's going on?" Because there were, like, a lot of people on the porch. Everywhere. I was, like, super scared . . . . And like, they took her. And she gave me the last hug, and um . . . She walked out of the door. And I was like, "You can't leave us!" [Christina's voice cracks, and she starts to cry quietly] So . . . me seeing my mom go away, it was very hard for me.

Christina recounted how she retreated into herself following her mother's arrest. As she explained, "I quit my grades, and with, like, everything." Christina's eventual healing occurred only after she found a space to vocalize her experience. Still, when Christina reflected on that horrible night, she actively wished that she could erase, not only her mother's arrest, but also her presence during it: "If I could change anything in my life, I would probably change that. I would wish not to be there whenever they took my mom. I wish I would never see that."

Not a single participant in our study described having a plan in place that would help guide and assist children about what to do in the event that a parent was arrested and detained. In this way, the cultural script of silence seemed to thwart the implementation of emergency plans for children and their families. As a result, participants described intense emotional experiences during the arrest and detention of a parent, and in turn, active efforts to mute the painful memories associated with such experiences. For example, thirteen-year-old Guillermo described the arrest and detention of his father this way: "Like sometimes it comes to my mind, but mostly I don't think about that. I don't know. When I'm about to go to sleep, it just comes up." The middles of the night, when he would wake from nightmares about his father, were some of the bleakest times for Guillermo.

It is important that the cultural script of silence was not static or unchanging in its manifestation. The salience of the script, both in guiding family dynamics and the extent to which it affected the well-being of citizen children, depended on the quality of resources available to children and their families. Although the script of silence operated as a kind of mediating force that shaped specific patterns of emotions, thoughts, behaviors, and dynamics within the mixed-status family, the well-being of citizen children was more than the simple presence or absence of a cultural script. Rather, well-being was also shaped by the availability and distribution of and access to social and material resources.

DISTRIBUTION OF RESOURCES

All of the participants in our study came to feel, experience, and understand the sociopolitical condition of illegality via their encounters with public institutions and broader community settings. Health care, employment, housing, neighborhood violence, and discrimination emerged as salient nodes around which citizen children came to understand the meaning of their parents' undocumented status, the political and economic constraints associated with lack of citizenship, and their own location within the constellation of discourses surrounding perceptions of individuals deemed illegal. The political and economic consequences of illegality reverberated across families of mixed-status through everyday experiences. Varied assemblages of legal statuses within and across families—citizen, authorized, undocumented—shaped the everyday experiences of citizen children differently, and the distribution of resources was often the driving force behind these differential experiences. As figure 1 illustrates, access to financial, education, extracurricular, mental health, legal, and immigration-related resources often translated to the differences between suffering, on the one hand, and resiliency, on the other.

In mixed-status families with one authorized or citizen parent, citizen children described less acute financial and housing struggles. In this way, legal status operated as a definitive resource. Nevertheless, the condition of illegality reverberated across the household even when only one parent was undocumented. In these cases, issues related to the institutional invisibility of the undocumented parent loomed large. For example, Cecilia, the ten-year-old daughter of an undocumented mother and citizen father, recounted that "the school doesn't know my mom's name. She can't sign our paperwork, and they only see my dad." Her mother's undocumented status altered the domestic organization of responsibilities within the household, and her father was charged with acting as both mother and father in the public sphere.

Among citizen children whose parents were detained, chronic experiences of political and economic marginalization sometimes shaped family decisions to accept deportation. In the case of Jennyfer, a fourteen-year-old who lived with her undocumented grandmother and undocumented mother, her mother became gravely ill. Her mother had been diagnosed with hepatitis C, which Jennyfer thought had been the result of a blood transfusion her mother received during childbirth. The family considered returning to Mexico to enable her mother to receive health care, but soon after this discussion, Jennyfer's grandmother was arrested and detained. Given the status of the mother's health, the grandmother accepted deportation so that the mother could receive the care she needed in Mexico. Although Jennyfer felt "sad" to leave the United States, she noted, "I would prefer that we moved here so that my mother could get better rather than stay there and watch her get worse." For Jennyfer and her family, barriers to accessing health care influenced the conditions under which they would "accept" deportation. In the end, Jennyfer decided that she would do whatever it would take to stay close to her mother.

Many participants who relocated to Mexico to reunite with their deported parents described how they initially missed the conveniences and material abundance associated with life in the United States, such as shopping at big box stores. However, these experiences gave way to more profound sensations of loss about their potential futures and resources. As twelve-year-old Clarissa explained, "If I stay here [in Mexico] I won't have the chance to have any kind of future." Participants described Mexico as a place with limited educational and employment opportunity. Twelve-year-old Luciana narrated a particularly difficult adjustment to the school setting in Mexico. She described repeatedly asking for help in her studies, but her teachers did not respond to her requests. They would tell her they were "too bored" by her questions. As a result, she lost any desire to do well in school: "I see that my grades have dropped a lot because I'm like, why would I try if no matter what I do, the teachers aren't even going to notice?"

Cases such as these reveal the various ways in which access to resources might have contributed to different outcomes for children in our study. Although legal status excluded many families from accessing resources, such as safe employment and healthcare, key players within institutional and family settings figured prominently in facilitating participants' access to what limited resources were available. For example, soon after the arrest and detention of Christina's mother, described above, her father was detained and deported. Although her mother was eventually released, Christina and her siblings experienced major disruptions in terms of housing and access to material resources. Desolate, Christina broke the script of silence and reached out to her school counselor: "I told my counselor that we really needed help 'cause, like, it was more than ten people living at my aunt's house. And she didn't have enough money for us. So [my counselor] got most of the teachers, they donated food and clothes. I remember coming home from school with a lot of bags full of like food and diapers and other stuff." For Christina and members of her family, the school staff provided material resources needed to sustain family life. Moreover, the counselor created a supportive environment for Christina to process her emotional reactions to her father's deportation.

For other citizen children, extended kin emerged as key brokers to accessing resources. Karla, twelve years old, described the significance of extended kin in shaping her experience of reuniting with her family in Mexico following her father's deportation. Her grandfather helped ease the transition economically by providing Karla's family with a house in Mexico and giving her father a job working in his painting business. On occasion, Karla's grandfather would supplement the family's income when they needed the extra money. With this additional money, Karla was able to maintain her involvement in sports, which helped to provide continuity between her former life in the United States and her new life in Mexico. Karla had participated in club boxing in the United States and was able to join a boxing gym in Mexico. During the interview, Karla noted excitedly that she was anticipating her first boxing match. She had been training for "a long, long time. They put me up against a ninth grader, and I am barely in sixth grade. But she's tiny! And I've been training for this . . . for the day that I'll fight."

The cases of Christina and Karla reveal how access to resources was shaped by relationships between citizen children and other individuals within their social network. In this way, social support functioned as a critical resource, particularly when trusted family and friends constructed a space to dismantle the cultural script of silence. Fourteen-year-old Elena, for example, described how she became withdrawn and uncommunicative on learning that her father had been detained. In response, her mother reached out to her and enrolled her in dance class to provide an outlet for her "frustration." In this way, Elena's mother provided support by finding a space in which Elena could process her emotions. In addition to family, trusted peers operated as a strong system of social support, buffering against the trauma associated with immigration enforcement by breaching the script of silence. Elena described school as a kind of second family: "We all know each other. We've been knowing each other since fifth grade. So we already have really strong connections because we've been growing and our school, they're like, team and family. So all of us are like our family." Close friendships at school created spaces of perceived safety in which citizen children could divulge their worst fears, worries, and anxieties. As Elena noted,

> There is this girl. She is my best friend, and we have known each other since the second grade. And I know that her parents don't have any papers too, so I mostly tell her everything about my life. Because, um, she told me everything about her life, and how she feels scared that she could lose her parents if they are ever sent to Mexico. So we tell each other everything, and we try to help each other out.

School enabled citizen children like Elena to foster relationships based on their shared experiences. Moreover, the school administration facilitated classroom curricula designed to break the script of silence and raise awareness about immigration:

> See, in our school, like in our history class they teach us about different topics and one of the topics has been, um, immigration. We can connect a lot to that since our school is 99.9 percent Hispanics. We already know most of the things so sometimes, like sometimes, it's an emotional class where we stay strong. So, it's kind of good to know something else that could help you.

Unfortunately, Elena's experience was rare. Her story reveals the ways in which her links to institutional resources and supportive relationships contributed to her well-being during her father's detention. Yet, the constellation of individual and family characteristics within her mixed-status family niche also facilitated positive outcomes as well. For example, Elena's parents had divorced many years before her father was detained. Although her family often spent time together in activities that included both her parents, such as family dinner, Elena did not live with her father. This is not to say that the detention of Elena's father was no less distressing to her, but rather that her well-being was shaped by the complex interaction of various factors, including those within the mixed-status family niche.

THE MIXED-STATUS FAMILY NICHE

Figure 1 illustrates the elements that make up the micro-setting of daily life in mixed-status families, or the mixed-status family niche. The niche represents the dynamic interplay between characteristics and behaviors at the individual and family level. Parent characteristics and family cohesion were cited as key to the capacity for the family to act as a system of social support and foster well-being.

Participants noted that their well-being was deeply tied to their parents' vulnerabilities and strengths, and thus that parental well-being held the potential to be a source of comfort or of stress for citizen children. Among participants, family histories of substance abuse or trauma were perceived as particularly stressful, capable of exacerbating the negative effects of immigration enforcement experiences. For example, Marisa, a thirteen-year-old who had reunited with her parents in Mexico after their deportation, noted that her father's history of substance abuse overshadowed her own adjustment to living in a new environment. Marisa had hoped that in reuniting with her parents in Mexico she would recover the parental love and support that she needed and desired. Yet, her relationship with her father was strained, and she described him as distant and uncommunicative. As she explained, "With my father taking drugs, he can't work and he spends a lot [on drugs]. And my mom has to work to be able to keep up the house. He has promised us so many times, he has sworn to us, that he is going to quit, but he never does. Sometimes he just spends the day in the house sleeping."

In reuniting with her family in Mexico, Marisa was forced to renegotiate her expectations for parental care. Her father's substance abuse affected his capacity to act as an engaged father and family member, but also produced financial strain. In turn, Marissa's mother worked extended hours and was rarely home. Marissa noted that the family did not agree about the reorganization of family life in Mexico, which generated significant family conflict.

In contrast, personal strengths were perceived as diminishing the negative effects or stressors that stemmed from immigration enforcement. For example, Marco, a fourteen-year-old boy, described the importance of a strong work ethic, which was instilled in him by his father. He noted that his father "wants to teach me how to work so I can get our family a better future. I work. I find anything I can do. I help my mom." Marco's narrative reflected the way in which he was becoming socialized to become the patriarch of the family, a process that had been accelerated by the fact that his father was facing deportation. Marco sometimes struggled with his newfound responsibilities but nevertheless accepted them. He explained:

> I don't really have my childhood anymore. I don't get to play around anymore. I always have to be there. I have to be strong for my brothers. I guess I miss when I was smaller and everything being so innocent for me. The world just being there as a playground for me. A place for me to have fun. Now it's kind of more like a... How would you call it? Um... obstacle ground. With obstacles. Obstacles I have to go through. I don't like it, but there's nothing I can do to take it off of me. I have to be there. It's my responsibility, and I have to hold it up, and I have to be there.

For Marco, like many citizen children, age and gender shaped the ways that parents organized household roles and responsibilities. The effects of immigration policies and practices often made it difficult for families to build consistent routines for children, which frequently resulted in confusion or resentment about their roles and responsibilities within the household. This was particularly the case among older girls who reunited with their families in Mexico. For example, in the case of fifteen-year-old Melina, she felt that the task of sibling and domestic care detracted from her personal motivation to focus on her education. Both her parents were required to work long hours outside of the household, and they charged Melina with caring for the household. As she explained, "[In the United States], I didn't have to clean, or work in the kitchen, or anything. It was pure studying because that is what I spent my time doing. But here, no, here it is different. Here, you spend all your time cleaning the house, taking care of your siblings. Now it's no longer about studying."

Reflecting on the change in routines in Mexico, Melina noted that she felt resentful toward her new responsibilities in the household. She said that she often took it out on her younger siblings by ignoring them. As her case illustrates, the ways that participants interpreted sudden changes in their routines and responsibilities could produce resentment, frustration, and angst, particularly when new household practices were perceived as thwarting their individual expectations and needs. In contrast, older boys and younger girls in our sample sometimes embraced the opportunity to contribute to the household. Thus, consensus among family members regarding the gendered and age-based organization of household responsibilities contributed to supportive interactions, whereas conflict between personal and family expectations could lead to tension. Individual characteristics and behaviors of children and parents were perceived as shaping the quality of family dynamics, yet many participants were cognizant of the ways in which family dynamics were singularly constrained by the broader political economy of U.S. immigration policy. This recognition led numerous citizen children to declare, "Things would be better in my family if only my parents had papers."

CHILD OUTCOMES

Figure 1 illustrates how, within the context of the political economy of U.S. immigration policy and encounters with enforcement agencies, the distribution of resources, the arrangement of factors in the mixed-status family niche, and the cultural script of silence interact to shape outcomes for citizen children. A range of effects on well-being is suggested, from negative to positive in terms of social and material well-being, the mental and emotional status of children, levels of stress, sense of identity and belonging, and academic performance. In this regard, an important theme in our research is that no single and definitive profile encapsulates the experiences of citizen children in mixed-status families. As illustrated in figure 1, the effects of immigration encounters on the well-being of citizen children depend heavily on many factors, reflecting the combined and continued effects associated with the political economy of U.S. immigration policy, the resources available to children and their families, the organization of the mixed-status family niche, and the cultural scripts that individuals draw on to navigate daily life.

Across participants, well-being was experienced differently depending on family circumstances. Without legal status, wage earners were subject to the realities of participating in an unskilled and informal labor market. As a result, most youth hoped their parents could get papers one day so that they would be able to find more satisfying—and better paying—work. As Jose, thirteen years old, noted, if his parents had papers, "they could be here and be comfortable. I just know that my dad says that he wants the papers because he wants a better job."

Additionally, some participants described confusion about their national, ethnic, and legal identities. Having an undocumented parent imposed boundaries of exclusion within school and community settings, even among those who had never experienced parental deportation. For example, twelve-year-old Anna recalled, "a lot of people are very racist at my school. And a lot of them say, 'Go back where you came from.'" Experiences of discrimination had a disempowering effect on children's understandings of their social location within these broader settings. As fourteen-year-old David explained, "I don't feel like other kids in school. I feel kind of like an outlaw." For youth who experienced parental deportation, some participants described not knowing where they belonged. Ten-year-old Daniel, who accompanied his deported father to Mexico, described "being between two worlds. I have family here and family over there, in both places. I'm like in the middle of Mexico and the U.S."

The potential threats to well-being could bring heightened stress and emotional and mental distress. Fear and worries about their parents' status, or experiences of parental deportation, made it difficult for youth to engage actively in daily life. One eleven year old, Emma, recounted that every time she left her mother's side, even at school, she became increasingly nervous that something would happen to her mother and she would not be nearby to help: "It's just worrying. Like [if I] leave her side. Like not be there to support her." In another case, Manny, who was fourteen years old, began to experience intense headaches and nausea when his father was deported to Mexico. At the time, he was living with his mother, a U.S. citizen, and younger brother. As he described the experience, "It was nerves. Pure nerves. I was scared that something would happen to my mom. Like, someone would hurt her or kidnap her, or something like that, because my dad wasn't there." As time passed, his symptoms worsened, and he began to vomit at school, almost daily. In response, the school sent him home because, as he said, "I couldn't be without my mom. It scared me." Finally, his mother took him to a psychologist, who recommended that the family reunite for Manny's emotional well-being. The family heeded the psychologist's advice and moved to Mexico to rejoin Manny's father, whereupon Manny's symptoms disappeared.

In our sample, Manny was not alone in his experience of intense distress. Nearly 30 percent of participants in the study described symptoms often associated with anxiety and depression, including intense bouts of crying, loss of interest in activities, difficulties sleeping, loss of appetite, feelings of fear, and suicidal thoughts. Although intense suffering was experienced across our sample, citizen children who were in the midst of parental deportation processes reported suffering more frequently than children in other groups. Among children who accompanied their deported parents to Mexico, the majority described difficulties adjusting to the different ecocultural environment, and these difficulties could be experienced more intensely depending on the constellation of factors outlined in figure 1.

Such experiences were not universal, however, as described in many of the cases, and some citizen children exhibited extraordinary resilience in the face of the many adversities they confronted. Unfortunately, narratives of well-being were described with less frequency across all groups. This was especially so among citizen children experiencing parental separation due to detention and deportation at the time of the interview: no child in this group reported doing well. In comparison, only seven citizen children whose parents had never been deported and only six who accompanied their parents to Mexico described feeling safe, emotionally secure, and socially connected. Among these children, access to resources to nurture well-being appeared to be a key leverage point in shaping how participants were able to manage their everyday lives. The most fundamental resource, at least from the perspective of citizen children across groups, was family cohesion. As Karla eloquently described it after her family reunification in Mexico,

> Really, I am happy there [in the United States], and I am happy here [in Mexico]. I am happy as long as I have my parents with me. If I am separated from one of them, I don't know what to do. It hurts. I can't be as happy as I would if I lived with both of them. I have always lived with both of them.

DISCUSSION

In this paper, we describe a framework for conceptualizing the effects of immigration enforcement on the well-being of citizen children living with their undocumented Mexican parents. The framework illustrates the complex multidimensional, and often multidirectional, factors citizen children vulnerable to or directly facing parental deportation experience. Our findings suggest that the everyday realities facing citizen children—and the ways in which these realities shape well-being—cannot be reduced to simple explanations. Thus, we situate youth well-being against a backdrop of multiple factors to understand how indirect and direct encounters with immigration enforcement, the mixed-status family niche, and access to resources shape differential child outcomes.

Participants in our study described well-being in terms of a dynamic relationship between personal qualities and the social context surrounding them. In this configuration, the presence or absence of parents emerged as a significant theme. Forced family separations were perceived to be the worst stressor facing participants in our sample. Among citizen children without experiences of parental deportation, the potential for a forced separation was never far from their minds. Indeed, the "deportability" of their parents was described overwhelmingly as a major cause for emotional distress (De Genova 2002). For citizen children facing parental deportation, families were forced to confront whether they should separate so that children could remain in their citizen country or relocate to Mexico to keep the family together. In deciding, citizen children had to evaluate the potential emotional, social, and material costs, and brace themselves for the aftermath.

The adverse circumstances citizen children faced were not limited to forced family separations and reflected the broader consequences associated with the political economy of U.S. immigration policy. Participants described the varied financial and emotional costs associated with illegality, supporting research that describes the ways in which citizen children suffer the consequences of their parents' undocumented status (Chavez et al. 1997; Guendelman et al. 2006; Kersey, Geppert, and Cutts 2007; Perreira and Ornelas 2011). Our results reveal how the personal strengths of parents and children had the potential to shield children from the negative effects of stressors that stemmed from indirect and direct encounters with immigration enforcement. Strengths were often entwined with the availability of resources that could enhance well-being. Access to financial, educational, extracurricular, mental health, legal, and immigration-related resources buttressed individual strengths and buffered against traumatic experiences related to immigration enforcement and forced family separations. Extended kin and individuals in school and religious institutions emerged as supportive networks that facilitated access to those resources that were important to well-being. Social connection, however, was not without its risks.[1] A strong social network was key to the facilitation of well-being among citizen children, but its loss could exacerbate the emotional costs of relocation to Mexico after parental deportation.

In our findings, we point to the cultural script of silence as an additional risk factor that is unique to the experience of mixed-status families. The presence and pragmatics of cultural silence have been well documented among families and communities of undocumented individuals (De Genova 2002, 2009; Fassin 2001; Menjívar and Kanstroom, 2014). Yet, as Joanna Dreby convincingly argues, U.S. immigration policies have "a profound impact on children in Mexican families regardless of the parents' or children's legal status or the family's actual involvement with the Department of Homeland Security" (2012, 843). The consequences of illegality, and the cultural logics of silence, extend beyond the boundaries of legal status to affect the lives of citizen children as well (Zayas 2015; Zayas and Bradlee 2015), and our findings point to the different ways in which silence operates. Although all participants knew that their parents were undocumented, the cultural script of silence manifested through other processes that encouraged youth to be silent about their experiences of suffering with kin, their peers, and even themselves.[2] Arguably, silencing not only leads to emotional and mental distress, but also fractures citizen children's understanding of their place in the world (Fivush 2010). Without a community to safely break the code of silence, citizen children—and their undocumented peers—must risk the potential integrity of their families should they choose to voice their experiences. It is for this reason that any resistance to the cultural script of silence will be found in the most closed, trusted, and intimate spaces. The experiences of immigrant families will remain, for the most part, hidden, camouflaged, and unspoken. Continued research on the effects of silence on well-being is warranted, especially comparative research that examines the differential experiences of citizen children and the spectrums of silence.

The categories and factors illustrated in figure 1 are derived from a rigorous approach to qualitative data analysis. Nevertheless, additional research is warranted to test our model and to determine the extent to which certain factors affect citizen children in immigrant families of different national origin. Additionally, we did not examine the unique circumstances of children living with psychiatric, cognitive, or developmental disability. Living with disability poses unique opportunities and challenges for families, which might distinguish their experiences as citizen children living in mixed-status families (Farrell and Krahn 2014). Research is still needed that examines the intersections of disability and legal status. Our framework opens the door for a critical discussion of the different factors that affect citizen children, and it is our hope that subsequent revisions are made to the framework based on the results of additional research. Of particular importance is the need to investigate how resources available in citizen children's local environment shape the degree to which cultural scripts, such as the script for silence, and individual coping mechanisms become helpful or harmful.

Our findings provide opportunities to influence immigration enforcement policies and practices. Experiences of family cohesion and dissolution hold particular relevance for this population, signifying potential avenues to reorganize programs and policies to enhance the well-being of citizen children. For example, the significance of the theme of family separation suggests the need to reconsider detention procedures that thwart family togetherness. Current practices that detain parents in locations that are geographically distant from family households pose serious risks to the emotional

---

1. Thanks to an anonymous reviewer for the suggestion regarding this point.

2. Our participants were aware of their parents' legal status, and this distinguishes our results from other research that reveals that many children, especially those who are undocumented, remain unaware of their families' legal status until they attend college (Gonzales 2011). This points to the diversity of experiences within immigrant families, both in terms of how children become aware of legal status differences and the experiences that such knowledge engenders.

well-being of citizen children (Zayas 2015). In the end, our results point to many resources that were perceived as mattering most. It is our hope, in offering a comprehensive account of the effects of immigration enforcement, that the framework can be used to modify leverage points that offer the potential for change in micro and macro settings in ways that appreciate the diversity of citizen children's experiences.

REFERENCES

Bronfenbrenner, Urie. 1979. *Ecology of Human Development: Experiments by Nature and Design.* Cambridge, Mass.: Harvard University Press.

———. 1993. "The Ecology of Cognitive Development: Research Models and Fugitive Findings." In *Development in Context: Acting and Thinking in Specific Environments*, edited by Robert H. Wozniak and Kurt W. Fisher. Hillsdale, N.J.: Lawrence Erlbaum.

Bronfenbrenner, Urie, and Pamela A. Morris. 1998. "The Ecology of Developmental Process." In *Handbook of Child Psychology: Theoretical Models of Human Development*, edited by William Damon and Richard M. Lerner. New York: John Wiley & Sons.

Cavazos-Rehg, Patricia A., Luis H. Zayas, and Edward L. Spitznagel. 2007. "Legal Status, Emotional Well-being and Subjective Health Status of Latino Immigrants." *Journal of the National Medical Association* 99(10): 1126–31.

Chavez, Leo R., F. Allan Hubbell, Shiraz I. Mishra, and R. Burciaga Valdez. 1997. "Undocumented Latina Immigrants in Orange County, California: A Comparative Analysis." *International Migration Review* 31(1): 88–107.

De Genova, Nicholas, P. 2002. "Migrant 'Illegality' and Deportability in Everyday Life." *Annual Review of Anthropology* 31 (October): 419–47.

———. 2009. "Conflicts of Mobility, and the Mobility of Conflict: Rightlessness, Presence, Subjectivity, Freedom." *Subjectivity* 29(1): 445–66.

Dreby, Joanna. 2012. "The Burden of Deportation on Children in Mexican Immigrant Families." *Journal of Marriage and Family* 74(4): 829–45.

———. 2013. "The Ripple Effects of Deportation Policies on Mexican Women and Their Children." In *The Other People: Interdisciplinary Perspectives on Migration*, edited by Meg Wilkes Karraker. New York: Palgrave Macmillan.

Farrell, Anne F., and Gloria L. Krahn. 2014. "Family Life Goes On: Disability in Contemporary Families." *Family Relations* 63(1): 1–6.

Fassin, Didier. 2001. "The Biopolitics of Otherness: Undocumented Foreigners and Racial Discrimination in French Public Debate." *Anthropology Today* 17(1): 3–7.

Fivush, Robyn. 2010. "Speaking Silence: The Social Construction of Silence in Autobiographical and Cultural Narratives." *Memory* 18(2): 88–98.

Gonzales, Roberto G. 2011. "Learning to Be Illegal: Undocumented Youth and Shifting Legal Contexts in the Transition to Adulthood." *American Sociological Review* 76(1): 602–19.

Gonzales, Roberto G., and Leo R. Chavez. 2012. "Awakening to a Nightmare." *Current Anthropology* 53(3): 255–81.

Guendelman, Sylvia, Megan Wier, Veronica Angulo, and Doug Oman. 2006. "The Effects of Child-Only Insurance Coverage and Family Coverage on Health Care Access and Use: Recent Findings Among Low-Income Children in California." *Health Services Research* 41(1): 125–47.

Guest, Greg, and Kathleen M MacQueen. 2008. "Re-evaluating Guidelines in Qualitative Research." In *Handbook for Team-Based Qualitative Research*, edited by Greg Guest and Kathleen M. MacQueen. New York: Altamira.

Guest, Greg, Kathleen M. MacQueen, and Emily E. Namey. 2012. *Applied Thematic Analysis.* Los Angeles: Sage Publications.

Kersey, Margaret, Joni Geppert, and Diana B. Cutts. 2007. "Hunger in Young Children of Mexican Immigrant Families." *Public Health Nutrition* 10(4): 390–95.

Mack, Natasha, Arwen Bunce, and Betty Akumatey. 2008. "A Logistical Framework for Enhancing Team Dynamics." In *Handbook for Team-Based Qualitative Research*, edited by Greg Guest and Kathleen M. MacQueen. New York: Altamira.

Menjívar, Cecilia, and Daniel Kanstroom. 2013. *Constructing Immigrant 'Illegality': Critiques, Experiences, and Responses.* Cambridge: Cambridge University Press.

Miles, Matthew B., and A. Michael Huberman. 1994. *Qualitative Data Analysis: An Expanded Source Book.* Thousand Oaks, Calif.: Sage.

Negrón-Gonzales, Genevieve. 2014. "Undocumented, Unafraid and Unapologetic: Re-Articulatory Practices and Migrant Youth 'Illegality'." *Latino Studies* 12(2): 259–78.

Ochs, Elinor, and Lisa Capps. 1996. "Narrating the Self." *Annual Review of Anthropology* 25 (October): 19–43.

Panter-Brick, Catherine. 2014. "Health, Risk, and Resilience: Interdisciplinary Concepts and Applications." *Annual Review of Anthropology* 43 (October): 431–48.

Perreira, Krista M., and India J. Ornelas. 2011. "The Physical and Psychological Well-being of Immigrant Children." *Future of Children* 21(1): 195–218.

Peutz, Nathalie, and Nicholas De Genova. 2010. "Introduction." In *The Deportation Regime: Sovereignty, Space, and the Freedom of Movement*, edited by Nicholas De Genova and Nathalie Peutz. Durham, NC: Duke University Press.

Pew Hispanic Research Center. 2013. "A Nation of Immigrants: A Portrait of the 40 Million, Including 11 Million Unauthorized." Washington, D.C.: Pew Research Center. Accessed March 1, 2017. http://www.pewhispanic.org/files/2013/01/statistical_portrait_final_jan_29.pdf.

Potochnick, Stephanie R., and Krista M. Perreira. 2010. "Depression and Anxiety Among First-Generation Immigrant Latino Youth: Key Correlates and Implications for Future Research." *The Journal of Nervous and Mental Disease* 198(7): 470–77.

Sobo, Elisa J. 2009. *Culture and Meaning in Health Services Research: A Practical Field Guide*. Walnut Creek, Calif.: Left Coast Press.

Spradley, James P. 1979. *The Ethnographic Interview*. New York: Holt, Rinehart and Winston.

Suárez-Orozco, Carola, and Hirokazu Yoshikawa. 2013. "Undocumented Status: Implications for Child Development, Policy, and Ethical Research." *New Directions for Child and Adolescent Development* 2013(141): 61–78.

Super, Charles M., and Sara Harkness. 1986. "The Developmental Niche: A Conceptualization at the Interface of Child and Culture." *International Journal of Behavioral Development* 9(4): 545–69.

Tudge, Jonathan. 2008. *The Everyday Lives of Young Children: Culture, Class, and Child Rearing In Diverse Societies*. Cambridge: Cambridge University Press.

Ungar, Michael, Mehdi Ghazinour, and Jörg Richter. 2013. "Annual Research Review: What Is Resilience Within the Social Ecology of Human Development?" *Journal of Child Psychology and Psychiatry* 5(4): 348–66.

Weisner, Thomas S. 2002. "Ecocultural Understanding of Children's Developmental Pathways." *Human Development* 45(4): 275–81.

——. 2010. "Well-being, Chaos and Culture: Sustaining a Meaningful Daily Routine." In *Chaos and Its Influence on Children's Development*, edited by Gary W. Evans and Theodore D. Wachs. Washington, D.C.: American Psychological Association.

Worthman, Carol. 2010. "Survival and Health." In *Handbook of Cultural Developmental Science*, edited by Marc H. Bornstein. New York: Taylor and Francis.

Yoshikawa, Hirokazu. 2011. *Immigrants Raising Citizens: Undocumented Parents and Their Children*. New York: Russell Sage Foundation.

Zayas, Luis. 2015. *Forgotten Citizens: Deportation, Children, and the Making of American Exiles and Orphans*. Oxford: Oxford University Press.

Zayas, Luis H., and Mollie H. Bradlee. 2015. "Children of Undocumented Immigrants: Imperiled Developmental Trajectories." In *Race, Ethnicity and Self: Identity in Multicultural Perspective*, edited by Elizabeth P. Salett and Diane R. Koslow. Washington, D.C.: National Association of Social Workers.

Employer Sanctions and the Wages of Mexican Immigrants

PETER BROWNELL

Wage differences between authorized and unauthorized Mexican immigrants can be explained by human capital factors prior to the 1986 passage of employer sanctions, which prohibited knowingly hiring unauthorized aliens. However, a significant post-1986 wage differential has been interpreted as employers "passing along" expected costs of sanctions through lower wages for unauthorized immigrants. I test this explanation using administrative data on employer sanctions enforcement, finding employer sanctions enforcement levels are related to Mexican immigrants' wages but have no statistically significant differential effect based on legal status. Estimated savings to employers due to the pay gap are orders of magnitude larger than actual fines.

Keywords: unauthorized immigrants, wages, employer sanctions

Historically, immigrants' low pay relative to the native-born has been popularly understood to stem from their "docility" and "desperation" (Higham 1955; Saxton 1971). In 1916, the economist Frank Julian Warne wrote that the immigrant "combines bodily vigor with a docility and meager physical demands that make it practicable to obtain his labor at the low cost of the coarsest subsistence" (175). Such formulations tend to portray the docility that causes low wages as an almost innate characteristic of immigrants, resulting from the poor conditions in the countries of their birth.[1]

In 1959, the sociologists Seymour Martin Lipset and Reinhard Bendix suggested "that foreign-born workers are less oriented toward occupational achievement than their native-born colleagues" (49), but the discussion of nativity was both overshadowed and confounded by discussions of the relationship between occupational mobility and religious affiliation. It seems that the low levels of immigration at mid-century made immigration a less salient topic for the social sciences.

However, as immigration increased in the wake of the 1965 Immigration Act, social scientists turned their gaze once again to its causes and effects. By the early 1970s, sociologists began rejecting the notion that immigrants' lower pay was due to docile dispositions, attributing it instead to immigrants' vulnerable position vis-à-vis the state (Castells

---

Peter Brownell is research director at the Center on Policy Initiatives and adjunct social scientist at the RAND Corporation.

© 2017 Russell Sage Foundation. Brownell, Peter. 2017. "Employer Sanctions and the Wages of Mexican Immigrants." *RSF: The Russell Sage Foundation Journal of the Social Sciences* 3(4): 70–96. DOI: 10.7758/RSF.2017.3.4.05. Direct correspondence to: Peter Brownell at peter@peterbrownell.net, Center on Policy Initiatives, 3727 Camino del Rio South, #100, San Diego, CA 91208.

1. Similarly, when immigrants proved not to be docile, the cause was also to be found abroad in the form of foreign tendencies toward communism or anarchism (Higham 1955).

1975; Portes 1978, 1977; Bach 1978; Jenkins 1978; Sassen-Koob 1978). That is, immigrants, as foreigners, lack political membership and rights, and are therefore more vulnerable to labor exploitation than the native born. Following this logic, "illegal" immigrants occupy an even more vulnerable position and are subject to more extreme "superexploitation" (Jenkins 1978; Portes 1977, 1978; Bach 1978). This literature focused on the higher profits that employers of undocumented immigrants earned by paying lower wages for labor that was assumed to be equally productive (see also Wilson 1993).

However, many economists took the opposite view, disputing that differences in average wages between legal and "illegal" immigrants were due to a pay penalty imposed on workers of comparable productive capacities. Instead, they argued, the differences in pay stemmed from differences in human capital, particularly education, English ability, and U.S. job experience (Borjas 1990; Chiswick 1978, 1984, 1988; Bailey 1985; see also Cornelius 1978). In other words, unauthorized and legal immigrants were not experiencing different treatment. Authorized and unauthorized immigrant workers with the same human capital should earn the same wage; in fact, they should be interchangeable substitutes in the eyes of employers. In this view, the difference in average wages is due to average differences in human capital. That is, unauthorized immigrants have, on average, less education, less U.S. work experience, and worse English abilities than legal immigrants, making them on average less productive and therefore on average less well paid. A number of empirical studies found that measured human capital variables explained much, but not necessarily all, of the wage differential between authorized and unauthorized immigrants (Bailey 1985; Heer and Falasco 1984 [cited in Heer 1990]; Kossoudji and Ranney 1986; Morales 1983). However, in 1987, the sociologist Douglas Massey, analyzing data from Mexican immigrant sending communities, found that controls for human capital explained the wages differences between legal and unauthorized Mexican immigrant workers. The economists George Borjas (1990) and Barry Chiswick (1988), relying heavily on Massey's results, argued forcefully against any effect of vulnerability or exploitation. With leading migration scholars in economics, sociology, as well as political scientist Wayne Cornelius (1978) supporting this view, there seemed, for a time, to be consensus across the social sciences for the human capital explanation.

However, as Douglas Massey and his Mexican Migration Project (MMP) collaborators continued collecting data, they began to find that, for more recent observations, human capital could not completely explain the difference in wages between authorized and unauthorized Mexican immigrants (Phillips and Massey 1999; Donato and Massey 1993; see also Massey and Gentsch 2014). However, these new findings did not contradict Massey's earlier findings (1987), but instead indicated that something had changed. Newer retrospective observations relating to the period prior to 1986 still indicated that human capital sufficed to explain differences in wages across legal status. However, post-1986 observations showed significant and large effects of immigration status that could not be explained by human capital or any other measured variable.[2]

A plausible explanation for this change was readily available. In 1986, Congress passed the Immigration Reform and Control Act (IRCA), which made it illegal, for the first time, for employers in the United States to knowingly hire aliens who did not have valid work authorization. Soon after its passage, and before any sanctions were implemented, Michael Todaro and Lydia Maruszko hypothesized that "any expected fines for hiring illegal migrants will be passed on to illegal workers as a further reduction in their wages relative to those of legal workers" (1987, 108). Since that time, a number of other economists have theorized that employers pass along the expected costs of employer sanctions fines to unauthorized workers (Crane et al. 1990; Taylor 1992; Cobb-Clark, Shiells, and Lowell 1995; Ise and Perloff 1995; Davila and Pagan 1997) and "potentially unauthorized workers" (Bansak 2005). Katharine Donato and Douglas Massey argue that after the passage of IRCA's employer sanctions provisions,

---

2. The later studies also found reduced returns to education in the post-IRCA period.

"employers responded to the added costs and risks of hiring undocumented workers by lowering their wages" (1993, 539). Similarly, Julie Phillips and Douglas Massey maintain that "employers continue to hire undocumented migrants, but transfer the costs and risks of doing so to workers in the form of lower pay" (1999, 234; see also Massey, Durand, and Malone 2002, 120).

Although it certainly is plausible that the significant post-IRCA wage penalty for unauthorized immigrants could be explained by employers passing along the expected costs of IRCA's employer sanctions provisions, the low level of employer sanctions enforcement calls this hypothesis into question (Bruno 2015; Brownell 2005; Pritchard 2003).

THE RISK OF FINES UNDER IRCA'S EMPLOYER SANCTIONS PROVISIONS

Employers' risk of fines for violations of IRCA's employer sanctions provisions is low for two reasons. The first is that safe harbor provisions in IRCA and subsequent amendments protect employers from fines if they make good faith efforts to comply. The second is the relatively low levels of enforcement effort devoted to sanctions.

Under IRCA, employers are legally required to request and examine documents establishing the identity and work authorization of new hires and document this on an I-9 form. If they do not complete a form for each new employee hired or if it is filled out incorrectly, employers are liable for "paperwork" fines (8 USC 1324a(e)(5)). However, employers who comply with the verification procedures by examining a document that "reasonably appears on its face to be genuine" (8 USC 1324a(b)(1)(A)), gain a defense from prosecution under IRCA's "knowing hire" provision (8 USC 1324a(a)(3)) which the government can overcome only with proof that the employer knew or should have known that the worker was unauthorized (*Collins Foods International, Inc. v. INS*, 948 F.2d 549 [9th Cir. 1991]).

Kitty Calavita argues that the legislative process redefined employers who do, in fact, knowingly hire unauthorized immigrants as *compliers* because they have met the paperwork requirements (1990). This makes compliance more likely, but works at counter purposes with the goal of reducing the employment of unauthorized immigrants.

Calavita's post-IRCA interviews with both employers and employees in southern California demonstrate this.[3] About 48 percent of the employers surveyed *thought* some of their employees were undocumented. Another 11 percent volunteered that they *knew* they had hired undocumented workers after IRCA had gone into effect. Of the workers interviewed (from the same firms), 30 percent acknowledged being undocumented at the time they were hired. Of these, 35 percent reported having used fraudulent documents. Slightly more than 4 percent of the undocumented workers reported being *told by their employer* to obtain false documents (Calavita 1990). Robert Bach and Howard Brill report that "the majority of employers accept documents even though they suspect and even know that the applicant is unauthorized" (Bach and Brill 1991, 62). As one employer told researchers, "the compliance procedures are not that difficult. You don't have to verify the person's documents are *valid*, so there's no hazard in hiring someone with fraudulent documents" (Cornelius 1989, 44 [emphasis added]). Thus the standard for "knowingly hire" (or "substantive") violations of IRCA's employer sanctions provisions creates a high bar that makes prosecution of employers who do, in fact, knowingly hire unauthorized aliens difficult, provided they have met their obligations to examine prospective employees' documents and correctly completed the I-9 form.

Moreover, the Illegal Immigration Reform and Immigrant Responsibility Act (IIRAIRA) of 1996 amended IRCA's sanctions provisions regarding paperwork violations. Under the original IRCA regulations, inspectors were required to give at least three days notice prior to inspecting an employer's I-9 forms

---

3. The interviews were conducted in 1987 and 1988, after IRCA's employer sanctions provisions had gone into effect. This survey was a collaboration between Cornelius, Calavita, and other researchers (see also Cornelius 1989).

Figure 1. Worksite Immigration Investigations

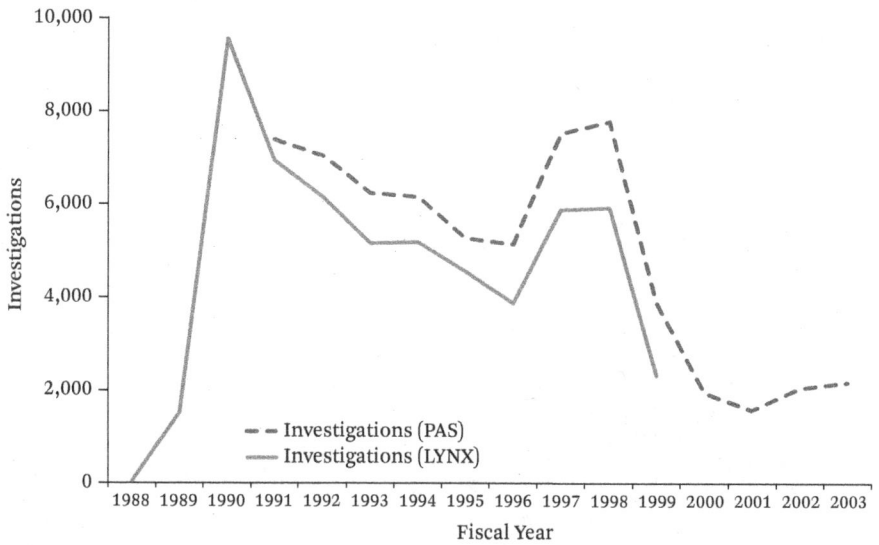

Source: INS 1997 and OIS 2003 (PAS) and author's calculations (LYNX).

(8 CFR 274a.2(b)(2)(ii); see also Fix 1991). Under the IIRAIRA amendments, so long as employers have made a "good faith effort" to properly complete the I-9 forms, they have ten additional days after an inspection to correct any "technical or procedural" errors before being considered out of compliance and liable for fines for paperwork violations (8 USC 1324a(b)(6)).

In addition to (or perhaps in part because of) the high bar that IRCA created for prosecuting employers for knowingly hiring unauthorized immigrants, the former Immigration and Naturalization Service (INS) and current Immigration and Customs Enforcement (ICE) have focused a relatively small share of their enforcement resources on employer sanctions (Siskin et al. 2006; GAO 1999). The General Accounting Office reported that in 1998, worksite investigations accounted for 2 percent of INS's enforcement work-years for overall (interior and border) enforcement activities (1999). The Congressional Research Service reported that investigations targeting employers accounted for about 15 percent of interior enforcement work-years between fiscal years 1992 and 1998 (Siskin et al. 2006). However, during fiscal years 2000 through 2003, employer investigations had declined to the point that they accounted for 5 percent or less of interior enforcement work-years (Siskin et al. 2006).

Figure 1 presents the number of completed worksite investigations by fiscal year from two data sources. The Worksite Enforcement Activity Record and Index (LYNX) data is publicly available for fiscal years (FY) 1988 to 1999, but is less complete than the Performance Analysis System (PAS) data published in the Department of Homeland Security's *Yearbook of Immigration Statistics* and the INS *Statistical Yearbook* (OIS 2002, 2003; INS 1997). The PAS data is available starting only in FY 1992, but continues through FY 2003. Comparable data for the period since INS investigations were reorganized into ICE is not available. At the peak level of audits, INS audited (or "investigated") approximately ten thousand employers in FY 1990, about 0.2 percent of the more than five million employers in the United States at that time (Small Business Administration, n.d.). The number of worksite investigations completed declined to a low of 5,149 in FY 1996, increasing again in FY 1997 and FY 1998 to a high of 7,788. Completed investigations declined again in FY 1999 to 3,868, hitting a low of 1,595 in FY 2001 before rebounding to 2,194 in FY 2003.

The number of employers to whom INS is-

Figure 2. Worksite Immigration Final Orders Imposing Fines

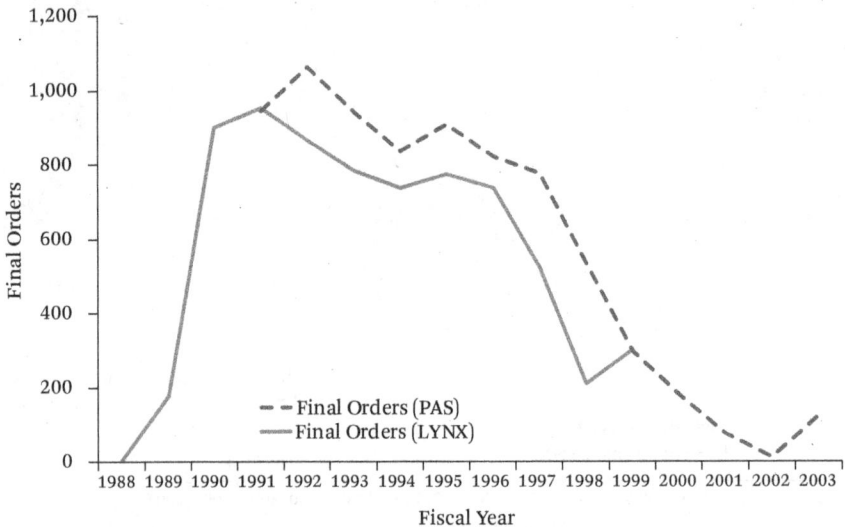

Source: INS 1997 and OIS 2003 (PAS) and author's calculations (LYNX).

sued final orders imposing fines for employer sanctions violations also began relatively low and declined through most of the period for which data are available. Figure 2 shows this downward trend, dropping 82 percent from a peak of nearly one thousand in FY 1991 to 124 in FY 2003. Although the data may not be directly comparable, the Congressional Research Service reports fewer than twenty per year between FY 2004 and FY 2008 (Bruno 2015).

The available data for FY 1990 to FY 1996 shows that the aggregate dollar value of employer sanctions fines imposed on final orders peaked in FY 1990 at $8.1 million, but that only $5.8 million in fines were actually collected that year (DOJ 1995; Jenks 1997). Fines imposed in one fiscal year may have been collected in later years, and in fact, fines collected peaked at $6.2 million in FY 1992, even though only $6.0 million in fines were ordered that year (DOJ 1995; Jenks 1997). The peak of collected fines at $6.2 million averages less than $0.07 per employee in the United States for 1992.[4]

To put these enforcement levels into broader perspective, in FY 2001 the Department of Labor Wage and Hour Division concluded 38,051 cases, assessing $10.5 million in civil monetary penalties and collecting $132 million in back wages (DOL 2002). The same year, $153 million in penalties were assessed for violations of the Occupational Safety and Health Act (DOL 2004). Similarly, over the period from 1989 to 1999, total back-pay awards ordered by the National Labor Relations Board ranged from $44.4 million to $89.9 million per year (NLRB 2001).

Given the low levels of employer sanctions enforcement, can employers' expected costs due to fines really explain the 18 to 22 percent wage penalty that MMP researchers find for unauthorized Mexican workers after 1986 (Phillips and Massey 1999; Donato and Massey 1993)? It is possible to test this hypothesis using INS administrative data on employer sanctions fines and survey data on the wages of individual Mexican immigrants. As figures 1 and 2 show, variation in the level of employer sanctions enforcement over time has been considerable. Because the INS had a decentralized structure that granted district offices and border patrol sectors a great deal of autonomy in determining enforcement priorities and practices, employer sanctions enforcement levels and strategies also varied considerably across space (Fix and Hill 1990; Fix 1991). Moreover, at both the

---

4. The Small Business Administration reports an employment figure of 92,825,797 for 1992, based on data from the U.S. Census Bureau, Statistics of U.S. Business and Nonemployer Statistics.

national and district levels, INS targeted particular industries for greater scrutiny in employer sanctions enforcement (GAO 1999). All in all, variation is considerable in the employer sanctions enforcement effort across years, states, and industries. Although previous research has identified that undocumented immigrants' pay declined relative to legal immigrants at about the same time that IRCA went into effect, researchers have thus far not managed "to isolate the *reasons* for this change" (Phillips and Massey 1999, 233). No direct test has been made of the relationship between levels of employer sanctions fines and the difference in wages between authorized and unauthorized Mexican immigrant workers. If the hypothesis that employers are merely passing along the expected costs of fines is correct, we should expect the post-IRCA wage gap to covary over time, place, and industry with the level of sanctions enforcement. If it does not, this would suggest that the post-IRCA difference in pay is not due directly to fines, and we should explore other changes that occurred during this period, which may or may not relate directly to the passage of IRCA. The regression methods described will allow us to determine the extent to which the wage gap can be explained by the level of employer sanctions fines.

DATA

The analysis requires survey data that include data on Mexican immigrants' U.S. wages, as well as key wage determinants such as age, education, duration in the United States, and English ability. An additional requirement is that the survey data include information on respondents' immigration status or work authorization. This requirement rules out the use of many U.S. sources of data on wages, such as the Current Population Survey (CPS) and Decennial Census Public Use Microdata Samples (PUMS). Instead, I turn to data from the Mexican Migration Project.

Mexican Migration Project Data

Data from the MMP has been used by Douglas Massey and his co-authors in analyses that have found a significant wage gap between authorized male Mexican immigrant workers and their unauthorized counterparts (Massey 1987; Phillips and Massey 1999; Donato and Massey 1993).

The MMP collects data primarily in Mexico, randomly sampling households within purposively selected migrant-sending communities. The survey also includes a small nonrandom sample of Mexican immigrants settled in the United States. The survey is administered to Mexican communities from December through January, when many U.S. migrants return to Mexico. Household heads are asked to give a retrospective migration history as well as detailed information about their last trip to the United States. Based on referrals in each sending community, six to twenty households of settled migrants in the United States are also surveyed during July and August (Phillips and Massey 1999).

Given both the selective nature of the migration process and the difficulties in sampling both sending communities and migrants in the United States, it is important that sampling weights be applied to the data to derive the best estimates of population parameters (Phillips and Massey 1999).[5] Except when stated otherwise, all analyses reported were carried out using the weights, both to make estimates closely representative of the population of Mexican immigrants to the United States, and to maintain comparability to the weighted analyses of Julie Phillips and Douglas Massey (1999).

This project picks up where Phillips and Massey left off, looking for the cause of the post-IRCA wage gap between authorized and unauthorized Mexican male immigrant workers. I begin my investigations by attempting to replicate the key finding that wage differences between legal and unauthorized immigrants

---

5. For the Mexican community samples, the sampling weights are the inverse of the proportion of households sampled in the community. For the out-migrants surveyed in the United States, weights are the inverse of estimated sampling fractions derived by dividing the actual sample size by estimates of the number of U.S. households based on information gathered from informants within the sending community (for more detail on the sampling procedure, see Massey and Espinosa 1997; for detail on the sample weights for the U.S. sample, see Massey and Parrado 1994).

can be explained by human capital factors in the pre-IRCA period, but not after IRCA's passage. Following Phillips and Massey, I limited the analysis to male household heads (due to small female household head sample size), who worked in the United States since 1970. The logged hourly wages used as the dependent variable in this ordinary least squares (OLS) regression analysis are adjusted to constant 1982 to 1984 dollars based on the Bureau of Labor Statistics' Consumer Price Index (CPI) for all urban consumers at the Metropolitan Statistical Area (MSA) level, where such a series exists, otherwise to the regional urban CPI.[6]

Because some models involve matching respondents' occupations (coded using the Mexican Classification of Occupations—CMO) to industries, respondents in occupations common to multiple industries were dropped from the analysis. A total of 149 cases (4.5 percent) that would otherwise have been included were dropped for this reason. Of these, about 27 percent were clerical workers, about 29 percent were professionals, technicians, business owners, or supervisors; about 19 percent were drivers or vehicle operators; about 13 percent reported nonworking classifications (student, homemaker, tourist, and the like) despite reporting a wage; about 3 percent were in the armed forces; and the remaining approximately 9 percent were ambulatory workers such as street vendors. Thus the sample used is not necessarily representative of all Mexican immigrant workers, but is generally representative of Mexican men in most blue-collar occupations in the United States.

Additionally, the MMP contains a small number of cases that appear to have coding errors in the hourly wage (HRWAGE) variable, resulting in unreasonably high (and perhaps unreasonably low) hourly wages. To address this, I have dropped from the analysis all "severe outliers," that is, all values of logged hourly real wages greater than or equal to 3.5 interquartile ranges (IQRs) from the median.

Thus, thirty cases with hourly wages (in 1982 to 1984 dollars) lower than $0.60 or greater than $30.08 per hour are excluded. Although doing so improves the fit of the models and the significance of many control variables, it does not significantly change the sign, magnitude, or significance level of the variables of interest (immigration status or enforcement measures).

Phillips and Massey (1999) include in their models the correction for selectivity bias that James Heckman proposes (1976, 1979). Katharine Donato and Massey test such a correction and find that it makes no significant difference in the wage equations based on the MMP data then available (1993). Ross Stolzenberg and Daniel Relles argue that the Heckman "correction" sometimes produces "corrected" parameter estimates that are further from the true population parameter than the uncorrected OLS estimate, even when the assumptions of the Heckman procedure are not violated (1997). Furthermore, it is not clear that a correction for selection is necessary or desirable unless one is substantively interested in the wages *potential* Mexican immigrants would have received *if they had migrated* to the United States. For these reasons, no term attempting to correct for any selectivity bias is included in the models presented here.

My initial models also included many fewer variables than Phillips and Massey, in part because many variables were not relevant to this project, in part because of methodological and causation issues, especially with social capital variables (see Livingston 2005), and finally because the prior study (Phillips and Massey 1999) found many of them not to have statistically significant relationships with wages. Among these were local unemployment rates and the rate of change in proportion of the local Mexican population with legal status (legalization rate), suggesting that post-IRCA wage differences were not driven by changes in the labor supply.[7]

---

6. For the CPI adjustments and all other measurements relating to the year in which the wage was earned, I assume that migrants interviewed in Mexico reported the wage earned at the end, rather than beginning of a U.S. trip. Wages reported by migrants interviewed in the United States are attributed to the year of the interview.

7. As of this writing, the MSAYEAR file on the MMP website that includes MSA level legalization rates and unemployment rates is dated March 1999 and includes data through 1996. Although the effort to update these

Table 1. Variable Descriptions

Variable	Description
Real wage	Hourly wage adjusted to constant 1982–1984 dollars for year last U.S. trip ended
Logged wage	Natural logarithm of hourly real wages in constant 1982–1984 dollars
Age	Age in years at end of last U.S. trip
Prior U.S. experience	U.S. experience in months prior to beginning of last U.S. trip
U.S. trip duration	Duration of last U.S. trip in months
Number of U.S. trips	Number of U.S. trips (including current trip)
Education	Years of schooling in four categories (1–3, 4–5, 5–11, 12+) with none as reference
English ability	Three categories: "Understands Some," "Speaks Some," Speaks Well," with none as reference
Immigration status	
Authorized	Legal permanent residents, U.S. citizens, other visas or statuses allowing work
Guestworker	H-2(A), cases coded "Temporary work," and immigrants who entered as Braceros
Unauthorized	No valid entry documents or documents not permitting work (such as a student visa)
Pre-IRCA	Unauthorized, last U.S. trip ended prior to 1986
Trip spans IRCA	Unauthorized, last U.S. trip began during or before 1986 and ended during or after 1986
Post-IRCA	Unauthorized, last U.S. trip began after 1986
Enforcement measures	
Expected fine	Average employer sanction fine in industry and state during twelve months beginning two months prior to calendar year (see equation [1])
Probability of audit	Probability of audit in industry and state during twelve months beginning two months prior to calendar year (see equation [2])

Source: Author's compilation.

Nonetheless, using models with variables for age, U.S. experience, education and English ability (see table 1), I was able to replicate the finding that the wages of unauthorized Mexican immigrant workers are significantly lower than the wages of comparable authorized workers only during the post-IRCA period. The results of regressions on a sample limited to cases from communities included in the MMP at the time of Phillips and Massey's analysis (not reported here), imply that the hourly wages of unauthorized immigrants were about 16 percent lower than legal immigrants ($p < .01$).

The question remains as to the causes of the post-IRCA wage penalty for unauthorized immigrants. Can it be explained by employers passing along the costs of expected fines? Or has some other factor tilted the playing field such that unauthorized immigrants earn less regardless of the level of employer sanctions enforcement directed at workplaces in their industry and area?

CASE-BASED FINES DATA TO MEASURE EXPECTED FINES

To answer this question, I constructed measures of actual levels of fines based on INS ad-

variables to include more recent data seems of limited value, the appendix includes results that use these measures on a limited sample.

ministrative data on employer sanctions enforcement activities. I use the Employer Sanctions Database obtained by the Center for Immigration Studies (CIS) through the Freedom of Information Act (FOIA). This database contains records from the INS/ICE database known as LYNX from the beginning of sanctions implementation through early 2000 (for more information on the LYNX database, see GAO 1999). The data are case level; that is, each observation corresponds to one "case" in which an employer was investigated (audited). The dataset contains the results of cases in which the employer was found to be in compliance as well as cases resulting in warnings or fines. However, relative to the aggregate counts of enforcement activities reported through the INS-DHS (Department of Homeland Security) Performance Analysis System, the CIS database suffers from considerable incompleteness (see figures 1 and 2). Moreover, relative to aggregate information publicly available from the LYNX system (DOJ 1996; GAO 1999), the CIS database also seems to be missing data that are included in LYNX. If the data are not missing at random, results could be biased. The incompleteness of the LYNX system relative to the PAS system should be worst for years prior to FY 1996, when LYNX was designated the primary system for recording sanctions enforcement activities (GAO 1999). The process leading to incompleteness in the CIS database relative to LYNX is unknown. Nonetheless, relative to PAS data on enforcement actions at the level of the INS District Office, the correlation between the number of final orders per fiscal year as recorded in the CIS data and the number of final orders reported in PAS is 0.61.[8] Although less than ideal, the CIS data capture a considerable share of the variation in employer sanctions enforcement. Moreover, it is the best publicly available dataset exported from the LYNX system. Unfortunately, although the PAS system reports aggregate national numbers of enforcement activities, for example, in the *Yearbook of Immigration Statistics*, the PAS data do not allow detailed analysis of enforcement by industry (OIS 2003, 2004).

Without going into great detail in describing the enforcement process, I describe the measure of expected fines and how it is calculated. The expected fines measure is an estimate of the mean fine paid (by employers) for violations of IRCA's employer sanctions provisions averaged across all workers employed in the same industry, state and year.[9] The measure used here combines both fines for "knowingly" hiring or employing unauthorized immigrants, as well as violations for failure to properly complete I-9 paperwork. Good arguments can be made for and against including "paperwork only" fines in the measure of average fines.[10] On the one hand, all employers are theoretically subject to fines for failing to properly fill out I-9 forms, even if all of their employees are in fact authorized to work. Because employers are subject to paperwork fines regardless of the status of their employees, we might not expect fines to cause the differences in wages based on legal status we seek to explain. Relatedly, one study found that paperwork and knowing hire fines had effects in the opposite directions on aggregate metropolitan wages, expected paperwork fines reducing wages and expected knowing hiring fines increasing wages (Fry, Lowell, and Haghighat 1995).

On the other hand, evidence suggests that INS reserved paperwork fines for cases that investigators believed but could not prove knowing employment (INS 1987, Section III-E-2; Fix and Hill 1990, 113). Moreover, after the 1996 amendments mentioned earlier, employers

---

8. Data from the PAS Investigations G-23.19 through G-23.20 at the INS district or Border Patrol Sector level were provided to the author for fiscal years 1994 to 2003 by the Office of Immigration Statistics and are available from the author on request.

9. To be clear, fines are levied against employers based only on the number of employees for whom the employer has either failed to properly complete a form I-9 or knowingly employed. Employees found to be out of status are not subject to fines, but rather to arrest and removal (deportation).

10. An anonymous referee for an earlier version of this article strongly suggested using only knowing hire fines, and a referee for a later version advocated using all employer sanctions fines. Although the main paper follows the latter suggestion, the appendix shows similar results using only knowing hire fines.

who made a "good faith effort" to comply were given ten days to correct any violations that were purely "technical or procedural," which is to say, "paperwork only" violations (8 USC 1324a(b)(6)). So it seems likely that many paperwork only fines were issued in cases that involved the employment of unauthorized aliens, but the burden of proving that the employer had knowingly hired such workers was not met. If this is the case, then both paperwork and knowing hire fines might be expected to affect differences in wages between authorized and unauthorized workers.

One reason to combine paperwork and knowing hire fines is practical: in a few investigations resulting in fines (forty-six), the type of violation is not recorded in the administrative data. The analysis that follows uses a measure of all employer sanctions fines (combining paperwork and knowing violations). Ultimately, however, using only knowing hire fines or all fines does not affect the direction or significance of the effects (for results of analysis based only on fines for knowing violations for comparison, see table A2).

The expected fines measure is based on a denominator of employees (of any status) for three main reasons. First, it estimates the cost (in employer sanctions fines) that an informed, employer in a given industry and state would anticipate upon considering hiring a new employee. Second, firms with more employees may face larger fines, as employers are liable for $100 to $10,000 in fines for *each* employee hired or employed in violation of IRCA.[11] Third, the regression models that follow take employees as the unit of analysis. All of these facts make it most appropriate to have a measure that estimates fines per employee rather than per firm.

The expected fines measure is the average employer sanctions fine per worker for a given industry, year, and state. More formally, it is calculated as

$$E(F_{ijk}) = \frac{(\Sigma F_{ijk})}{(N_{ijk})} \quad (1)$$

where $E(F_{ijk})$ is the expected fine in industry i, for year j, and state k. Similarly, ΣF_{ijk} is the sum of all fines and N_{ijk} is an estimate, based on the Current Population Survey, of the overall size of the workforce, both for industry i, year j, and state k.

A second measure of enforcement is used in the analysis to examine the causal direction between enforcement effort and wages. This measure is the probability of audit, $P(A)$. More precisely, it is the probability that a worker works at an audited firm. It is calculated by summing the total number of workers at audited firms (from the CIS data) for each industry, year, and state cell and dividing by the CPS-based estimate of the overall size of the workforce for that cell:

$$P(A_{ijk}) = (a_{ijk})/(N_{ijk}) \quad (2)$$

where a_{ijk} is the sum of workers at audited firms in industry i, for year j, and state k and where N_{ijk} is the CPS-based estimate of the overall workforce as defined in equation (1).

These enforcement measures are then attributed to respondents from the MMP who worked in occupations matched to these industries, in the corresponding year and state.[12]

---

11. Paperwork violations can result in fines from $100 to $1,000 for each employee with a missing or incorrect I-9 form (8 USC 1324a(e)). For substantive violations, fines are $250 to $2,000 for each unauthorized alien knowingly hired, for a first offender. For the second offense, the range increases to $2,000 to $5,000 per alien, and for the third or greater offense fines are $3,000 to $5,000 per unauthorized alien.

12. The Mexican Migration Project classifies occupations using the Clasificación Mexicana de Ocupaciones (Mexican Occupation Classification), which has the benefit, for the present purposes, of dividing production occupations by industry. The fifteen industry groups used here are agriculture, retail, domestic services, services (nondomestic), transportation, and industrial production in the following categories: food-beverage-tobacco, mines-quarries-wells, textile-leather, wood-paper, electrical-metal-automobile, ceramic-glass-tile, construction, electrical utilities-installation-repair, chemical-oil-plastics, and other production. Respondents with CMO occupational codes that could not be matched uniquely to an industry (such as clerical occupations) were excluded from the study.

Figure 3. Means of Enforcement Measures for MMP Sample

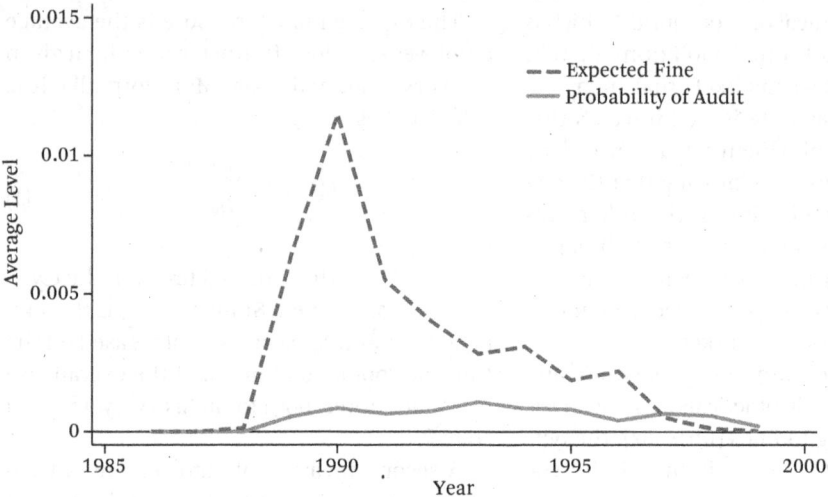

Source: Author's calculations.

These enforcement measures are equal for workers within a given state, year, and industry cell. This clustering could produce estimates of regression standard errors that are too low if not corrected.

Table 2 shows that, within the MMP sample, the average levels of expected fines were about $0.003 per employee during the years since the passage of IRCA, but vary considerably (SD = 0.0085). Figure 3 shows the average levels of $E(F_{ijk})$ and $P(A_{ijk})$ experienced by immigrants in the MMP sample used here.[13] Expected fines peaked in 1990 (at $0.012), declining to less than 5 percent of this level ($0.0005) by 1997. Figure 3 shows some correlation ($r = 0.69$) between expected fines and probability of audit, although the former exhibits much more variation due to differences over time in the certainty and size of fines experienced by noncompliant employers. However both measures reach all-time lows in 1999, the last full year in the series.

Although we see considerable variation over time in sanctions enforcement, I have no strong a priori assumptions about how long it might take for information regarding enforcement actions to diffuse to other employers. To find the empirically best-fitting time lag, I tested the effects of expected fines for one-year periods beginning zero to twelve months prior to the beginning of the year in which a migrant reported earnings (results not reported here). I found the best fit to the data with a two month lag, that is, the effect of enforcement for which a Notice of Intent to Fine was issued between November 1 of year $t\text{-}1$ and October 31 of year t on wages reported for calendar year t.

RESULTS

Table 3 shows the results of ordinary least squares regression models taking logged hourly wages adjusted to 1982 to 1984 dollars as the dependent variable. Model I replicates past findings regarding a post-IRCA wage gap using a sample that includes nearly two thousand additional (newer) observations, for a total sample size of 3,249 (Phillips and Massey 1999; Donato and Massey 1993). Including these newer observations, the results imply a post-IRCA wage penalty of about 11.5 percent for unauthorized immigrants, controlling for age, and human capital factors (education, English ability, and measures of U.S. experience). This

---

13. Note that because the male Mexican immigrant workers in the MMP are not a random sample of all U.S. employees, they are likely to experience levels of employer sanction enforcement that differ from the average levels for all U.S. employees discussed earlier.

Table 2. Summary Statistics

	Unauthorized		Authorized		Overall			
Variable	Mean/Percentage	SD	Mean/Percentage	SD	Mean/Percentage	SD	Min	Max
Real wage	4.95	2.83	6.04	3.25	5.33	3.07	0.61	29.48
Age	34.40	11.10	40.81	11.20	36.64	11.62	14.17	86.00
Prior U.S. experience (months)	18.89	36.59	95.18	78.59	45.55	68.20	0.00	431.00
U.S. trip duration (months)	55.13	86.28	88.70	108.57	66.86	97.97	1.00	612.00
Number of U.S. trips	2.56	3.00	6.04	5.76	3.78	4.68	1.00	44.00
Guestworker	1.08%		3.08%					
Education								
None	9.67%		6.90%		8.70%			
One to three years	20.57		18.74		19.93			
Four to five years	11.56		9.86		10.97			
Six to eleven years	46.00		49.69		47.29			
Twelve or more years	12.20		14.81		13.11			
English ability								
None	37.17%		9.50%		27.51%			
Understands some	34.44		23.43		30.59			
Speaks some	19.17		38.60		25.96			
Speaks well	9.22		28.47		15.94			
Trip timing								
Pre-IRCA	33.99%		4.56%		23.71%			
Trip spans IRCA	22.40		29.90		25.02			
Post-IRCA	43.60		65.54		51.27			
Enforcement measures								
Expected fine (1987–1999)	0.0027	0.0085	0.0056	0.0117	0.0040	0.0104	0.0000	0.1574
Audit probability (1987–1999)	0.0006	0.0011	0.0007	0.0009	0.0006	0.0010	0.0000	0.0091
Observations	2,291		958		3,249			

Source: Author's calculations.
Note: Table based on weighted data.

wage penalty is not due to changes in the distribution of immigrants across industries or states after IRCA. Holding state and industry constant results a small and statistically insignificant *increase* in the estimate of the post-IRCA wage gap (see table A1).[14]

Neither is the growing divergence in wages the result of increasing wages for legal Mexican immigrants. As model I indicates, the post-IRCA real wages of authorized immigrants (the reference group and period) were lower than their real wages prior to IRCA, net of all the other factors in the model. Comparing across legal statuses during the pre-IRCA period, the wages of unauthorized immigrants are statistically indistinguishable from the wages of legal immigrants ($p = .20$). The wages of those unauthorized immigrants whose last U.S. trip began before, but ended after, IRCA are also not significantly different from the post-IRCA wages of authorized immigrants. These immigrants were subject to a grandfather clause that made it legal for employers to continue to employ them, provided they had been hired prior to IRCA's passage.

Model II in table 3 shows the addition of the expected fines measure to model I. The fines measure does have a statistically significant negative effect on wages, implying a decrease in wages of about 1.4 percent at the mean (post-IRCA) level of enforcement, relative to no enforcement.[15] Each standard deviation increase in expected fines implies an average decrease in wages of 4.3 percent.[16] Although expected fines have a large and statistically significant coefficient, the low level of observed fines (averaging $0.003 per employee annually) means that the substantive effect on Mexican immigrants' wages is small.

With regard to the role of expected fines in explaining the post-IRCA wage gap between authorized and unauthorized Mexican immigrants, once expected fines are added to the model the magnitude of the coefficient representing the wage gap increases slightly and statistically significantly. Had employer sanctions enforcement caused the wage differential, we would have expected a large decrease in the magnitude of this coefficient. Thus, this model implies that the level of fines cannot explain the wage gap.

This conclusion is further supported by model III, which includes an interaction term allowing the effect of fines to vary between legal and unauthorized workers. The results show no statistically significant difference in the effects of expected fines on the wages of authorized and unauthorized Mexican immigrants. So, although fines do seem to affect wages, they are not a valid explanation of the post-IRCA difference in wages based on legal status. Instead, they seem to affect all Mexican male immigrants equally, a result consistent with IRCA-induced national-origin discrimina-

---

14. Because of a lack of agreement on the best formula for estimating the standard deviation of the difference in coefficients across nested models (Clogg et al. 1995; Allison 1995), I used bootstrap estimation or Stata's "seemingly unrelated estimation" (-suest-) procedure to test the significance of such changes (Weesie 1999).

15. It is possible that a statistically significant effect in these models is related to the expected fines measure being calculated, and thus clustered, at the year-state-industry level. That expected fines are not independent within year-state-industry cells should lead to an estimate of the standard error that is too small. Table A1 shows results from models similar to model II with the addition of fixed effects for state and the fourteen industry categories used in calculating the expected fines and with robust standard errors corrected for clustering on years. These models should correct for the clustering of expected fines by industry, state, and year, but the fixed effects should now capture the average effect of enforcement in each state and industry category, reducing the effect of expected fines. In model IIa, we see that under such a specification the expected fines measure calculated using all employer sanctions fines is not statistically significant. However, the expected fines measure calculated using only knowing hire fines remains significant. Unweighted mixed models with crossed random effects for year, state, and industry category (not reported here) also show statistically significant effects for both expected fine measures.

16. The predicted change in hourly wage as expected fines go from zero to the mean post-IRCA value of 0.0027 is $e^{(-5.139 \times 0.0027)} - 1 = -0.0138$. Similarly, the predicted change in hourly wage as expected fines increase from zero to the post-IRCA standard deviation of 0.0085 is $e^{(-5.139 \times 0.0085)} - 1 = -0.0427$.

Table 3. Regression of Logged Hourly Wages on Selected Predictors

Variable	Model I	Model II	Model III	Model IV
Age	0.010	0.010	0.009	0.010
	(0.006)	(0.006)	(0.006)	(0.006)
Age squared	−0.0002**	−0.0002**	−0.0002**	−0.0002**
	(0.0001)	(0.0001)	(0.0001)	(0.0001)
U.S. experience	0.001*	0.001	0.001	0.001
	(0.000)	(0.000)	(0.000)	(0.000)
U.S. duration	0.002***	0.002***	0.002***	0.002***
	(0.000)	(0.000)	(0.000)	(0.000)
Number of U.S. trips	0.002	0.004	0.003	0.004
	(0.003)	(0.003)	(0.003)	(0.003)
Education (reference = none)				
One to three years	0.065	0.072	0.070	0.072
	(0.057)	(0.056)	(0.057)	(0.056)
Four to five years	0.094	0.101	0.101	0.102
	(0.066)	(0.066)	(0.066)	(0.066)
Six to eleven years	0.094	0.096	0.095	0.097
	(0.056)	(0.057)	(0.057)	(0.057)
Twelve or more years	0.204**	0.206**	0.205**	0.206**
	(0.064)	(0.064)	(0.064)	(0.064)
English (reference = none)				
Understands some	0.093**	0.088**	0.088**	0.088**
	(0.032)	(0.032)	(0.032)	(0.032)
Speaks some	0.148***	0.146***	0.147***	0.146***
	(0.039)	(0.039)	(0.039)	(0.039)
Speaks well	0.252***	0.242***	0.244***	0.242***
	(0.063)	(0.063)	(0.063)	(0.063)
Immigration status (reference = authorized post-IRCA)				
Authorized pre-IRCA	0.152	0.106	0.113	0.105
	(0.104)	(0.106)	(0.107)	(0.106)
Guestworker	−0.460	−0.463	−0.461	−0.465
	(0.345)	(0.345)	(0.344)	(0.344)
Unauthorized				
Pre-IRCA	0.023	−0.022	−0.015	−0.023
	(0.064)	(0.067)	(0.068)	(0.067)
Post-IRCA	−0.122**	−0.132**	−0.118**	−0.132**
	(0.042)	(0.042)	(0.044)	(0.042)
Grandfathered	−0.058	−0.073	−0.063	−0.073
	(0.060)	(0.062)	(0.062)	(0.062)
Enforcement measures				
Expected fine		−5.139***	−3.612	−4.670**
		(1.544)	(1.906)	(1.798)
Expected fine*unauthorized			−4.161	
			(3.188)	
Probability of audit				−9.355
				(15.147)
Time trend	−0.003	−0.005	−0.005	−0.004
	(0.004)	(0.004)	(0.004)	(0.004)
Constant	1.236***	1.290***	1.285***	1.285***
	(0.138)	(0.139)	(0.139)	(0.139)
N	3,249	3,249	3,249	3,249
R^2	0.1914	0.1964	0.1971	0.1965

Source: Author's calculations.
Note: Robust standard errors in parentheses.
*p < .05; **p < .01; ***p < .001

tion (see also Bansak 2005; Bansak and Raphael 2001; GAO 1990).

One other possibility is that the relationship between fines and wages might be due to INS enforcement efforts targeted at industries with low wages. Thus, low wages could lead to increased fines, rather than causation running in the opposite direction. Alternatively, some third factor could cause both low wages and higher fines, resulting in a spurious relationship between fines and wages. However, if enforcement were focused on sectors with low wages, then the probability of audit would be negatively related with wages. Model IV shows that when both expected fines ($E(F)$) and probability of audit ($P(A)$) are included, there is a negative relationship between $P(A)$ and wages that is not statistically significant. However, the change in the $E(F)$ coefficient due to the addition of $P(A)$ is neither large nor statistically significant. This suggests that the expected fines effect on wages is driven primarily by variation in the certainty and size of fines, rather than a spurious relationship stemming from INS efforts targeted at low wage industries.

Regardless of the relationship between probability of audit and expected fines, the post-IRCA wage gap for unauthorized workers does not change significantly when controlling for both enforcement factors. In fact, none of the models including any variation of enforcement measures yield any statistically significant decreases in the magnitude of the coefficient for the post-IRCA wage gap for unauthorized Mexican immigrants. Put somewhat differently, none of the enforcement measures explains the significant post-IRCA wage penalty for unauthorized Mexican immigrants, contradicting the commonly offered explanation that this wage penalty results from employers passing along the expected costs of fines to their unauthorized employees.

These results give us one other way to test the hypothesis; we can compare the aggregate wage loss by unauthorized immigrants to total fines paid by employers. The most recent estimate places the size of the unauthorized labor force at about eight million (Passel and Cohn 2015). If we assume each unauthorized employee to work an average of thirty-five hours per week and forty-four weeks of the year at the current federal minimum wage of $7.25 per hour, then an 11.5 percent wage penalty implies an aggregate loss of more than $10 billion in wages per year. Compare this with less than $52 million in combined administrative and criminal fines and asset forfeitures in FY 2014 (Bruno 2015; see also Jenks 1997; DOJ 1995). Clearly, the wage savings to employers is orders of magnitude larger than the fines paid. In other words, employers of unauthorized immigrants seem to be profiting handsomely.

DISCUSSION

Analysis of MMP survey data on Mexican male immigrants' wages, combined with administrative data on employer sanctions enforcement, contradicts the broadly held hypothesis that the post-IRCA wage gap between authorized and unauthorized Mexican immigrants is due to employers passing along expected enforcement costs to their unauthorized workers. Although employer sanctions enforcement does have a statistically significant negative relationship with all Mexican immigrant men's wages, the difference in the magnitude of this relationship based on legal status is not statistically significant. In other words, sanctions enforcement seems to drive down all Mexican immigrants' wages, but does not explain why the wages of unauthorized immigrants are lower than that of their authorized counterparts in the post-IRCA period.

One alternative explanation is that changes in the relative supply of authorized and unauthorized Mexican labor may have caused differences in wages. As Elaine Sorensen and Frank Bean note, "the effect of IRCA's legalization programs has been to increase the supply of legal immigrant labor" (1994, 3). Specifically, the share of unauthorized Mexican immigrants dropped from 57 percent immediately before IRCA to 27 percent immediately after as 2.3 million Mexicans legalized (Woodrow and Passel 1990; see also Massey and Bartley 2005). By 2000, the share of unauthorized was about 53 percent, still slightly below the pre-IRCA figure (INS 2003). This relative increase in the supply of authorized Mexican labor would lead us to predict a decrease in the relative returns to legal status as millions of previously unauthorized Mexicans were legalized. However, we ob-

Figure 4. Estimates of Pay Penalty for Unauthorized Immigrants

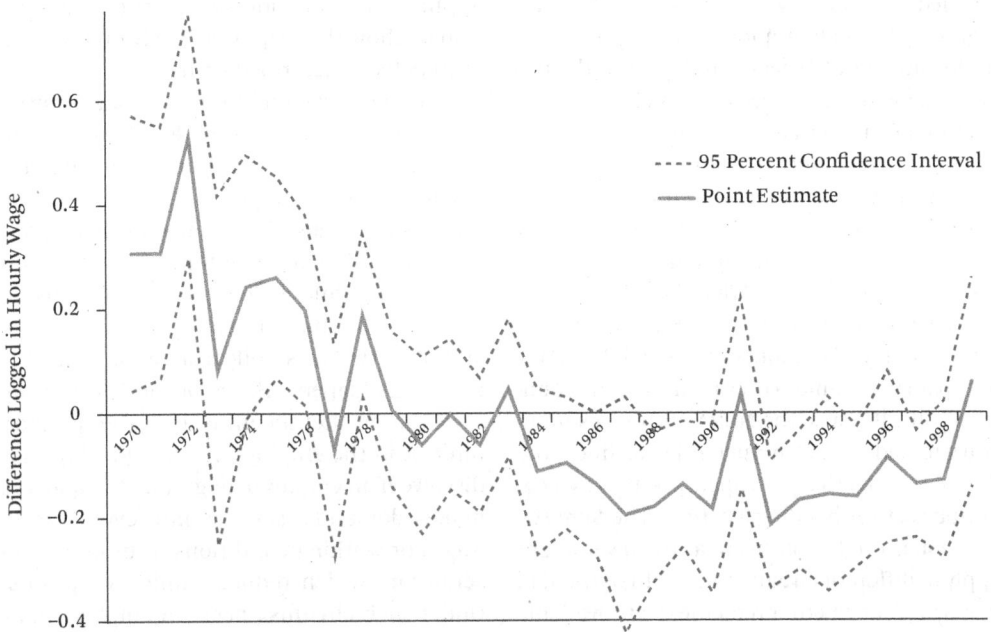

Source: Author's calculations.
Notes: Calculated with year*unauthorized interaction terms net of all factors in model I, table 3 except immigration status.

serve (and are attempting to explain) an increase in wages received by authorized Mexican immigrants relative to compatriots who remained unauthorized. Also, recall that Phillips and Massey (1999) find small and nonsignificant effects of both the local legalization rate and metro-area level unemployment on wages (see appendix). A more recent study finds a negative association between the share of the Mexican immigrant population that was undocumented and all Mexican immigrants' wages (Massey and Gentsch 2014). However, in their study, the share undocumented failed to explain the decline in Mexican immigrants' wages in the decade immediately following the passage of IRCA in 1986. Instead, period dummies representing this decade reflect significant wage losses that are not explained by any variable in the model (Massey and Gentsch 2014, table 2 and figure II). The particular timing at which the wage penalty for unauthorized Mexican immigrant workers arose cannot be explained by changes in the relative labor supply or share of the Mexican immigrant population that was undocumented.

Given that neither human capital factors nor sanctions enforcement nor local labor market conditions explain the difference in wages by legal status, we must conclude that some other change that roughly coincided with the Immigration Reform and Control Act of 1986 reduced the wages of unauthorized immigrants relative to their authorized counterparts. Two related developments are worthy of future investigation.

One event that may explain the wage differences took place slightly before the passage of IRCA. Although research has focused on IRCA as the most likely source of significant changes in Mexican immigrants' labor market outcomes, research has not established that the changes coincided exactly with IRCA's passage or implementation. Figure 4 shows year-by-year estimates of the effect on wages of unauthorized status (net of other factors in model I). This analysis suggests that the changes may have begun in 1984 or earlier, but the estimates are not precise enough to identify exactly which year undocumented immigrants began experiencing a wage penalty.

It was in 1984 that the U.S. Supreme Court decided *Sure-Tan v. NLRB* (467 U.S. 883), a case regarding a small employer who reported his undocumented Mexican employees to the INS after losing a union recognition election. The Court reaffirmed that undocumented workers were covered under the National Labor Relations Act (NLRA) and that the employer's letter to the INS was illegal retaliation that effectively fired the workers for their union support. However, the Court also ruled that the workers, who had been taken by the INS to Mexico because of the employer's action, were ineligible for any backpay award unless they reentered the country legally. Because the NLRA authorizes monetary remedies, but no penalties or fines, the employer effectively escaped paying any economic cost for his illegal action. The *Sure-Tan* decision brought confusion as to how it might apply to different circumstances. In particular, it was unclear whether remedies were available under the NLRA to undocumented immigrants who remained in the country and whether *Sure-Tan* also limited remedies available under other labor laws, such as for violations of the Fair Labor Standards Act (Blum 1988). It is possible that, in light of *Sure-Tan*, unauthorized employees were less likely to join unions, but also less likely to demand legally mandated minimum wages or overtime or even to ask for higher wages, for fear that they would be summarily fired or reported to INS and would have no legal recourse.

Second, the enactment of IRCA may have further eroded the ability of undocumented immigrants to assert their workplace rights. IRCA's sanctions provisions created a process in which employers are supposed to request documentation to complete the I-9 form and to use the information they gain to discriminate in hiring against the unauthorized. However, to avoid the appearance of (and potential liability for) using the I-9 process to discriminate against authorized immigrants or U.S. citizens, most employers only request documents to complete the I-9 form after an offer of employment has been made and accepted. Thus, employers typically complete the I-9 form only after they have concluded an applicant is likely to be a productive and profitable employee. At this point, employers have little incentive not to hire unauthorized immigrants, provided the applicant can provide sufficient documentation to allow the employer to rely on the good faith defense described earlier.

In other words, employers have an incentive to accept questionable or even false documents. As Kitty Calavita's interviews suggest, a small minority of employers explicitly told applicants to get false documents (1990). Employers are occasionally directly involved in procuring the fraudulent documents necessary to allow them to hire or continue to employ unauthorized workers while maintaining what Calavita calls "paperwork compliance" (ICE 2008).

However, after the initial hire, the common interest in the employment relationship may dissolve if an employee or group of employees makes demands, such as improvements in wages or working conditions or union representation, which reduce employers' profits. Under such circumstances, an employer may wish to fire employees making such demands, but employees' actions may be protected under the NLRA, Fair Labor Standard Act (FLSA), the Occupational Safety and Health Act (OSHA) or other federal, state, or local labor laws. In some such cases, employers may use information about workers' immigration status to do what the employer in *Sure-Tan* did: make threats or actual reports to the immigration authorities to intimidate or retaliate against unauthorized employees asserting legally protected workplace rights. Such actions may have chilling effects on similarly situated undocumented workers who do not directly experience threats (Gleeson 2010).

Evidence of Threats and Retaliation

A 2005 report by Human Rights Watch offers insight into the environment of implicit and explicit threats experienced by unauthorized workers. One Nebraska Beef worker interviewed explained: "[The top personnel manager] knows who is undocumented and who isn't, and he holds that over us" (Human Rights Watch 2005, 111). Similarly, a poultry plant worker told Human Rights Watch, "They have us under threat all the time. They know most of us are undocumented—probably two-thirds. All they care about is getting bodies into the plant. My supervisor said they say they'll call the INS if we make trouble" (Human Rights Watch 2005, 111).

When unauthorized workers make demands for improvements in wages or working conditions, union representation or compliance with legal labor standards, employers may threaten to report workers to the Immigration authorities. Kate Bronfenbrenner studied employer threats using a random sample of union organizing campaigns at firms with fifty employees of more during the two-year period from 1998 to 1999 (2000). Although the report focuses on threats to move production abroad, it finds that employers threatened to report workers to the INS in 7 percent of all campaigns and in 52 percent of campaigns where the union's lead organizer reported that the bargaining unit included undocumented workers. So, not only were such threats common in campaigns involving undocumented workers, they were about 8.5 times more likely in these campaigns than in those that organizers did not report included undocumented workers.[17]

For example, in a Teamster/UFW campaign to organize apple packers employed by Stemilt in Washington state, the employer required workers to attend anti-union presentations (captive audience meetings). Separate meetings were held for Latino workers, at which the company's consultant told Latino workers "there hasn't been a union here yet, and the INS hasn't done any raids. But with a union, the INS is going to be around" (NNIRR 1998; Human Rights Watch 2000). Employers make similar threats with regard to other efforts to improve wages and working conditions. For example, after workers at a New York delivery company filed claims for unpaid wages and overtime, five workers were fired and the employer required the remaining employees to submit proof of immigration status and threatened to report undocumented workers to the INS (NILC 2001).

Although it is perhaps not surprising that employers frequently make intimidating threats to immigrant workers attempting to assert their workplace rights, the frequency with which employers are able to make good on threats to have workers detained and removed from the country is surprising. As one particularly frank onion grower confidently told the *Chicago Tribune*, "If a bad one slipped in, we'd just call the INS to take them away" (Thompson 1998). Certainly employers can call in their tips or leads to the immigration authorities, but doing so does not guarantee any enforcement action. Employers reporting their own workers are by no means the sole source of leads for worksite immigration enforcement. Some calls come from members of the public who are genuinely concerned about illegal immigration and have no ulterior motive. Others come from parties with an ax to grind, either with the employer, who may be subject to fines, or with one or more unauthorized employee who may be arrested and removed from the country. Aside from employer retaliation, examples include divorcing spouses, business competitors, feuding neighbors, and disgruntled former employees (on the long history of tips to immigration authorities based on spite or personal conflicts, see Clark 1931, 324; Van Vleck 1932, 124). The INS received tens of thousands more leads each year than it had the resources to investigate (DOJ 1996, 1995). Yet employers seem to have been particularly successful in getting their complaints about their own employees acted upon. In fact, in 2000 then INS Associate Commissioner Robert Bach told the *New York Times* that undocumented immigrants are at little risk of workplace raids, "unless the employer turns a worker in, and employers usually do that only to break a union or prevent a strike or that kind of stuff" (Uchitelle 2000, A1).

A study by law professor Michael Wishnie

---

17. Threats were made in 7 percent of cases overall, but in just over 6 percent not reported to involve undocumented workers. This figure is derived from calculating conditional probabilities of threat given the lead organizer's report of whether the unit included undocumented workers. The result relies on the Bronfenbrenner's report that 2 percent of campaigns were reported to involve undocumented workers. The probability of threat and undocumented is (0.02 x 0.52) = 0.0104. Because the reported overall probability of threat is 0.07, the probability of threat and not undocumented is 0.07 − 0.0104 = 0.0596. Because the not undocumented cases account for 98 percent of the total, the probability of threat given not undocumented is 0.0596÷0.98 = 0.0608.

provides empirical evidence that such calls to INS frequently resulted in arrests and deportations (2004).[18] He requested records relating to labor standards complaints and union organizing campaigns for each of the 184 businesses raided by INS in the New York City area during a thirty-month period between 1997 and 1999. He found that 55 percent of raided businesses were subject to at least one other labor proceeding or investigation at the time. Wishnie argues that these raids are "likely prompted by a labor dispute"—that is, are retaliatory.

Even absent widespread threats, we might hypothesize that after the implementation of IRCA's sanctions provisions, once unauthorized immigrants had secured a job, they were less likely than legal immigrants to respond to poor wages by looking for a new job (which would require going through the I-9 process and potentially exposing them as lacking valid documents). After IRCA, perhaps unauthorized immigrants have been willing to stick with their current employer despite low pay, and similarly situated legal immigrants might seek a new employer willing to pay more for the experience and skills they had built up on the job. These labor market frictions could give employers what economists would call monopsony power over unauthorized employees.[19]

The statistical analysis presented earlier does not provide any way to directly test the relationship between employers' implicit or explicit threats of immigration raids and the post-IRCA differential in pay between unauthorized male Mexican immigrant workers and their legal counterparts. Nor does it provide a way to adjudicate between such threats and monopsony power due to a reduced willingness to change jobs. However, the analysis does show that this pay penalty for unauthorized immigrants is not due to employers simply passing along the expected costs of employer sanctions fines. Given the evidence that employers often meet demands for improvements in wages and working conditions or other legally protected workplace rights with threats of immigration raids, further research into the relationship of such threats and raids to the post-IRCA pay penalty for unauthorized workers is warranted. Whatever the cause may be, the lower pay received by unauthorized workers in the post-IRCA period amounts to billions of dollars in annual savings to the firms that employ unauthorized immigrants. The low wages accepted by unauthorized immigrants in the post-IRCA period strongly suggest that IRCA's employer sanctions provisions have failed to create disincentives to the hiring and employment of unauthorized immigrants.

APPENDIX: ALTERNATIVE MODEL SPECIFICATIONS

Table A1 shows models I and II from table 3, as well as these same models with the addition of fixed effects for state and each of fifteen categories of industry and occupations. These models (Ia and IIa) also have standard errors corrected for clustering on year. This table is included in the appendix for two reasons. The first is to show that the post-IRCA wage gap does not result from some change in the geographic or industry-occupation distribution that coincides with the timing of IRCA. The second is to examine the effect of including fixed effects for industry-occupation and state on the coefficient of the expected fines measure or measures. The models with fixed effects and standard errors adjusted for clustering on years should address the deflation of standard

---

18. Technically, few apprehended unauthorized immigrants go through formal deportation or removal proceedings. Most waive their right to such a proceeding in return for a speedy repatriation to their country of origin.

19. I hesitate to hypothesize that a set of employers unwilling to hire unauthorized immigrants created a restricted labor market for them which gave employers monopsony power. Even if this was the case immediately following the passage of IRCA, when employers might have expected significant enforcement, the reality is that strong employer demand for undocumented immigrant workers was the key factor that attracted millions of Mexican immigrants to cross the border to the United States without valid documents throughout the 1990s (Lowell, Pederzini, and Passel 2008). It seems unlikely that limited employment opportunities reduced wages in the same period that huge expansions of employment opportunities drew millions to work in the United States.

errors due to clustering of expected fine measures on industry-occupation, state, and year. However, the fixed effects also capture both time-constant effects of employer sanctions enforcement and other fixed characteristics of each industry-occupation category and state. Including the fixed effects (and adjusting standard errors for clustering of observations by year) does decrease the magnitude of the expected fine measure calculated using all (knowing and paperwork) fines and renders it statistically insignificant. However, this is one instance in which the choice of expected fines measures does lead to different conclusions. Model IIb shows that an expected fines measure calculated only on knowing hire fines remains statistically significant with state and industry-occupation fixed effects.

Table A2 reports results from models that use such a knowing hire only expected fine measure which are otherwise the same as those reported in table 3. This table shows that the paper's primary conclusions are not dependent on the choice of expected fines measures. The coefficients for the (knowing) expected fine measure in models IIc-IVc are larger than in models II-IV, largely because the expected fine measure here, calculated using only knowing fines, is generally smaller than that in table 3. Unlike the expected fines measure in table 3, the knowing fines measure main effect remains significant in model IIIc. Neither the measures used in table 3 nor those in table A2 suggest a statistically significant differential relationship between either expected fine measure and unauthorized status; nor does any evidence indicate that either measure explains the post-IRCA wage penalty for unauthorized Mexican immigrant men.

Table A3 addresses the role of local labor market conditions, specifically, the unemployment rate and the legalization rate. As noted earlier, Phillips and Massey (1999) find that neither of these factors was statistically significant. Given this, effort spent updating these series seems unlikely to yield much payoff. To complicate matters somewhat, MSAYEAR, the MMP file containing data on these variables through 1995, is currently available with only geographic codes for Metropolitan Statistical Areas from older versions of the MMP. The currently available MMP uses Census Bureau codes for MSAs. The MMP staff is in the process of updating this file.

In the meantime, I have made a match of MSAs to the older MMP geographic codes, which, though imperfect, is hopefully sufficient to briefly revisit the effects of local labor market on Mexican immigrants' wages. Some cases from areas with small populations of Mexican immigrants were not matched, but the majority of immigrants are included.

All three models in table A3 are limited to cases for which both unemployment rates and legalization rates are available in the MSAYEAR file, thus they span the years from 1970 to 1995.

Column I shows results similar to table 3, model II, but limited to this smaller sample of 1969 cases. Column II includes the unemployment rate and the legalization rate, which is basically the number of Mexicans granted permanent legal status (green cards) from INS data divided by the size of the Mexican foreign-born population within the MSA (for more detail, see Phillips and Massey 1999). Here, however, unlike Phillips and Massey's results, some statistically significant relationship between legalization rate and wages is indicated. However, including these variables does not significantly decrease the magnitude of the post-IRCA legal status wage gap. Along these same lines, column III includes interactions with legalization rate and unauthorized status and unemployment rate and unauthorized status. These interactions terms are small, positive, and statistically insignificant, which suggests that these factors do not differentially affect unauthorized Mexican immigrants and therefore do not explain the differences in wages. Based on the data available, there is no basis for revising Phillips and Massey's 1999 conclusion that the post-IRCA wage gap cannot be attributed to local unemployment or legalization rates.

Table A1. Regressions of Logged Hourly Wages with and Without Fixed Effects for State and Industry/Occupation Categories

Variable	Model I	Model Ia	Model II	Model IIa	Model IIb
Age	0.010	0.009	0.010	0.009	0.010
	(0.006)	(0.005)	(0.006)	(0.005)	(0.005)
Age squared	−0.0002**	−0.0002**	−0.0002**	−0.0002**	−0.0002**
	(0.0001)	(0.0001)	(0.0001)	(0.0001)	(0.0001)
U.S. experience	0.001*	0.001	0.001	0.001	0.001
	(0.000)	(0.000)	(0.000)	(0.000)	(0.000)
U.S. duration	0.002***	0.002***	0.002***	0.002***	0.002***
	(0.000)	(0.000)	(0.000)	(0.000)	(0.000)
Number of U.S. trips	0.002	0.005	0.004	0.006*	0.006*
	(0.003)	(0.003)	(0.003)	(0.003)	(0.003)
Education (reference = none)					
One to three years	0.065	0.072	0.072	0.076	0.080
	(0.057)	(0.061)	(0.056)	(0.059)	(0.059)
Four to five years	0.094	0.104	0.101	0.108	0.106
	(0.066)	(0.058)	(0.066)	(0.058)	(0.059)
Six to eleven years	0.094	0.092	0.096	0.094	0.094
	(0.056)	(0.052)	(0.057)	(0.052)	(0.052)
Twelve or more years	0.204**	0.191**	0.206**	0.195**	0.196**
	(0.064)	(0.063)	(0.064)	(0.062)	(0.062)
English (reference = none)					
Understands some	0.093**	0.075**	0.088**	0.074**	0.076**
	(0.032)	(0.023)	(0.032)	(0.023)	(0.023)
Speaks some	0.148***	0.140**	0.146***	0.142**	0.140**
	(0.039)	(0.046)	(0.039)	(0.045)	(0.044)
Speaks well	0.252***	0.225**	0.242***	0.223**	0.226**
	(0.063)	(0.076)	(0.063)	(0.076)	(0.076)
Immigration status (reference = authorized post-IRCA)					
Authorized pre-IRCA	0.152	0.126	0.106	0.097	0.097
	(0.104)	(0.113)	(0.106)	(0.123)	(0.118)
Guestworker	−0.460	−0.488	−0.463	−0.489	−0.495
	(0.345)	(0.253)	(0.345)	(0.252)	(0.252)
Unauthorized					
Pre-IRCA	0.023	−0.021	−0.022	−0.049	−0.048
	(0.064)	(0.080)	(0.067)	(0.091)	(0.084)
Post-IRCA	−0.122**	−0.139***	−0.132**	−0.146***	−0.139***
	(0.042)	(0.030)	(0.042)	(0.032)	(0.031)
Grandfathered	−0.058	−0.076	−0.073	−0.085	−0.081
	(0.060)	(0.083)	(0.062)	(0.087)	(0.085)
Time trend	−0.003	−0.008	−0.005	−0.009	−0.009
	(0.004)	(0.005)	(0.004)	(0.005)	(0.005)
Expected fine (all)			−5.139***	−2.925	
			(1.544)	(1.664)	
Expected fine (knowing only)					−21.018***
					(4.066)
Constant	1.236***	2.023***	1.290***	2.039***	2.036***
	(0.138)	(0.300)	(0.139)	(0.302)	(0.300)
State fixed effects	No	Yes	No	Yes	Yes
Industry fixed effects	No	Yes	No	Yes	Yes
N	3,249	3,249	3,249	3,249	3,249
R^2	0.1914	0.2430	0.1964	0.2444	0.2499

Source: Author's calculations.
Note: Robust standard errors corrected for clustering on year in parentheses.
*$p < .05$; **$p < .01$; ***$p < .001$

Table A2. Regressions of Logged Hourly Wages with Expected Fines Measures Based on Knowing Hire Fines Only

Variable	Model IIc	Model IIIc	Model IVc
Age	0.010	0.010	0.010
	(0.006)	(0.006)	(0.006)
Age squared	−0.0002**	−0.0002**	−0.0002**
	(0.0001)	(0.0001)	(0.0001)
U.S. experience	0.001	0.001	0.001
	(0.000)	(0.000)	(0.000)
U.S. duration	0.002***	0.002***	0.002***
	(0.000)	(0.000)	(0.000)
Number of U.S. trips	0.003	0.003	0.004
	(0.004)	(0.003)	(0.004)
Education (reference = none)			
One to three years	0.074	0.073	0.076
	(0.056)	(0.056)	(0.056)
Four to five years	0.096	0.097	0.100
	(0.066)	(0.066)	(0.066)
Six to eleven years	0.094	0.093	0.097
	(0.056)	(0.057)	(0.056)
Twelve-plus years	0.204**	0.203**	0.205**
	(0.064)	(0.064)	(0.064)
English (reference = none)			
Understands some	0.091**	0.091**	0.090**
	(0.031)	(0.031)	(0.031)
Speaks some	0.145***	0.146***	0.146***
	(0.039)	(0.039)	(0.039)
Speaks well	0.247***	0.248***	0.244***
	(0.063)	(0.063)	(0.063)
Immigration status (reference = authorized post-IRCA)			
Authorized pre-IRCA	0.123	0.125	0.112
	(0.104)	(0.104)	(0.104)
Guestworker	−0.460	−0.459	−0.464
	(0.344)	(0.344)	(0.342)
Unauthorized			
Pre-IRCA	−0.003	−0.002	−0.014
	(0.064)	(0.064)	(0.065)
Post-IRCA	−0.122**	−0.117**	−0.123**
	(0.041)	(0.042)	(0.041)
Grandfathered	−0.065	−0.062	−0.070
	(0.060)	(0.060)	(0.061)
Enforcement measures			
Knowing fines	−25.48***	−21.67***	−24.87***
	(4.774)	(5.913)	(4.795)
Knowing fines*unauthorized		−9.214	
		(9.328)	
Probability of audit			−22.80
			(13.149)
Time trend	−0.004	−0.004	−0.004
	(0.004)	(0.004)	(0.004)
Constant	1.261***	1.262***	1.261***
	(0.137)	(0.137)	(0.137)
N	3,249	3,249	3,249
R^2	0.2023	0.2027	0.2036

Source: Author's calculations.
Note: Robust standard errors corrected for clustering on year in parentheses.
*$p < .05$; **$p < .01$; ***$p < .001$

Table A3. Regressions of Logged Hourly Wages with Local Labor Market Variables

Variable	Model I	Model II	Model III
Age	0.017*	0.016*	0.016*
	(0.008)	(0.008)	(0.008)
Age squared	−0.0003**	−0.0003**	−0.0003**
	(0.0001)	(0.0001)	(0.0001)
U.S. experience	0.001	0.000	0.000
	(0.000)	(0.000)	(0.000)
U.S. duration	0.002***	0.002***	0.002***
	(0.000)	(0.000)	(0.000)
Number of U.S. trips	0.009*	0.009*	0.009*
	(0.004)	(0.004)	(0.004)
Education (reference = none)			
One to three years	0.162**	0.162**	0.162**
	(0.062)	(0.062)	(0.062)
Four to five years	0.201*	0.206*	0.212**
	(0.080)	(0.080)	(0.081)
Six to eleven years	0.198**	0.202**	0.201**
	(0.065)	(0.064)	(0.065)
Twelve-plus years	0.277***	0.276***	0.278***
	(0.075)	(0.074)	(0.074)
English (reference = none)			
Understands some	0.068	0.064	0.063
	(0.035)	(0.035)	(0.035)
Speaks some	0.163**	0.151**	0.147**
	(0.051)	(0.050)	(0.050)
Speaks well	0.202*	0.192*	0.185*
	(0.087)	(0.087)	(0.087)
Immigration status (reference = authorized post-IRCA)			
Authorized pre-IRCA	−0.051	−0.068	−0.081
	(0.125)	(0.129)	(0.131)
Guestworker	−0.174	−0.169	−0.168
	(0.160)	(0.159)	(0.159)
Unauthorized			
Pre-IRCA	−0.106	−0.131	−0.186
	(0.080)	(0.088)	(0.140)
Post-IRCA	−0.180**	−0.171**	−0.231*
	(0.055)	(0.055)	(0.112)
Grandfathered	−0.027	−0.027	−0.084
	(0.084)	(0.085)	(0.132)
Expected fine	−4.475*	−5.084*	−5.255**
	(1.956)	(1.981)	(1.984)
Unemployment rate		−0.009	−0.012
		(0.007)	(0.013)
Unemployment*unauthorized			0.004
			(0.016)
Legalization rate		−0.003*	−0.007*
		(0.001)	(0.003)
Legalization rate*unauthorized			0.006
			(0.003)
Time trend	−0.017**	−0.017**	−0.018**
	(0.005)	(0.006)	(0.006)
Constant	1.261***	1.363***	1.423***
	(0.179)	(0.177)	(0.202)
N	1,979	1,979	1,979
R^2	0.2235	0.2279	0.2301

Source: Author's calculations.
Note: Robust standard errors in parentheses.
*$p < .05$; **$p < .01$; ***$p < .001$

REFERENCES

Allison, Paul D. 1995. "The Impact of Random Predictors on Comparisons of Coefficients Between Models: Comment on Clogg, Petkova, and Haritou." *American Journal of Sociology* 100(5): 1294–305.

Bach, Robert L. 1978. "Mexican Immigration and the American State." *International Migration Review* 12(4): 536–58.

Bach, Robert L., and Howard Brill. 1991. *Impact of IRCA on the U.S. Labor Market and Economy: Final Report to the U.S. Department of Labor*. Binghamton: State University of New York.

Bailey, Thomas. 1985. "The Influence of Legal Status on the Labor Market Impact of Immigration." *International Migration Review* 19(2): 220–38.

Bansak, Cynthia. 2005. "The Differential Wage Impact of the Immigration Reform and Control Act on Latino Ethnic Subgroups." *Social Science Quarterly* 86(5): 1279–98.

Bansak, Cynthia, and Steven Raphael. 2001. "Immigration Reform and the Earnings of Latino Workers: Do Employer Sanctions Cause Discrimination." *Industrial & Labor Relations Review* 54(2): 275–95.

Blum, Richard E. 1988. "Labor Standards Enforcement and the Realities of Labor Migration: Protecting Undocumented Workers After *Sure-Tan*, the IRCA, and *Patel*." *New York University Law Review* 63(6): 1342–75.

Borjas, George J. 1990. *Friends or Strangers: The Impact of Immigrants on the U.S. Economy*. New York: Basic Books.

Bronfenbrenner, Kate. 2000. "Uneasy Terrain: The Impact of Capital Mobility on Workers, Wages, and Union Organizing." Washington: U.S. Trade Deficit Review Commission. Accessed March 1, 2017. http://purl.access.gpo.gov/GPO/LPS30669.

Brownell, Peter B. 2005. "The Declining Enforcement of Employer Sanctions." *Migration Information Source*. September 1. Accessed March 1, 2017. http://www.migrationpolicy.org/article/declining-enforcement-employer-sanctions/.

Bruno, Andorra. 2015. "Immigration-Related Worksite Enforcement: Performance Measures." CRS Report No. R40002. Washington: Congressional Research Service. Accessed August 15, 2016. https://www.fas.org/sgp/crs/homesec/R40002.pdf.

Calavita, Kitty. 1990. "Employer Sanctions Violations—toward a Dialectical Model of White-Collar Crime." *Law & Society Review* 24(4): 1041–69.

Castells, Manuel. 1975. "Immigrant Workers and Class Struggles in Advanced Capitalism—Western European Experience." *Politics & Society* 5(1): 33–66.

Chiswick, Barry R. 1978. "Immigrants and Immigration Policy." In *Contemporary Economic Problems, 1978*, edited by William Fellner. Washington, D.C.: American Enterprise Institute.

———. 1984. "Illegal Aliens in the United States Labor Market: Analysis of Occupational Attainment and Earnings." In "Irregular Migration: An International Perspective." Special issue, *International Migration Review* 18(3): 714–32.

———. 1988. *Illegal Aliens: Their Employment and Employers*. Kalamazoo, Mich.: W. E. Upjohn Institute for Employment Research.

Clark, Jane Perry. 1931. *Deportation of Aliens from the United States to Europe*. New York: Columbia University Press.

Clogg, Clifford C., Eva Petkova, and Adamantios Haritou. 1995. "Statistical Methods for Comparing Regression Coefficients Between Models." *American Journal of Sociology* 100(5): 1261–93.

Cobb-Clark, Deborah A., Clinton R. Shiells, and B. Lindsay Lowell. 1995. "Immigration Reform: The Effects of Employer Sanctions and Legalization on Wages." *Journal of Labor Economics* 13(3): 472–98.

Cornelius, Wayne A. 1978. *Mexican Migration to the United States: Causes, Consequences and U.S. Responses*. Cambridge, Mass.: Massachusetts Institute of Technology.

———. 1989. "The U.S. Demand for Mexican Labor." In *Mexican Migration to the United States: Origins, Consequences, and Policy Options*. San Diego: Center for U.S.-Mexican Studies, University of California.

Crane, Keith, Beth J. Asch, Joanna Heilbrunn, and D. C. Cullinane. 1990. *The Effect of Employer Sanctions on the Flow of Undocumented Immigrants to the United States*. Santa Monica, Calif.: RAND Corporation.

Davila, Alberto, and Jose A. Pagan. 1997. "The Effect of Selective INS Monitoring Strategies on the Industrial Employment Choice and Earnings of Recent Immigrants." *Economic Inquiry* 35(1): 138–50.

Donato, Katharine M., and Douglas S. Massey. 1993.

"Effect of the Immigration Reform and Control Act on the Wages of Mexican Migrants." *Social Science Quarterly* 74(3): 523–41.

Fix, Michael. 1991. *The Paper Curtain: Employer Sanctions' Implementation, Impact, and Reform*. JRI-10. Santa Monica, Calif.: RAND Corporation.

Fix, Michael, and Paul T. Hill. 1990. *Enforcing Employer Sanctions: Challenges and Strategies*. JRI-04. Santa Monica, Calif.: RAND Corporation.

Fry, Richard, B. Lindsay Lowell, and Elhum Haghighat. 1995. "The Impact of Employer Sanctions on Metropolitan Wage Rates." *Industrial Relations* 34(3): 464–84.

Gleeson, Shannon. 2010. "Labor Rights for All? The Role of Undocumented Immigrant Status for Worker Claims-Making." *Law & Social Inquiry* 35(3): 561–602.

Heckman, James. 1976. "The Common Structure of Statistical Models of Truncation, Sample Selection and Limited Dependent Variables and a Simple Estimator for Such Models." *Annals of Economic and Social Measurement* 5(4): 475–92.

———. 1979. "Sample Selection Bias as a Specification Error." *Econometrica* 47(1): 153–61.

Heer, David M. 1990. *Undocumented Mexicans in the United States*. Cambridge: Cambridge University Press.

Heer, David M., and Dee Falasco. 1984. "Determinants of Earnings Among Three Groups of Mexican-Americans: Undocumented Immigrants, Legal Immigrants and the Native Born." Paper presented at the Annual Meeting of the Population Association of America, Minneapolis, Minn. (May 3–5).

Higham, John. 1955. *Strangers in the Land; Patterns of American Nativism, 1860–1925*. New Brunswick, N.J: Rutgers University Press.

Human Rights Watch. 2000. *Unfair Advantage: Workers' Freedom of Association in the United States Under International Human Rights Standards*. New York: Human Rights Watch. Accessed December 11, 2015. http://www.hrw.org/reports/pdfs/u/us/uslbr008.pdf.

———. 2005. *Blood, Sweat, and Fear: Workers' Rights in U.S. Meat and Poultry Plants*. New York: Human Rights Watch. Accessed December 11, 2015. http://www.hrw.org/en/reports/2005/01/24/blood-sweat-and-fear.

Ise, Sabrina, and Jeffrey M. Perloff. 1995. "Legal Status and Earnings of Agricultural Workers." *American Journal of Agricultural Economics* 77(2): 375–86.

Jenkins, J. Craig. 1978. "The Demand for Immigrant Workers: Labor Scarcity or Social Control?" *International Migration Review* 12(4): 514–35.

Jenks, Rosemary. 1997. Prepared Statement. *Legislation Concerning Immigrant Issues: Hearing Before the Subcommittee on Immigration and Claims of the Committee on the Judiciary, House of Representatives*. 105th Congress, 1st session. H.R. 231, H.R. 429, H.R. 471, H.R. 1493, May 13, 1997. Washington: Government Printing Office.

Kossoudji, Sherrie A., and Susan I. Ranney. 1986. "Legal Status as Union Membership: Legal and Illegal Wage Rates of Mexican Immigrants." Unpublished paper, Population Studies Center, University of Michigan, Ann Arbor.

Lipset, Seymour Martin, and Reinhard Bendix. 1959. *Social Mobility in Industrial Society*. Berkeley: University of California Press.

Livingston, Gretchen. 2005. "Re-assessing the Relationship Between Migrant Kin Networks and Wages Among Mexican Migrant Men." Paper presented at the Annual Meeting of the Population Association of America, Philadelphia, Pa. (April 30).

Lowell, B. Lindsay, Carla Pederzini, and Jeffrey Passel. 2008. "The Demography of Mexico/US Migration." In *Mexico US Migration Management: A Binational Approach*, edited by Augustín Escobar Latapí and Susan F. Martin. Lanham, Md.: Lexington Books.

Massey, Douglas S. 1987. "Do Undocumented Migrants Earn Lower Wages Than Legal Immigrants? New Evidence from Mexico." *International Migration Review* 21(2): 236–74.

Massey, Douglas S., and Katherine Bartley. 2005. "The Changing Legal Status Distribution of Immigrants: A Caution." *International Migration Review* 39(2): 469–84.

Massey, Douglas S., Jorge Durand, and Nolan J. Malone. 2002. *Beyond Smoke and Mirrors: Mexican Immigration in an Era of Economic Integration*. New York: Russell Sage Foundation.

Massey, Douglas S., and Kristin E. Espinosa. 1997. "What's Driving Mexico-U.S. Migration? A Theoretical, Empirical, and Policy Analysis." *American Journal of Sociology* 102(4): 939–99.

Massey, Douglas S., and Kerstin Gentsch. 2014. "Undocumented Migration to the United States and the Wages of Mexican Immigrants." *International Migration Review* 48(2): 482-99.

Massey, Douglas S., and Emilio Parrado. 1994. "Migradollars—the Remittances and Savings of Mexican Migrants to the USA." *Population Research and Policy Review* 13(1): 3-30.

Massey, Douglas S., and René Zenteno. 2000. "A Validation of the Ethnosurvey: The Case of Mexico-U.S. Migration." *International Migration Review* 34(3): 766-93.

Morales, Rebecca. 1983. "Transitional Labor: Undocumented Workers in the Los Angeles Automobile Industry." *International Migration Review* 17(4): 570-96.

National Immigration Law Center (NILC). 2001. *Ansoumana, et al. v. Gristede's Operating Corp. et al.: Workers Protected from Further Retaliation and Threats of Being Reported to the INS. Immigrants' Rights Update* 15, no. 8 (December 20). Accessed December 11, 2015. http://www.nilc.org/document.html?id=719.

National Labor Relations Board (NLRB). 2001. *Sixty-Fourth Annual Report of the National Labor Relations Board for the Fiscal Year Ended September 30, 1999*. Washington, D.C.: NRLB. Accessed December 11, 2015. https://www.nlrb.gov/sites/default/files/attachments/basic-page/node-1677/nlrb1999.pdf.

National Network for Immigrant and Refugee Rights (NNIRR). 1998. "Portrait of Injustice: The Impact of Immigration Raids on Families, Workers, and Communities." Oakland, Calif.: NNIRR.

Passel, Jeffrey S., and D'Vera Cohn. 2015. "Share of Unauthorized Immigrant Workers in Production, Construction Jobs Falls Since 2007." Washington, D.C.: Pew Research Center. Accessed December 10, 2015. http://www.pewhispanic.org/2015/03/26/share-of-unauthorized-immigrant-workers-in-production-construction-jobs-falls-since-2007/.

Phillips, Julie A., and Douglas S. Massey. 1999. "The New Labor Market: Immigrants and Wages After IRCA." *Demography* 36(2): 233-46.

Portes, Alejandro. 1977. "Labor Functions of Illegal Aliens." *Society* 14(6): 31-37.

———. 1978. "Introduction: Toward a Structural Analysis of Illegal (Undocumented) Immigration." *International Migration Review* 12(4): 469-84.

Pritchard, Justin. 2003. "Despite Wal-Mart Case, Raids for Illegal Workers Are Rare." *Honolulu Advertiser*, December 1. Accessed November 18, 2016. http://the.honoluluadvertiser.com/article/2003/Dec/01/bz/bz03a.html.

Sassen-Koob, Saskia. 1978. "The International Circulation of Resources and Development: The Case of Migrant Labour." *Development and Change* 9(4): 509-45.

Saxton, Alexander. 1971. *The Indispensable Enemy: Labor and the Anti-Chinese Movement in California*. Berkeley: University of California Press.

Siskin, Alison, Andorra Bruno, Blas Nuñez-Neto, Lisa Seghetti, and Ruth Ellen Wasem. 2006. "Immigration Enforcement Within the United States." CRS Report for Congress no. RL33351. Washington, D.C.: Congressional Research Service. Accessed March 23, 2010. http://digitalcommons.ilr.cornell.edu/crs/15.

Sorenson, Elaine, and Frank D. Bean. 1994. "The Immigration Reform and Control Act and the Wages of Mexican Origin Workers: Evidence from Current Population Surveys." *Social Science Quarterly* 75(1): 1-17.

Stolzenberg, Ross M., and Daniel A. Relles. 1997. "Tools for Intuition About Sample Selection Bias and Its Correction." *American Sociological Review* 62(3): 494-507.

Taylor, J. Edward. 1992. "Earnings and Mobility of Legal and Illegal Immigrant Workers in Agriculture." *American Journal of Agricultural Economics* 74(4): 889-96.

Thompson, Ginger. 1998. "Immigration Clash Leaves Vidalia Onion Farmers Bitter." *Chicago Tribune*, May 28, A1. Accessed March 1, 2017. http://articles.chicagotribune.com/1998-05-28/news/9805280124_1_vidalia-onion-g-r-farms-farmers.

Todaro, Michael P., and Lydia Maruszko. 1987. "Illegal Migration and US Immigration Reform: A Conceptual Framework." *Population and Development Review* 13(1): 101-14.

Uchitelle, Louis. 2000. "I.N.S. Is Looking the Other Way as Illegal Immigrants Fill Jobs." *New York Times*, March 9, A1.

U.S. Department of Justice, Office of the Inspector General (DOJ). 1995. "Immigration and Naturalization Service Select Enforcement Activities." Audit Report No. 95-30. Washington: Government Printing Office.

———. 1996. "Immigration and Naturalization Service Efforts to Combat Harboring and Employing Illegal Aliens in Sweatshops." Report No. I-96-08. Washington: Government Printing Office.

U.S. Department of Labor, Occupational Safety and

Health Administration (DOL). 2004. "OSHA Facts." Accessed November 18, 2016. http://web.archive.org/web/20041204084157/http://www.osha.gov/as/opa/oshafacts.html.

U.S. Department of Labor, Wage and Hour Division (DOL). 2002. "2002 Statistics Fact Sheet." Accessed March 30, 2010. http://www.dol.gov/whd/statistics/200212.htm.

U.S. General Accounting Office (GAO). 1990. "Immigration Reform Employer Sanctions and the Question of Discrimination." GAO/GGD-90-62. Washington: Government Printing Office. Accessed November 18, 2016. http://www.gao.gov/assets/150/148824.pdf.

———. 1999. "Illegal Aliens: Significant Obstacles to Reducing Unauthorized Alien Employment Exist." GAO/GGD-99-33. Washington: Government Printing Office. Accessed November 18, 2016. http://www.gao.gov/assets/230/227062.pdf.

U.S. Immigration and Customs Enforcement (ICE). 2008. "Agriprocessors and Management Criminally Indicted." Accessed April 1, 2010. http://www.ice.gov/pi/nr/0811/081121cedarrapids.htm.

U.S. Immigration and Naturalization Service (INS). 1987. *Immigration Officer's Field Manual for Employer Sanctions*. Washington, D.C.: American Immigration Lawyers Association.

———. 1997. *Statistical Yearbook of the Immigration and Naturalization Service*. Washington: Government Printing Office.

———. 2003. "Estimates of the Unauthorized Immigrant Population Residing in the United States: 1990 to 2000." Washington: Office of Policy and Planning, January. Accessed December 11, 2015. http://www.dhs.gov/xlibrary/assets/statistics/publications/Ill_Report_1211.pdf.

U.S. Office of Immigration Statistics (OIS). 2002. *Yearbook of Immigration Statistics*. Washington: Government Printing Office.

———. 2003. *Yearbook of Immigration Statistics*. Washington: Government Printing Office.

———. 2004. *Yearbook of Immigration Statistics*. Washington: Government Printing Office.

U.S. Small Business Administration (Small Business Administration). n.d. "Firm Size Data." Accessed November 18, 2016. http://www.sba.gov/advo/firm-size-data.

Van Vleck, William Cabell. 1932. *The Administrative Control of Aliens: A Study in Administrative Law and Procedure*. New York: Commonwealth Fund.

Warne, Frank Julian. 1916. *The Tide of Immigration*. New York: D. Appleton.

Weesie, Jeroen. 1999. "sg121: Seemingly Unrelated Estimation and the Cluster-Adjusted Sandwich Estimator." *Stata Technical Bulletin* 52 (November): 34–47.

Wilson, Tamar Diana. 1993. "Theoretical Approaches to Mexican Wage Labor Migration." *Latin American Perspectives* 20(3): 98–129.

Wishnie, Michael J. 2004. "The Border Crossed Us: Current Issues in Immigrant Labor." *New York University Review of Law and Social Change* 28: 389–95.

Woodrow, Karen A., and Jeffrey S. Passel. 1990. "Post-IRCA Undocumented Immigration to the United States: An Assessment Based on the June 1988 CPS." In *Undocumented Migration to the United States: IRCA and the Experience of the 1980s*, edited by Frank D. Bean, Barry Edmonston, and Jeffery S. Passel. Santa Monica, Calif.: RAND Corporation.

Revisiting Ethnic Niches: A Comparative Analysis of the Labor Market Experiences of Asian and Latino Undocumented Young Adults

ESTHER YOONA CHO

Drawing on thirty in-depth interviews with Korean- and Mexican-origin undocumented young adults in California, this comparative analysis explores how the intersection of immigration status and ethnoracial background affects social and economic incorporation. Respective locations of principal ethnic niches, and access to these labor market structures, lead to divergent pathways of employment when no legal recourse exists. Despite similar levels of academic achievement, Korean respondents were more likely to enter into a greater diversity of occupations relative to Mexican respondents. However, the experiences of Mexican respondents varied depending on their connection to pan-ethnic Latino nonprofit organizations. Illegality, therefore, is conditioned by opportunity structures that vary strongly by membership in different ethnoracial communities, leading to structured heterogeneity in experiences with undocumented status.

Keywords: undocumented, illegality, ethnic niche, ethnicity, race

Although scholars have explored how undocumented youth and young adults navigate barriers to higher education, their experiences in the labor market are much less understood. Some studies have pointed to the converging employment outcomes of undocumented young adults despite varying levels of education, suggesting that they often have access only to low-wage blue-collar industries of the labor market regardless of their academic and professional qualifications and aspirations (for example, Gonzales 2011; Abrego and Gonzales 2010; Gleeson 2010). However, we still know little about the *processes* by which undocumented young adults gain access to these jobs. More important, because these studies draw solely on data from the Latino population, it has been difficult to know whether all undocumented young adults share these employment experiences, or to what degree there exists variation by ethnoracial background. Given the highly racialized discourse surrounding illegal immigration, as well as the diverse resources available to diverse immigrant communities, one might well expect that undocumented young adults inhabiting diverse ethnoracial categories will experience differentiated employment trajectories.

Therefore, drawing on in-depth interviews of Korean and Mexican 1.5-generation undocumented young adults, I explore how ethnoracially diverse undocumented immigrants navigate transitions into and within the labor market when no legal recourse for barriers to employment is available. Within this group, I focus specifically on highly educated individu-

Esther Yoona Cho is a PhD candidate in the Department of Sociology at the University of California, Berkeley.

© 2017 Russell Sage Foundation. Cho, Esther Yoona. 2017. "Revisiting Ethnic Niches: A Comparative Analysis of the Labor Market Experiences of Asian and Latino Undocumented Young Adults." *RSF: The Russell Sage Foundation Journal of the Social Sciences* 3(4): 97–115. DOI: 10.7758/RSF.2017.3.4.06. Direct correspondence to: Esther Yoona Cho at eyc@berkeley.edu, Department of Sociology at the University of California, Berkeley, 410 Barrows Hall, Berkeley, CA 94720.

als covered by Deferred Action for Childhood Arrivals (DACA)—those who may be considered among the most advantaged within the undocumented population—to demonstrate how even strong advantages along traditional axes of incorporation are significantly constrained by legal status. Then, by highlighting these undocumented individuals who have similar ambitions, skills, and education but who nevertheless differ with respect to their membership in diverse immigrant communities, I seek to isolate the critical role of one's ethnoracial background in mediating access to socioeconomic opportunities. In this undertaking, I take seriously the call for a shift in studying undocumented migrants from a general perspective to examining the nuanced ways in which everyday illegality can be constructed across spaces and contexts (Coutin 2000; De Genova 2002; Ngai 2004; Willen 2007). I add to this growing literature on the everyday lives of undocumented youth by demonstrating the significance of meso-level ethnic structures in determining individual-level access to differentially embedded work opportunities.

In this study, I find that the distinct experiences of Korean and Mexican 1.5-generation undocumented immigrants manifest acutely in the area of work, arguably the most important marker of transition into adulthood and a fundamental aspect of social identity. Ethnoracial background, especially how that background activates different social and structural resources, shapes the range of jobs undocumented young adults to which they have access, and in turn, their material and social well-being. That is, this study shows that the divergent collective human capital of Asian[1] and Latino populations (Nee and Holbrow 2013; Lee and Zhou 2015; Massey and Pren 2012) has a spillover effect on the labor market outcomes of those undocumented in their respective co-ethnoracial communities. Namely, I find that the labor market structures of ethnic niches assume a critical role in the social and economic integration of 1.5-generation Korean and Mexican undocumented young adults. The term *ethnic niche* has historically been used to describe for-profit businesses serving as occupation networks for ethnic communities. However, I expand the scope of this term to encompass opportunity structures, both for-profit organizations and nonprofit organizations, in which the majority of occupants are co-ethnic. Access to ethnic niches, and the location of these structures in the broader occupational hierarchy in particular, have consequential effects on the work experiences of undocumented Korean and Mexican young adults, at times providing opportunities beyond those conventionally associated with undocumented labor. Previous literatures have examined variation across ethnic niches: for example, Cubans in Miami (Portes and Bach 1985), Chinese in New York City (Zhou and Logan 1989), and Koreans in Los Angeles (Light and Bonacich 1991). The consequences of these differences have been understudied, however, especially for ethnically diverse 1.5-generation immigrants. My goal, therefore, is not to interrogate why such differences exist, but *how* these structuring conditions affect the incorporation of the 1.5-generation undocumented young adults of diverse ethnic origin.

My findings show that although all undocumented young adults struggle with barriers to employment because of their legal situation, the everyday experience of illegality is conditioned by opportunity structures that vary strongly by membership in different ethnoracial communities, leading to *structured heterogeneity* in the experience of illegality. The nature of the work they ultimately do find is significantly shaped by the primary location of their respective immigrant networks and, in particular, their access to ethnic niches. Despite comparable levels of educational achievement, Korean respondents were more likely to have access to a broader range of occupations than their Mexican counterparts. Given the extensive web of Korean employers in California (Frauenfelder 2016), jobs in these niches were within

---

1. Employing the vast category of "Asian" elides the internal heterogeneity that exists within this group; Asian Americans exhibit a bimodal pattern on structural indicators such as socioeconomic status and education. However, I deploy the broader racial term "Asian" throughout the paper as a rhetorical strategy to begin interrogating the ways in which race and ethnicity condition experiences with illegality.

relatively easy reach. In contrast, the work experiences of Mexican respondents varied depending on their relationship to the predominantly Latino network of nonprofit organizations supporting undocumented immigrants. Those with connections to these organizations were able to access information about creative ways to work beyond traditional low-wage jobs. That is, labor market outcomes were bifurcated among the Mexican young adult population, either more constrained or less constrained, depending on the primary type of ethnic niche in which they were embedded. All of these individuals felt trapped within immigrant enclave occupations that were categorically incommensurate with their educational background, career aspirations, and desire to be employed lawfully. However, my findings suggest that opportunities to work in a greater diversity of industries within capital-rich ethnic niches could be a path to greater material stability, particularly for those who receive work authorization through DACA or have the chance to regularize their status in the future. By examining the pre-DACA labor market experiences of Korean and Mexican undocumented young adults, therefore, this study highlights the impact of collective ethnic resources as a consequential mechanism of stratification among the lives of diverse undocumented immigrants, complicating and adding to the body of scholarship on the importance of disaggregating the variegated material and symbolic consequences of illegality (see, for example, Patler 2014; Gonzales, Terriquez, and Ruszczyk 2014).

THE CONVERGENCE OF RACE AND ILLEGALITY

Despite a growing presence of undocumented Asian immigrants in the United States (Rosenblum and Ruiz Soto 2015), sociological understandings of the undocumented immigrant experience have largely come from studying Latinos. This focus is not surprising considering that the vast majority of undocumented immigrants are from Mexico and other Latin American countries such as El Salvador, Guatemala, and Honduras. Nevertheless, four of the top ten countries of origin of the undocumented population are in Asia. One in five Korean, one in six Filipino, one in six Chinese, and one in six Vietnamese immigrants are undocumented (Hoefer, Rytina, and Baker 2011). Considering the racialization of illegal immigration in political and public discourse, it is important to examine how the experience of illegality is shaped by ethnoracial background.

Research suggests that the Hispanicization of undocumented immigration coupled with the model minority stereotype may protect Asians from the constant anxiety of being profiled as undocumented (Chan 2010; Dozier 1993). However, because this rhetoric leads to assumptions regarding the legal status of Latinos, undocumented Latinos may "come out" more readily both in personal relationships and public spheres, increasing the likelihood of fostering collective and coalitional relationships. On the other hand, the legal and racial invisibility of Asians may lead to intensified feelings of shame, loneliness, and isolation as they strategically avoid revealing their undocumented status for fear of stigmatization. Unaware of the large presence of other undocumented Asians who share their struggles (Chan 2010), they might think they have more to lose on both personal and institutional levels from divulging their situation. Having a cloak of legal and racial invisibility, therefore, could function as a double-edged sword (Chan 2010). Given these racial dynamics, Asian undocumented youth might have an easier time getting jobs because they are not associated with unauthorized status, but conversely, for the very same reason, they might be more reluctant to seek help in securing employment—a difficult task given their status.

SOCIAL NETWORKS IN TRANSITIONS INTO ILLEGALITY

Ethnoracial background not only is important as symbolic material used in the construction of racialized notions of illegality, but also can have structural implications when considering access to formal and informal resources and networks, and especially, employment opportunities in ethnic niches. Scholars have illustrated the importance of social networks in shaping the experiences of the undocumented population in work, school, and family (Gonzales 2015; Abrego 2006; Abrego and Gonzalez 2010; Gonzalez 2011; Perez and Cortes 2011;

Menjívar and Abrego 2012). For 1.5-generation undocumented youth in particular, research has highlighted the significant effects of social networks on transitions into postsecondary education. As they exit the protection of the K–12 education system, key intermediaries such as supportive school personnel can help "cushion the blow," minimizing structural and psychological barriers to higher education (Gonzalez 2011; Abrego 2006; Abrego and Gonzalez 2010; Enriquez 2011; Gonzales, Suárez-Orozco, Dedios-Sanguineti 2013). However, less well understood is the subsequent stage of transition out of higher education and the structural factors that may mediate their entrance into the labor market within which no legal recourse is available. Undocumented young adults have been shown to dampen their professional aspirations and simply join their first-generation parents in harsh, exploited labor markets (Gleeson and Gonzales 2012). However, these studies do not take into account the significant variation in opportunities available in the broader labor market, and furthermore, how this variation may be associated with the ethnoracial diversity of the undocumented population.

ETHNIC NICHES AND LABOR MARKET OUTCOMES

Beyond social networks, we can consider the structural role of ethnic niches in shaping the material outcomes of undocumented young adults. The work of Alejandro Portes and colleagues suggests that they develop in part from a dearth of employment opportunities for immigrants in the primary labor market due to language barriers, a lack of cultural capital, and workplace discrimination (see, for example, Portes and Bach 1980; Wilson and Portes 1980; Portes and Bach 1985). Drawing from segmented labor market and ethnic solidarity theories (Reich, Gordon, and Edwards 1973; Light 1972), they first proposed an enclave-economy hypothesis that the returns of the enclave labor market are commensurate to the primary labor market for immigrants. Some scholars, however, have found limits to ethnic enclave economies—material benefits outside the niches surpass those within, particularly for the employees of ethnic niches relative to their employers (Borjas 1986, 1990; Bates 1987, 1989; Sanders and Nee 1987). Min Zhou and John Logan also demonstrate that the advantages of working in ethnic businesses are stratified by gender, providing more economic advantages for men than women (1989). On the whole, then, the benefits of ethnic niches appear mixed, but can provide some first-generation immigrants with material and social advantages.

Scholars have also examined how ethnic niches affect the patterns of integration for second-generation immigrants. They find that second-generation youth desire to escape the ethnic economy and that many are successful in doing so (Waldinger 1996; Light and Gold 2000). Philip Kasinitz and his colleagues argue that though ethnic enclaves might have been advantageous for first-generation immigrants, little evidence indicates that they are a significant source of upward mobility for the second generation (2008). Instead, the economic future of children of immigrants is tied more closely to the overall economy than it is to "protective ethnic enclaves," which act more as "safety nets" than "springboards" for this generation.

But what about the 1.5-generation immigrant youth, notably those lacking legal status? Scholars have not sufficiently theorized legal differentiation among the children of immigrants. Second-generation youth in the United States are granted jus soli (birthright) citizenship, expanding their capacity for labor market integration and social mobility. However, the 1.5-generation undocumented population lacks this legal security. If employment in the primary labor market is simply a matter of linguistic and cultural socialization, they, like the second generation, should not benefit from ethnic niches. Like their legal peers, 1.5-generation undocumented immigrants may also desire to evade the ethnic economies. However, given legal barriers into the primary labor market, these niches might serve as protective safety nets.

Furthermore, the potential for jobs in ethnic niches to be an economic springboard for undocumented immigrant young adults may vary. Korean for-profit niches are distributed across a diverse range of professional industries, whereas Mexicans occupy less favorable for-profit niches in a narrower subset of retail and service industries (Waldinger 2001). The principal locations of readily accessible niches in an ethnoracial community could significantly shape the types of positions available, in turn affecting not only one's career trajectory but also one's sense of self-worth and identity. Many studies have suggested that, for individuals belonging to disadvantaged social groups, using homophilous social ties to find employment has at best a negligible, and often negative, effect on their employment outcomes (Battu, Seaman, and Zenou 2011; Elliott 1999). These findings have led sociologists to argue that these individuals have the "wrong networks," preventing them from achieving more desirable employment outcomes, and instead channeling them to low-paying, low-status, and ethnically homogenous jobs (Fernandez and Fernandez-Mateo 2006). However, this perspective unduly focuses only on the micro-level relationship between the individual's network resources and that individual's employment outcomes. Especially for the immigrant case, this perspective fails to take into account that individuals are actors embedded in larger structures and organizations that purposively and nonpurposively affect social capital (Small 2009). Work outcomes are not only contingent on an individual's job search strategies and social ties. They also depend on the structural conditions within which these ties are situated that determine how and whether one can, in fact, activate these ties (Menjívar 2000; Small 2009; Smith 2010). Moreover, niches vary not only by ethnic composition and occupational prestige, but also by entrepreneurial objectives. Research on undocumented youth's civic and political engagement points to the importance of grassroots and nonprofit advocacy organizations in positively shaping the experiences and outcomes of the undocumented community (Nicholls 2013). Given that the vast majority of undocumented immigrant organizations are composed of Mexican-origin individuals, we would expect that involvement in nonprofit niches would not only foster collective empowerment, but also shape tangible individual-level employment outcomes through direct employment as well as information capital.

Considering these complex contextual dynamics, a broader institutional setting must be considered in the conceptualization of ethnic niches. Therefore, I adopt the idea of ethnic niches, which the literature has historically characterized exclusively as for-profit businesses, to encompass both for-profit and nonprofit organizations in which most of its occupants are co-ethnics. Building on the long history of research on ethnic economies, I further suggest that there are two conceptually distinct levels: *ethnic industries* and *ethnic organizations*. Ethnic industries are the types of occupations certain ethnoracial groups are likely to occupy (for example, Mexicans in agriculture or Filipinos in nursing), whereas ethnic organizations are instantiations of these ethnic industries, when the work is owned and operated by co-ethnics (such as a Korean-owned laundromat or an Indian-owned liquor store); ethnic organizations can be for-profit businesses or nonprofit organizations.

Although the wrong networks perspective suggests that ethnic niches are unproductive for the 1.5-generation undocumented immigrant community, we must recognize that, particularly for individuals without work authorization, these structures can facilitate crucial material and social benefits. The prevailing literature finds that the beneficial role of ethnic niches diminishes with each generation. However, although far from an ideal employment situation, being able to mobilize collective ethnic capital and access different types of ethnic industries and organizations in particular may be instrumental for 1.5-generation undocumented young adults who face barriers to the broader labor market.

RESEARCH DESIGN

This article draws on thirty semi-structured in-depth interviews with "DACAmented" Asian and Latino undocumented young adults from the greater San Francisco and Los Angeles areas. California is the most appropriate site for this research as it has the highest share and greatest ethnic diversity of undocumented immigrants and the largest number of DACA-approved youth and young adults (Migration Policy Institute 2014). To be eligible for this study, respondents had to be twenty-one years old or older, be of Korean or Mexican descent, and have DACA. I restricted my sample to

DACA beneficiaries in part for methodological reasons: interviewing individuals who are temporarily protected by this program minimized risk of detrimental legal consequences and thus facilitated data collection. Further, focusing on this subgroup reveals that even strong advantages along traditional lines of incorporation are significantly circumscribed by immigration status.

In an effort to overcome some of the selection bias in chain-referral sampling common in research on vulnerable populations while seeking to maximize the trust and comfort of respondents, I used two strategies to recruit program participants: a convenience sample and a snowball sample. First, I reached out to a broad range of individuals in my personal network and asked them to provide my contact information to anyone they knew who would be eligible for the study. Respondents found in this way contacted me directly to express their interest in participating. Because these respondents were often unable to provide referrals to other undocumented peers due to the latter's desire to remain "in the shadows," I also reached out to a small group of undocumented student activists who were more readily able to provide referrals because of their activist network. However, because I found that their interviews were often qualitatively different from nonactivist respondents, I limited this subsample to nine.[2]

The thirty respondents include sixteen undocumented young adults of South Korean origin, thirteen of Mexican origin, and one of Indian origin (see table 1). Most of the interviews were conducted between the summer of 2013 and spring of 2014; five were conducted in 2016. All of my respondents had received DACA benefits by this time. Interviews lasted one to three hours and included questions about their migration experience, school experiences, work experiences, relationships with family and friends, and how DACA may have affected these spheres. Nineteen of the respondents were female and eleven were male; they ranged between the ages of twenty-one and thirty. I intentionally focused my sample to include young adults over twenty-one in order to understand transitions to adulthood that would not be captured with a younger cohort. Educationally, my respondents were high achievers: the majority had graduated from college (or had some college) and two had received master's degrees.

In this article, I focus primarily on their labor market experiences *before* receiving work authorization through DACA. Limiting my analysis to pre-DACA employment allows for a clearer understanding of how high-achieving undocumented young adults navigate the labor market and mobilize ethnic resources in the midst of their inhibiting legal situations. I highlight the experiences of high-achieving DACAmented individuals because they have been given special attention by local, state, and federal governing bodies and therefore warrant close examination by scholars. A focused examination on this subgroup provides important theoretical insights into the processes by which the absence of legal status shapes the everyday experiences of undocumented immigrants, constraining the lives of even those who would be considered advantaged relative to the broader undocumented community.

FINDINGS: HOW ETHNIC NICHES MATTER

My research suggests that undocumented young adults' work experiences are significantly shaped by the ethnic niches they are able to access and mobilize in light of their constrained conditions. Hence, the interaction of the availability of ethnic niches and demand for ethnic labor leads to different outcomes for my sample. I demonstrate, first, that the transition to and navigation of work has been one of the most significant, formative aspects of respondents' lives as college graduates without legal status. To be excluded from the professions toward which they had invested all their academic efforts is one of the harshest realities they must

---

2. Nine respondents were involved in the undocumented activist movement to varying degrees from occasional volunteer to vocal leader (four Korean and five Mexican). I found it more difficult to garner responses situated in personal, concrete details from my activist interviewees unless specifically probed, because they seemed to be accustomed to sharing their experiences in a more abstract, politicized manner. In my analysis, I was therefore more sensitive to any potential differences between activist and nonactivist responses.

Table 1. Respondent Demographic and Pre-DACA Job Characteristics

Pseudonym	Ethnicity	Gender	Age	Education	Parental Education[b]	Employment	Ethnic Niche
Jayani	Indian	Female	28	Bachelor's	n/a	Korean advertising agency	Ethnic organization (for-profit)
Christine	Korean	Female	22	Bachelor's[a]	Some college	Tutor/Korean media	Ethnic organization (for-profit)
Elaine	Korean	Female	22	Bachelor's	High school	No work	–
Grace	Korean	Female	26	Bachelor's[a]	College	Korean café	Ethnic organization (for-profit)
Helen	Korean	Female	22	Bachelor's[a]	College	Tutor/Korean café	Ethnic organization (for-profit)
Julie	Korean	Female	24	Bachelor's[a]	College	Korean restaurant/café	Ethnic organization (for-profit)
Miyoung	Korean	Female	21	Bachelor's	n/a	n/a	Ethnic organization (for-profit)
Nancy	Korean	Female	27	High school	n/a	Korean fashion merchandising	Ethnic organization (for-profit)
Rachel	Korean	Female	24	Bachelor's	College	No work	–
Sana	Korean	Female	23	Bachelor's	Some college	Korean law firm	Ethnic organization (for-profit)
Edward	Korean	Male	25	Bachelor's	Master's	Korean contracting firm	Ethnic organization (for-profit)
Jeff	Korean	Male	24	Bachelor's	n/a	Korean restaurant	Ethnic organization (for-profit)
Kenny	Korean	Male	26	Bachelor's	College	Korean restaurant	Ethnic organization (for-profit)
Kevin	Korean	Male	26	Bachelor's	College	Software engineering	Entrepreneurship
Paul	Korean	Male	27	Bachelor's	High school	Korean law firm	Ethnic organization (for-profit)
Sun	Korean	Male	23	Master's[a]	Some college	Korean restaurant	Ethnic organization (for-profit)
Young	Korean	Male	25	Master's[a]	College	Korean tennis academy	Ethnic organization (for-profit)
Ana	Mexican	Female	25	Master's	Some college	Fast food chain/franchise	Ethnic industry (for-profit)
Ashley	Mexican	Female	27	Master's	High school	Italian restaurant	Ethnic industry (for-profit)
Gabriela	Mexican	Female	27	Master's[a]	n/a	Community health clinic program	Ethnic organization (nonprofit)
Isabel	Mexican	Female	27	Bachelor's	High school	IT company	–
Lucia	Mexican	Female	26	Bachelor's[a]	n/a	Movie theater, administration	Ethnic industry (for-profit)
Mariana	Mexican	Female	26	Bachelor's[a]	Elementary	Nannying/babysitting	Ethnic industry (for-profit)
Miriam	Mexican	Female	24	Bachelor's[a]	n/a	Cleaning/housekeeping	Ethnic industry (for-profit)
Roslyn	Mexican	Female	30	Bachelor's[a]	Elementary	American restaurant	Ethnic industry (for-profit)
Sara	Mexican	Female	22	High school	n/a	Cleaning/fast food chain	Ethnic industry (for-profit)
Alejandro	Mexican	Male	22	Bachelor's	High school	Immigrant advocacy organization	Ethnic organization (nonprofit)
Felipe	Mexican	Male	26	Bachelor's	High school	Fast food chain	Ethnic industry (for-profit)
James	Mexican	Male	30	Master's	Some college	Afterschool program	Ethnic organization (nonprofit)
Tomas	Mexican	Male	23	Bachelor's	College	Financial services	Entrepreneurship

Source: Author's compilation.

[a]In progress at time of interview.

[b]Parental education is the highest level of education received by one or both parents; n/a indicates that the respondent chose not to answer.

confront. Second, I show that the divergent trajectories of labor market incorporation of Korean- and Mexican-origin respondents differ qualitatively because of the characteristics of their respective ethnic niches. Despite similar academic achievement, professional aspirations, and psychological resilience, Korean respondents were more likely to enter into a greater diversity of occupations than their Mexican counterparts because of their access to a greater variety of for-profit ethnic organizations. Mexican respondents, on the other hand, varied in their employment trajectories depending on their connection to the nonprofit undocumented immigrant advocacy movement. All Mexican respondents felt constrained in low-wage jobs in restrictive ethnic industries, but those who participated in ethnic organizations, namely, nonprofit agencies for undocumented immigrants, discovered alternative pathways to work deemed more fulfilling.

To be clear, the enclave occupations held by all of these high-achieving individuals are incommensurate with their educational attainment, professional aspirations, and desire to be employed lawfully. However, opportunities to work in a wider range of industries due to available ethnic resources could have beneficial long-term implications such as expedited incorporation into the primary labor market, particularly after DACA approval or potential legalization.

Transition into the Labor Market: Confronting Illegality

A recurring theme in interviewee responses was the centrality of work to their social identity regardless of their educational attainment. However, the findings discussed in this section are based primarily on the majority of the sample, who received at least a bachelor's degree. These individuals represent a small segment of the undocumented young adult population: they were not only able to matriculate into a postsecondary institution, but also to overcome the numerous structural barriers that often hindered educational progress. For these individuals, the question "What's next?" was a substantial source of trauma reminiscent of the anxiety and hopelessness that plagued them in their transition out of high school.

Twenty-six-year-old Mexican Felipe, who graduated from a prestigious university with Latin honors, described his concerns as a bomb that could explode at any moment: "It gave me some anxiety. I was like 'what's going to happen after I graduate?' It was like *a ticking time bomb*.... It was a nagging worry that would come up a lot" [emphasis added].

Despite the awareness of their inability to work legally, the sheer hope for a pathway to legalization sustained respondents' motivation to piece together funds to pay for tuition and prepare themselves for life after college. When Kevin, who emigrated from Korea when he was three, entered college, he realized that "the glory days" of high school were "all gone." "There's that trite saying 'College is the best four years of my life, and like high school is terrible.' Mine was the exact opposite," he told me. As a student in a competitive university, the pressure to obtain summer internships to secure a job after graduation had plagued him. He shared his experience of applying to jobs regardless of the legal barriers: "I lied and said I was a U.S. citizen just so I could get interviews. I got interviews from like all the big companies. I graduated cum laude so I had a good GPA and all that stuff ... but *I knew I couldn't do it*" [emphasis added].

Twenty-four-year-old Korean college graduate Rachel said much the same, that her legal situation presented itself as a more salient issue in college. "I think in high school, I didn't really think about it too much. It wasn't really a big part of my life. But in college, I was like, what do I do now after college, you know? I'm here in college, I'm studying and all of that, but then what am I doing this for? I would question that. And I'd be like *how long do I have to live like this*, you know?" [emphasis added]. As Rachel explained, although hurdles continue to persist for undocumented youth pursuing education, confronting the impenetrable door to a professional career is equally daunting, if not more so.

The hopelessness that came with navigating legal status also peaked during college for Paul, who grew up in Koreatown. All he ever wanted was "to work for an American company," but when he realized that he could not obtain any jobs or internships, he "blamed

[his] parents" for his situation. He recounted seriously considering "self-deportation" to Korea, his parents' heritage country, or France, where he was born. He poignantly told me, "After I graduated from college, *I had nowhere to go*" [emphasis added]. Despite his internal turmoil, he did not communicate his frustrations to his parents. No one, not even his parents, could allay his feelings of isolation and helplessness through this transition into the labor market.

My findings illustrate that, for high-achieving individuals, the transition out of college is one of the most traumatic moments at which they must "learn to be illegal" (Gonzales 2011). In addition to this juncture in high school when many undocumented youth discover the magnitude of the consequences of their legal situation (Gonzales 2011), the transition out of higher education into the labor market is a qualitatively distinct season of crisis. Entering the workforce full time is difficult not only because of the lack of preparation for physically demanding, restrictive labor (Gleeson and Gonzales 2012), but also because of the sheer deprivation from their long-held aspirations. Although those who have the combination of academic resilience and financial means to pursue higher education are but a small fraction of the undocumented population, as long as they are somehow able to find the resources, the opportunity to attend school legally exists. Afterward, however, the options are but two: no work or illegal work.

For this reason, a few respondents, when weighing their options after college graduation, decided to continue in higher education to remain "protected" by their status as students. Graduate school was the safest route, a legitimate "excuse not to have a job," as twenty-seven-year-old Mexican Ashley explained:

INTERVIEWER: Were there any points through high school or college when you felt really burnt out?
ASHLEY: Not in high school so much, but in college, especially when I was about to be done with my B.A., because . . . I was thinking like, [my friends] are going to be able to get a job, and I'm not going to be able to get a job . . . It was like "What am I going to do now?" I went to college, but I can't work in something related to what I studied.
INTERVIEWER: So the decision to go to the master's program was . . .
ASHLEY: In part because I knew I couldn't get a job. It was like going to a master's program was like an *excuse for me not to have a job*. Oh okay, I can't get a job because I'm doing my master's [emphasis added].

The trauma of an uncertain future was more salient for Ashley in college than it was in high school. Fear, anxiety, and shame plagued her as she realized the insurmountable barriers to entering occupations related to her undergraduate studies. Meanwhile, her documented friends had opportunities to enter the labor market without these obstacles. Despite the financial burden of educational expenses, for Ashley, continuing to learn and improve her credentials provided a sense of security that would at least temporarily shield her from the stigma of unemployment. Similarly, twenty-three-year-old Korean Sun strategically chose to attend graduate school immediately after college in hopes that a pathway to work and legalization would open up in the near future: "I thought my best bet was just to go to grad school . . . and then maybe afterwards everything would just work out step by step."

Although only a few respondents were able to enter graduate studies, their choice is not surprising. Their desire to stay in school reflects the protected, "legitimate" identity that undocumented college students in California find in AB540, an assembly bill allowing them to pay in-state tuition given they fulfill certain qualifications (Abrego 2008). However, despite the bleakness of their career prospects, the majority still had to find employment regardless of their level of education. As children of immigrant parents who have instilled in them a strong work ethic, and an equally strong belief in the American promise of opportunity (Gleeson and Gonzales 2012), their careers are a defining aspect of their social identities. In the next section, I describe the integral role of ethnic niches in the divergent employment trajectories of the undocumented young adults in my sample. Despite similar levels of aptitude and drive, the nature of employment ultimately achieved varied according to my respondents' access to and activation of their co-ethnic resources.

THE ROLE OF ETHNIC NICHES ON WORK TRAJECTORIES

Diverse Employment Possibilities in Korean Niches

"It was Korean-owned definitely. It was through a connection through my mom, or else it was really hard to find jobs working under the table."

Korean-owned *definitely*. To Sun and the other Korean respondents, the availability of work in co-ethnic organizations was a presumed reality that provided basic material benefits despite their legal status. All of them worked for Korean entrepreneurs leading to a diversity of work experiences for this group: restaurants, law firms, afterschool educational centers, a tennis academy, and a fashion merchandising company. Having a range of for-profit ethnic organizations readily accessible that willingly paid them "under the table" proved to be a significant source of material support for Korean respondents who otherwise would not be able to work at all due to their legal status. Although it was often still difficult to make ends meet, because their income was critical for the financial survival of the family, the Korean interviewees had more opportunities to work that extended beyond occupations conventionally characterized as low-wage, blue-collar labor.

All Korean respondents would search for employment primarily in Korean businesses because they knew that the chance of being hired despite their legal status was higher. "Actually I would look for places that were Korean-owned because those were the ones who pay you cash. Like even if you have your documents, they pay you cash, because they wanna avoid tax and all that stuff," twenty-seven-year-old Nancy explained. The Korean young adults in the sample used a variety of methods to find their jobs, but primarily through their parents or other family members, all of whom worked in Korean businesses. Christine, however, applied formally through a Korean media company. When I asked whether her employers were aware of her status, she explained that, though it was never explicitly discussed, they were sympathetic to her undocumented position: "Well, so the person who worked before me, he was from my high school and he's Korean. He is in the same situation as me, and he was getting paid by cash. And he knew me, and yeah ... I think he told the owner that I am in the same situation, and they were understanding."

Christine continued to explain the generosity of her other employers. As a private tutor for young Korean students, she was paid $20 an hour. She described getting "more money than she deserved" at a Korean restaurant where she had worked temporarily one summer. To Christine, finding jobs easily in Korean niches was possible because of the cultural sentiment of 정 (*jung*), which roughly translates to a deep emotional bond stemming from shared experience and social responsibility. Whether Korean entrepreneurs' motivation to hire undocumented co-ethnics stems from *jung* or from a desire to evade taxes (as Nancy thought), these readily accessible for-profit organizations are sources of material security for my Korean-origin respondents.

Because of their access to jobs in co-ethnic niches, a work authorization card through DACA was therefore described by some respondents as more of a symbol of security and freedom to do things the "right way" than a significant quantitative increase in income. For Paul, more than by any of the other barriers that come with undocumented status, he had felt most deprived by the inability to work in an American company in the formal labor market. After graduating from college, Paul never went without a paid job—in fact, he worked in two law firms—but each time was employed by a Korean enterprise. Although these organizations provided material stability and work in a professional industry, Paul described the employment as tedious and irrelevant to his bachelor's degree in business. Having developed transferable skills at the Korean-operated law firms, he quickly secured a job in a "more Americanized company" once he had received work authorization through DACA.

For Nancy, who mostly worked in the Korean niche of the fashion industry in Los Angeles, "money was never an issue" because she "never had problems looking for work":

I'm looking for a job where I can work legally.... I mean, I'm not going to be making enough money obviously, because I was making a lot more before [DACA]. Obviously I wasn't paying taxes.... I had five to six years of experience in the industry, and they have like a going rate for how experienced you are, so I was making pretty good money. And it was all in cash, so I just put everything in my safe. I get paid, I put it in my safe. I didn't have a bank account, nothing. Money was never an issue for me actually. God—He's always provided. I've never had problems looking for work.

Shortly after obtaining her DACA benefits, Nancy was able to find a steady job at a major American clothing brand and finish her bachelor's. Although she has continued to struggle to make ends meet with both full-time work and full-time school, her years of working in the Korean ethnic economy provided her the means to pursue her career aspirations once a legal avenue opened up.

The experiences of 1.5-generation Korean-origin undocumented respondents demonstrate the variation in occupational location and prestige among undocumented immigrants. Previous studies have suggested that the children of immigrants avoid working in ethnic niches and that such work may even adversely affect their social mobility. However, my findings demonstrate that their undocumented peers, who have also been raised, educated, and culturally conditioned in the United States, may actually benefit from mobilizing these ethnic resources. Access to a diversity of for-profit ethnic organizations, from a law firm to a fashion merchandising company, provided opportunities for Korean respondents to work beyond industries that are often associated with undocumented labor. Contrary to prior arguments affirming the ineffectual role of ethnic niches for 1.5- and second-generation immigrants, my findings show that working in ethnic organizations can indeed serve as an economic and professional springboard for the 1.5 generation who face legal barriers to the formal labor market.

Latino Niches: Limits and Opportunities

Despite comparable educational backgrounds and aspirations for upward mobility, Mexican-origin respondents experienced qualitatively different occupational pathways than their Korean-origin counterparts. Most worked in more physically intensive occupations, such as food service, swap meets, and domestic labor as nannies or cleaners. Years of excelling in their academic careers proved useless in the labor market, severely constraining their professional prospects. Hence, differences in the principal types, levels, and availability of ethnic niches—a diversity of for-profit Korean organizations versus Latino-dominated industries of largely low-wage, blue-collar labor—led to divergent trajectories for these undocumented young adults.

Within this overall pattern, however, some Mexican respondents were able to access an alternative pathway to employment through pan-ethnic Latino organizations in the burgeoning realm of undocumented youth advocacy.[3] Nonprofit organizations, particularly those tailored to support undocumented immigrants, acted not only as direct employers, but also as a springboard for employment through the dissemination of invaluable information. That is, I find bifurcated outcomes among the Mexican undocumented 1.5-generation young adult population: one constrained and one less constrained. The employment decisions and experiences of Mexican respondents varied depending on their re-

---

3. The descriptor *pan-ethnic* more accurately captures the composition of the Latino nonprofit niches in which these respondents were involved. Because of a shared Spanish language heritage, it is easier for pan-ethnic Latino organizations to emerge and be sustained (compared to pan-ethnic Asian niches). Furthermore, I do not mean to suggest that undocumented immigrant organizations are explicitly exclusionary. However, similar to for-profit Korean niches, where owners, managers, and employees are all likely to be Korean (but not necessarily so), in an analogous way, nonprofit Latino niches tend to be predominantly Latino and draw from co-ethnoracial resources and funders. Despite increasing pan-ethnic mobilization among all undocumented communities, in sheer numbers, the vast majority are of Latino origin, and, as a few Asian respondents explained, the isolated nature of niches for undocumented immigrants make them conceptually similar to market-based niches.

lationship to the predominantly Latino niche of undocumented immigrant advocacy.

The experiences of Felipe, who grew up in the suburbs of Los Angeles, highlight the difficulties in navigating barriers to the labor market despite strong individual-level credentials and the significant potential role of ethnic niches in structuring outcomes. Felipe has been working as a cashier at a fast-food restaurant for the past several years even though he graduated with Latin honors from a prestigious university. In fact, he enjoyed the intellectual stimulation of college so much that he stayed an extra semester after completing his requirements. However, as it came time to confront life after college, anxiety loomed over him. Felipe became angry and frustrated over the restricted options for employment as he did not have access to networks that could offer information about working without legal status.

> I was nervous about getting work, like I didn't know where to look for it or who would hire me with my status. I mean, I didn't really have a network, you know what I mean? Since we didn't really tell anyone about it, we didn't have like a network of like 'oh these people would hire.' And I guess a lot of it was unwillingness to try, because I didn't wanna do a lot of the kind of things that were like.... You know? I mean I was like, I friggin graduated college. *I don't want to be like a dishwasher, that kinda thing.* You know what I mean? [emphasis added]

When he described not "really [having] a network," he was not referring to any network, but one that would lead him to a profession that was reputable, remunerative, and relevant to his studies. He was aware that his networks could provide jobs, such as dishwashing, but the dearth of a diversity of ethnic niches that extended beyond blue-collar labor was a structural reality that Felipe could not overcome despite his human capital. In fact, even with work authorization through DACA, Felipe has been struggling for months to secure a job in the primary labor market. He lamented that, even with magna cum laude on his resume, his limited employment experience in food service has hindered him from advancing as a job candidate.

Socialized by the merit-based American education system to work hard and aim high (Gleeson and Gonzales 2012), all the Mexican respondents echoed Felipe's feelings of entitlement to more rewarding careers that reflected their academic achievement and professional potential. Twenty-five-year-old Ana, who came to the United States as a toddler, also had no other choice but to work at restaurant franchises even after graduating from a top state university. It was clear that Ana sensed a stark dissonance between the menial line of labor to which she felt limited and the career trajectories she felt she deserved.

> *I hated it.* I mean, I don't know, you just feel so useless, having a degree from one of the best institutions in the world and working as a waitress, getting yelled at by your customers for doing something, forgetting to bring this, the food taking too long. I hated it. So I always knew I wanted to go back to school. I never saw myself stopping at a bachelor's. Especially being from [my university], where everyone just talks about going to medical school.... All my friends are in medical school right now. I honestly came from the AP world, the science world, where everyone wants to go get an MD.... So I even looked down on master's programs honestly. I had a really big head coming from [my university]. [emphasis added]

Having been surrounded by high-achieving, ambitious peers throughout her schooling, Ana struggled not only with the insurmountable barrier to her professional aspirations but also with the threat that legal status posed on her social identity among her friends. Feelings of inadequacy and failure manifested acutely for educationally successful young adults like Felipe and Ana.

Alejandro had also been an outstanding student throughout his academic career, but when he had to confront a future without job prospects, he described his "dread of failure":

> Well I just felt desperate. Not knowing what I was going to do. And I felt that if I didn't do

anything, I was going to fail my parents and my sister. Like I dreaded going back [home] and saying, "Hey Lucia [my younger sister], after I graduate from college, I can't do anything." I didn't want to go back and tell her, you're going to try really hard to get into college and be a top student so you could get a scholarship, and then go to college. And then after college, you're not going to get anything done because you can't get a job. I just couldn't do that ... and I didn't want to go back and work construction with my dad, because I also felt like that would be a failure.

Despite his impressive academic achievement and assertive, outgoing personality, Alejandro felt that he had no other immediate options beyond working in conventional industries, such as construction. Anxieties surrounding the bleakness of employment opportunities stemmed not only from financial concerns, but also from being unable to pursue a profession he deemed himself worthy for. The inability to obtain a job that reflects academic trajectory is a matter of not only material stability, but also security in social identity, even among close family members.

Hence, desperate for a job other than construction with his father, Alejandro made myriad plans to be an entrepreneur, considering ventures such as opening a cafe, monetizing a blog, and contracting for financial firms. In fact, he had decided to major in economics even though he preferred humanities and social sciences, because he had acquired "insider" knowledge from undocumented student groups that entrepreneurship was a viable route for undocumented immigrants: "Finally I ended up deciding on economics because it was like a skill that I could very easily use to start my own business or to do consulting or any kind of contract, since undocumented individuals could own their own businesses as independent contractors."

Ultimately, however, like most other respondents, Alejandro did not become an independent contractor by starting a business. Instead he was able to secure a job under independent contractor status at a nonprofit undocumented student advocacy group in which he was actively involved. Alejandro therefore benefited from the timely job opening in a nonprofit Latino organization. However, if it were not for these resources garnered from his co-ethnoracial community, his most tangible option would have been working in blue-collar labor like many of his undocumented peers.

Like Alejandro, a few other Mexican respondents were able to avoid low-wage jobs through nonprofit organizations composed primarily of co-racial Latino peers and mentors. Hence, although Korean respondents appeared to be better situated in terms of their access to readily available for-profit ethnic organizations, Mexican respondents often circumvented barriers to legal employment in the formal labor market by undertaking either entrepreneurship or employment with pan-ethnic nonprofits.[4] Like second-generation immigrants who have been found to engage in "expressive entrepreneurship" as a way to avoid conventional low-wage occupations (Fernandez-Kelly and Konczal 2005), Mexican respondents used their knowledge of independent contracting to pursue more meaningful employment. Unlike the documented second generation, this sample of undocumented 1.5-generation Latinos pursued this path out of necessity as well as for personal satisfaction. For undocumented young adults, satisfaction does not come simply from engaging in a different type of work from their first-generation parents who primarily sought self-employment for financial stability, but also from liberation from racialized blue-collar labor.

Twenty-seven-year-old Gabriela was also able to gather information about "creative ways to work and get paid" by participating in an institutionalized network of high-achieving undocumented peers and allies. After a few years of working various jobs, such as a parking attendant, a cashier, and a telemarketer,

---

4. Independent contractors perform work for other individuals or entities, but are not their employees. Because independent contractors are not obligated by immigration law to verify legal status, creating a company or becoming an independent contractor has been a way for undocumented immigrants to work and get around immigration enforcement.

she found full-time work as a program manager at a nonprofit community health clinic serving underprivileged youth. She attributed her ability to find this job that would "give [her] skills that were going to lead to some sort of career path" to her involvement in an undocumented student group.

> I think luckily I had a good network. Like, my friend Miguel who was working at this nonprofit.... I was like whoa, you know? He could do that?... So I think that opened up my mind a little bit more, like to different possibilities. Like, okay, maybe I could try this somewhere else, as long as I can talk to people who are already working there, or who are in the same situation. So it was always about networks, like who do I know who's already doing something.

Gabriela recognized that she would not have been able to gain access to work beyond Latino-dominated service industries had she not been familiar with individuals who had already creatively navigated their legal situation. Some of the Mexican undocumented young adults in my sample, therefore, leveraged their educational background and involvement in nonprofit Latino organizations to strategize innovative ways to work in occupations beyond low-wage industries. These findings are echoed by a *Los Angeles Times* article that illustrated ways young undocumented immigrants found to be employed by becoming "their own bosses" (Carcamo 2013). However, entrepreneurial spirit, academic background, and resiliency are not enough on their own. These individuals were well connected to the undocumented student movement, which provided unique resources specifically targeting the empowerment of this community. Not only did they form new individual and institutional ties through their participation, which would lead to an expansion of viable options for employment, they also found significant relief from other material stressors such as navigating the application for DACA. These organizations, therefore, opened up tangible opportunities for career development, but more important, were critical in instilling new hope for a better future in solidarity with other undocumented young adults.

The vast majority of respondents, therefore, drew on co-ethnoracial resources, but the structural location of these resources was qualitatively distinct. Korean respondents were able to rely on the collective capital of their co-ethnic community and Korean-owned businesses. However, Mexican young adults—though they were able to access paid work in low-wage ethnic industries—did not end up in what they perceived as the "right" jobs. Mexican respondents who found their employment trajectories relatively more personally satisfying did so by virtue of their participation in heavily Latino nonprofit organizations. My data suggest, therefore, that the types of ethnic (and pan-ethnic) networks and niches to which undocumented young adults have access assume a significant role in shaping their employment trajectories.

DISCUSSION AND CONCLUSION

Studies have shown that 1.5-generation undocumented immigrants' labor market opportunities are stratified by legal status (Gleeson and Gonzales 2012). These findings, however, illustrate that the opportunities are also stratified by ethnoracial background by way of the collective capital and resources in an immigrant community. All respondents, both Korean- and Mexican-origin, placed enormous value on their work, seeking a career of integrity and relevance to their academic backgrounds. Work not only was integral to the formation of their social identities, but also fulfilled their pragmatic need to sustain themselves and their families financially. However, their employment trajectories were significantly shaped by the structural conditions of accessible ethnic niches. Korean participants collectively occupied a diversity of occupations beyond those typically associated with undocumented labor, owing to a wide variety of readily available for-profit ethnic organizations. Mexican participants, in otherwise similar situations, generally lacked access to comparable organizations and took on menial low-wage labor instead. However, some Mexican undocumented young adults found employment through involvement in the pan-ethnic organizations of undocumented youth advocacy. Occupational stratification therefore exists within the undocumented Mexican young adult community based on access to different types and levels of ethnic niches. Supportive immigrant networks, then, coupled with access to high-performing ethnic organizations—whether for-profit or nonprofit—significantly affect the material well-being of young job-seekers without documentation. Only by understanding the interaction of personal resilience, close networks, and ethnic niches can we begin to capture the nuanced mechanisms by which undocumented young adults navigate their immigration status.

It may not be surprising that ethnoracial background often shapes connections to ethnic niches. However, I emphasize that the primary mechanism here is not ethnic identity, but instead access to ethnic niches. Jayani, a twenty-eight-year-old Indian college graduate, worked at a Korean advertising agency for nearly five years. Although not Korean herself, she was able to secure a position through a Korean friend who helped her gain "experience in a lot of different areas." Jayani remained at this job until receiving DACA approval, immediately after which she found a legal position with comprehensive benefits and started pursuing a master's degree part time. Even though the Korean ethnic economy was neither situated in her ideal occupational industry nor immediately accessible to her as a non-Korean, the structural conditions of the Korean ethnic economy made it possible for her to cultivate skills that were marketable after obtaining the opportunity to work legally with DACA. Hence, looking solely at an individual's cultural background is not enough: particular opportunity structures that transmit ethnic capital lead to divergent work experiences for Asian and Latino undocumented young adults.

These experiences are likely to have profound long-term implications for undocumented young adults and their families. Previous studies have argued that working in ethnic niches adversely affects the mobility of 1.5- and second-generation immigrant youths (such as Kasinitz et al. 2008). Considering the consequential barrier of legal status reveals a different story. English-language skills and cultural competency allow them to navigate ethnic organizations in strategic, innovative ways distinct from their first-generation parents. Although mainstream economic conditions may be the primary structural factor influencing employment outcomes for documented immigrant youth and young adults, ethnic organizations can play a vital role for their undocumented peers in providing immediate material resources and potentially long-term benefits, pending work authorization.

These findings suggest that the primary source of difference between Asian and Latino undocumented immigrants with respect to material circumstances may lie in the availability of ethnic niches capable of addressing their immediate needs. Scholars have pointed to the institutional mechanisms of legal entry and hyperselectivity of Asian immigrants to understand their higher human capital (Nee and Holbrow 2013; Lee and Zhou 2015), particularly when contrasted with the Latino population at the opposite end of the documentation and class spectrum (Massey 2007; Massey and Pren 2012). This study shows how the collective capital of Asian immigrants, particularly with regard to legal status and economic resources, has consequential spillover effects for their co-ethnoracial undocumented counterparts. The relative impact of documentation on work, therefore, is influenced by the broader proportion of documentation of the co-ethnic community. Among Asians in California, opportunities for employment are likely to be more extensive given a readily accessible network of co-ethnoracial entrepreneurs (Frauenfelder 2016). This study's Korean respondents (and single Indian respondent) benefited from the broader Korean community in which they were embedded, mitigating legal violence, at least in part (Menjívar and Abrego 2012). An understanding that they were undocumented was often tacit between Korean respondents and their employers, but these same individuals generally remained "in the shadows" within their personal networks and even with many of their coworkers because of the intense shame and stigma associated with their residency status. Their ethnoracial identity nevertheless provided a kind of protective cloak that allowed them to accumulate financial resources and achieve a modicum of legitimacy in their jobs, the frustrations of legally barred aspirations notwithstanding.

However, the most salient support for Mexican respondents may not be stable employment opportunities in co-ethnic niches but instead greater access to institutionalized resources outside the traditional sphere of work: a large and vibrant undocumented Latino community. Hence, though they may not enjoy equal access to employment in for-profit ethnic organizations, some have found creative ways to take advantage of institutionalized networks through nonprofit advocacy organizations. This may also be true for Asian and other non-Latino undocumented young adults (particularly with increasing pan-ethnic mobilization), but given the sheer size of the Latino undocumented population, Latinos are the primary recipients of resources for undocumented immigrants. For instance, although Sun was civically and politically engaged in the undocumented student movement, he described experiencing the added disadvantage of being an *Asian* undocumented student. Because many scholarships were "specifically for [those of] Latino or Hispanic descent, and my mom was struggling, my sister was struggling, . . . I just found my own way to hustle," Sun explained. Relative to the undocumented Asian community, nonprofit Latino niches not only provide instrumental support but also offer spaces for greater solidarity and empowerment. That is, both Korean and Mexican undocumented young adults gain resources through their respective ethnic organizations, but the nature and strength of these supports vary. This variation may explain diverging group-level patterns of economic, social, and civic integration, including the likelihood of political mobilization in the undocumented community.

Furthermore, the collective ethnic capital across some Asian groups may be one explanation for the disproportionately low DACA application rates among Asian-origin youth and young adults. Although additional study is necessary, these findings suggest that the capacity to address immediate financial concerns through employment at ethnic niches may delay the exigency of requesting DACA, the primary material benefit of which is work authorization. This, coupled with the persistent stigmatization of undocumented status and relatively sparse institutionalized support systems for Asian American and Pacific Islander (AAPI) undocumented immigrants, may contribute to the fact that more than 85 percent of those eligible have not requested DACA. That is, they may not perceive the benefits as outweighing the costs of coming forward, placing their unprotected undocumented relatives at risk and bringing shame to themselves and their families.

The substantive and theoretical implications of this research point to important, new directions of inquiry. In light of the potential short-term and long-term consequences of participation in diverse ethnic niches, further work should be undertaken to examine these key support structures for undocumented immigrants. Advancing extant scholarship, I suggest that ethnic niches be differentiated into ethnic industries and ethnic organizations for greater theoretical and empirical precision. Particularly because of the evolving character of ethnic niches in contemporary society, further work should examine them in light of this conceptual distinction. Moreover, although not the primary focus of this article, respondents' changes in employment experiences after work authorization through DACA offer strong evidence that working in certain ethnic organizations, though far from ideal professional circumstances, may equip 1.5-generation undocumented young adults with occupational skills that may lead to expedited career advancement if and once they are legalized.

By examining the role of ethnic niches on employment trajectories of Korean and Mexican undocumented 1.5-generation young adults, I have sought to highlight *structured heterogeneity* in the experience of illegality. In this study, I demonstrate how the economic consequences of illegality are conditioned by ethnoracial background via the mediating structures of ethnic niches. Mexican-origin Felipe had graduated from a top university with Latin honors and Korean-origin Paul's academic credentials were not nearly as strong. However, their memberships in different ethnoracial communities led Felipe to stay on as a cashier of a fast-food franchise for several years and to remain trapped in that position even after receiving work authorization through DACA, while Paul managed to work in Korean-operated law firms after college graduation and then, with DACA benefits, quickly transition into a job with benefits in the formal labor market. Future research may usefully interrogate other potential sources of heterogeneity—such as gender, socioeconomic status, educational background, family composition of immigration status, and so on—that may further modify the material and symbolic ramifications of illegality. Especially in light of record high deportation rates and heightened struggles around immigration law and policy, scholars must consider the complexities of the constitutive role of legal status on the livelihoods of immigrants, particularly as those who are differentially stratified in the broader fabric of American society.

REFERENCES

Abrego, Leisy J. 2006. "'I Can't Go to College Because I Don't Have Papers': Incorporation Patterns of Latino Undocumented Youth." *Latino Studies* 4(3): 212–31.

———. 2008. "Legitimacy, Social Identity, and the Mobilization of Law: The Effects of Assembly Bill 540 on Undocumented Students in California." *Law & Social Inquiry* 33(3): 709–34.

Abrego, Leisy J., and Roberto G. Gonzales. 2010. "Blocked Paths, Uncertain Futures: The Postsecondary Education and Labor Market Prospects of Undocumented Latino Youth." *Journal of Education for Students Placed at Risk* 15(1–2): 144–57.

Bates, Timothy. 1987. "Self-Employed Minorities: Traits and Trends." *Social Science Quarterly* 68(3): 539–51.

———. 1989. "The Changing Nature of Minority Business: A Comparative Analysis of Asian, Nonminority, and Black-Owned Business." *Review of Black Political Economy* 18(2): 25–42.

Battu, Harminder, Paul Seaman, and Yves Zenou. 2011. "Job Contact Networks and the Ethnic Minorities." *Labour Economics* 18(1): 48–56. DOI: 10.1016/j.labeco.2010.07.001.

Borjas, George J. 1986. "The Self-Employment Experience of Immigrants." *Journal of Human Resources* 21(4): 485–506.

———. 1990. *Friends or Strangers: The Impact of Immigrants on the U. S. Economy*. New York: Basic Books.

Carcamo, Cindy. 2013. "Immigrants Lacking Papers Work Legally—as Their Own Bosses." *Los Angeles Times*, September 14.

Chan, Beleza. 2010. "Not Just a Latino Issue: Undocumented Students in Higher Education." *Journal of College Admission* 206 (Winter): 29–31.

Coutin, Susan B. 2000. *Legalizing Moves: Salvadoran Immigrants' Struggle for U.S. Residency*. Ann Arbor: University of Michigan Press.

De Genova, Nicholas. 2002. "Migrant 'Illegality' and Deportability in Everyday Life." *Annual Review of Anthropology* 31: 419–47.

Dozier, Sandra Bygrave. 1993. "Emotional Concerns of Undocumented and Out-of-Status Foreign Students." *Community Review* 13(1): 33–38.

Elliott, James R. 1999. "Social Isolation and Labor Market Insulation." *Sociological Quarterly* 40(2): 199–216. DOI:10.1111/j.1533-8525.1999.tb00545.x.

Enriquez, Laura E. 2011. "Because We Feel the Pressure and We Also Feel the Support: Examining the Educational Success of Undocumented Immigrant Latina/o Students." *Harvard Educational Review* 81(3): 476–99.

Fernandez, Roberto M., and Isabel Fernandez-Mateo. 2006. "Networks, Race, and Hiring." *American Sociological Review* 71(1): 42–71.

Fernández-Kelly, Patricia, and Lisa Konczal. 2005. "'Murdering the Alphabet' Identity and Entrepreneurship Among Second-Generation Cubans, West Indians, and Central Americans." *Ethnic and Racial Studies* 28(6): 1153–81.

Frauenfelder, Mary. 2016. "Asian-Owned Businesses Nearing Two Million." *Random Samplings* [blog], July 27, 2016. Accessed August 23, 2016. http://blogs.census.gov/2016/07/27/asian-owned-businesses-nearing-two-million/.

Gleeson, Shannon. 2010. "Labor Rights for All? The Role of Undocumented Immigrant Status for Worker Claims Making." *Law & Social Inquiry* 35(3): 561–602.

Gleeson, Shannon, and Roberto G. Gonzales. 2012. "When Do Papers Matter? An Institutional Analysis of Undocumented Life in the United States." *International Migration* 50(4): 1–19.

Gonzales, Roberto G. 2011. "Learning to Be Illegal: Undocumented Youth and Shifting Legal Contexts in the Transition to Adulthood." *American Sociological Review* 76(4): 602–19.

———. 2015. *Lives in Limbo: Undocumented and Coming of Age in America*. Berkeley: University of California Press.

Gonzales, Roberto G., Carola Suárez-Orozco, and Maria Cecilia Dedios-Sanguineti. 2013. "No Place to Belong: Contextualizing Concepts of Mental Health Among Undocumented Immigrant Youth in the United States." *American Behavioral Scientist* 57(8): 1173–98. DOI: 0002764213487349.

Gonzales, Roberto G., Veronica Terriquez, and Stephen P. Ruszczyk. 2014. "Becoming DACAmented: Assessing the Short-Term Benefits of Deferred Action for Childhood Arrivals (DACA)." *American Behavioral Scientist* 58(14): 1852–72.

Hoefer, Michael, Nancy Rytina, and Bryan C. Baker. 2011. "Estimates of the Unauthorized Immigrant Population Residing in the United States: January 2010." Washington: U.S. Department of Homeland Security.

Kasinitz, Philip, John H. Mollenkopf, Mary C. Waters, and Jennifer Holdaway. 2008. *Inheriting the City: The Children of Immigrants Come of Age*. New York: Russell Sage Foundation.

Lee, Jennifer, and Min Zhou. 2015. *The Asian American Achievement Paradox*. New York: Russell Sage Foundation.

Light, Ivan Hubert. 1972. *Ethnic Enterprise in America: Business and Welfare Among Chinese, Japanese, and Blacks*. Berkeley: University of California Press.

Light, Ivan, and Edna Bonacich. 1991. *Immigrant Entrepreneurs: Koreans in Los Angeles, 1965–1982*. Berkeley: University of California Press.

Light, Ivan Hubert, and Steven J. Gold. 2000. *Ethnic Economies*. San Diego: Academic Press.

Massey, Douglas S. 2007. *Categorically Unequal: The American Stratification System*. New York: Russell Sage Foundation.

Massey, Douglas S., and Karen A. Pren. 2012. "Unintended Consequences of US Immigration Policy: Explaining the Post-1965 Surge from Latin America." *Population and Development Review* 38(1): 1–29.

Menjívar, Cecilia. 2000. *Fragmented Ties: Salvadoran Immigrant Networks in America*. Berkeley: University of California Press.

Menjívar, Cecilia, and Leisy Abrego. 2012. Legal Violence: Immigration Law and the Lives of Central American Immigrants. *American Journal of Sociology* 117(5): 1380–421.

Migration Policy Institute. 2014. "Profile of the Unauthorized Population: California." Accessed July 17, 2015. http://www.migrationpolicy.org/data/unauthorized-immigrant-population/state/CA.

Nee, Victor, and Hilary Holbrow. 2013. "Why Asian Americans Are Becoming Mainstream." *Daedalus* 142(3): 65–75.

Ngai, Mae. 2004. *Impossible Subjects: Illegal Aliens and the Making of Modern America*. Princeton, N.J.: Princeton University Press.

Nicholls, Walter. 2013. *The DREAMers: How the Undocumented Youth Movement Transformed the Immigrant Rights Debate*. Stanford, Calif.: Stanford University Press.

Patler, Caitlin. 2014. "Racialized Illegality: The Convergence of Race and Legal Status among Black, Latino, and Asian American Undocumented Young Adults." In *Scholars and Southern California Immigrants in Dialogue*, edited by Victoria Carty, Tekle Woldemkael, and Rafael Luévano. Lanham, Md.: Lexington Press.

Perez, William, and Richard Douglas Cortes. 2011. *Undocumented Latino College Students: Their Socioemotional and Academic Experiences*. Dallas, Tex: LFB Scholarly Publishing.

Portes, Alejandro, and Robert L. Bach. 1980. "Immigrant Earnings: Cuban and Mexican Immigrants in the United States." *International Migration Review* 14(4): 315–41.

———. 1985. *Latin Journey: Cuban and Mexican Immigrants in the United States*. Berkeley: University of California Press.

Reich, Michael, David M. Gordon, and Richard C. Edwards. 1973. "A Theory of Labor Market Segmentation." *American Economic Review* 63(2): 359–65.

Rosenblum, Marc R., and Ariel G. Ruiz Soto. 2015. "An Analysis of Unauthorized Immigrants in the United States by Country and Region of Birth." Washington, D.C.: Migration Policy Institute.

Sanders, Jimmy M., and Victor Nee. 1987. "Limits of Ethnic Solidarity in the Enclave Economy." *American Sociological Review* 52(6): 745–73.

Small, Mario L. 2009. *Unanticipated Gains: Origins of Network Inequality in Everyday Life*. New York: Oxford University Press.

Smith, Sandra Susan. 2010. *Lone Pursuit: Distrust and Defensive Individualism Among the Black Poor*. New York: Russell Sage Foundation.

Waldinger, Roger David. 1996. *Still the Promised City? African-Americans and New Immigrants in Postindustrial New York*. Cambridge, Mass.: Harvard University Press.

———. 2001. *Strangers at the Gates: New Immigrants in Urban America*. Berkeley: University of California Press.

Willen, Sarah S. 2007. "Towards a Critical Phenomenology of 'Illegality': State Power, Criminalization, and Abjectivity Among Undocumented Migrant Workers in Tel Aviv, Israel." *International Migration* 45(3): 7–38.

Wilson, Kenneth L., and Alejandro Portes. 1980. "Immigrant Enclaves: An Analysis of the Labor Market Experiences of Cubans in Miami." *American Journal of Sociology* 86(2): 295–319.

Zhou, Min, and John R. Logan. 1989. "Returns on Human Capital in Ethnic Enclaves: New York City's Chinatown." *American Sociological Review* 54(5): 809–20.

Crossing the Mexico-U.S. Border: Illegality and Children's Migration to the United States

KATHARINE M. DONATO AND SAMANTHA L. PEREZ

Recent public debates reveal that the experiences of child migrants are not well understood. This study is a child-centered analysis of Mexican migration. We examine whether and how conditions in origin communities, and the attributes of children and parents, affect the propensities that children undertake a first migrant trip to the United States. From event history and other multivariate models used to assess children's undocumented migration and how conditions in origin and sending communities explain its variation, our findings reveal close links between violence in Mexico and unauthorized child migration, and important variation in children's likelihoods to initiate migration related to parents' migration, origin migrant networks, and period of U.S. entry.

Keywords: children, unauthorized migration, illegality, Mexico-U.S. migration

For several years, more unaccompanied children have been detained at the Mexico-U.S. border for attempting to cross without legal documents. In 2014 alone, the U.S. Customs and Border Protection reports that 15,634 unaccompanied children from Mexico were encountered at the border, versus 16,404 from El Salvador, 17,057 from Guatemala, and 18,244 from Honduras (2015). These numbers reveal dramatic growth in unaccompanied minors from Central America, but since 2009 also show that the number of unaccompanied children from Mexico well exceeds those from other nations. Together, they signal that children are migrating in large numbers to the United States.[1]

Katharine M. Donato is Donald C. Herzberg Professor of International Migration and director of the Institute for the Study of International Migration at Georgetown University. **Samantha L. Perez** is a doctoral student in the Department of Sociology at Vanderbilt University.

© 2017 Russell Sage Foundation. Donato, Katharine M., and Samantha L. Perez. 2017. "Crossing the Mexico-U.S. Border: Illegality and Children's Migration to the United States." *RSF: The Russell Sage Foundation Journal of the Social Sciences* 3(4): 116–35. DOI: 10.7758/RSF.2017.3.4.07. This paper was presented at Undocumented Immigration and the Experience of Illegality, a conference held at the Russell Sage Foundation in October 2015. We are grateful to Steven Raphael and Roberto Gonzales, and to two anonymous reviewers, for their helpful comments. We also thank the Russell Sage Foundation and the College of Arts and Science at Vanderbilt University for their generous support of this project. Direct correspondence to: Katharine M. Donato at kmd285@georgetown.edu, Edmund Walsh School of Foreign Service, Georgetown University, 3300 Whitehaven Rd., Washington, D.C. 20007; and Samantha L. Perez at samantha.l.perez@vanderbilt.edu, Department of Sociology, Vanderbilt University, PMB 351811, Nashville, TN 37235.

1. Children are also among those fleeing conflict in Syria and the Middle East, and among the Rohingya leaving Myanmar. The World Bank estimates that young people, defined as those between twelve and twenty-four years of age, make up one-third of all international migrants (2006). UNICEF estimates that children represent 51

The presence of many unaccompanied children has fueled public and academic debates about humanitarian protection, such as whether and how children are eligible for refugee and asylum status, and administrative concerns about how to best manage the many minors requesting protection. These debates illustrating children's experiences are not well understood, in part because many have long presumed that children are dependents joining families already in the United States, therefore subsuming children's experiences into those of their parents and families. Some studies have begun to redress this situation by articulating how migration affects the lives of families and children (Abrego 2014; Dreby 2007, 2010, 2012, 2015; Levitt 2009; Donato and Duncan 2011; Gonzales 2011, 2015; Mazzucato and Schans 2011; Nobles 2011; Adserà and Tienda 2012; Donato and Sisk 2015). Less is known, however, about the prevalence of child migration, what pushes children to migrate without legal status, and whether and how unauthorized children cross borders with family members. Most of our knowledge derives from journalistic accounts, which offer rich detailed accounts of the conditions and experiences of children as they cross borders but which do not broadly analyze the systemic factors that push children to migrate from particular countries or regions (see Nazario 2006, 2014).

This study is a child-centered analysis of Mexican children's unauthorized migration. We seek to disentangle whether and how conditions in communities of origin, as well as the characteristics of children and their parents, affect the propensity that children undertake a first migrant trip to the United States. Thus, we examine the extent to which children from Mexico make an initial U.S. trip with and without legal documents, whether and how violence and an historical legacy of out-migration in sending communities are related to children's migration, and the ways in which unauthorized children enter the United States.

To our knowledge, these research questions have not been addressed in prior studies, a situation likely related to the limits of existing data about child migrants. We solve this problem by using data from the Mexican Migration Project (MMP), which is an ongoing data collection effort that began in the 1980s and now contains substantial information about children and child migrants in Mexican households. Its size, merged with data that describe conditions in origin communities, permit the use of multivariate techniques to assess children's undocumented migration and how conditions in origin and sending communities explain its variation. Overall, our findings reveal close links among violence and migrant social networks in Mexican origins, parents' migration experience, when children enter the United States, and unauthorized child migration.

VIOLENCE, FAMILIES, AND ECONOMIC OPPORTUNITY

We review studies that consider the factors that push children to migrate. Much of this work relates to the recent growth of unaccompanied minors at the Mexico-U.S. border and the serious neglect of children in past migration studies. Wherever possible, we also review studies that mention children or adolescents in the process of Mexico-U.S. migration even if they are not central actors in these studies.

Despite a lack of clarity about the "precise combination of motives" that underlie recent child arrivals in the United States (Kandel et al. 2014, 12), some agreement has been reached about the key factors that underlie this migration (Chishti and Hipsman 2014). Three stand out: violence, family separation and reunification, and limited economic opportunity. Among these, drug-related and organized crime-style violence has been well documented. In Honduras, El Salvador, and Guatemala, for example, murder rates are among the world's highest. Mexico's homicide rates are somewhat lower, but between 2007 and 2012, they grew more quickly than in any country (from 8.1 per hundred thousand to 21.5). This rise correlates with the timing of Mexican Pres-

---

percent, or 2.4 million, of the Syrian refugee population (www.unicef.org/appeals/syrianrefugees.html, accessed November 4, 2016).

ident Calderón's decision to go after all drug trafficking organizations in 2007, which subsequently intensified violence and geographically dispersed it across the entire nation (Guerrero-Gutiérrez 2011). In addition, in the last few years, although Mexico's homicide rate has dropped somewhat, violence has become increasingly tied to organized crime groups whose influence infiltrates down into local community institutions, including the police (Heinle, Rodríguez Ferriera, and Shirk 2015). Reports also suggest that smugglers are recruiting young children to migrate to carry various forms of illegal contraband (Kennedy 2014).

One well-known case of organized crime and violence is the disappearance of forty-three students who were traveling by bus in the state of Guerrero in 2014. Initially detained by local police affiliated with an organized crime group, most of the students were taken away and presumably killed (their remains have yet to be found). As this occurred, the town's mayor and his wife went into hiding; they, and some other believed perpetrators, were eventually found and charged for kidnapping and organized crime activity. A year later, no one had been charged with murder; an Inter-American Commission report suggested the attack was a coordinated effort between organized crime, local police, and federal security forces. Jo Tuckman also speculates that the reason for the students' disappearance was corrupt police who thought the bus carrying the students contained heroin or drug money (2015). Although just one case, it illustrates how difficult it is to understand the extent of drug-related violence in Mexico and its impacts. Accompanying drug-related violence in Mexico are the many who have gone missing since 2006, albeit with far less publicity. Kimberly Heinle, Octavio Rodríguez Ferriera, and David Shirk estimate the number to be more than twenty thousand people between 2006 and 2012—including approximately 1,200 children ten years old or younger (2015, n. 60).

How violence and organized crime, real or perceived, affect the experiences of children and their behavior in Mexico is not well understood. Generally, studies suggest that children, no matter where they live, may develop symptoms related to post-traumatic stress disorder if exposed to violence (Martinez and Richters 1993; Berman et al. 1996; Osofsky et al. 2004). Exposure may also affect how parents relate to, and monitor, children including whether they permit them to go to school (Bryk et al. 2010; Harding 2010). In Mexico, Pedro Orraca Romano shows that in 2011 approximately 7 percent of students reported they stopped attending school because they feared becoming a victim of crime (2015, table 1). Using school-level data, he finds that homicide exposure at a young age reduced Mexican children's academic achievement, more so in secondary than elementary schools. Valentina Duque reports a negative effect of violence exposure on children's educational outcomes in Colombia (2013).

In 2011 and 2012, the United Nations High Commissioner for Refugees interviewed approximately four hundred unaccompanied children from Mexico, El Salvador, Guatemala, and Honduras to understand the reasons they left their homes for the United States (UNHCR 2014). Although findings show complexity in children's reasons, approximately one-third of those from Mexico describe violence in their communities, 17 percent mention violence in their homes, and another 12 percent report both (UNHCR 2014). Moreover, unlike children from Central America, a sizeable share (almost 40 percent) of Mexican children in this sample reported being recruited into the human smuggling industry. Together, these findings suggest that children migrate to escape violence and are "in need of international protection" (UNHCR 2014, 6).

Not surprisingly, conditions of violence are likely to intensify "the desire for family reunification" between children in Mexican origins and their parents in the United States (Kandel et al. 2014, 15). In fact, many unaccompanied children who enter from Mexico have ties to parents in the United States. Descriptive results from the UNHCR report reveal that 22 percent of unaccompanied children entering the United States from Mexico had at least one parent living in the United States (2014). Katharine Donato and Blake Sisk also find a very strong relationship between the migration of children and parents (2015). Although the likelihood of a Mexican child making a first U.S. trip was quite low, it was practically nonexistent for children whose parents have no U.S. experience. For children with migrant parents in the United States, children's cumulative chances of making a first trip by age seventeen were very high: 69 percent for trips made between 1970 and 1986, 75 percent between 1987 and 1996, and 55 percent between 1997 and 2011. Thus, although annual rates of Mexico-U.S. migration have declined, Donato and Sisk suggest continued and strong linkages between migrant parents and their children (Villarreal 2014; Donato and Sisk 2015).

In addition, parents' attributes, especially legal status, may also influence children's migration. Prior studies suggest that having a father as an undocumented migrant was positively associated with children migrating without documents. These studies mention children, but only in the context of understanding the larger process of Mexico-U.S. migration. For example, studies describe Mexico-U.S. undocumented migration from small rural villages as being passed down from one generation to the next, especially from fathers to sons (Reichert and Massey 1979; Massey and Liang 1989; Massey et al. 1987). Studies also note that children followed their fathers, who initially migrated without documents for agricultural work but subsequently obtained legal permanent residency, to reunify with their families (Reichert and Massey 1979, 1980; Massey, Goldring, and Durand 1994; Fonseca and Moreno 1988; Goldring 1990; Durand and Massey 1992; Donato 1993, 1994; Cerrutti and Massey 2001; Donato, Wagner, and Patterson 2008; Creighton and Riosmena 2013). Theoretically, Oded Stark and Richard Taylor recognize that children are involved in the migration process when they argue that households—and not individuals—make migration decisions to diversify household risks and costs (1991).

In contrast to these studies, Christine Tucker and her colleagues (2013) interviewed forty-seven Mexican youth, age fourteen through twenty-four, in two origin communities about their reasons for migration. Like many adults migrating northward, youth with U.S. experience reported that economic hardship and difficulty finding a job were their main reasons to migrate. Yet, the decision of most interviewed youth to migrate depended on their parents because they accompanied parents on U.S. trips. The remaining, smaller group of young adults whose parents had never migrated wanted to remain in Mexico. They had no plans to migrate because they envisioned economic opportunities in their origin communities and because they feared the difficulties related to crossing the border without authorization.[2]

Finally, in addition to personally threatening violent conditions and the motivation to reunify with parents, children in Mexico face limited economic and social mobility. Although economic opportunities are changing somewhat because of moderate annual rates of recent economic growth (World Bank 2015), Mexico ranks near the top of all countries for high income and wealth inequality. Income is highly concentrated among the top 1 percent of the population, and the wealthiest 10 percent control 64 percent of the nation's total wealth (Esquivel Hernandez 2014). These indicators suggest children's access to economic opportunities, and the skills and training needed to access them, will be—at best—uneven. Along these lines, student performance in Mexico's schools remains well behind that of other Organization for Economic Cooperation and Development (OECD) countries, despite the government's sizeable investments in Mexico's educational system since the 1990s (Acevedo and Salinas 2000; OECD 2013). In 2012, although Mexico reported one of the highest rates of preschool enrollment, its effectiveness was challenged by high student-teacher ratios. In addition, although Mexico expanded compulsory attendance to the secondary level in 1993, upper secondary school graduation rates remain quite low (approximately 36 percent).

---

2. Tucker and her colleagues do not mention violence as a factor that pushes young adults to migrate, but that they do not is related to when the authors collected their data, in 2006—a year before Mexican President Calderon employed the military to stop drug trafficking and the proliferation of violence began.

SHIFTING U.S. CONTEXT FOR CHILD MIGRATION

The United States has witnessed two key shifts likely to influence Mexican children's propensities to migrate. The first is related to U.S. immigration policy. The second is related to the Great Recession; although the recession officially began in late 2007 and ended in June 2009, its shadow on the U.S. labor market continues to loom large (Shierholz 2014).

The U.S. policy provision that directly influenced children's out-migration was the amnesty provision of the 1986 Immigration Reform and Control Act (IRCA). Approximately two million Mexicans received permanent residency after a five-year waiting period, when they became able to sponsor spouses and children for permanent residency. IRCA also set the groundwork for subsequent policies by dramatically increasing funds for enforcement and removal operations throughout the United States. Together, these policies have had the unintended effect of increasing settlement and family reunification in the United States (Massey, Durand, and Malone 2002). Thus, like many women entering immediately after IRCA, many children entered both with and without documents after 1986 (Donato 1993; Donato and Armenta 2011). Some were quickly able to adjust their status after their fathers received permanent residency, but many others continue to reside in the United States without documents, or with temporary legal status under the Deferred Action for Childhood Arrivals (DACA) program started in 2012. As a result, Roberto Gonzales argues that a broken immigration system has led to many child migrant residents unable to move forward and fully integrate into U.S. society (2015).

Together with record high deportations in recent years, unauthorized immigrants face higher risks of being deported and with their families and children have suffered substantial consequences (on deportations, Gonzalez-Barrera and Krogstad 2014; on consequences, Abrego 2014; Dreby 2012, 2015; Massey 2013). Thus, the last three decades have proved a labyrinth of restrictive policies that have made the lives of immigrants more difficult in the United States. One recent study suggests that border militarization has disrupted the lives of transnational families and lowered the odds that the children of Mexican farm workers reside in Mexico (Hamilton and Hale 2016).

Understanding the effects of these conditions is even more challenging given that certain migrant children are treated differently than others. For example, not all child migrants are unaccompanied minors encountered by officials at the Mexico-U.S. border. Provisions of the William Wilberforce Trafficking Victims Protection Reauthorization Act of 2008 (Public Law 110-457) mean that unaccompanied minors from Mexico and Canada are treated differently than those from Central America. Mexican minors are quickly processed and then deported if, after screening, they are not deemed trafficking victims or have asylum claims based on a credible fear of persecution or torture. In contrast, minors from noncontiguous countries are placed in formal removal proceedings, and released to parents or relatives who care for them until they appear in front of a U.S. immigration judge.[3]

Such a confusingly intricate state of affairs can easily create a complex set of perceptions about whether and how children crossing the border receive humanitarian protection once in the United States (Chishti and Hipsman 2014). For example, some may positively, but wrongly, perceive DACA as a form of permanent legal status even though it is temporary, subject to renewal, and available only to children who entered as unauthorized with their parents and meet other criteria. Others, after the Department of Homeland Security's recent announcement to deport minors who recently received removal orders, may perceive that children have slim prospects of receiving protection and legal status (Markon and Nakamura 2015).

The second salient shift likely to affect children's propensities to make a first U.S. trip is related to the U.S. economy. Before the Great

---

3. Most unaccompanied minors from Central America encountered in the summer of 2014 had waiting periods of approximately two years due to backlogs.

Recession began in 2007, the United States witnessed four decades of sustained immigration and foreign-born workers made up approximately 16 percent of the U.S. labor force (Newburger and Gryn 2009). Late in 2007, however, the U.S. economy sank into a deep recession that was especially devastating for low-skilled workers, of whom approximately half were immigrants (Bean et al. 2012; Orrenius and Zavodny 2013). By 2010, those with less than a high school degree faced a 15 percent unemployment rate, versus the overall rate of 10 percent (Hout, Levanon, and Cumberworth 2011; BLS 2013). Sisk and Donato find that the recession's impact on Mexican immigrant men was mixed (2017). Although they weathered the Great Recession well in some respects, for example, they were more likely than native whites and blacks to remain employed during the recession, Mexican men's relative success was not without its costs as they were also more likely to become underemployed by transitioning into involuntary part-time work. Compounding this situation, especially for unauthorized Mexican immigrants, is a set of deteriorating working conditions, including lower wages and precarious working conditions, under way since the 1980s (Donato et al. 1992; Donato and Massey 1993; Phillips and Massey 1999; Donato and Sisk 2013; Hall and Greenman 2015; Durand, Massey, and Pren 2016; Massey, Durand, and Pren 2016).

In addition to worsened labor market outcomes, the Great Recession is also associated with fewer Mexicans migrating to the United States. Although some describe this downward shift as a standstill (Passel and Cohn 2011) and others as a decline (Warren 2016), the shift is unprecedented in recent decades and led to more recent immigrants entering from China and India than from Mexico (Chishti and Hipsman 2014). It is also associated with a decline in U.S. demand for Mexicans to work in industries, such as construction, which had employed them in large numbers in the past (Villarreal 2014). These conditions, then, are likely to lower the chances that Mexican children will make a first U.S. trip after 2006.

EXPECTATIONS

Based on this review of the literature, we argue that children's unauthorized migration results from a set of decisions associated with conditions in Mexico and the United States. Thus we expect the following three hypotheses:

H1: Exposure to violence will affect children's chances of making an initial trip; greater violence will stimulate children's out-migration, with and without documents.

H2: Parents' migration experience and legal status will influence children's likelihood of making a trip because children's migration is often linked to parents.

H3: Period of entry will positively influence the odds of children's initial migration. We expect higher odds of authorized and unauthorized migration after 1986, when an amnesty program regularized the status of approximately two million Mexicans. However, after 2006, the Great Recession will be associated with lower likelihoods of making a first U.S. trip.

DATA AND METHODS

This study uses data from the Mexican Migration Project (MMP154), a collaborative ongoing research project launched in 1982 and based at Princeton University and the University of Guadalajara.[4] Because the MMP is an ongoing data collection effort, it now represents 154 origin communities derived from interviews with more than 25,000 households and 160,000 people.[5] Derived from randomly selected households in these communities, this is an established data source that contains, among other things, information about labor and marital histories, family composition and other demographics, and household assets. For each household member, the MMP154 includes data on first and most recent migrant trips to the United States, and attributes of these trips, including legal status, when they occurred, and duration.

Like most studies of migration, the MMP was not primarily designed to understand chil-

---

4. See http://mmp.opr.princeton.edu/ (accessed November 4, 2016).

5. See http://mmp.opr.princeton.edu/home-en.aspx (accessed November 4, 2016).

dren's migration. However, its substantial size, merged with data that describe conditions in origin communities, permit us to go beyond results from journalists and others, who often use ethnographic or U.S. Customs and Border Patrol data to examine unaccompanied children crossing the border. Therefore, like Donato and Sisk (2015), we analyze MMP data using sophisticated statistical techniques to examine children's migration.

Although we construct two samples that correspond to different parts of the following analysis, both samples are restricted to children residing in two-parent households and to those with at least one biological parent in households from 149 of the 154 MMP communities. The first sample permits us to use event history models to examine children's migration from Mexico. Given each child's date of birth and year of the survey, we construct a year-by-year child life history up to the date of his or her first U.S. trip.[6] The outcome measure is whether the child migrated within the person-year in question. If they did not migrate in a given year, the migration variable is coded 0; if they did, it is coded 1, and all later years of that child's life are excluded from the file. In every year when migration occurred, we also record legal status (authorized or unauthorized). Legal—that is, authorized or documented—child migrants had valid U.S. documents to enter and reside in the United States; illegal—that is, unauthorized or undocumented—child migrants did not. Thus, the first sample is a large set of person years that refer to respondents who are age seventeen or younger at the time of migration, from households surveys conducted from 1984 to 2013.

Using this sample, we estimate person-year event history models, in which we regress the 0–1 migration variable on indicators representing legal status, gender, age, metropolitan type, parent's migration, homicide rates, migration prevalence in origin communities, and period of first U.S. migrant trip. We measure legal status and gender as two dummy variables, where 1 = without documents, 0 = with legal documents, and 1 = female, 0 = otherwise. We include age as a set of dummy variables (two to eleven years = 1, 0 = otherwise; twelve to seventeen years = 1, 0 = otherwise) and use less than two years as the reference category. Metropolitan type captures the urbanicity of Mexican origins in a set of four dummy variables, with large urban as the reference category. Parent's migration is measured in two dummy variables. The reference category is when a child's parents had no migration experience, with two other dummy variables entered in the model (parents migrated in any year before the year the child migrated, and parents migrated in the same year the child migrated).

At the national level, we include national homicide rates per hundred thousand people per year (from 1972 to 2010) as a continuous variable.[7] Following Douglas Massey and Steven Alvarado, we use homicide rates because they reliably measured across years (2010). We then merge these rates with MMP event history data to assess the effect of violence on the odds that children make a first U.S. trip. We also examine the effect of migration networks, included as the percentage of adults (fifteen years and older) in the origin community with U.S. migration experience of all adults in that community in a given year. Finally, to measure period differences, we use the year of the child's first U.S. trip and construct four dummy variables: 1987 to 1996, which refers to the amnesty period; 1997 to 2006, when border enforcement activity significantly increased; 2007 to 2010, years that correspond to the Great Recession; and 1972 to 1987, the reference category.[8]

---

6. That is, we built a discrete-time person-year file that followed each child from birth to the date of his or her seventeenth birthday or to the first U.S. trip, whichever came first.

7. Although we wanted to use a yearly measure of violence in origin communities, instead of a national measure, this information does not exist for a long time span. For example, the MMP contains this variable for its origin communities but only for 1990 to 2013.

8. With respect to control variables, we expect, overall, less unauthorized versus authorized child migration. Girls (boys) will be less likely than boys (girls) to make a first authorized (unauthorized) trip because Mexican families

To better understand the specific ways in which unauthorized children enter relative to the migration of their parents and siblings, we create a second sample that contains everyone who reported being a child (biological, adopted, or stepchild) of the household head and made a first unauthorized U.S. trip before age eighteen. From a universe of 102,612 children of household heads in the data set, 4,286 (or 4.2 percent of all children) reported migrating on a first trip before age eighteen. From this total, we removed 719 children in female-headed households because children in these households may have different migration experiences.[9] We also removed 167 children for whom we did not have complete migration information for either their mothers or fathers, twenty-two because legal status on first trip was missing, and twelve whose biological mother was not the spouse of the household. Thus, from the 2,497 child migrants for whom migration and legal status information for themselves and their parents is complete, we use a sample of 1,928 children who made a first U.S. trip without documents.

The analysis using this second sample examines characteristics associated with variation in undocumented children's migration. We operationalize two dependent variables: whether children migrate without authorization but with at least one unauthorized parent in the same year, and whether children make an unauthorized trip alone (without parents or siblings migrating in the same year, including parents and siblings who did not report a U.S. trip). We coded each as one if the unauthorized child migrated on his or her first trip in that family arrangement, and zero otherwise. In these models, we control for gender, age, parent's education, and parent's age; we expect that boys will be more likely than girls to make an unauthorized trip with an unauthorized parent or alone. We also expect older children to be more likely than younger ones to make unauthorized trips alone, and younger children to be more likely than their older counterparts to make authorized trips. The chance that children make a first unauthorized trip will be negatively correlated with parent's education and age.

We include mother's and father's prior unauthorized migration experience, and include these as controls in the form of two dummy variables. We expect that mother's and father's prior undocumented status is related to children's unauthorized entry. Father's prior unauthorized status will increase the likelihood that children make a first trip, but mother's prior undocumented status will reduce the likelihood, especially for girls. Violence and migrant social networks will be especially important predictors of children migrating alone. Undocumented children will be most likely to enter with parents during the period of amnesty, between 1987 and 1996. Furthermore, relative to those making a first trip before 1987, children entering between 1987 and 1996 and 1997 and 2005 will be more likely to migrate alone than those entering afterward, between 2006 and 2010.[10]

Thus, our analysis strategy is as follows. First, we examine variation in children's migration, separately for those making an initial trip with and without documents. We assess

---

have protected girls more than boys in the migration process (Donato, Wagner, and Patterson 2008). Older children and those from larger metropolitan areas will be more likely than younger children and those from smallest communities to make a first unauthorized trip. Because studies suggest that access to migrant networks facilitates adults' out-migration by passing on information and resources to potential migrants that, then, lower the costs and risks of making a trip (Massey and Espinosa 1997), we expect migrant networks will facilitate children's authorized first trips. However, we also expect that access to those same networks are associated with lower odds of children making a first unauthorized trip, so that knowledge about migration will protect children from making an initial unauthorized trip.

9. These children were in households where the spouse of the household head was either younger than the child or in households where the difference between children's and spouse's age was less than twelve years.

10. Note that the two most recent period dummies are slightly different than those in the first analysis because of small sample sizes. We made small adjustments to these period variables, as needed, to accommodate the smaller sample sizes of unauthorized children (see tables 2, 3, and 4).

whether and how violence, as well as other characteristics, influence children to make a first U.S. trip. To illustrate differences by legal status and period, we calculate and present predicted probabilities that children make a first U.S. trip. Second, we estimate models that predict whether unauthorized children who migrate do so in the same year as an unauthorized parent, or alone (without parents or siblings). We estimate these models for all children, and separately for boys and girls, to investigate gender differences in children's unauthorized migration arrangements.

CHILDREN MAKING A FIRST U.S. TRIP

Table 1 contains three regression models: one for all children, and two separate models for unauthorized and legally authorized children's migration. The models that predict whether a child makes a first U.S. trip up through age seventeen. The first set of columns refers to all first trips, the next two sets to unauthorized and authorized trips. The separate legal status models are justified by Chow test results that reveal coefficients for the unauthorized differ significantly from coefficients for the authorized.[11]

We begin by summarizing the coefficients in the pooled model. As we expected, net of other attributes, being unauthorized significantly reduces the likelihood that children migrate on a first trip. In addition, relative to boys, girls are more likely to migrate. Relative to those less than two years of age, being a young adolescent up to age seventeen significantly increases the chance of making a first trip. However, children from urban areas are no different from children originating in smaller places, whether towns or smaller ranchos.

Consistent with Donato and Sisk, having parents with U.S. experience, especially those migrating in the same year as their child, increases the risk of children's out-migration (2015). Violence, as measured by national homicide rates, operates as a push factor and is positively associated with children migrating on a first trip. However, migration prevalence in origin communities significantly reduces

that likelihood. In addition, when a child makes a first trip also matters. Compared with before 1987, the three coefficients for 1987 to 1996, 1997 to 2006, and 2007 to 2010 are positive and significant. Thus, children's migration grows with time, and although it appears to peak between 1997 and 2006, it still remains substantially higher during the period of the Great Recession, between 2007 and 2010, relative to before 1987.

Comparison of the next two sets of models reveals a decidedly different process of first-trip migration for children making unauthorized and authorized trips. Beginning with the gender effect, we see that although being female is associated with a greater likelihood of making a first legal trip, it is not associated with making a first illegal trip. Age, too, operates differently across the two models. The risk of making a first undocumented trip is considerably higher for adolescents, but no different for those age two to eleven years relative to very young children. In contrast, no significant age coefficients predict the likelihood of making a documented U.S. trip. Moreover, although metropolitan area does not influence children's unauthorized first trips, originating from a small town reduces a child's chance of making an authorized first trip relative to those from large urban areas.

Whether we consider unauthorized or authorized first trips, children are much more likely to make a first trip in the year their parents migrate than children whose parents have never migrated. In both models, these coefficients are significant and large. In addition, although somewhat smaller in size, coefficients for parents migrating in the past suggest that children are also more likely to make an undocumented or documented first U.S. trip if their parents had U.S. experience.

Once again, rates of violence are also significant and positive, suggesting that exposure to violence can encourage children to migrate with or without documents. Interestingly, although the effect of social networks, as measured by the prevalence of migration in origin communities, affects the likelihood that children make a first trip, its effect has different

---

11. These results are available on request.

Table 1. First U.S. Migration

	Total Migration	Unauthorized	Authorized
Children's attributes			
Undocumented (reference = documented)	−0.543***	NA	NA
	(0.105)		
Female (reference = male)	0.184**	0.055	0.403***
	(0.088)	(0.102)	(0.156)
Age (reference = 0–1)			
Two to eleven	−0.187	−0.230	−0.077
	(0.141)	(0.163)	(0.213)
Twelve to seventeen	1.583***	1.528***	0.287
	(0.167)	(0.175)	(0.251)
Metropolitan type (reference = urban)			
Small urban	−0.158	−0.095	−0.234
	(0.177)	(0.200)	(0.294)
Town	−0.166	0.211	−1.073***
	(0.170)	(0.190)	(0.327)
Rancho	−0.104	0.067	−0.471
	(0.180)	(0.203)	(0.313)
Parents' migration (reference = no parent migration)			
Parents migrated before child	0.424***	0.338***	1.147***
	(0.119)	(0.124)	(0.344)
Parents migrated in the same year as child	3.918***	3.176***	4.130***
	(0.140)	(0.140)	(0.332)
National homicide rate	0.221***	0.218***	0.138***
	(0.036)	(0.036)	(0.039)
Migration prevalence	−0.016***	−0.025***	0.014**
	(0.004)	(0.004)	(0.006)
Period of migration (reference = 1972–1986)			
1987–1996	1.384***	1.435***	0.733***
	(0.120)	(0.140)	(0.199)
1997–2006	2.955***	2.677***	2.299***
	(0.348)	(0.356)	(0.392)
2007–2010	1.787*	0.565	3.560***
	(0.953)	(1.142)	(0.926)
Intercept	−8.050***	−8.448***	−8.915***
	(0.700)	(0.701)	(0.854)
Person years (N)	10,675	10,675	10,675
Wald chi²	1,332.90	1,169.61	617.96
Pseudo R^2	0.3839	0.3135	0.3128

Source: MMP154 data set (Mexican Migration Project 2015).
Note: Standard errors are included in parentheses.
NA = not applicable.
*p < .1; **p < .05; ***p < .01

signs in the two models. Having more adult migrants in a Mexican origin decreases the likelihood that children make an unauthorized first trip, but increases the chance that children make a first legal trip. T-tests of these two coefficients reveal a significant difference: that is, social networks operate differently when predicting the likelihood that a child makes a first

Figure 1. Predicted Probabilities of Children Making a First U.S. Trip

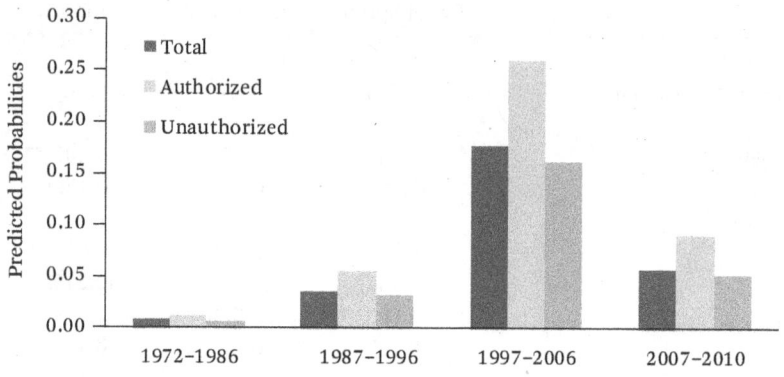

Source: MMP154 data set (Mexican Migration Project 2015).
Note: Probabilities generated from model 1 in table 1.

unauthorized trip rather than an authorized one.

Coefficients for the period variables reveal that the risks of children's first-time unauthorized and authorized migration has shifted over time. Relative to before 1987, the likelihood that children migrate on a first trip without documents is higher in two of the three subsequent periods: from 1987 to 1996 and from 1997 to 2006, but no different from 2007 to 2010. With respect to authorized migration, however, all three periods are significantly different from before 1987. Moreover, results from a t-test of the 2007 to 2010 coefficients across the two models (not shown here) reveal that this effect is significantly different across the two models. Together, these results suggest that children were less likely to initiate a U.S. trip without documents during the period corresponding to the Great Recession, but in the same period were more likely to do so with documents than before 1987.

Figure 1 presents predicted probabilities of children making a first trip from Mexico by legal status and period of entry, calculated from coefficients in the first model in table 1. These probabilities depict four important findings. First, before 1987, the chances that a child would make a first trip are negligible and we see no legal status differences. Second, from 1987 to 1996, immediately following IRCA's passage, though they remain low, the chances that children make a first unauthorized or authorized trip grow somewhat but they are higher for children making an authorized versus unauthorized trip. Third, between 1997 and 2006, the overall chances of children making a first trip dramatically rise, up to 18 percent for all trips, 26 percent for authorized trips, and 15 percent of unauthorized trips. Fourth, between 2007 and 2010, the chances that children will make a first U.S. trip drop. They are highest among those making an authorized first trip, at just less than 10 percent; the chance of making a first illegal trip drops down to 5 percent.

UNAUTHORIZED CHILD MIGRATION ARRANGEMENTS

Table 2 presents descriptive statistics about children who made a first unauthorized U.S. trip, boys and girls, before their eighteenth birthday. From our analytic sample of 1,928 unauthorized child migrants, 75 percent were boys and 25 percent were girls. Approximately 23 percent of these entered in a year when at least one parent also migrated or when that parent was already in the United States; 21 percent were unauthorized children migrating in the same year that at least one unauthorized parent migrated, and 60 percent were at least twelve years old migrating alone, without parents or siblings in the United States. Among children making an unauthorized first trip, their average age was close to fourteen. Their parents combined education averaged less than seven years of school. Many more children had fathers (55 percent) with unauthorized migration experience than mothers (40

Table 2. Descriptive Statistics, First Trip, Unauthorized Children

	All	Boys	Girls
Gender composition of unauthorized children on first trip	NA	75.0	25.0
Percent unauthorized children, at least one parent	22.6	16.9	39.5***
Percent unauthorized children, at least one unauthorized parent	20.8	15.4	36.7***
Percent unauthorized children, twelve-plus, alone	60.3	66.4	41.8***
Mean age at first migration (0–17)	13.7	14.2	12.0***
Mean combined parent education (0–46)	6.7	6.3	7.6***
Mean combined parent age (35–146)	86.2	87.4	82.7***
Percent mother prior unauthorized migration (reference = no)	5.5	4.7	7.7**
Percent father prior unauthorized migration (reference = no)	40.0	37.8	46.8***
Mean Mexican homicide rate (8.2–22.9)	17.4	17.4	17.5
Mean migration prevalence ratio (0–65.4)	24.0	24.1	23.5
Percent migrated in or before 1986	45.5	46.2	43.5
Percent migrated between 1987 and 1996	40.1	38.8	44.1**
Percent migrated between 1997 and 2005	13.3	13.8	11.6
Percent migrated between 2006 and 2010	1.1	1.2	0.8
N	1,928	1,445	483

Source: MMP154 data set (Mexican Migration Project 2015).
Note: NA = not applicable.
$*p < .1; **p < .05; ***p < .01$

percent). Homicide rates were 17.4 deaths per hundred thousand, and approximately 24 percent of origin communities had adults with U.S. experience. As the table makes clear, fewer than half of the sample migrated in 1986 or earlier, another 40.1 percent migrated between 1987 and 1996, 13.3 percent from 1997 to 2005, and 1.1 percent from 2006 to 2010.

Key among the gender differences are the migration arrangements of undocumented children. They suggest that more girls are accompanied by, or migrate in the same year as, parents. Girls are significantly more likely than boys to enter in the same year as a parent, regardless of status. Among the authorized, 39.5 percent of girls entered in the same year as a parent, compared to 16.9 percent of boys. Similarly, 36.7 percent of unauthorized girls entered in the same year as a parent, compared to 15.4 percent of unauthorized boys. However, boys were much more likely than girls (66.4 to 41.8 percent) to migrate without parents. In addition, girls are younger than boys, and girls' parents had significantly more education and were younger. Girls were also more likely than boys to have mothers with unauthorized migration experience (7.7 to 4.7 percent), and girls were also more likely than boys to have fathers with such experience (46 or 48 to 37.8 percent). The only other significant gender difference is in the share of children who migrated between 1987 and 1996, when boys were less likely to enter.

Multivariate logistic regression models that predict the likelihood of unauthorized children migrating in the same year as at least one unauthorized parent clarify the specific arrangements in which unauthorized children enter, and the extent to which violence and other factors matter (see table 3). The first column of table 3 refers to all children, the second two columns to boys and girls.

The first column reveals that girls are significantly more likely than boys to migrate on a first U.S. trip without documents in the same year as an undocumented parent. Unauthorized children with older parents are less likely to make a first trip with an unauthorized parent. In addition, the effect for mothers with prior unauthorized experience is negative but for fathers is strongly positive. Homicide rates are negatively associated with the likelihood

Table 3. Regressions, Unauthorized Children First Trip, with Unauthorized Parent

	All Children	Boys	Girls
Children's attributes			
Female (reference = male)	0.824***	NA	NA
	(0.155)		
Age at first migration	−0.244***	−0.274***	−0.206***
	(0.020)	(0.026)	(0.031)
Parent education	0.008	−0.004	0.020
	(0.015)	(0.020)	(0.024)
Parent age	−0.030***	−0.032***	−0.026***
	(0.006)	(0.007)	(0.009)
Parents' migration (reference = no parent migration)			
Mother prior unauthorized migration (reference = no)	−0.596**	−0.370	−0.929**
	(0.294)	(0.373)	(0.473)
Father prior unauthorized migration (reference = no)	0.718***	0.874***	0.442*
	(0.154)	(0.198)	(0.251)
Mexican homicide rate	−0.092**	−0.126**	−0.051
	(0.045)	(0.057)	(0.075)
Migration prevalence ratio	0.018***	0.027***	0.006
	(0.006)	(0.007)	(0.010)
Period of migration (reference = 1972–1986)			
1987–1996	0.644***	0.848***	0.419
	(0.166)	(0.217)	(0.264)
1997–2005	−0.147	0.060	−0.487
	(0.383)	(0.472)	(0.669)
2006–2010	−0.766	−0.215	−1.410
	(0.911)	(1.054)	(1.360)
Intercept	4.478***	5.285***	4.310***
	(0.914)	(1.146)	(1.550)
N	1,928	1,445	483
LR chi²	719.52	456.03	188.00
Pseudo R^2	0.366	0.367	0.296

Source: MMP154 data set (Mexican Migration Project 2015).
Note: Standard errors in parentheses.
NA = not applicable.
*$p < .1$; **$p < .05$; ***$p < .01$

that children make a first unauthorized trip with at least one parent. However, the migration prevalence ratio for a child's place of origin has the opposite effect: the likelihood of first unauthorized trip with at least one parent increases with higher prevalence of U.S. migration. Moreover, as expected, unauthorized child migration is more likely in the amnesty period, immediately after IRCA, than before 1987. Furthermore, an examination of the models for boys and girls (columns 2 and 3 of table 3) reveals covariate effects that are similar across the two groups.

Table 4 presents models that predict unauthorized children, between twelve and seventeen years old, migrating alone. In the first model for all children, we see that girls are significantly less likely than boys, but older children are more likely than younger ones, to migrate alone. Once again, we observe negative effects for parent's education and for parent's age. We also see that having a mother who

Table 4. Regressions, Unauthorized Children First Trip, Alone

	All Children	Boys	Girls
Children's attributes			
Female (reference = male)	−0.789***	NA	NA
	(0.121)		
Age	0.192***	0.207***	0.165***
	(0.017)	(0.021)	(0.032)
Parent education	−0.021*	−0.014	−0.040*
	(0.011)	(0.013)	(0.022)
Parent age	−0.011***	−0.010**	−0.014*
	(0.004)	(0.004)	(0.008)
Parents' migration (reference = no parent migration)			
Mother prior unauthorized migration (reference = no)	−1.073***	−0.967***	−1.397***
	(0.255)	(0.297)	(0.525)
Father prior unauthorized migration (reference = no)	−0.485***	−0.567***	−0.281
	(0.112)	(0.131)	(0.222)
Mexican homicide rate	0.005	−0.003	0.034
	(0.031)	(0.036)	(0.064)
Migration prevalence ratio	−0.011***	−0.013***	−0.008
	(0.004)	(0.005)	(0.008)
Period of migration (reference = 1972–1986)			
1987–1996	−0.279**	−0.497***	0.261
	(0.121)	(0.143)	(0.232)
1997–2003	−0.161	−0.408	0.561
	(0.258)	(0.301)	(0.516)
2004–2010	−0.393	−0.811*	1.133
	(0.430)	(0.471)	(1.007)
Intercept	−0.346	−0.307	−1.362
	(0.644)	(0.745)	(1.312)
N	1,832	1,399	433
LR chi²	305.19	187.41	53.06
Pseudo R^2	0.125	0.106	0.089

Source: MMP154 data set (Mexican Migration Project 2015).
Note: Standard errors in parentheses.
NA = not applicable.
*$p < .1$; **$p < .05$; ***$p < .01$

made a prior unauthorized trip reduces the likelihood that an unauthorized child migrates alone. In contrast to the findings in table 3, however, we also see that having a father who made a prior unauthorized trip also reduces the likelihood that an unauthorized child migrates alone. Moreover, the coefficient for mothers is at least twice as large as that for fathers. Although homicide has no significant effect, but social networks have a significant and negative effect, suggesting that larger networks in origin communities reduce unauthorized children's chances of migrating alone. Of the remaining coefficients, only that for 1987 through 1996 is significant. Children were less likely than before 1987 to make a first unauthorized trip alone immediately after IRCA became law.

Examining the models separately for boys and girls reveals that, although children's demographic attributes are mostly similar in their effects on the likelihood that unauthorized children migrate alone, having parents with prior unauthorized experience operates differently for boys and girls. Among boys, having either a mother or father with prior undocumented experience lowers the risk they migrate alone. Among girls, only mother's prior undocumented status negatively affects this risk. Moreover, although violence has no effect, migrant networks lower the likelihood of migrating alone only for girls. Finally, period effects in the boys model suggest that, relative to those who migrated before 1987, boys were less likely to migrate alone in two of the three subsequent periods. Among girls, however, none of the period coefficients are significant. Results from tests that compare these effects for boys and for girls (not shown here) substantiate that the observed effects for period of first trip are significantly different. Thus, although the propensity to migrate alone did not shift over time for girls, it shifted downward for boys both during the amnesty period immediately after IRCA was passed and after 2003, when the Great Recession emerged.

DISCUSSION

In the context of contemporary U.S. immigration, children have become an important topic of study. Yet, although scholars have begun to examine how migration affects the lives of family and children, few researchers have systematically investigated the factors that push children to migrate (on how migration affects families, see Abrego 2014; Dreby 2007, 2010, 2012, 2015; Levitt 2009; Donato and Duncan 2011; Gonzales 2011, 2015; Mazzucato and Schans 2011; Nobles 2011; Adserà and Tienda 2012; Donato and Sisk 2015). This study attempts to fill that void by estimating a series of event history models to predict the likelihood that children from Mexico take an initial U.S. trip, with and without documents, as a function of violence, migrant social networks, period of a child's first trip, and other child and parent attributes. In addition, we consider two of the ways that unauthorized children enter the United States, with parents or alone, and examine the factors that are associated with variation in these outcomes.

Using MMP data merged with national rates of homicide in Mexico, we find evidence consistent with our first hypothesis. Exposure to serious violence—in the form of homicide—operates to push children to make a first trip with or without documents. In addition, as expected, parent's migration is strongly associated with that of children. Those migrating in the same year as or before their parents had higher odds of making an initial trip. Having larger migrant social networks reduced the overall likelihood that a child migrated on first U.S. trip, but reduced the odds of unauthorized and increased the odds of authorized migration. In addition, well-defined period differences in the likelihood that children initiate a first trip emerged. Children were much more likely to make a first authorized trip after 1987—in any period—than before. However, among those making a first undocumented trip, the odds between 2007 and 2010 were no different than those for before 1987. The Great Recession thus appears to have diminished the odds that children initiated unauthorized migration.

To visually display some of these effects, we present predicted probabilities. Two striking findings emerge from these results. First, the chances that children initiate a U.S. trip were dramatically higher between 1997 and 2006, after the initial period of amnesty but before the Great Recession. The chances of migrating on a first authorized trip was approximately 26 percent, up from 5 percent between 1987 and 1996. Correspondingly, the chances of making an initial unauthorized trip also rose to 16 percent from 3 percent between 1987 and 1996. Thus, although many migrants regularized their status after 1986, the odds that children made a first trip rose well after the initial legalization period. Second, the probabilities reveal greater variation by legal status over time. Before IRCA's amnesty program, that is, between 1972 and 1986, the odds that children initiated migration with and without documents were near zero. Beginning in the 1987 to 1996 period, legal status began to stratify the chances that a child migrated. The largest difference appeared in the 1997 to 2006 period, and the second largest in the 2007 to 2010 period (25 to 16 percent, and 9 to 5 percent, respectively).

In the second half of our analysis, we consider the drivers of two types of unauthorized children's migration, that is, whether entry was linked to that of parents and siblings, and within these arrangements, whether boys and girls differed. For example, the likelihood that unauthorized children migrate when an unauthorized parent migrates appears to be driven by children's attributes (of themselves and their parents) and period of entry. As expected, we see higher odds for boys who make an illegal first trip with at least one parent, but not girls, from 1987 to 1996 versus before 1987. However, we also see that boys have a lower likelihood of migrating alone between 1987 and 1996.

In contrast, key predictors of the odds that children migrate alone also include mother's and father's prior unauthorized migration status, migrant social networks, and period of entry, though showing some gender differences across the models. In particular, father's prior unauthorized migration does not matter when predicting girls migrate alone. What matters for boys, but not girls, is the prevalence of migration. Moreover, among boys, the odds of making an unauthorized trip alone were substantially lower after 1987 than before.

One limitation of this study is that it is limited to existing MMP data. As a result, our findings derive from an analytic sample of children defined by parents' first and most recent U.S. trip, rather than their complete migration histories. Thus, when parents had made more than two trips, we are unable to discern whether children migrated with them and therefore exclude children from the analysis. A second limitation is that, although the MMP contains information about children who migrated earlier in the twentieth century, that is, before 1972, we restricted our analysis to children who migrated between 1972 and 2010 because we had Mexican homicide and migration prevalence rates only for these years.

Despite limitations, our findings suggest that legal status is an important stratifier of children's chances of initiating migration. Legal status impacts are well documented for Mexican adult out-migration and for labor market outcomes (see Donato and Massey 2016). This analysis, however, reveals how legal status stratifies the odds of children initiating migration, and how exposure to violence, access to migrant social networks, period of entry, as well as other attributes of children and parents, operate differently to help explain variation in children's propensities to make an initial migrant trip.

Throughout the analysis, we also see clear signs that children's migration is part of a slow process of family reunification. Yet despite connections to family residing in the United States, most Mexican children do not receive special protections in the migration process—even though many arrive as a by-product of the strong labor demand provided by their parents. As Jacqueline Bhabha suggests, this situation does not result from a lack of awareness about the problems that child migrants face; rather, it reflects society's ambivalence about integrating migrant children (2014). Thus, although presidential executive actions, like DACA, may temporarily resolve some of the problems that these children and young adults face, until political will to fix the immigration policy regime is strong, they and many other migrant children will remain either invisible or unequal or both.

REFERENCES

Abrego, Leisy. 2014. *Sacrificing Families: Navigating Laws, Labor, and Love Across Borders*. Stanford, Calif.: Stanford University Press.

Acevedo, Gladys López, and Angel Salinas. 2000. "How Mexico's Financial Crisis Affected Income Distribution." *Policy Research* working paper no. 2406. Washington, D.C.: World Bank.

Adserà, Alícia, and Marta Tienda. 2012. "Comparative Perspectives on International Migration and Child Well-being." *Annals of the American Academy of Political and Social Science* 643(1): 6–15.

Bean, Frank D., Susan K. Brown, James D. Bachmeier, Zoya Gubernskaya, and Christopher D. Smith. 2012. "Luxury, Necessity, and Anachronistic Workers: Does the United States Need Unskilled Immigrant Labor?" *American Behavioral Scientist* 56(8): 1008–28.

Berman, Steven L., William M. Kurtines, Wendy K. Silverman, and Lourdes T. Serafini. 1996. "The Impact of Exposure to Crime and Violence on Urban Youth." *American Journal of Orthopsychiatry* 66(3): 329–36.

Bhabha, Jacqueline. 2014. *Child Migration & Human Rights in a Global Age*. Princeton, N.J.: Princeton University Press.

Bryk, Anthony S., Penny Bender Sebring, Elaine Allensworth, John Q. Easton, and Stuart Luppescu. 2010. *Organizing Schools for Improvement: Lessons from Chicago*. Chicago: University of Chicago Press.

Bureau of Labor Statistics. 2013. *Unemployment Rate: Less than a High School Diploma*. Washington: Bureau of Labor Statistics. Accessed November 4, 2016. http://data.bls.gov/timeseries/LNS14027659.

Cerrutti, Marcela, and Douglas S. Massey. 2001. "On the Auspices of Female Migration from Mexico to the United States." *Demography* 38(2): 187–200.

Chishti, Muzaffar, and Faye Hipsman. 2014. "Dramatic Surge in the Arrival of Unaccompanied Children Has Deep Roots and No Simple Solutions." *Migration Policy Institute*. Accessed November 4, 2016. http://www.migrationpolicy.org/article/dramatic-surge-arrival-unaccompanied-children-has-deep-roots-and-nosimple-solutions.

Creighton, Matthew J., and Fernando Riosmena. 2013. "Migration and the Gendered Origin of Migrant Networks Among Couples in Mexico." *Social Science Quarterly* 94(1): 79–99.

Donato, Katharine M. 1993. "Current Trends and Patterns in Female Migration: Evidence from México." *International Migration Review* 27(4): 748–71.

———. 1994. "U.S. Policy and Mexican Migration to the United States, 1942–92." *Social Science Quarterly* 75(4): 705–29.

Donato, Katharine M., and Amada Armenta. 2011. "What We Know About Unauthorized Migration." *Annual Review of Sociology* 37(1): 529–43.

Donato, Katharine M., and Ebony M. Duncan. 2011. "Migration, Social Networks, and Child Health in Mexican Families." *Journal of Marriage and Family* 73(4): 713–28.

Donato, Katharine M., Jorge Durand, and Douglas S. Massey. 1992. "Changing Conditions in the U.S. Labor Market: Effects of the Immigration Reform and Control Act of 1986." *Population Research and Policy Review* 11(2): 93–115.

Donato, Katharine M., and Douglas S. Massey. 1993. "Effect of the Immigration Reform and Control Act on the Wages of Mexican Migrants." *Social Science Quarterly* 74(3): 523–41.

———. 2016. "Twenty-First Century Globalization and Illegal Migration." *Annals of the American Academy of Social and Political Science* 666(1): 7–26.

Donato, Katharine M., and Blake Sisk. 2013. "Shifts in the Employment Outcomes Among Mexican Migrants to the United States, 1976–2009." *Research in Social Stratification and Mobility* 30(1): 63–77.

———. 2015. "Children's Migration from Mexico and Central America to the United States: Evidence from the Mexican and Latin American Migration Projects." *Journal of Migration and Human Security* 3(1): 58–79.

Donato, Katharine M., Brandon Wagner, and Evelyn Patterson. 2008. "The Cat and Mouse Game at the México-U.S. Border: Gendered Patterns and Recent Shifts." *International Migration Review* 42(2): 330–59.

Dreby, Joanna. 2007. "Children and Power in Mexican Transnational Families." *Journal of Marriage and Family* 69(4): 1050–64.

———. 2010. *Divided by Borders: Mexican Migrants and Their Children*. Berkeley: University of California Press.

———. 2012. "The Burden of Deportation on Children in Mexican Immigrant Families." *Journal of Marriage and Family* 74(4): 829–45.

———. 2015. *Everyday Illegal: When Policies Undermine Immigrant Families*. Berkeley: University of California Press.

Duque, Valentina. 2013. "The Hidden Costs and Lasting Legacies of Violence on Education: Evidence from Colombia." Paper presented at the Population Association of America Annual Meeting. New Orleans (April 11–13).

Durand, Jorge, and Douglas S. Massey. 1992. "Mexican Migration to the United States: A Critical Review." *Latin American Research Review* 27(2): 3–42.

Durand, Jorge, Douglas S. Massey, and Karen A. Pren. 2016. "Double Disadvantage: Unauthorized Mexicans in the U.S. Labor Market." *Annals of the American Academy of Social and Political Science* 666(1): 78–90.

Esquivel Hernandez, Gerardo. 2014. *Extreme Inequality in Mexico: Concentration of Economic and Political Power*. Mexico City: OXFAM. Accessed November 4, 2016. https://is.cuni.cz/studium/predmety/index.php?do=download&did=113954&kod=JMM591.

Fonseca, Omar, and Lilia Moreno. 1988. "Consideraciones historico-sociales de la migración de trabajadores michoacanos a los Estados Unidos de America: El caso de Jaripo." In *Migración en el*

Occidente de México, edited by Gustavo López Castro and Sergio Pardo Galván. Zamora de Hidalgo, México: El Colegio de Michoacán.

Goldring, Luin. 1990. "Development and Migration: A Comparative Analysis of Two Mexican Migrant Circuits." Commission working paper no. 37. Washington, D.C.: Commission for the Study of International Migration and Cooperative Economic Development.

Gonzales, Roberto G. 2011. "Learning to Be Illegal: Undocumented Youth and Shifting Legal Contexts in the Transition to Adulthood." *American Sociological Review* 76(4): 602–19.

———. 2015. *Lives in Limbo: Undocumented and Coming of Age in America*. Berkeley: University of California Press.

Gonzalez-Barrera, Ana, and Jens Manuel Krogstad. 2014. "U.S. Deportations of Immigrants Reach Record High in 2013." Washington D.C.: Pew Research Center. Accessed November 4, 2016. http://www.pewresearch.org/fact-tank/2014/10/02/u-s-deportations-of-immigrants-reach-record-high-in-2013/.

Guerrero-Gutiérrez, Eduardo. 2011. *Security, Drugs, and Violence in Mexico: A Survey*. Survey carried out for the 7th North American Forum. México: Lantia Consultores. Accessed November 4, 2016. http://fsi.stanford.edu/sites/default/files/93.securitydrugs.pdf.

Hall, Matthew, and Emily Greenman. 2015. "The Occupational Cost of Being Illegal in the United States: Legal Status, Job Hazards, and Compensating Differentials." *International Migration Review* 49(2): 406–42.

Hamilton, Erin R., and Jo Mhairi Hale. 2016. "Changes in the Transnational Family Structures of Mexican Farm Workers in the Era of Border Militarization." *Demography* 53(5): 1429–51. DOI:10.1007/s13524-016-0505-7.

Harding, David J. 2010. *Living the Drama: Community, Conflict, and Culture Among Inner-City Boys*. Chicago: University of Chicago Press.

Heinle, Kimberly, Octavio Rodríguez Ferriera, and David A. Shirk. 2015. "Drug Violence in Mexico: Data and Analysis Through 2014, Special Report." San Diego: Justice in Mexico Project, Department of Political Science, University of San Diego.

Hout, Michael, Asaf Levanon, and Erin Cumberworth. 2011. "Job Loss and Unemployment." In *The Great Recession*, edited by David B. Grusky, Bruce Western, and Christopher Wimer. New York: Russell Sage Foundation.

Kandel, William A., Andorra Bruno, Peter J. Meyer, Clare Ribando Seelke, Maureen Taft-Morales, and Ruth Ellen Wasem. 2014. "Unaccompanied Alien Children: Potential Factors Contributing to Recent Immigration." CRS Report no. R43628. Washington: Congressional Research Service.

Kennedy, Elizabeth. 2014. "No Childhood Here: Why Central American Children Are Fleeing Their Homes." Special Report. Washington, D.C.: American Immigration Council. Accessed November 4, 2016. https://www.americanimmigrationcouncil.org/research/no-childhood-here-why-central-american-children-are-fleeing-their-homes.

Levitt, Peggy. 2009. "Roots and Routes: Understanding the Lives of the Second Generation Transnationally." *Journal of Ethnic and Migration Studies* 35(7): 1225–42.

Markon, Jerry, and David Nakamura. 2015. "U.S. Plans Raids to Deport Families Across the Border." *Washington Post*, December 23. Accessed November 4, 2016. https://www.washingtonpost.com/politics/us-plans-raids-to-deport-families-who-surged-across-border/2015/12/23/034fc954-a9bd-11e5-8058-480b572b4aae_story.html.

Martinez, P., and J. E. Richters. 1993. "The NIMH Community Violence Project: II. Children's Distress Symptoms Associated with Violence Exposure." *Psychiatry* 56(1): 22–35.

Massey, Douglas S. 2013. "America's Immigration Policy Fiasco: Learning from Past Mistakes." *Daedalus* 142(3): 5–15.

Massey, Douglas S., Rafael Alarcón, Jorge Durand, and Humberto González. 1987. *Return to Aztlan: The Social Process of International Migration from Western Mexico*. Berkeley: University of California Press.

Massey, Douglas S., and Steven E. Alvarado. 2010. "In Search of Peace: Structural Adjustment, Violence, and International Migration in Mexico and Central America 1979–2002." *Annals of the American Academy of Political and Social Science* 630(1): 137–61.

Massey, Douglas S., Jorge Durand, and Nolan Malone. 2002. *Beyond Smoke and Mirrors: Mexican Immigration in an Era of Economic Integration*. New York: Russell Sage Foundation.

Massey, Douglas S., Jorge Durand, and Karen A. Pren. 2016. "The Precarious Position of Latino

Immigrants in the United States: A Comparative Analysis of Ethnosurvey Data." *Annals of the American Academy of Social and Political Science* 666(1): 91–109.

Massey, Douglas S., and Kristin Espinosa. 1997. "What's Driving Mexico-U.S. Migration? A Theoretical, Empirical and Policy Analysis." *American Journal of Sociology* 102(4): 939-99.

Massey, Douglas S., Luin Goldring, and Jorge Durand. 1994. "Continuities in Transnational Migration: An Analysis of Nineteen Mexican Communities." *American Journal of Sociology* 99(6): 1492–533.

Massey, Douglas A.; and Zai Liang. 1989. "The Long-Term Consequences of a Temporary Worker Program: The US Bracero Experience." *Population Research and Policy Review* 8(3): 199–226.

Mazzucato, Valentina, and Djamila Schans. 2011. "Transnational Families and the Well-being of Children: Conceptual and Methodological Challenges." *Journal of Marriage and Family* 73(4): 704–12.

Mexican Migration Project. 2015. MMP154 data set. Princeton University and the University of Guadalajara. Accessed January 23, 2016. http://mmp.opr.princeton.edu.

Nazario, Sonya. 2006. *Enrique's Journey: The True Story of a Boy Determined to Reunite with His Mother*, 2nd ed. New York: Ember.

———. 2014. "The Children of the Drug Wars: A Refugee Crisis, Not an Immigration Crisis." *The New York Times*. July 11.

Newburger, Eric C., and Thomas Gryn. 2009. *The Foreign-Born Labor Force in the United States: 2007*. Washington: U.S. Department of Commerce, Economics and Statistics Administration, U.S. Census Bureau.

Nobles, Jenna. 2011. "Parenting from Abroad: Migration, Nonresident Father Involvement, and Children's Education in Mexico." *Journal of Marriage and Family* 73(4): 729–46.

Organisation for Economic Cooperation and Development (OECD). 2013. "Mexico, Country Note: Education at a Glance." Paris: OECD. Accessed November 4, 2016. http://www.oecd.org/edu/Mexico_EAG2013%20Country%20Note.pdf.

Orraca Romano, Pedro Paulo. 2015. "Crime Exposure and Educational Outcomes in Mexico." Paper presented at the 18th IZA European Summer School in Labor Economics conference. Inning, Germany (May 27). Accessed November 4, 2016. http://www.iza.org/conference_files/SUMS_2015/orraca_romano_p5554.pdf.

Orrenius, Pia M., and Madeline Zavodny. 2013. "Immigrants in the U.S. Labor Market." Working Paper no. 1306. Dallas, Tex.: Federal Reserve Bank. Accessed November 22, 2016. https://www.dallasfed.org/assets/documents/research/papers/2013/wp1306.pdf.

Osofsky, Joy D., Michael Rovaris, Jill Hayes Hammer, Amy Dickson, Nancy Freeman, and Katherine Aucoin. 2004. "Working with Police to Help Children Exposed to Violence." *Journal of Community Psychology* 32(5): 593–606.

Passel, Jeffrey S., and D'Vera Cohn. 2011. *Unauthorized Immigrant Population: National and State Trends, 2010*. Washington, D.C.: Pew Hispanic Center.

Phillips, Julie A., and Douglas S. Massey. 1999. "The New Labor Market: Immigrants and Wages After IRCA." *Demography* 36(2): 233–46.

Reichert, Joshua, and Douglas S. Massey. 1979. "Patterns of US Migration from a Mexican Sending Community: A Comparison of Legal and Illegal Migrants." *International Migration Review* 13(4): 599–623.

———. 1980. "History and Trends in US Bound Migration from a Mexican Town." *International Migration Review* 14(4): 475–91.

Shierholz, Heidi. 2014. "Six Years from Its Beginning, the Great Recession's Shadow Looms over the Labor Market." Issue Brief no. 374. Washington, D.C.: Economic Policy Institute. Accessed November 4, 2016. http://www.epi.org/publication/years-beginning-great-recessions-shadow/.

Sisk, Blake, and Katharine M. Donato. 2017. "Weathering the Storm? The Great Recession and the Employment Status Transitions of Low-Skill Male Immigrant Workers in the United States." *International Migration Review* 51(2) (June). DOI: 10.1111/imre.12260.

Stark, Oded, and J. Edward Taylor. 1991. "Migration Incentives, Migration Types: The Role of Relative Deprivation." *Economic Journal* 101(408): 1163–78.

Tucker, Christine M., Pilar Torres-Pereda, Alexandra M. Minnis, and Sergio A. Bautista-Arredondo. 2013. "Migration Decision-Making Among Mexican Youth Individual, Family, and Community Influences." *Hispanic Journal of Behavioral Sciences* 35(1): 61–84.

Tuckman, Jo. 2015. "Mexico Ayotzinapa Massacre:

New Theory suggests Illicit Cargo Motivated Attack." *The Guardian*, September 23. Accessed November 4, 2016, http://www.theguardian.com/world/2015/sep/23/mexico-bush-ambush-43-missing-students-new-report.

United Nations High Commissioner for Refugees (UNHCR). 2014. *Children on the Run: Unaccompanied Children Leaving Central America and Mexico and the Need for International Protection*. Washington, D.C.: UNHCR. Accessed November 4, 2016. http://www.unhcrwashington.org/sites/default/files/1_UAC_Children%20On%20the%20Run_Executive%20Summary.pdf.

U.S. Customs and Border Protection. 2015. "Southwest Border Unaccompanied Alien Children Statistics FY 2015." Accessed November 4, 2016. http://www.cbp.gov/newsroom/stats/southwest-border-unaccompanied-children/fy-2015.

Villarreal, Andres. 2014. "Explaining the Decline in Mexico-U.S. Migration: The Effect of the Great Recession." *Demography* 51(6): 2003–28.

Warren, Robert. 2016. "US Undocumented Population Drops Below 11 Million in 2014, with Continued Declines in the Mexican Undocumented Population." *Journal on Migration and Human Security* 4(1): 1–15. Accessed November 4, 2016. http://jmhs.cmsny.org/index.php/jmhs/article/view/58.

World Bank. 2006. *World Development Report 2007: Development and the Next Generation*. Washington, D.C.: The World Bank. Accessed November 4, 2016. http://www-wds.worldbank.org/external/default/WDSContentServer/IW3P/IB/2006/09/13/000112742_20060913111024/Rendered/PDF/359990WDR0complete.pdf.

———. 2015. "Mexico: Overview." Accessed November 4, 2016. http://www.worldbank.org/en/country/mexico/overview.

Parental Legal Status and the Political Engagement of Second-Generation Mexican Americans

SUSAN K. BROWN AND ALEJANDRA JAZMIN SANCHEZ

This paper invokes a theoretical model of immigrant membership exclusion to assess the political integration of second-generation Mexican Americans. Specifically, we examine the extent to which the migration status of parents, especially mothers, is associated with the political engagement, community engagement, and voting registration of their adult offspring. In each type of engagement, respondents whose mothers have remained unauthorized show lower overall levels of political incorporation. The effect is indirect in that it is mediated by the respondents' educational level, in keeping with prior research showing that persistent unauthorized status by mothers reduces the years of schooling of children. This study thus contributes to the literature finding that the unauthorized status of parents has repercussions for the overall integration of their offspring.

Keywords: unauthorized migration, membership exclusion, political integration

A substantial body of research on U.S. immigration covering the last thirty years shows the harmful consequences of unauthorized status for immigrants and the benefits of legalization (see, for example, Bean et al. 2014; Fussell 2011; Gleeson and Gonzales 2012; Kossoudji and Cobb-Clark 2000; Massey 2013; Orrenius and Zavodny 2012). A more recent literature based largely on qualitative research finds negative effects of unauthorized status on children, including on their cognitive and emotional development (Gonzales 2015; Yoshikawa 2011). Even more recently, data show the depressing effects on adult offspring of long-term unauthorized status of parents (Bean, Brown, and Bachmeier 2015). The effects of unauthorized status probably have grown since the late twentieth century because of public derision and strong sanctions from authorities (Chavez 2008; Massey and Pren 2012). Drawing on this literature, a new immigrant-integration perspective known as *membership exclusion* holds that legal status operates as a critical first stage of the integration of immigrant groups (Bean and Brown 2014; Bean, Brown, and Bachmeier 2015; Brown and Bean 2016). Without the early political membership afforded by legal status, immigrants may adapt socioculturally but often be hamstrung by structural barriers when attempting to advance socioeconomically.

Susan K. Brown is professor of sociology at the University of California, Irvine. **Alejandra Jazmin Sanchez** graduated magna cum laude with bachelor's degrees in education sciences and sociology and received a teaching credential at the University of California, Irvine.

© 2017 Russell Sage Foundation. Brown, Susan K., and Alejandra Jazmin Sanchez. 2017. "Parental Legal Status and the Political Engagement of Second-Generation Mexican Americans." *RSF: The Russell Sage Foundation Journal of the Social Sciences* 3(4): 136–47. DOI: 10.7758/RSF.2017.3.4.08. We thank workshop organizers Roberto G. Gonzales and Steven Raphael, other workshop participants, and Frank D. Bean for helpful comments. Direct correspondence to: Susan K. Brown at skbrown@uci.edu, Department of Sociology, University of California, 3151 Social Science Plaza, Irvine, CA 92697–5100; and Alejandra Jazmin Sanchez at alejanjs@uci.edu.

With legal status, however, immigrants and their children show substantial mobility.

This paper assesses whether the membership-exclusion perspective applies to the political engagement of the adult offspring of Mexican immigrants and, if so, whether the effect of influence operates directly or through other factors. To our knowledge, research has not yet addressed how parents' legal status affects children's political engagement and the potential for children's political incorporation. Insofar as legal status is a necessary precursor to political incorporation, its absence would be expected to affect the second generation's engagement in politics through voting, activism, and even awareness of issues, all of which are later stages in the political integration process (Hochschild and Mollenkopf 2009). We argue that this first step of legalization is necessary to achieving many types of political engagement, not only in the first generation but also in the second.

We test the membership-exclusion perspective on the offspring of Mexican immigrants because Mexicans are a plurality of all immigrants and slightly more than half of all undocumented U.S. immigrants. In 2010, Mexico accounted for 29 percent of the foreign-born population (Passel, Cohn, and Gonzalez-Barrera 2012). Despite a steep decline in Mexican migration since the Great Recession, the total number of unauthorized Mexicans in the United States by 2012 was still about 5.9 million, 52 percent of all unauthorized residents. More than 27 percent of these live in one state—California (Gonzalez-Barrera and Krogstad 2015).

POLITICAL INCORPORATION AND ENGAGEMENT

Broadly, political incorporation involves the extent to which immigrants have been integrated into a host country's political processes and structures. The earliest form of political incorporation is the legal right to remain in a nation; the most advanced form is the ability to influence government policies, especially by holding high political office (Hochschild and Mollenkopf 2009). Because political incorporation is both a process and an outcome, it is a challenge to define, let alone operationalize (Minnite 2009). Political incorporation manifests itself in degrees along a continuum, beginning with legalization and naturalization, advancing to participation in nonelectoral and electoral forms of politics, and ending when the immigrant group participates in the formulation and implementation of government policies (Jones-Correa 2005; Minnite 2009). As new citizens demonstrate high levels of civic engagement, they begin to influence policy and move toward such higher forms of political activity as running for elective office (Jones-Correa 2005).

Jennifer Hochschild and John Mollenkopf present both rudimentary and full models of immigrant political incorporation (2009). To achieve full political incorporation, the children of immigrants must follow a necessary progression: first entry into (or birth in) the host country, then entry into membership, then involvement in the political arena, and finally responsiveness to and from the political system. The form of entry into the host country should prove critical to later political participation because entry into membership is necessary though not sufficient for many of the later steps. Many factors may mitigate the effect of form of entry and the attainment of membership on political participation. For example, participation depends on knowledge of politics, which may be limited even among native-born citizens. For example, in 2011, a national survey of thirty thousand Americans found that only 50 percent could name all three branches of government (Lee 2012). In general, whites, males and older, financially more secure citizens are more likely to have solid knowledge about national politics, and education remains the single most powerful predictor of political knowledge (Delli Carpini and Keeter 1996). Thus, any examination of how parental legal status affects the political engagement of offspring should also examine the effects of such factors, especially education.

UNAUTHORIZED MIGRANTS AND THEIR CHILDREN

In 2010, an estimated 5.5 million children in the United States had at least one unauthorized parent. Of these children, an estimated 4.5 million were born in the United States and have birthright citizenship (Passel and Cohn 2011). A growing literature on the children of unauthorized parents suggests that parents' legal status powerfully affects children from young ages on because parents may be less likely to access the sorts of public programs, health services, and subsidies available to low-income families (Berk and Schur 2001; Castañeda and Melo 2015). Hirokazu Yoshikawa describes how the stress of precarious finances and fear of deportation exacerbate parental stress and depression to the detriment of children's development of language and cognitive skills (2011). Leisy Abrego argues that children of one or two undocumented parents commonly fear separation from their parents (2014a). Roberto Gonzales shows how youths have to learn to be illegal and how they feel they must hide their unauthorized status and isolate themselves, thereby reducing their educational opportunities (2011).

In particular, educational deficits may restrict the mobility of even legal or citizen offspring. Frank Bean, Susan Brown, and James Bachmeier assess the degree to which the legal status of parents (particularly mothers) affects the success and overall integration of Mexican American immigrant children in the 1.5 and second generations. Long-term unauthorized status among mothers limits the integration of offspring across multiple structural dimensions, such as education, income, and neighborhood attainment (2015). Children of authorized mothers average slightly more than thirteen years of schooling, and those whose mothers are unauthorized average a year and a quarter less—or the difference between not finishing high school and attaining some college (Bean et al. 2011). The long-term unauthorized status of mothers also negatively influences linguistic integration, a key factor in determining other kinds of integration (Bean, Brown, and Bachmeier 2015). Although such findings highlight the effects of mothers' legal status on integration across several dimensions, analyses have not yet been extended to examining effects on the political integration of the next generation.

The literature on the political effects of unauthorized status is sparse. The low socioeconomic status and difficult lives of most unauthorized Mexican immigrant parents would suggest that they would be relatively unengaged politically, and, of course, their status forecloses their possibility of voting. Moreover, parents pass their political proclivities on to their children (Verba, Schlozman, and Brady 1995; Vecchione and Caprara 2009). Yet for undocumented parents, the causal direction can be reversed given that children may provide a bridge to political or civic institutions (see Bloemraad and Trost 2008; Waters and Pineau 2015). Still, the increased vulnerability of unauthorized families and their lack of sense of belonging may undermine the potential for offspring to influence their parents (Abrego 2014b; Getrich 2008). Moreover, because education is related to political engagement, a lack of education among the children of unauthorized parents may mediate their potential to become more politically integrated.

MEMBERSHIP EXCLUSION

Membership exclusion is a theoretical perspective about how lack of initial societal membership, reinforced by institutional and organizational factors, limits the structural integration of immigrants and their children (Bean, Brown, and Bachmeier 2015; Brown and Bean 2016). Societal membership refers to both legal and social citizenship, the latter elaborated by T. H. Marshall to argue that social citizenship involves access to political, civil, and social rights (1950). Thus, societal membership refers not only to legal status but also to a much broader sense of membership. Membership exclusion underscores the signature role that the absence of societal membership may play in the integration process.

Immigration exemplifies the idea of societal membership, because newcomers are often excluded to varying degrees, with those subject to the most exclusion being most hindered in their integration (Bean et al. 2012; Koopmans 2010; Nee and Holbrow 2013). As a result, the integration of the unauthorized and their offspring may be slow and incomplete, even after three generations (Bean, Brown, and Bachmeier 2015). Some scholars have noted the potential negative effects of lack of membership (Hondagneu-Sotelo 1994; Waldinger 2013). Other research, however, emphasizes that even though integration is multidimensional, structural integration is contingent on basic legal and societal membership (Bean et al. 2012; Bean, Brown, and Bachmeier 2015; Bean and Brown 2014; Brown and Bean 2016). For example, many (though not all) forms of political integration depend on societal membership, not least because voting is generally restricted to citizens. Particularly when boundaries are formalized in law, those immigrants who fall outside of them not only face persistent stigmatization and marginalization, they are also ineligible for many forms of structural participation, and the likelihood is that the effects spill over into the next generation.

RESEARCH QUESTIONS

In this paper, we examine at the individual level how the earliest form of immigrant political incorporation (legal status) relates to later forms in the next generation. In other words, does having one or two unauthorized parents influence the desire and ability of offspring to participate in organizations that have political influence and to vote? Evidence of effects of unauthorized status on the political incorporation of the next generation would lend support for the concept of membership exclusion, which highlights the crucial role initial political membership may have on the integration process. We are less interested in examining the adult individual-level correlates of political behavior, because these are limited depending on whether migrants and their families have legal status. Rather, we are interested in the consequences of earliest form of political membership, legal status, on the political variables involving the second generation. For us, the key independent variable is *parental* legal status, because membership exclusion holds that the long-term absence of legal status undercuts the ability of offspring to integrate across multiple structural dimensions regardless of a child's status. Certainly, an unauthorized adult unable to attain even the temporary protection of Deferred Action for Childhood Arrivals faces more challenges than legalized siblings, but the disadvantages of parental unauthorized status affect all children.

The analysis below thus examines how parents' legal status influences children's political engagement, broadly defined. Guided by the tenets of membership exclusion and the findings of research, we limit our focus to mother's legal status, which has more effect than father's status on both sons and daughters across such dimensions of integration as education, income and neighborhood attainment (Bean et al. 2011; Bean, Brown, and Bachmeier 2015). Given previous research emphasizing the impact of parents' legal status, we first hypothesize that mother's authorization status is related to the political outcomes of offspring.

If indeed we find that mother's long-term legal status affects the political integration of offspring, the next question of interest is to examine the potential mechanisms. The effect can be direct, in that if parents remain unengaged politically because their migration status makes them wary, their offspring may also hesitate to participate, even though the children are often citizens.

Immigrants with unauthorized status live in "the shadow of the law" and are denied the "set of rights an individual has by virtue of belonging to a national community" (Menjívar 2006, 1032). Even when granted residency or work permits, immigrants remain in a state of "legal limbo," experiencing "liminal legality"— suspended legality under which immigrants may secure temporary statuses but can "easily slip back into the realm of nonlegality" (Menjívar 2006, 1008). Unauthorized immigrants often take extreme measures to avoid deportation, by confining themselves as much as possible to the safety of their homes (Chavez 1998). The children of unauthorized mothers, having never seen their parents participate in politics, might withdraw from the political arena. They might view the U.S. government as unresponsive to the needs of their group and, consequently, might be pessimistic about the influence their political involvement could have. In such a case, parents' legal status would have a direct effect on children's political involvement.

Alternatively, because education and income are positively related to political engagement, the effect on offspring of parental unauthorized status may be indirect. That is, it may keep children from maximizing their socioeconomic potential and thus probably lower their socioeconomic status and political engagement. This hypothesis maintains that other factors may mediate the effect of unauthorized mothers. Political incorporation is often affected by a variety of factors, including income and education. Unauthorized immigrants' vulnerability to deportation, low-wage employment and lack of access to public amenities may reduce their socioeconomic status relative to families with authorized backgrounds. Because children of unauthorized mothers receive less schooling than their counterparts, the effect of an unauthorized mother on political participation could be mediated by education (Delli Carpini and Keeter 1996).

DATA AND MEASURES

This analysis uses data from a survey called Immigration and Intergenerational Mobility in Metropolitan Los Angeles, or IIMMLA (Rumbaut et al. 2004). Conducted in 2004 by telephone, IIMMLA covered the five-county metropolitan area of Los Angeles, included 4,780 respondents, and was designed to parallel a previous study also supported by the Russell Sage Foundation, the Immigrant Second Generation in New York. The goal behind both studies was to see how the offspring of recent immigrants across multiple groups fare in the different contexts of Los Angeles and New York, the two cities in the United States with the largest immigrant populations. With its more than 6.5 million residents of Mexican origin, Los Angeles is the preeminent site for studying Mexican American integration (Ruggles et al. 2010). Respondents were asked about their basic demographic information, sociocultural orientation, economic mobility, geographic mobility, and civic and political engagement. The survey targeted the 1.5 and second generations among the area's six largest immigrant groups—Mexicans, Central Americans (Salvadoran and Guatemalan), Vietnamese, Filipinos, Koreans, and Chinese—along with a catch-all group of other immigrants. It also targeted the third and higher generations of Mexican Americans, non-Hispanic whites, and blacks. Respondent ages were limited to between twenty and forty because for most immigrant groups arriving in the United States after 1965, the second generation was still in young adulthood. This study examines only the 1.5 and second generations of Mexican Americans, all of whom were accessed through random-digit dialing.

One of the distinctive characteristics of the IIMMLA study is the retrospective information obtained on the legal and citizenship status of the respondents' parents, both when they first entered the United States and at the time of the interview. This information has been used to estimate status trajectories on migration, legalization, and citizenship jointly for each parent of the respondents, as well as respondents themselves (Bean et al. 2011; Bean, Brown, and Bachmeier 2015). This analysis uses the actual combinations of parental trajectories developed through latent-class analysis (Bean et al. 2011). The measure is based on the findings that initial unauthorized status matters less to children's outcomes than whether that unauthorized status persists, and that the combinations of parents' trajectories shape children's lives. Although the data do not permit determination of exactly how long parents remained in unauthorized status, the timing of the survey suggests that many of the parents of respondents in the IIMMLA survey would have been eligible to legalize under provisions of the Immigration Reform and Control Act of 1986.

Apart from allowing the creation of combinations for parents' legal status trajectories, the IIMMLA survey also included an abundance of data derived from respondents' answers to questions regarding political attitudes, electoral behavior, and community involvement, thus allowing us to tap into the respondents' level of civic engagement. Our analysis involves indicators of political behaviors, attitudes, and community involvement. We combine three of the behavioral indicators into an index after preliminary principal components analysis (not shown) suggested that they tapped into a latent factor. Questions on voting, political knowledge, and community involvement represent different dimensions and are therefore included separately. The questions are as follows:

> In the past twelve months, have you contacted a government office about a problem or to get help or information either by telephone or email or in person; attended any

political meetings, rallies, speeches, or dinners in support of a political candidate; taken part in any form of protest, such as picketing, a march, demonstration or boycott?

Do you strongly agree, somewhat agree, somewhat disagree, or strongly disagree with the following statement: I have a pretty good understanding of the important political issues facing our country?

Do you belong to any community organizations, work-related organizations, sports teams, or other nonreligious organizations?

Are you registered to vote in the precinct where you now live, are you registered to vote somewhere else, or are you not registered to vote?

On the understanding question, any kind of agreement was coded as a 1; any disagreement was coded as 0 to avoid variation in respondents' self-perception and their interpretation of what it means to have a "good understanding." On the registration question, any form of registration was coded as a 1, not registered as 0. The latter question was asked only of respondents who reported being naturalized or born in the United States, so the sample size for this question is smaller.

RESULTS

Because authorization status has such a powerful impact on the immigrant experience in the United States, the children of long-term unauthorized mothers have lower socioeconomic status than their counterparts. For example, the average annual household income of respondents with an unauthorized mother was about $17,000 less than those with an authorized mother, a statistically significant difference (see table 1). In addition, respondents with an unauthorized mother tend to be much less educated, completing an average of 11.1 years of schooling, than their counterparts with an authorized mother, who attain an average of 13.3 years. Unauthorized parents themselves also tend to have less education. Authorized mothers received an average of 8.8 years, and unauthorized mothers an average of seven. Similarly, fathers coupled with authorized mothers received a mean 8.7 years, and their counterparts coupled with unauthorized mothers had 7.7. Relatively few respondents appear to be themselves unauthorized. Using the strictest interpretation of who might be unauthorized based on a series of questions about auspices of entry and changes in visa status, we estimate that fifty-five respondents in the 1.5 generation are unauthorized, and that the correlation between authorized status of mother and offspring appears to be 0.49. In this sample, 34.5 percent of the respondents were 1.5 generation, who came to the United States before age fourteen, as opposed to the second generation, members of which were born in the United States. However, the 1.5 generation is disproportionately represented among those whose mothers remained unauthorized. More than 65 percent of the respondents whose mothers remained unauthorized were 1.5 generation, whereas only 28.8 percent were among those with legalized or citizen mothers.

On indicators of political behaviors, respondents with authorized mothers scored significantly higher than those with unauthorized mothers in every category of political behavior: participating in a protest, attending a political gathering, and contacting government. In addition, respondents with authorized mothers were more likely to report good political understanding and to belong to a community organization, suggesting more general engagement as well. In voting registration, respondents with authorized mothers were significantly more likely than those with unauthorized mothers to be registered. However, active participation in political behaviors is relatively rare, ranging from 6.6 percent of all respondents attending a political gathering to 25.1 percent contacting government. Fewer than 15 percent belong to a community organization. Political understanding and voter registration are far more common: 80.1 percent of citizen respondents reported that they had registered.

Table 2 regresses political behaviors, civic engagement, and political understanding on mothers' and respondents' legal status, respondents' nativity, parents' and respondents' education level, and respondents' household income. Respondents' age and gender are also

Table 1. Means and Standard Deviations, Respondent Characteristics

	Mothers Authorized		Mothers Unauthorized		All	
	Mean	SD	Mean	SD	Mean	SD
Independent variables						
Age	28.1	6.0	28.3	5.9	28.1	6.0
Women (percent of sample)	51.5	50.0	46.0	50.0	50.7	50.0
1.5 generation (percent of sample)	28.8	45.3	67.7***	46.9	34.5	47.6
Father's education (in years)	8.7	4.1	7.7*	4.0	8.5	4.1
Mother's education (in years)	8.8	3.8	7.0***	3.6	8.5	3.8
Education (in years)	13.3	2.1	11.1***	3.1	13.0	2.4
Household income	$46,664	43,072	$29,254***	32,682	$44,106	42,168
Dependent variables	%	SD	%	SD	%	SD
Political behaviors						
Attended political gathering	7.6	26.5	2.1*	14.3	6.6	24.9
Participated in protest	14.0	35.7	8.8†	28.4	13.0	33.7
Contacted government	26.7	44.2	17.6*	38.2	25.1	43.4
Good political understanding	87.0	33.7	77.0**	42.2	85.2	35.5
Belong to community organization	16.8	37.4	4.4***	20.6	14.6	35.3
Registered voter	80.9	40.2	71.1†	45.4	80.1	40.0
N	720		124		844	

Source: Authors' compilation based on IIMMLA 2004.
Note: Significance levels refer to differences between respondents with authorized mothers and unauthorized mothers. Household income is presented as a 5 percent trimmed mean.
†$p < .1$; *$p < .05$; **$p < .01$; ***$p < .001$

controlled, though results are not shown. Model 1 shows the effect of mother's legal status for each of three dependent variables. In each case, having a mother who remained unauthorized is negatively related to engaging in any form of political behavior, belonging to a community organization, or a sense of having a good understanding of politics. For example, those whose mothers were unauthorized were more than 70 percent less likely than those with legal mothers to belong to a community organization. They were less than half as likely to say they had a good understanding of politics.

Being foreign born (that is, in the 1.5 generation) accounts for a small part of the disadvantage among respondents in political engagement, as model 2 shows. Respondents who are foreign born are likely to have less overall family exposure to the U.S. political system. For the political behavior and understanding variables, foreign birth has a negative effect apart from mother's legal status. Still, the question remains whether the respondents themselves are unauthorized. Model 2 also examines whether the respondent's legal status has an independent effect on political behavior and understanding. In none of these cases is the result significant. Despite failing to achieve significance, the coefficients for attending protests (the realm of the disenfranchised) and expressing understanding of politics are positive for unauthorized respondents, suggesting perhaps a tendency for those who grew up in the United States to be less likely to remain in the shadows. Nevertheless, the lack of a significant result suggests strongly that it is mothers' legal status—which remains a significantly depressing effect on the political engagement and understanding of offspring—more than the respondents' own status that influences their political behaviors.

The story changes in model 3 for all three dependent variables. These models control for the education of the respondents and their parents as well as respondents' income. Respon-

Table 2. Regression of Political Behaviors and Understanding, Mexican Americans, Ages Twenty to Forty

	Model 1	Model 2	Model 3
Index of attending political gathering, participating in protest, and/or contacting government			
Mother unauthorized	-0.527**	-0.409*	-0.151
1.5 generation		-0.318**	-0.218†
Respondent unauthorized		0.006	0.187
Father's education			0.005
Mother's education			0.021*
R's education			0.170***
R's household income (000s)			-0.001
Intercept	-0.702***	-0.620***	-3.157***
χ^2	10.30**	17.73**	72.79***
N	839	839	839
Belong to community organization			
Mother unauthorized	-1.261**	-0.940*	-0.599
1.5 generation		-0.125	0.126
Respondent unauthorized		-1.646	-1.363
Father's education			0.000
Mother's education			0.032
R's education			0.196***
R's household income (000s)			0.007**
Intercept	-2.379***	-2.304***	-5.131***
χ^2	22.39***	27.31***	69.77***
N	843	843	843
Good understanding of politics			
Mother unauthorized	-0.814**	-0.693*	-0.245
1.5 generation		-0.598**	-0.420†
Respondent unauthorized		0.350	0.508
Father's education			-0.014
Mother's education			0.014
R's education			0.164**
R's household income (000s)			0.012**
Intercept	1.189*	1.21*	-1.319
χ^2	22.01***	28.79***	57.69***
N	837	837	837

Source: Authors' compilation based on IIMMLA 2004.
Note: All models also control for respondent's age and gender. Index is run using negative binomial regression. Other variables use logistic regression.
†$p < .1$; *$p < .05$; **$p < .01$; ***$p < .001$

dents' education far and away influences their political and civic engagement. Each additional year of education raises the likelihood of belonging to a community organization by nearly 22 percent. It raises the likelihood of expressing a good understanding of politics by nearly 18 percent. It is far more important than parents' education and even more important than household income, which has no effect on political behavior but a significant one on

Table 3. Logistic Regression of Voting Registration, Mexican Americans, Ages Twenty to Forty

	Model 1	Model 2	Model 3
Mother unauthorized	−0.735*	−0.695*	−0.262
1.5 generation		−0.480†	−0.486†
Respondent unauthorized		N/A	N/A
Father's education			−0.040
Mother's education			0.021
R's education			0.368***
R's household income (000s)			0.003
Intercept	−0.802	−0.920	−5.510***
χ^2	30.55***	33.96***	79.56***
N	677	677	677

Source: Authors' compilation based on IIMMLA 2004.
Note: All models also control for respondent's age and gender.
†$p < .1$; *$p < .05$; **$p < .01$; ***$p < .001$

belonging to a community organization and expressing a good understanding of politics. Respondents' achieved status also attenuates the effect of mothers' legal status, suggesting that education is a strong mediating variable. The children of unauthorized mothers get less schooling, and this lack is strongly related to their lack of political involvement. These findings suggest that the effect of mothers' unauthorized status on political behaviors, civic engagement, and political understanding is indirect, operating mainly by suppressing the level of the child's education.

Table 3 regresses voting registration on the same sets of predictors. The sample size for this regression is smaller because the question about voter registration was asked only of those who were eligible to vote, that is, citizens. The results are similar to those found in table 2. Having a persistently unauthorized mother dampens the likelihood that offspring who are citizens will register to vote, in this case by more than half, as the exponentiated version of the coefficient in model 1 shows. Very little of the effect of mother's legal status is related to the respondent's generation, as model 2 shows. However, naturalized citizens are marginally less likely to register to vote than the native-born second generation. Again, the education of the respondent becomes the critical factor relating to voter registration, as shown in model 3. Each additional year of schooling raises the chances by 44 percent that a respondent will register to vote, mostly regardless of income. Registering to vote is fairly late-stage type of political incorporation, inaccessible to those who have not yet attained citizenship, regardless of their education. Yet the results show the same pattern that education mediates the effect of mother's unauthorized status on respondent's voter registration. Foreign birth still marginally drives down the chances of registering to vote, probably as a result of less family exposure to U.S. politics. Nevertheless, net of education, parents' unauthorized status does not affect the chances of their offspring registering to vote.

DISCUSSION AND CONCLUSION

This paper provides what we believe is the first examination of how unauthorized status of parents may limit the overall political integration of offspring. Across all indicators, mothers' lack of legal status does indeed negatively influence offspring's political engagement. The results consistently show that having an unauthorized mother is significantly and negatively associated among offspring with a lack of political engagement or understanding and a lack of community involvement and voter registration. Such a consistent finding provides support for the provisions of the membership-exclusion hypothesis. The results confirm the significant role legalization plays in the political integration of immigrant children. In this case, though, the legalization of parents matters more than that of respondents, because even the citizen children of unauthorized migrants are handicapped by their parents' status.

Second, across all the tested forms of political incorporation, the effect of mothers' legal status is indirect and mediated by respondents' education. It is not the mothers' liminal legal status that influences the children's political engagement so much as the structural limitations such liminality imposes on children's mobility, limitations such as lack of access to education and better opportunities. Indeed, previous research has shown that parents' legal status may limit the overall integration of offspring in several dimensions: childhood development, education, income, neighborhood, and language (Bean, Brown, and Bachmeier 2015; Yoshikawa 2011).

The question of whether any effect of unauthorized parental status is direct or indirect is important for the policy implications. This indirect effect suggests that much of the political integration of the children of immigrants relates to socioeconomic mobility, so that more opportunities for the offspring of unauthorized immigrants may encourage greater political involvement on their part. The literature on political engagement has long stressed the critical impact of education. The children of unauthorized mothers remain disadvantaged in many respects, particularly in terms of education, compared with their counterparts whose parents have legalized or naturalized (Bean, Brown, and Bachmeier 2015).

These results also support the perspective of membership exclusion, which emphasizes how the formal lack of societal membership adversely influences integration. In this analysis, respondents with authorized mothers, on average, showed greater political engagement on every indicator. Other studies examining dimensions of mobility have found that educational attainment is directly affected by parents' legal status and that forms of mobility that are related to education, such as neighborhood attainment, are thus only indirectly related to parents' migration status (Bean, Brown, and Bachmeier 2015). This study provides further evidence of such an indirect effect, this time on political aspects of integration. Further work may examine more attitudes toward the political process, such as belief in the efficacy of government.

The results of this study show that children of unauthorized mothers, children who are overwhelmingly citizens or legal immigrants, are less likely to be politically engaged than those with authorized mothers. Basic social membership of immigrant parents is necessary for better structural integration of the next generation. These findings matter for policy. The most straightforward policy to encourage greater political participation among the children of immigrants would be to enable unauthorized migrants to find a pathway to legalization. Without immigration reform, a greater proportion of unauthorized working parents will remain in the shadows than of their predecessors who arrived in the United States in the 1960s and 1970s. The persistence of their unauthorized status will affect their children, even though many of those children may be citizens themselves. Reasonable pathways that are neither difficult nor punitive will enable the children of the unauthorized to realize their political voice as well as their potential in other arenas of public and private life.

REFERENCES

Abrego, Leisy J. 2014a. "Latino Immigrants' Diverse Experience of 'Illegality.'" In *Constructing Immigrant "Illegality": Critiques, Experiences, and Responses*, edited by Cecilia Menjívar and Daniel Kanstroom. New York: Cambridge University Press.

———. 2014b. *Sacrificing Families: Navigating Laws, Labor, and Love Across Borders.* Stanford, Calif.: Stanford University Press.

Bean, Frank D., James A. Bachmeier, Susan K. Brown, Jennifer Van Hook, and Mark A. Leach. 2014. "Unauthorized Mexican Migration and the Socioeconomic Integration of Mexican Americans." In *Diversity and Disparities: America Enters a New Century*, edited by John R. Logan. New York: Russell Sage Foundation. Accessed November 25, 2016. https://www.russellsage.org/publications/diversity-and-disparities.

Bean, Frank D., and Susan K. Brown. 2014. "Demographic Analyses of Immigration." In *Migration Theory: Talking Across Disciplines*, 3rd ed., edited by Caroline Brettell and James P. Hollifield. New York: Routledge.

Bean, Frank D., Susan K. Brown, and James D. Bachmeier. 2015. *Parents Without Papers: The Progress and Pitfalls of Mexican-American Integration*. New York: Russell Sage Foundation.

Bean, Frank D., Susan K. Brown, James D. Bachmeier, Tineke Fokkema, and Laurence Lessard-Phillips. 2012. "The Dimensions and Degree of Second-Generation Incorporation in U.S. and European Cities: A Comparative Study of Inclusion and Exclusion." *International Journal of Comparative Sociology* 53(3): 181–209.

Bean, Frank D., Mark A. Leach, Susan K. Brown, James D. Bachmeier, and John R. Hipp. 2011. "The Educational Legacy of Unauthorized Migration: Comparisons Across U.S.-Immigrant Groups in How Parents' Status Affects Their Offspring." *International Migration Review* 45(2): 348–85.

Berk, Marc L., and Claudia L. Schur. 2001. "The Effect of Fear on Access to Care Among Undocumented Latino Immigrants." *Journal of Immigrant Health* 3(3): 151–56.

Bloemraad, Irene, and Christine Trost. 2008. "It's a Family Affair: Intergenerational Mobilization in the Spring 2006 Protests." *American Behavioral Scientist* 52(4): 507–32.

Brown, Susan K., and Frank D. Bean. 2016. "Migration Status and Political Knowledge Among Latino Immigrants." *RSF: The Russell Sage Foundation Journal of the Social Sciences* 2(3): 22–41.

Castañeda, Heide, and Milena Andrea Melo. 2015. "Health Care Access for Latino Mixed-Status Families: Barriers, Strategies, and Implications for Reform." *American Behavioral Scientist* 58(14): 1891–909.

Chavez, Leo R. 1998. *Shadowed Lives: Undocumented Immigrants in American Society*, 2nd ed. Stamford, Conn.: Thomson Learning.

———. 2008. *The Latino Threat: Constructing Immigrants, Citizens, and the Nation*. Stanford, Calif.: Stanford University Press.

Delli Carpini, Michael X., and Scott Keeter. 1996. *What Americans Know About Politics and Why It Matters*. New Haven, Conn.: Yale University Press.

Fussell, Elizabeth. 2011. "The Deportation Threat Dynamic and Victimization of Latino Migrants: Wage Theft and Robbery." *Sociological Quarterly* 52(4): 593–615.

Getrich, Christina M. 2008. "Negotiating Boundaries of Social Belonging: Second-Generation Mexican Youth and the Immigrant Rights Protests of 2006." *American Behavioral Scientist* 52(4): 533–56.

Gleeson, Shannon, and Roberto G. Gonzales. 2012. "When Do Papers Matter? An Institutional Analysis of Undocumented Life in the United States." *International Migration* 50(4): 1–19.

Gonzales, Roberto G. 2011. "Learning to Be Illegal: Undocumented Youth and Shifting Legal Contexts in the Transition to Adulthood." *American Sociological Review* 76(4): 602–19.

———. 2015. *Lives in Limbo: Undocumented and Coming of Age in America*. Berkeley: University of California Press.

Gonzalez-Barrera, Ana, and Jens Manual Krogstad. 2015. "What We Know About Illegal Immigration from Mexico." Washington, D.C. Pew Research Center, July 15. Accessed September 11, 2015. http://www.pewresearch.org/fact-tank/2015/07/15/what-we-know-about-illegal-immigration-from-mexico/.

Hochschild, Jennifer L., and John H. Mollenkopf. 2009. *Bringing Outsiders In: Transatlantic Perspectives on Immigrant Political Incorporation*. Ithaca, N.Y.: Cornell University Press.

Hondagneu-Sotelo, Pierrette. 1994. *Gendered Transitions: Mexican Experiences of Immigration*. Berkeley: University of California Press.

Jones-Correa, Michael. 2005. "Bringing Outsiders In: Questions of Immigrant Incorporation." In *The Politics of Democratic Inclusion*, edited by C. Wolbrecht and R. E. Hero. Philadelphia, Pa.: Temple University Press.

Koopmans, Ruud. 2010. "Trade-Offs Between Equality and Difference: Immigrant Integration, Multiculturalism and the Welfare State in Cross-National Perspective." *Journal of Ethnic and Migration Studies* 36(1): 1–26.

Kossoudji, Sherrie A., and Deborah A. Cobb-Clark. 2000. "IRCA's Impact on the Occupational Concentration and Mobility of Newly-Legalized Mexican Men." *Journal of Population Economics* 13(1): 81–98.

Lee, Ann. 2012. *What the U.S. Can Learn from China: An Open Minded Guide to Treating Our Greatest*

Competitor as Our Greatest Teacher. San Francisco: Berrett-Koehler.

Marshall, T. H. 1950. *Citizenship and Social Class and Other Essays*. Cambridge: Cambridge University Press.

Massey, Douglas S. 2013. "America's Immigration Policy Fiasco: Learning from Past Mistakes." *Daedalus* 142(3): 5–15.

Massey, Douglas S., and Karen A. Pren. 2012. "Origins of the New Latino Underclass." *Race and Social Problems* 4(1): 5–17.

Menjívar, Cecilia. 2006. "Liminal Legality: Salvadoran and Guatemalan Immigrants' Lives in the United States." *American Journal of Sociology* 111(4): 999–1037.

Minnite, Lorraine C. 2009. "Lost in Translation? A Critical Reappraisal of the Concept of Immigrant Political Incorporation." In *Bringing Outsiders In: Transatlantic Perspectives on Immigrant Political Incorporation*, edited by Jennifer L. Hochschild and John H. Mollenkopf. Ithaca, N.Y.: Cornell University Press.

Nee, Victor, and Hilary Holbrow. 2013. "Why Asian Americans Are Becoming Mainstream." *Daedalus* 142(3): 65–75.

Orrenius, Pia M., and Madeline Zavodny. 2012. "The Economic Consequences of Amnesty for Unauthorized Immigrants." *Cato Journal* 32(1): 85–106.

Passel, Jeffrey S., and D'Vera Cohn. 2011. "Unauthorized Immigrant Population: National and State Trends, 2010." *Pew Research Center, Hispanic Trends*. Accessed March 24, 2015. http://www.pewhispanic.org/2011/02/01/unauthorized-immigrant-population-brnational-and-state-trends-2010/.

Passel, Jeffrey S., D'Vera Cohn, and Ana Gonzalez-Barrera. 2012. "Characteristics of Mexican-Born Immigrants Living in the U.S." *Pew Research Center, Hispanic Trends*. Accessed March 20, 2015. http://www.pewhispanic.org/2012/04/23/vi-characteristics-of-mexican-born-immigrants-living-in-the-u-s/.

Ruggles, Steven, J. Trent Alexander, Katie Genadek, Ronald Goeken, Matthew B. Schroeder, and Matthew Sobek. 2010. Integrated Public Use Microdata Series: Version 5.0 [Machine-readable database]. Minneapolis: University of Minnesota.

Rumbaut, Rubén G., Frank D. Bean, Leo R. Chavez, Jennifer Lee, Susan K. Brown, Louis DeSipio, and Min Zhou. 2004. "Immigration and Intergenerational Mobility in Metropolitan Los Angeles (IIMMLA)." Ann Arbor: Inter-University Consortium for Political and Social Research [distributor], 2008-07-01. DOI: 10.3886/ICPSR22627.

Vecchione, Michele, and Gian Vittorio Caprara. 2009. "Personality Determinants of Political Participation: The Contribution of Traits and Self-Efficacy Beliefs." *Personality and Individual Differences* 46(4): 487–92.

Verba, Sidney, Kay Lehman Schlozman, and Henry E. Brady. 1995. *Voice and Equality: Civic Voluntarism in American Politics*. Cambridge, Mass.: Harvard University Press.

Waldinger, Roger. 2013. "Crossing Borders: International Migration in the New Century." *Contemporary Sociology: A Journal of Reviews* 42(3): 349–63.

Waters, Mary C., and Marisa Gerstein Pineau, eds. 2015. *The Integration of Immigrants into American Society*. Panel on the Integration of Immigrant into American Society and the Committee on Population, Division of Behavioral and Social Sciences and Education. Washington, D.C.: National Academies Press.

Yoshikawa, Hirokazu. 2011. *Immigrants Raising Citizens: Undocumented Parents and Their Young Children*. New York: Russell Sage Foundation.

"Don't Let the Illegals Vote!": The Myths of Illegal Latino Voters and Voter Fraud in Contested Local Immigrant Integration

ROBERT COURTNEY SMITH

This paper analyzes how the belief and fear by mostly older, white voters, politicians, and poll workers that "illegal" Latino immigrants were seeking to vote in local elections led to stigmatization of and discrimination against some Latino citizen voters in Port Chester, New York. Stoked by and closely echoing national voter ID law rhetoric, this fear fueled an "illegal Latino voter threat" narrative. This article documents how Port Chester's leaders and citizens repeated this narrative in public life, sometimes enacting it in politics, including in voting. The resultant stigma denies Latino voters the presumed legitimacy other citizens enjoy, discrediting them in one word: illegal. Such processes harm democracy in Port Chester and America, and were on display in the 2016 presidential election.

Keywords: myth of voter fraud, myth of illegal Latino voters, voting rights act, democracy, immigrants, citizens

"Don't let the illegals vote!" Port Chester poll workers discussing why they wanted to ask some Latino voters for ID before allowing them to vote in 2010.

This article analyzes how the belief and fear by mostly older, white voters, politicians and poll workers that "illegal" Latino immigrants are seeking to vote in local elections has led to stigmatization of and discrimination against some Latino citizen voters in the Village of Port Chester, New York. This fear—stoked by and closely echoing national voter ID law rhetoric (Minnite 2010)—has fueled an "illegal" Latino voter threat myth whereby mostly white residents fear that illegal Latino voters threaten their group position in Port Chester and what they see as their American way of life (Blumer 1958). Port Chester's leaders and citizens repeated these narratives in public life, sometimes enacting them in the political process, including in voting. The resultant stigma denies Latino voters the presumed legitimacy (Goffman 1963) other citizens enjoy, creates an unwelcoming climate, and discredits them in one word, *illegal*. Such processes harm democracy in Port

Robert Courtney Smith is professor of sociology, immigration studies, and public affairs at the Marxe School of Public and International Affairs, Baruch College, and Sociology Department, Graduate Center, CUNY.

© 2017 Russell Sage Foundation. Smith, Robert Courtney. 2017. "'Don't Let the Illegals Vote!': The Myths of Illegal Latino Voters and Voter Fraud in Contested Local Immigrant Integration." *RSF: The Russell Sage Foundation Journal of the Social Sciences* 3(4): 148–75. DOI: 10.7758/RSF.2017.3.4.09. I would like to thank the volume editors, anonymous reviewers, Suzanne Nichols, and other staff at the Russell Sage Foundation for their especially diligent work on my paper and this volume. I also thank Manuel Garcia y Griego, Lori Minnite, John Mollenkopf, Jeffrey Passel, and Harel Shapira for giving insightful comments on an earlier version of the paper; and Andrew A. Beveridge for collaborating on the survey. Robert Smith and Andrew A. Beveridge gratefully acknowledge the support of the CUNY Collaborative Incentive Research Grant #1857, Cycle 18, "Contested Immigrant Integration and American Institutions, 2011–2012." Direct correspondence to: Robert Courtney Smith at robert.smith@baruch.cuny.edu, Marxe School of Public and International Affairs, Baruch College, Box D0901, 1 Bernard Baruch Way, New York, NY 10010.

Chester and America, but could be counteracted. They raise questions about how we will address the current version of our American dilemma in our integration of immigrants and their children (Myrdal 1964; DiTomaso 2013). The 2016 presidential campaign remarkably juxtaposed a Democratic candidate openly discussing implicit bias in American life, and a Republic candidate who claimed massive voter fraud by illegally voting immigrants both when it looked as if he would lose the election and after he won.

PORT CHESTER'S VOTING RIGHTS ACT CASE

Port Chester is a strategic case study of immigrant political integration and exclusion in small-town America. It is like so many other small towns that have become immigrant destinations in recent decades, which simultaneously integrate and exclude newcomers.[1] But Port Chester is exceptional because it was sued in 2006 by the Department of Justice (DOJ) for harming the ability of Latino voters to "elect candidates of their choice," in violation of the Voting Rights Act (VRA). The VRA trial, resulting change of voting system, and DOJ supervision through 2016 made otherwise usually hidden processes visible for study for years. My role as an expert witness and DOJ ethnographer in 2006 and 2007, coupled with my later research as a City University of New York (CUNY) professor, enables me to observe these processes over time. I offer a brief overview of the case to properly contextualize this analysis of the myths of voter fraud and illegal Latino voters.

Port Chester's case juxtaposes a long history of immigrant integration with a DOJ lawsuit for violating the 1965 Voting Rights Act, the main legal tool to address unconstitutional minority exclusion in politics. Port Chester is both an old and a new immigrant destination. Many Port Chester natives and older European immigrants or their children feel that the mostly Latino immigration since the 1980s has changed their town dramatically, and not always positively.[2] In the 2007 trial, the DOJ alleged that Latino voters had been discriminated against in Port Chester by racial appeals in voting, not recruiting Latinos as candidates, an apparent outright theft of an earlier election, and in other ways. Judge Michael Robertson, as I call him, agreed, and permanently enjoined Port Chester's at-large voting system—in which candidates for Port Chester's six-member Board of Trustees (which, with its mayor, is its governing body) could live anywhere (no geographic, representative districts were defined)—because racial bloc voting meant that the white majority always defeated the Latino minority. In 2007, no Latino or black had ever been elected in Port Chester even though Latinos were 49 percent of its population and blacks were 12 percent. Moreover, DOJ was able to show at trial that virtually all Latinos had voted for the candidate I call Aldo Rodriguez, the only Latino candidate in the 2001 trustee election, who still lost.

Judge Robertson's remedy was to order early voting and cumulative voting from 2010 to 2016. In Port Chester's cumulative voting, each voter has six votes and may cast them for one or more candidates, enabling voters to show strength of preference by allotting more than one vote to a candidate.[3] If minority voters give all six votes to one candidate, they need be less than 15 percent of the voting population to elect one of six trustees. Cumulative voting seeks to systematically address racially polarized voting by enabling minorities to elect can-

1. Andrew A. Beveridge, using census data, reports more than eight hundred places in the United States that have at least 10 percent Latino citizen voting age population and at-large voting districts like the kind found to violate the VRA in Port Chester. Stories like the one in Port Chester will become increasingly common (personal communication, 2015).

2. The literature on new destinations, and the reception of immigrants in them, is growing (Marrow 2011; Flores 2014, 2015; Longazel 2016; Zuniga and Hernandez 2005; Massey and Sanchez 2008).

3. Each voter gets the same number of votes as there are open seats. Port Chester has six open seats, so voters get six votes (for contemporary public discussion from an interested party, see Slatky 2010). Cumulative voting is little known in the United States, but has been used here (Blair 1958; Goldburg 1994; Sawyer and McRae 1962; Guinier 1994).

didates of their choice within a system with no geographical electoral districts, in which candidates can live anywhere (Engstrom, Taebel, and Cole 1988; Cole, Taebel, and Engstrom 1990). Early voting is thought to raise turnout, especially among minority voters.[4]

To properly understand how the myths of voter fraud and illegal Latino voters combined to foster stigma and sometimes discrimination against Latino voters, I first frame the theoretical and policy questions engaged by these myths, and briefly discuss methods, before turning to Port Chester itself, including reviewing its history to the eve of the VRA lawsuit.

IMMIGRANT POLITICAL INTEGRATION, NARRATIVES, AND DISCRIMINATION IN VOTING

Political Incorporation of Immigrants, Writ Large

Social scientists have studied immigrant incorporation extensively in recent decades, but focused less explicitly on how political incorporation works on the ground. Sociology has mainly theorized group assimilation, centered on how ethnicity and related processes affect outcomes like social mobility.[5] Although sociological studies analyze how discrimination can inhibit integration, most do not explicitly focus on how such processes work in politics (Ramakrishnan and Bloemraad 2008; Alba and Foner 2009). Historians and political scientists have analyzed how political parties, unions, and churches have all served as institutions to integrate immigrants into political life in the late nineteenth to the mid-twentieth century, but do so less fully as their influence has declined; social movements, social media, and other institutions have come to matter more (Erie 1998; Junn and Haynie 2008; Anderson 2008; Wolbrecht and Hero 2005). Work on the political incorporation of minorities first focused squarely on the civil rights movement and African Americans securing the right to vote, and then analyzed African American, Latino, and Asian American political participation and representation (Browning, Marshall, and Tabb 1984; de la Garza, Falcon, and Garcia 1996; Epstein et al. 2006; Wong et al. 2011; Canon 1999; Junn and Haynie 2008). Research focused on immigrants analyzes which ones become U.S. citizens and vote; how national, state, and local institutions facilitate or inhibit immigrant political integration (Bloemraad 2006, 2013; Varsanyi 2010); how immigrant voters form coalitions (Mollenkopf 2013); how we should define and measure political integration (Minnite 2009; Jones-Correa 2009, 2013; Bloemraad 2013); how immigrant community organizations relate to civic and political integration (Ramakrishnan and Bloemraad 2008); and how Latino immigrants become American voters (DeSipio and de la Garza 2015; DeSipio 2013).[6] These studies less often specify how—the mechanisms by which—political integration occurs or does not for immigrants (Hochschild et al. 2013; Hochschild and Mollenkopf 2009). Research is needed especially on how immigrant incorporation can be passively or actively blocked (Minnite 2009; Jones-Correa 1998), how immigrants are framed in politics or media (Haynes, Merolla, and Ramakrishnan 2016), and how the VRA might help integrate naturalized U.S. citizens and their children (de la Garza and DeSipio 2006).

VRA trials are special cases of immigrant incorporation because they occur only when

---

4. This position is not universally held, but that debate is beyond the scope of this paper (see Gronke and Toffey 2008; Gronke, Galanes-Rosenbaum, and Miller 2007; Slatky 2010; Stein 1988).

5. In classical assimilation theory, most groups adapt by adopting American culture (Gordon 1964); in segmented assimilation, better-off immigrant groups use cultural coherence to more successfully integrate whereas others face the dangers of downward integration into a "rainbow underclass" (Portes and Rumbaut 2001); in "remade" assimilation, home and host culture both change by immigration, enabling surprising upward mobility (Alba and Nee 2003; Alba 2014); in "second-generation advantage," U.S.-raised children of immigrants pick elements of parental and U.S. culture to maximize their chances for success, thus gaining some advantages that later-generation native-born children do not have (Kasinitz et al. 2008).

6. A key issue this paper cannot address is the effects of the systematic exclusion of millions of immigrants from citizenship on the larger political system.

violations of the act are alleged to occur and are actually pursued. Passed in 1965, the VRA was renewed in 1982, 1992, and 2006. Initially designed to protect voting rights of African Americans, the VRA was extended in 1975 to language minorities, mostly Latinos and Asians. It promotes immigrant integration by targeting exclusionary mechanisms affecting members of protected racial or language minority groups.

Incorporation, Writ Small
This article analyzes the narratives about race and ethnicity in public life in Port Chester, and their sometimes discriminatory enactment by individuals, groups, and institutions in speech, inaction, or action. Narratives are stories that explain social reality, thus framing which policy responses are appropriate (Abbott 2001; Ewick and Silbey 1995; Somers 1994). Politicians and others use them to compete for power, create community, and legitimize policies (Gamson and Modigliani 1989; Snow and Benford 1992; Pease Chock 1995; Boyce 1995; Hajer 1995; Hajer and Laws 2006; Stone 1989). Racially divisive narratives can be enacted in discrimination, conduct that is legally proscribed (such as asking Latinos for ID to vote), or legally required but not enacted (such as Port Chester not having enough bilingual poll workers). Narratives can change with political circumstance and circulate within society. A "moral panic" occurs when a narrative about an issue legitimizes policies or actions that would be otherwise unacceptable (Cohen 1972; Costelloe 2006).

America is in a moral panic about immigration, driven by overlapping narratives about immigration, racism, local dispossession, and voting. The Latino threat narrative describes how whites feel that Latinos threaten America by having too many children, costing more in public services than they contribute in taxes, bringing crime and disease, and being unassimilable (Chavez 2008; Hochschild 2016; Skocpol and Williamson 2013; Parker and Barreto 2013). This Latino threat narrative works with another, the myth of voter fraud (Minnite 2010; Levitt 2007). Republican-sponsored voter ID laws posit widespread voter fraud, including voting by so-called illegal aliens. But a comprehensive review of voter fraud studies, covering roughly one billion votes cast, documented only thirty-one cases of voter impersonation, which such laws address. (This number increased to thirty-two when a Donald Trump supporter in Iowa voted twice in fear that the election was rigged.) Levitt estimates the incidence of voter fraud as between 0.00004 and 0.00009 percent, making it less likely than "being struck by lightning." Most voter fraud is by absentee ballot (Rutenberg 2015; Presidential Commission 2014). In contrast, many studies document thousands of voters disenfranchised by lack of required photo ID, and by inaccurate scrubbing of voter rolls undertaken via these laws (Rutenberg 2015; *New York Times* 2016; Weiser and Agraharkar 2012; Cobb, Greiner, and Quinn 2012).

Lorraine Minnite argues that this unsupported voter fraud narrative is used to justify restrictive ID laws to do "the political work" of preventing Democrat-inclined voters—poor, minority, immigrant—from voting (2010). The illegal Latino voter threat narrative analyzed in this paper combines the Latino threat narrative and the myth of voter fraud to analyze how white residents' fears of "illegal" Latino voting were acted upon in Port Chester's political life via the actions of politicians, poll workers, and others, sometimes resulting in discrimination. Such threat narratives can also emerge where immigrants are nearly all well-educated, naturalized citizens or U.S. permanent legal residents, who are "highly skilled but unwelcome," especially in electoral politics (Aptekar 2008).

Underlying both these narratives is a feeling of white dispossession—a refrain on alt-Right social media—whereby mainly older, white Americans feel they are being displaced from their homes by immigration, and, in Donald Trump's words, that they "Don't have a country anymore." This sense of white dispossession was heightened in Port Chester's VRA trial because such trials are unusual federal interventions into local elections. Under the U.S. Constitution, elections are under state, not federal, government authority (McCrary, Seaman, and Valelly 2006; Thernstrom 1987). The trial reinforced a larger belief, among some white voters especially, that the federal government is the problem and sides unfairly with minorities and immigrants, including "illegals," against the hard-working white working people who they feel "made America great." They believe that undeservings have cut in front of them in the line for the American Dream (Hochschild 2016). Eddie Lavoro of Port Chester feels that children of immigrants are being given the benefits of his and prior generations' hard work: "they are taking . . . [from] the ones that made this country . . . WWII, Korean War, Vietnam. . . . All illegal children should get free education—Why? A kid born in this country—an American citizen. [Yes.] But a kid who . . . comes at age fourteen is entitled to everything you and I sacrificed for? . . . bullshit, he's not an American citizen." Moreover, many in Port Chester felt the town was unjustly being accused of being racist by DOJ's lawsuit.

I focus on *enactments* of narratives because discriminatory action or inaction is legally regulated, and actionable. While discriminatory thought can motivate discriminatory action, it is not necessary to show discrimination. Non-bigoted people can also discriminate. Moreover, *showing* racist or bigoted beliefs is difficult, because it usually requires disclosure by the person. Finally, legal injury in a VRA case occurs if enacted discrimination abridges the ability of a protected class of voters to "elect candidates of their choice," regardless of a candidate's race.[7] Disparate outcome, and not racist intent, can demonstrate that injury, and has been the legal standard in VRA cases since the 1982 Senate amendments rejecting the Supreme Court's ruling in *Mobile v. Bolden* (446 U.S. 55 (1980)), requiring demonstrated discriminatory intent. The disparate outcome standard recognizes that discrimination can be *individual* or *structural* and must be considered in context (Allport 1958; Bobo, Kluegel, and Smith 1997; Feagin 2006; Feagin and Ekberg 1980; Butler 1978). The standard is not negated by nonracial rationales that whites may offer for actions or structures that have racial impacts (Bonilla-Silva 2006; DiTomaso 2013). The Port Chester VRA trial heard testimony on racially divisive actions by individuals—such as the anonymous flyer of Republican Barry Deutche, as I call him—and actions or inaction by institutions—such as Port Chester's not hiring enough Spanish-language poll workers—that supported a finding of discrimination.

Hostile narratives stigmatize by linking a group identity to discrediting traits—here, Latinos are "illegals"—thus denying the presumption of moral legitimacy enjoyed by other citizens (Goffman 1963). It can mobilize bias (implicit or explicit, discussed later). Its impact is stronger when done by, or within, institutions that should not tolerate it (Croom 2008; Matsuda et al. 1993), such as polling places. Stigmas are an exercise in power via a two-sided dynamic: the stigmatized person feels his or her group identity linked with discrediting traits in the gaze of a dominant group or institution, and the latter "sees" the stigmatized traits and not the actual person in front of them (Holmes 2012; Calogero 2004; Skelton 2010; Patterson and Elliott 2002; Foucault 1977; Pritchard and Morgan 2000). In a polling place, this white citizen gaze would be enacted by poll workers asking for extra ID to make sure that "illegals" do not vote, and would be felt by a U.S. citizen Latino being treated like an "illegal" when trying to vote. Because poll workers are state agents, when they treat some Latinos as potential "illegals," it is functionally the state seeing them with bias or stigma, creating

---

7. Finding a violation of the VRA is done by a two-part test. The first part asks whether the *Gingles* preconditions (*Thornburg v. Gingles*, 478 U.S. 30 (1986)) are met: Is there polarized white and minority racial bloc voting in which white candidates mostly defeat minority candidates, and is it possible to remedy this situation by creating majority-minority electoral districts? (If minority candidates lose because minorities split their votes substantively between minority and white candidates, the Gingles test is not met.) With preconditions established, step two assesses if discrimination occurred on seven Senate factors (such as racial appeals) and two other factors constituting a "totality of the circumstances" (see *U.S. v. Village of Port Chester*, https://www.justice.gov/crt/cases-raising-claims-under-section-2-voting-rights-act-0#portchester, accessed January 19, 2017). This broad review, like a sociological case study, analyzes all available evidence.

a hostile climate (Minnite 2009, 2010; Winders 2013; Delano 2014).

THE LONGITUDINAL, SATURATED, EMBEDDED ETHNOGRAPHIC CASE STUDY

This paper uses a longitudinal, saturated, embedded ethnographic case study approach, which is epistemically pragmatic, developing analytical opportunities emerging from long-term ethnographic immersion (George and Bennett 2005; Duneier 1999; Katz 1997, 2001, 2002; Black 2009; Smith 2006b; Gonzales 2016). The project began when my colleague Andrew Beveridge (Queens College, City University of New York) and I were expert witnesses for the DOJ's 2007 case against Port Chester, becoming very familiar with the legal evidence for a VRA violation. We continued this research as CUNY professors using varied sources, including a weighted, representative survey of Port Chester voters. Since 2007, I have regularly read local newspapers, websites, and other documents (such as court filings) and conducted one-off and repeat interviews. I have also regularly attended public events and meetings, especially when events presented opportunities to see otherwise hidden dynamics. For example, Barry Deutche's 2011 nomination as a Port Chester mayoral candidate sparked unusual, open accusations of racism by opponents, who were in turn accused of un-Americanism for protesting. The project is ethnographically embedded by starting with work in the VRA trial, is longitudinal by its decade of fieldwork, and is saturated by combining many sources. It follows Herbert Blumer's exhortation to contextualize analysis of the evolving meanings of intergroup relations, but also links these to later action (on meanings, Blumer 1958; Blalock 1967; Esposito and Murphy 1999; Bobo and Hutchings 1996; Quillian 1995, 2006, 2008; on action, Flores 2015, 2014; Longazel 2016). The study seeks not to generalize to all VRA cases, but to fully describe dynamics of this case—the sociological equivalent to the totality of circumstances test in VRA trials. Finally, this research differs from most on VRA trials and remedies like cumulative voting, which is usually short term, using one-off interviews and document review (Engstrom 1992; Engstrom and Brischetto 1997; Engstrom, Taebel, and Cole 1988; Cole, Taebel, and Engstrom 1990). This long-term research documents the downstream effects of a VRA trial and specific remedy, which should help in determining appropriate remedies in future cases.

Following ethnographic convention, I use pseudonyms for everyone in the paper, prefacing the first use of each name with a phrase indicating this (for example, "whom I call"). While there is no legal or ethical need to anonymize the names of public officials speaking on public issues, or of people who testified in open court, spoke in public meetings, or wrote a letter to the editor, I also draw on interviews where I agreed not to use their names. To avoid confusion on which names are real or pseudonyms, I have used fake names for everyone. Ethnography seeks to document and analyze the processes at work—related to but distinct from journalism's goal of reporting the news, where real names would be indicated.

This paper next analyzes how the illegal Latino voter narrative circulated in public life and leeched into Port Chester's political process, including into voting.

A BRIEF HISTORY OF PORT CHESTER TO THE EVE OF THE VRA TRIAL

The Village of Port Chester is a microcosm of an America that we need to understand better, as became clear in the surprising 2016 presidential election. In recent decades, Port Chester has experienced deindustrialization and related economic vulnerability, especially for those without college educations; an aging taxpayer base; dramatic demographic change; and a loosening of the monopoly on political life previously held by Port Chester–born white ethnics. Port Chester sits on 2.3 square miles about an hour north of New York City in wealthy Westchester County, New York. It has always been a commercial center surrounded by wealthier communities. In the colonial era, it was known as Saw Pit Landing for its saw mill, boat building, and shipping industries. In 1837, it became Port Chester. By 1950, Port Chester was a "leading factory town in the Lower Hudson Valley . . . and had [several] headquarters or production centers," supporting a strong working class through 1970s, when the factories began moving to cheaper areas.[8] Port Chester's last factory, Life Savers, closed in 1984. This is the period—the 1950s to the 1970s—whose passing Port Chester residents lament when decrying too much change in the Village (Coontz 2000). The 1970s to the 1980s saw economic struggle and demographic decline. Since the 1990s, Port Chester has rebounded as the self-proclaimed restaurant capital of Westchester County—driven by Latin American cuisine—and site of big box stores and professional offices. Its population grew by influxes of Latin American immigrants, mainly, and non–Port Chester-born young, mostly white, professionals who cannot afford other suburbs or value the town's diversity. Port Chester's population decreased from its postwar high in 1970 of 25,803 to 23,565 in 1980—a drop of 8.7 percent—rebounding to 24,728 in 1990, 27,867 in 2000, and 28,967 in 2010.[9]

Port Chester has a long, contradictory history of incorporating new immigrant groups, which shows a time-lagged entry into politics. The children of earlier Italian immigrants to Port Chester took the political lead during the 1940s and 1950s from the earlier Protestant and then Irish political elites. Locals say that the "Italians" (people of Italian ancestry and other white ethnics) have run Port Chester politics since the 1970s. In the 1960s, Port Chester incorporated Cuban refugees, most as anti-Communist Republicans; they are now 4 percent of Port Chester's population. Colombians, Peruvians, Ecuadorans, and Bolivians came in large numbers in the 1980s and 1990s, and Mexicans, Salvadorans, and Guatemalans have come since the 1990s. In 2010, Joe Nadal, as I call him, a Peruvian immigrant, was the first Latino elected as a trustee; he was reelected in 2013 and 2016. Will Jenkins, as I call him, was the first African American elected, also in 2010; he was reelected in 2013.

The imbalance in potential political influence in Port Chester for the 2001 trustee election that led to the VRA lawsuit can be seen in the dramatic differences in the proportion of each major group in the overall population versus in the citizen voting age population (table 1).[10] In 2000, Port Chester's total population was 49 percent Latino, 39 percent white, and 12 percent black; its voting age population (VAP) was 42 percent Latino, 46 percent white, and 11 percent black. However, the citizen voting age population (CVAP) was 27 percent Latino, 59 percent white, and 14 percent black. Moreover, only 34 percent of VAP Latinos were citizens (CVAP), versus 83 percent for whites and 76 percent for

---

8. "Village of Port Chester," http://www.portchesterny.com/pages/PortChesterNY_WebDocs/about (accessed December 8, 2016).

9. Port Chester's housing stock has more diversity than its neighboring communities, reflecting its more diverse population. Rather than solely single-family homes on large plots, Port Chester combines large pockets of highly concentrated multifamily housing, detached houses on small plots, and relatively smaller numbers of detached houses on large plots. Some 61 percent of Port Chester's population rents; 39 percent live in their own home (Port Chester Comprehensive Plan 2012, 55). On Google Earth, Port Chester's gray, built-up downtown contrasts markedly with the intense green of its wealthier, northern neighborhoods, or of the surrounding communities, or golf courses. Port Chester has the fourth lowest median house price of the twenty-three localities in Westchester County. In 2010, the median house price in Westchester County was $559,000 and for villages (Port Chester is a village) $701,000. Port Chester's median house value, however, was only $471,000 (Port Chester Comprehensive Plan 2012).

10. Contrary to the comments expressed by some at the Port Chester Hearing on redistricting on October 5, 2006, the census data suggest that Latinos in Port Chester who are able to legalize their status and become citizens do so. Most of the foreign born in Port Chester are Latino. According to the census, of the 2,392 foreign-born persons who entered the United States before 1980, 1,651 (69 percent) were naturalized U.S. citizens in 1999; whereas of the 3,140 who entered between 1980 and 1989, 1,047 (33 percent) had; of those who entered from 1990 to 2000, only 6 percent had done so. Those who arrived prior to 1985 had more opportunity to legalize and become citizens given the 1986 Immigration Reform and Control Act, and had generally easier access to legal status in prior decades (Smith 2006a).

Table 1. Port Chester Population and Voter Demography

	Total	Non-Hispanic White	Hispanic	Non-Hispanic All Other
Total	27,773	10,833	13,633	3,307
Percent of all		39.0%	49.1%	11.9%
Voting age population (VAP)	22,127	9,373	10,244	2,510
Percent of all		42.4%	46.3%	11.3%
Citizen voting age population (CVAP)	13,215	7,781	3,522	1,912
Percent of all		58.9%	26.7%	14.5%
Percent of CVAP by VAP by group	59.7%	83.0%	34.4%	76.2%

Source: Author's compilation based on 2000 U.S. Census; table prepared by Andrew A. Beveridge of Queens College.

blacks. Hence, in racially polarized elections, whites' electoral power ensured that no blacks or Latinos were ever elected to office. Such had been the case prior to the 2007 trial. The Department of Justice contended that, absent discrimination, Latinos' 27 percent of total CVAP should have been enough for them to elect some candidates of their choice, given Port Chester's six trustee seats.

The focus on discrimination in voting here should not obscure the fact that Port Chester has done a great deal to foster substantive immigrant integration, including by establishing a day labor site, and especially by its community schools model with afterschool and in-school medical programs that help children of immigrants in particular.[11] Port Chester's innovative work integrating children of immigrants in school was recognized by a 2005 U.S. Department of Education National Blue Ribbon School Award, and a 2006 EdTrust Dispelling the Myth Award; was profiled in the book *Turning High Poverty Schools into High Performing Schools* (Parrett and Budge 2012); and has been an anchor in developing a community schools training program at a local college (Ferrara, Nath, and Guadarrama 2014).[12] More-over, interethnic relations in daily life are mostly harmonious and unremarkable. How then, is there discrimination in politics? This apparent contradiction reflects America's larger stance on immigration. We pride ourselves as a nation of immigrants yet are deeply split on how or whether to fix our current immigration issues. This contradiction is analyzed more elsewhere, but we can start by recognizing that different logics of action govern the role of race and ethnicity in different spheres of public life. Absent political pressures, most teachers want to teach all children (Marrow 2011; Maxwell 2014; Jones-Correa 2009; Varsanyi 2010); business deals can have win-win outcomes. But winner-take-all elections yield zero-sum games where campaigns often mobilize voters by divisive appeals to group, including racial and ethnic identity. This helps explain how white Port Chester residents can get along with and even like their Latino neighbors, but ask some Latinos for ID when they try to vote.

Discrimination against Latino voters matters theoretically because it occurs at the end of the process wherein immigrants have done their part to incorporate by becoming law-

---

11. This assessment is complicated by the fact that these expenditures are contested by Port Chester natives even though they are largely funded by private donors or grants rather than directly by Port Chester school taxes. However, the rhetoric of many homeowners does not recognize that distinction. The overall point, though, is that Port Chester has done impressive work in its schools to help all children, especially children of immigrants.

12. The community schools model in Port Chester was developed by Dr. Eileen Santiago and Dr. JoAnne Ferrara and their partners in the Port Chester Public Schools. See "Thomas A. Edison Full-Service Community School," http://annex.mville.edu/graduate/academics/school-of-education/about/partnerships/professional-development-schools/thomas-a-edison.html (accessed December 8, 2016).

abiding, civically engaged citizens who seek to vote (Jones-Correa 2009, 76). Discrimination is active exclusion or nonincorporation attacking the heart of America's political project (Hochschild and Mollenkopf 2009). Given that stories of Latino apathy, illegality, or refusal to assimilate were used to explain why Latinos had never been elected in Port Chester, it is painfully ironic that Latino voters could be excluded for being Latino as they sought to exercise this central right of American citizens.

For clarity, before analyzing the myths of voter fraud and illegal Latino voters in Port Chester, I offer a simplified timeline of the events discussed in this paper.

Mid-2006—The Department of Justice sends Port Chester a letter telling of intent to sue and possibility of consent decree.

October 2006—Port Chester holds public hearings to discuss how Port Chester should respond to DOJ. In hearings, some voters express fear Latino voters may be "illegals."

February 2007—Preliminary injunction hearing; DOJ seeks to stop March 2007 election. Judge hears evidence of prior stolen election and of racial discrimination or hostile climate for Latinos in voting.[13]

Early March 2007—Republican trustee candidate Barry Deutche authors and mails anonymous, racially divisive pamphlet, giving DOJ evidence of racial appeals in voting.

Mid-March 2007—Judge stops Port Chester's March 2007 trustee election, finding VRA violation.

Late Spring 2007—VRA trial. Judge Robertson affirms VRA violation ruling.

December 2009—Judge Robertson accedes to Port Chester's request to do cumulative voting, and orders early voting. First cumulative voting and early voting in New York State are in Port Chester in June 2010.

Spring 2010—During training for cumulative voting, Port Chester voters regularly ask how they can know whether Latino voters are legal. Poll workers discuss asking Latinos for ID to ensure that no "illegals" vote.

March 2011—Barry Deutche is nominated for mayor by Republican and Conservative parties.

March 2014, 2015—A Latina voter I call Magda Votante is asked for ID; she does not vote in 2014. In 2015, she is asked for ID, shows it, and votes after repeated, failed attempts by poll workers to find her in voting book. Other Latinos are also asked for ID when voting.

I now delve into analyzing the expression, dissemination, and enactment of the myth of the illegal Latino voter.

EXPLANATIONS AND EMERGENCE OF THE ILLEGAL LATINO VOTER THREAT NARRATIVE

Port Chester's political leaders, and most white residents, were incredulous when they received DOJ's 2006 letter threatening to sue for VRA violations. They believed that Port Chester had integrated previous waves of immigrants, and many more than their richer neighbors in Rye, New York, or Greenwich, Connecticut. Why would DOJ target them? The lawsuit began when Aldo Rodriguez, a naturalized U.S. citizen and active Democratic party member, ran for office in 2001 and lost, but felt that Democratic party leaders and white Port Chester residents had not supported him because he was Latino. He contacted DOJ, who investigated, and in 2006 sent Port Chester a letter offering a corrective agreement called a consent decree, whereby Port Chester could, without admitting fault, remedy conditions violating the VRA by creating electoral districts, and avoid trial. Port Chester held public hearings in October 2006 to discern public sentiment on settling with or fighting DOJ. Soon after, Port Chester decided to fight.

13. A preliminary injunction hearing is a sort of pretrial that plaintiffs can ask for if there is imminent harm to justice in delay while waiting for a trial. Here the imminent harm was, in DOJ's view, an unfair election that would elect representatives using a system that discriminated against Latinos. One can get and win a preliminary injunction, as DOJ did, if the evidence presented shows it is very likely one will win in the actual trial.

The lawsuit and hearings catalyzed an unusual public conversation revealing Port Chester's contradictions on immigration. Mayor John Langdon, as I call him, who led the fight against DOJ, was recognized in the hearing for his work on the Workers Center (which serves Latino day laborers) by a Latina leader who supported DOJ's suit. Mayor Langdon's courtesy to all contrasted sharply with the heckling of Latinos by white Port Chester residents, which was so bad that two future trustee candidates criticized it. One, Barry Deutche, chastised hecklers, saying, "I'm ashamed by comments coming from the back of this room. . . . I'd hate to think" people would have treated his "Italian mother's side" of the family this way. But, emblematic of Port Chester's divisions, Deutche would go on five months later as a trustee candidate to author the racially divisive, anonymous pamphlet that underpinned Judge Robertson's subsequent finding of racial appeals in voting. Deutche would also get the most votes of the fourteen candidates in the first cumulative voting election in 2010, and be nominated for mayor on the Republican and Conservative party lines in 2011 (he lost) while protestors denouncing him as a racist walked outside the restaurant where he was being nominated.

Port Chester's divisions are reflected in the racial split on how to respond to the DOJ proposal: "81% (13 of 16) of those (comments) made by Latinos supported the DOJ's proposal of electoral districts, while 93.5% (17 of 18) of those by whites rejected it."[14] Speakers in the hearings enacted elements of the illegal Latino voter threat narrative. Several Latino leaders—directly answering white Port Chester residents' assertions that DOJ district plans would "divide" Port Chester—declared "we are already divided" and that Latinos lack "a seat at the table." Bianca Ibanez, as I call the Democrat who would be targeted in Barry Deutche's 2007 flyer, argued that DOJ's proposed remedy of electoral districts could help unite the Village by making geographic district representatives accountable to their constituents, including Latinos. Overall, Latinos felt excluded from public life and whites expressed confusion, as one put it, over "why we are even here. It's much ado about nothing." These statistics reflect the incommensurability of the white view—"Port Chester is united; DOJ don't divide it"—and the Latino view—"Port Chester is already divided because we are left out."

The Reverend Federico Perez, as I call him, of Port Chester asked perhaps the most insightful question in a later letter to the editor in the *Westmore News,* which points to the illegal Latino voter threat narrative. How did hearings meant to determine public sentiment on how to respond to DOJ's proposed plan to create electoral districts to remedy discrimination against Latino voters turn instead into a conversation about the threat Latinos, and "illegal" Latino voters, posed to Port Chester's quality of life and democracy?

We can understand how the meaning of the hearing changed by the three questions white Port Chester residents asked in it and the answers they gave then and in later conversations. The first asked, why had no Latinos ever been elected in the Village? Second, why is the federal government blaming us for the problem they created by letting these "illegal" immigrants in, and by dividing us by ethnicity? And, third, how do we know that the Latinos trying to vote are U.S. citizens and not "illegals"?

These questions, and white Port Chester residents' answers to them, show the white citizen gaze and linked illegal Latino voter threat narrative, creating a policy narrative leading Port Chester to fight DOJ. Both Latinos who spoke in the hearings and DOJ's allegations argued that Latinos did not get elected due to discrimination in how Port Chester conducted politics. In contrast, white Port Chester residents argued that no Latinos had been elected in Port Chester because of Latino apathy (La-

---

14. This is from my second report to DOJ (Smith 2007). A total of forty-three public comments at the microphone were made in the two hearings, and thirty-six expressed clear stands on redistricting. Seven people, four whites and three Latinos, did not express clear opinions. I discuss the number of public comments made, and not number of persons speaking, because some people spoke at both hearings. Only three Latinos rejected the plan, and only one white person—the former head of the Port Chester branch of the NAACP—supported the redistricting plan. These stark divisions indicate significant social and racial polarization.

Table 2. Fear of Undocumented Voters Among Port Chester's Registered Voters

Fear of noncitizen voters	White	Black	Latino	Asian	Total
Yes	33 (33.74%)	2 (22.2%)	2 (4.4%)	0	37 (24.7%)
No	62 (65.3)	7 (77.8)	42 (93.3)	1 (100%)	112 (74.7)
Declined to answer	0	0	1 (2.2)	0	1 (0.67)
Total	95 (100)	9 (100)	45 (100)	1 (100)	150 (100)

Source: Author's data; calculated by Guillermo Yrizar.

tinos don't care enough to vote), overload (Latinos are working too many jobs to vote), or ineligibility (Latinos are not citizens and cannot vote). I discuss the second and third questions shortly, but raise one point here. In the first hearing, four of eleven white speakers asked, "How do we know if Latino voters are actually citizens?" This question stigmatizes by making all Latino voters into potential "illegals" and threats to Port Chester's democracy, and to the group position of older, white, citizen voters.

In the following section, I analyze the myths of voter fraud and the illegal Latino voter. I first present data on aggregate beliefs about "illegals" in Port Chester, then on discussions of them in public hearings and electoral campaigns, and then in the polling place.

THE ILLEGAL VOTER THREAT NARRATIVE IN PORT CHESTER'S REGISTERED VOTERS

During the summer of 2012, Andrew A. Beveridge and I did a 153-person, weighted, random sample of doorstep interviews of registered voters in Port Chester, including appropriate numbers of voters in each of the categories of interest for our research.[15] Table 2 presents data on a key question, formulated from comments in Port Chester's October 2006 public hearings on the DOJ's Voting Rights lawsuit. I used *illegal immigrant* in the question because people in the public hearing used this language.

Q 20. Some people fear that, because no ID is required to vote, illegal immigrants will vote in Port Chester and change the outcome of elections. Do you share this fear? Y/N

Table 2 shows that 25 percent of Port Chester's registered voters fear that "illegal" immigrants will vote and change electoral outcomes: 35 percent of white registered voters and 22 percent of blacks, but only 4 percent of Latinos fear this. Fear of "illegals" trying to vote varies by birthplace. It is greater among those born in Port Chester than outside it. Only two of thirty-eight voters born in Latin America feared this; four of the ten voters born in Europe did. The only group whose majority feared it—three of four—was voters born in Italy. Given the rarity of voter fraud, these statistics are striking.

Why do one in three white Port Chester residents fear that undocumented immigrants will vote and change electoral outcomes in Port Chester? This fear was higher in two kinds of voting districts. (Voting districts here are simply catchment areas for organizing polling sites in at-large systems, not electoral districts electing a representative for that geographical area.) First, this fear was higher in whiter, wealthier districts with more voters, in the north end of

---

15. The sampling for this survey was done by Andrew A. Beveridge, and was designed to capture representative proportions of white, Latino, and black prime and nonprime voters. Prime voters are those who have voted in the last three elections, and are most likely to be courted by politicians. Nonprime voters have not voted in the last three elections and are less likely to be courted by candidates. The survey itself I developed, consulting with Beveridge, and fielded along with my team. The sample was weighted to ensure enough Latino voters. Professor Beveridge and I gratefully acknowledge the support of a 2011–2012 CUNY Collaborative Incentive Research Grant, "Contested Immigrant Incorporation and American Institutions: Race, ethnicity and immigration, and the violation and enforcement of Voting Rights."

These doorstep interviews were anonymous, in-person interviews conducted with the voters at their homes, and usually took about twenty-five minutes.

the Village. Some four of fifteen voters in District 18, seven of fifteen in District 19, and five of fifteen voters in District 25 feared "illegals" would vote. Districts with more Latinos but fewer overall voters feared illegal voters less: one of seven voters in Districts 6 and 10, none of the ten in District 13. Some districts were anomalous districts—more Latino voters and more reported fear of "illegals." But unraveling these anomalies supports my argument. In District 9, four of six whites interviewed, and one of three Latinos, feared illegal voters. In District 11, the three white voters interviewed all feared illegal voters, but the two Latino and one black voter did not. Drawing on my conversations with these white voters, these numbers reflect the feeling of whites who live in neighborhoods whose demographics have changed around them, and in their view, for the worse compared to the old days (Coontz 2000; Skocpol and Williamson 2013; Parker and Barreto 2013; Longazel 2016). Taken together, these anomalies and whiter districts' greater fears support the illegal Latino voter narrative threat argument. Having established this fear of illegal voters as a larger phenomenon in Port Chester, I trace the enactment of this narrative in various public arenas, in public hearings held by Port Chester, and then in the polling place.

THE ILLEGAL LATINO VOTER THREAT NARRATIVE IN OCTOBER 2006 PUBLIC HEARINGS

Perhaps the most impassioned, analytical, and applauded speaker was a local lawyer whom I call Dante Lauria. While saying that he spoke as a private citizen, he also reported having worked for local governments and being an expert in election law. He later advised the Voting Rights Commission, which was supposed to determine Port Chester's responses to DOJ's proposal, and was on the legal team that fought DOJ. This influential insider's words carried weight with the crowd.

Mr. Lauria offered a positive history of immigrant integration in Port Chester, and then an indignant two-sided indictment of the federal government for allowing the illegal immigration that profoundly changed Port Chester and caused it problems, and, in his view, unconstitutionally seeking to impose district voting on a place that already welcomed immigrants:

> How can a federal government that allows . . . illegal immigration . . . now have the *audacity* to seek to impose a district voting regimen on our community, which has tolerated and well accommodated the demographic changes? *Our community works.* The last thing we need is the federal government . . . formula . . . Our neighborhoods do not have fences . . . Only good people that know how to [live together . . . Districts will] create an unnecessary divisive parochialism . . . to the detriment of the community at large. Is this not redlining? . . . Port Chester has always been a community of hard-working immigrants . . . We have taken an influx of immigrants . . . created day labor center sites. We educate them in our schools.

He invites DOJ to "see the Columbus Day Parade" with all races marching, and see the "good, solid businesses" of Hispanics in Port Chester.

The view that DOJ was dividing a united Port Chester was reiterated in a Board of Trustees resolution creating the Voting Rights Commission days later, on October 23, 2006:

> Whereas, many of the speakers expressed concern that the threat of the federal lawsuit is divisive to a community that has accommodated, accepted and integrated waves of immigrants, while acknowledging that more can be done to engage all citizens including Hispanics in the political process . . . Whereas it is the intention of the Board of Trustees of the Village of Port Chester not to divide or polarize the community over . . . voting rights for any of our citizens.

These *whereas* clauses echo Mr. Lauria's words, and bolster a sense of white dispossession by errant DOJ action causing division. But they also completely ignore the racially disparate reactions to DOJ's lawsuit in the hearings—the authors did not or would not "see" that racial difference was important.

Mr. Lauria then describes the threat to democracy posed by *illegal* Latino voters who can vote due to weak election laws: "Right now, anyone can fill out a registration card, enter the last four digits of a social security number, and/or a driver's license number, and there's no verification process—they're added to the voting list! This does not sound like the barn door has been locked to prevent Hispanics from voting, legally or illegally." He enacts the illegal Latino voter narrative by posing the problem not as one of Latino candidates of choice always losing due to racially polarized voting, but as "illegal" Latinos voting illegally. With the moral panic induced by a belief that Latino immigrants are voting illegally, vigilance with Latino voters makes sense. This policy story normalizes such a stance.

Mr. Lauria's analysis emotionally anchors the town's policy response to fight DOJ.[16] Port Chester residents indignantly refused to settle DOJ's lawsuit because they felt it portrayed them as racists; settlement would implicitly admit racism. This position was clear among white speakers in the hearings, and in conversation with political leaders' over the next decade. Trustee Luigi Trastuilli regularly offered a friendly goading when I noted positive actions on immigration in Port Chester—Imagine that, in a racist little town like this? Trustee Will Jenkins's 2012 *Westmore News* op-ed explained that he supported fighting DOJ until the last appeal, despite long odds, because not fighting would forever "stain" Port Chester's reputation. The threat to white Port Chester residents' group position is not just from demographic change or "illegal" Latino voters, but from the DOJ's ill-informed intervention that paints white residents as racists. We can summarize this position as: federal incompetence has let "illegals" into Port Chester who vote and threaten to dispossess us of our Village, and DOJ calls us racists. Framed this way, these "illegal" Latino voters and this unjust accusation must be resisted, including by vigilance against illegal Latino voters.

The idea that noncitizen Hispanics were trying to vote even crept into the VRA trial in a report by Port Chester's redistricting expert, who wrote, "Indeed, Plaintiff's own expert, Professor Robert Smith, testified that he encountered instances in which noncitizen Hispanics in Port Chester had voted" (*U.S. v. Village of Port Chester*, Preliminary Injunction Hearings (S.D. N.Y. 2007), 1493). Under questioning by DOJ, he admitted he had heard this from a Port Chester attorney, but had not seen my deposition transcript. When shown the transcript—noting possible voting by two long-term, legal resident Italians—he withdrew his comment.

Mr. Lauria offered a policy fix that drew comment from the judge. Lauria asked, "I'd like to ask our federal representatives to sponsor amendments to the Voting Rights Act to protect us from having to raise taxpayers' taxes in defending this lawsuit. . . . These amendments are common in Congress. Have our representatives do their job." Finding no DOJ representatives present, he scornfully says that no one "has the courage" to admit they are from DOJ: "Shame on the U.S. Attorney's Office . . . [which] does not know Port Chester." This remarkable framing views the problem as DOJ's lack of understanding of Port Chester—right-thinking persons would not see discrimination in Port Chester—and fixable by exemption. The opinion of Judge Robertson found it "surprising" that a lawyer would propose exemption from the nation's main voting rights law. Mr. Lauria has since run for local office, and is still active in politics.

Mr. Lauria's framing supports the illegal Latino voter threat narrative. Because DOJ sued to protect the rights of U.S. citizen Latino voters to elect candidates of their choice, why even discuss "illegals"? They fit only if you believe that "illegals" are impersonating voters to vote, an unsupported belief in Port Chester, as nationally (Minnite 2010). Naturalized citizens vote, which could threaten the dominant group position of old-timer Port Chester residents. But a common belief in and fear of "illegal" Latino voting sets up the poll workers' question: How do we know if a Hispanic is a U.S. citizen voting legally or an "illegal" immigrant voting illegally? Such doubts show the perni-

---

16. Psychologists analyze how specific emotions, such as disgust or fear, are used to legitimize bias against outgroups, especially in situations that include no immediate threat (Hodson et al. 2014; Kteily et al. 2015).

cious, divisive impact of voter ID laws and rhetoric.

These positions contain various theories of how race works in public life. The self-check by white Port Chester residents—I am not a racist—dictates Port Chester's policy response—thus we must fight DOJ's offensive lawsuit. This position views racism as the agglomeration of individual racist acts or beliefs, and not inherent in larger structures or practices. In contrast, DOJ's allegations, and Judge Robertson's ruling, accommodate individual and systemic theories of racial dynamics. While a person can be racist, systems can discriminate by blocking minorities' chances to elect candidates without overt racism (Bonilla-Silva 2006). Systemic discrimination can occur by what people or procedures do—such as not recognizing Latino voters as registered or inciting white fears to win elections—and by what they do not do—such as not providing enough poll workers or Spanish-language translators or not training poll workers to see and prevent bias.

BARRY DEUTCHE'S ANONYMOUS, RACIALLY DIVISIVE CAMPAIGN FLYER

> "Bianca say's [sic] jump, fetch, beg or bark and Pino does it. The Hispanics are running the show already."
>
> —Anonymous campaign flyer, later acknowledged by Barry Deutche, Republican trustee candidate, early March 2007, just before Judge Robertson stopped the March 2007 election.

In the preliminary injunction hearing in February 2007, the Department of Justice won on all allegations except racial appeals in voting. Barry Deutche fixed that problem with his racially divisive, anonymous flyer, sent as the March 2007 trustee campaign began, before Judge Robertson stopped it.[17] The flyer tells a story about Port Chester contrary to what its residents believe about themselves. Many thought it exceeded the limits of Port Chester's often funny, often nasty, history of electoral flyering. Its blatant racial appeal was described to me by one white political leader as "trying to scare Whitey in the north end of the Village." It personally and divisively attacked an emerging Latina political leader, Bianca Ibanez, as such (as well as Aldo Rodriguez, the initial DOJ complainant). Its poor grammar ("what does Pino and Kingston want") irked the judge. Deutche also sent it secretly, unsigned, from a Connecticut post office, in the middle of a federal case. Absent DOJ's subpoena power, it is unlikely the flyer's author would have become publicly known. Deutche told the judge he sent the flyer out of "civic responsibility to the community" (*U.S. and Cesar Ruiz v. Village of Port Chester*, 06. Civ. 15173 SCR (S.D. N.Y. 2008), 40).

The flyer embodies elements of the illegal Latino voter threat narrative. While Deutche attacks mayoral candidate Charlie Pino, as I call him, for recommending settlement with DOJ after losing the preliminary injunction hearing, his attacks on Pino's campaign manager, Bianca Ibanez, are what went too far. The Republican nominee for mayor that year, whom I call Ricardo Vacarro, called the flyer "disturbing" in court, and thinks it cost him the election. In the flyer, Deutche attacks Ibanez as both a "double agent" and a "super secret triple agent!," saying she is a

> wolf in sheep's clothing . . . [who] want[s] for Port Chester—more affordable housing, more subsidized housing, more Section 8 housing. And she is going to get if [sic] because Ibanez and Pino are in bed together on the Village Affordable Housing SubCommittee [sic]. The wolf is in the House, thanks to Pino! . . . What Bianca cares about is only Hispanic!

Deutche laments that "Hispanics are running the show already" and exhorts Port Chester voters not to "elect carpetbaggers, elect people who care about hour history, heritage and what our kids will told about us in the future, are we to be known as Racists or Law Abiding Free Americans."

This flyer mattered so much because Ibanez and Deutche represent central images in Port Chester's community life, brought here into

---

17. Deutche claimed that the flyer was created with a sitting Republican trustee and the Board of Education president (whose students were majority Latino); they acknowledge only knowing of it.

open conflict. Bianca Ibanez is a model of the successful American integration of which Port Chester is rightly proud, as per Mr. Lauria's comments. Coming to the United States from Peru as a little girl, Ibanez attended Port Chester schools, went to college, got a master's degree in urban planning, and returned home to Port Chester to serve the town that had nurtured her, working to address the region's housing shortage. Deutche represents an older Port Chester—born and raised in Port Chester, he did not graduate from college, but developed his alarm business (valued at $25 to 50 million on ZoomInfo). In public speeches, he regularly remarks on his being born and raised in Port Chester.

Deutche's attack shows Port Chester at war with itself. How could this successful young professional child of immigrants and of Port Chester be targeted as a dangerous, divisive operative for Latinos—a secret agent—because she was active in politics? The attack implies that Bianca Ibanez—and those she represents—had gotten out of their place and should be put back into it. In symbolic, image-driven terms, the flyer implies that the Barry Deutches of Port Chester felt that the Bianca Ibanezs threatened their dominant group position and way of life. In Deutche's attack on Ibanez, as Pino's campaign manager and a secret agent, he suggests that Ibanez may act as if she is fully integrated into Port Chester's political life, but is in fact a kind of sleeper cell for Latinos who wish to change Port Chester forever. She "only cares about . . . Hispanic (s)" and will bring in cheap housing for them, ruining Port Chester's middle-class lifestyle (Parker and Barreto 2013; Skocpol and Williamson 2013). Hence, to vote for Pino was to vote to ruin Port Chester by fostering more immigration and a Latino takeover. Finally, Deutche's framing of old-time Port Chester residents' place in history—to be remembered as racists or true Americans— takes an indirect shot at DOJ's intervention, which was understood to depict Port Chester as racist. Next, we follow these open forum enactments of threat narratives into the intimacy of the polling place.

BIAS AND DISCRIMINATION IN VOTING

To properly understand these enactments in voting requires a brief theoretical discussion of an issue that, improbably, was part of the 2016 presidential campaign—bias, both implicit and explicit. Legal scholars document explicit and implicit bias and discrimination in polling places, especially in asking for ID. Rachel Cobb, James Greiner, and Kevin Quinn show that even where the law required all voters to be asked for ID, black and Latino voters were asked more than whites were (2012). Anthony Page and Michael Pitts see polling places as perfect sites to mobilize implicit bias because poll workers have time pressures, little information on each voter, and little review of their work (Page and Pitts 2009; Staats 2014). Minnite notes that agencies charged with administering elections are, in a Weberian sense, "prebureaucratic," because they do not create the rules they enforce, which are often politically motivated (2010). Moreover, the bureaucrats enforcing them—poll workers—work so infrequently and are trained so little they do not develop daily, routinized, bureaucratic expertise.[18] Conditions in Port Chester, and in many places in the United States, further raise chances for implicit bias because mostly white, older poll workers often personally know longtime white voters, but not newly naturalized, Latino voters, whose numbers have greatly increased in Port Chester. Implicit bias can be primed because racial signifiers (phenotype, accented English, need of translation, Hispanic last name) coincide with poll workers' personal information about different kinds of voters.

18. For example, New York State Election Law (§ 3-412 (2016)) requires them to be trained each year they work, and lists the things that should be covered, but does not specify how many hours the training should be or how it should be taught. Trainings in Port Chester have usually been part of a Saturday from nine o'clock in the morning to three o'clock in the afternoon. This is well above the national average of 2.5 hours (Presidential Commission 2014, 48). My point is that poll workers do not do their jobs all the time, and hence do not deepen their capacity on the job. I am not saying they do not work hard (they do), or do a good job. My point is the weakness of electoral bureaucracy, not of poll workers.

Most studies of implicit bias use either computer programs to document response time and associations with images to infer implicit bias, or experiments or audits to identify the effects of implicit bias (Staats 2014; Quillian 2008, 2006, 1995; Blanton and Jaccard 2008). This saturated case study's contribution is to trace, in situ and over an extended period, expression of public narratives that could promote bias by local leaders and citizens, and their enactment in voting, and the perception of this experience by some Latinos.

Election administration in Port Chester inadvertently accommodates mobilization of bias. First, under New York Election Law, poll workers may request proof of identity only if they legitimately think the person is an imposter or if the voter did not show proof of identity when first registering. In the latter case, the registry would have "ID" printed next to the name in the registry, telling poll workers they should request identification (New York State Election Law § 8.302.2 (2016)). The law also requires that challenges to a voter's identity be recorded. In federal, state, or county elections, New York State law requires poll workers to offer provisional ballots to persons not on the voter list but claiming to be registered. In Village of Port Chester elections, the law does not provide for a provisional ballot; the voter must get an order from a judge in White Plains (twenty minutes away) allowing him or her to vote, which is a decided burden. Space for indirect accommodation of bias opens because many voters do not know that they should get provisional ballots, or that they need not show ID, and hence do not challenge such actions. This reduces costs of discrimination because violations go unreported; individuals would not know that the law was unevenly enforced. Finally, aversion to believing one is being discriminated against can further inhibit perception of and response to it, as discussed in the next section.

DAVID CRUZ'S STOLEN 1991 ELECTION

Threatened group position dynamics were clearly enacted in the apparently stolen 1991 election for the Port Chester School Board. The candidate I call David Cruz, son of a Cuban immigrant, raised in Port Chester, ran for the Board of Education as a Republican against an incumbent Republican. Despite his family's long Republican party history and his service as a Parent Teacher Association copresident, Cruz's run "angered the hierarchy" of his party, which had tried to dissuade him. Turnout was unusually large because Cruz had registered many new voters, scores of whom were turned away by poll workers saying they were not registered. Cruz lost by thirty-eight votes, but submitted thirty-nine valid affidavits to the New York State Education Commissioner by registered Latino voters who were told they were not and could not vote (N.Y.S. D.O.E. Commissioner's Decision No. 12,704 (May 26, 1992)). The commissioner ordered a rare new election, which Cruz lost, he said, because his Latino supporters were "disgusted" at having been turned away at the polls and would not turn out again for what they felt was a rigged process.

A Cruz supporter told him that "the parents in the King Street School district, which is the white area, were not going to support me," and that a flyer had gone out there against him. Cruz saw his supporters being turned away when trying to vote; many then walked over to tell him. Cruz knew they were registered, because he or his family had personally registered them, and he had his supporters list with him. When he complained, election officials said that poll workers had "checked the rolls, [and] those people were not registered." Cruz testified that only Latinos were turned away from voting, and that, later, other Latinos (but no whites) called saying they had been told they were not registered.

The discussion of poll worker intent and conditions in the 2007 trial offers insight into the dynamics of racial bias. Port Chester's lawyer, whom I call Albert Pescatore, defined the problem as overwhelmed poll workers. There were close to two hundred new voters, mainly Cruz supporters, who, as first-time voters, had at that time to go through two lines to vote. The Westchester County voting roll—used then in hard copy—was not user friendly, and "elderly" white women poll workers struggled with Latino names. Pescatore twice asked Cruz about discriminatory intent, getting different answers:

PESCATORE: You didn't believe that any of your supporters got turned away because of their ethnicity, did you?

CRUZ: I believe that they were turned away not *strictly* for their ethnicity, but the fact that they were elderly people working that particular table, and they didn't know how to spell Hispanic names. (*U.S. v. Village of Port Chester*, Preliminary Injunction Hearings (S.D. N.Y. 2007), 311 [emphasis added]).

And:

CRUZ: I don't believe . . . these elderly ladies specifically turned away Hispanics . . . the way the system was set up, where these elderly ladies had to look up Hispanic names in the entire Westchester County roll . . . they had no other choice but to turn people away. (318)

Cruz's testimony and Pescatore's questions show that Port Chester had not taken enough measures to ensure that all voters could vote, creating conditions fostering discrimination against Hispanics (backlog at the new voter table and not enough poll workers who understood Latino names). Moreover, the slippage between Cruz's first answer—that Hispanics were turned away not strictly for their ethnicity—and the second—that elderly white ladies were set up to fail by the system—suggests that Cruz does not want to "see" discrimination, which psychologists note is a common response (Crosby 1984; Johnson, Ashburn-Nardo, and Leccil 2013). He recognizes that only Latinos were excluded, making it discriminatory, but does not want to believe his elderly, small-town neighbors would racially target his supporters. For Judge Robertson, that only Latinos were turned away was "telling" and discriminatory (*U.S. v. Village of Port Chester*, Preliminary Injunction Hearings (S.D. N.Y. 2007), 311).

Confirmation that the election had purposefully been stolen from Latinos came inadvertently in a 2010 conversation with Republican leaders whom I call Luigi Trastuli and Gary Pildulski. Trastuli told me that poll workers did not say they could not find the Latino voters' names because they were "racist," but because they wanted "their guy" to win. Cruz was being punished for disobeying Republican party leaders, who told "All the Republicans . . . [to] Stay away" from David. They see political rather than a racist exclusion:

PILDULSKI: . . . take the social engineering part out of it . . . the initial move there was not to exclude him because he was Spanish. . . .

TRASTULI: Yeah . . . it was a political move . . . It could've been me running. . . . It had nothing to do with that. And the only reason he got a second . . . bite at the apple was the idiots that were running the show there . . . put twenty of the Hispanics to the side. Cause they knew that's Cruz's votes.

In this telling, registered Latino voters were not excluded because of racial bigotry or racism (because they disliked Latinos as such), but rather because being Latino identified them to white poll workers as Cruz supporters. Trastuli further denies any racism by saying that "Cubans are like Italians in this Village"—Republican, Catholic, and integrated, with clean houses with "pictures of the Virgin" Mary. Fascinatingly, Trastuli and Pildulski helped Cruz gather affidavits used in the appeal to the education commissioner, but knew it would lead to a bigger defeat: "We had another election . . . which was bad . . . I told David, now you're gonna really get crushed . . . Cause now all the white people are coming after you." Trastuli and Pildulski's arguments make internal sense, but also document discrimination. They say that excluding Cruz's voters, identified by ethnicity, was a political, not racial, strategy. But party leaders punished Cruz for running when told not to—getting out of his proper place, threatening their dominant group position. Even if we accept Trastuli's analysis of no bigotry, poll workers still discriminated in violation of the VRA by using ethnicity as a marker to prevent registered minority voters from voting and electing a candidate of their choice.

POLL WORKER–VOTER INTERACTION

The climate for poll worker–voter interaction is partly set before election day, by law, and by action and inaction by electoral officials. With enough language-minority voters, the VRA requires signs, electoral materials, sample ballots in that language as well as translators and other accommodations (Jones-Correa 2005). Moreover, all voters must be well treated. Witnesses in the 2007 trial reported that Latinos were not welcomed like their white peers, but rather treated in "hostile" or "unfriendly" ways. Witnesses reported Latinos not in the voting registry were not offered provisional ballots, but similarly situated whites were. A 2005 consent decree with Westchester County, which covers Port Chester, agreed to provide enough Spanish translators, to ensure all voters were treated courteously, and to promptly notify DOJ of issues. I testified that Port Chester had not provided enough translators to comply with the consent decree, discriminating by what it failed to do.

The illegal Latino voter threat narrative was a staple during many trainings of voters and poll workers leading up to the first cumulative voting election in 2010, many of which I attended. Poll workers asked how one would know if those trying to vote, especially Hispanics, were registered voters or "illegals"? The question was so frequent that Village staff preempted it by explaining, up front, that noncitizens could not vote. After the 2010 elections, I suggested ways to address this apparent bias in poll worker training to a receptive Mayor Pino, but it was not done. The next Village clerk, a Republican party leader hired over Democratic protest, spent thirty to forty seconds on discrimination in poll worker training, simply saying that it was prohibited. In that training, a poll worker asked how one knows whether a Hispanic voter is legal or "illegal." Poll workers continued to discuss the threat of "illegal" Latinos voting while manning the polls, as seen in three confirming repetitions of the same story in the 2010, 2014, and 2015 elections, driven by the same fear of weak voting protections. If these conversations take place in a voting context, they constitute an enactment of bias that can lead to discrimination.

In the 2007 trial, a Latina poll worker, whom I call Elena Valdes, testified that some of her white counterparts openly declared the need to "make sure that the illegals don't vote." Noting inadequate protections from voting fraud—you don't even need to show an ID to vote!—they "asked certain kinds of Latinos for identification before letting them vote." Valdes's contemporaneous reporting of these events to the county was confirmed by an electoral official I spoke to. She showed great civic spirit, returning from Florida despite financial strain and testifying on crutches due to a recent injury. Ms. Valdes said she showed her voter registration card to vote, but was repeatedly asked for her driver's license. Only later, when she showed her poll inspector ID, was she not asked for her license.

VALDES: I brought my card register [voter registration card], and they ask me for my driver license. I had to show it all the time.

INTERVIEWER: And this happened more than once?

VALDES: Oh, yes.

INTERVIEWER: Does it happen every time you vote?

VALDES: In the last couple of years, no, because I bring my—the paper that say inspector, and they don't ask me for that [driver's license]. But before I have it [polling inspector ID] yes, I have to [show my license each time].

Ms. Valdes testified that other poll workers asked certain Latinos to show a driver's license to vote. Ms. Valdes speaks strongly accented English, with errors, so she likely would have been asked for extra ID.

VALDES: When the person speaks English, no, they don't asking. But when the person doesn't speak English, they ask. So Spanish people speak good English, they don't ask. But when they speak English, they have an accent, they asking. Sometime because they look Spanish ... (*U.S. v. Village of Port Chester*, Preliminary Injunction Hearings (S.D. N.Y. 2007), 888)

INTERVIEWER: Was every single Hispanic ... asked for their driver's license identification before they were permitted to vote?

VALDES: Okay. If they come ten Spanish, they ask for eight. If ten persons come in, they ask to eight people ... and two not ... When they [Spanish-speaking, -accented, -looking voters] going to speak, they [poll workers] gave them more hard time. They don't speak English, they give them more hard time. (890).

A related scene occurred in 2010. A woman I call Maria Moreno, a light-skinned Latina who speaks English well, is a naturalized U.S. citizen, was a long-time poll worker, and worked Port Chester's first cumulative voting and early voting election, three years after the trial. Aldo Rodriguez, who was widely disliked for starting the case, was shuttling voters to the polls for a candidate I call Joe Mano, a Latino running as a write-in candidate after being kicked off the ballot on technicalities. Port Chester has many such mobilizations.

Maria Moreno reported a conversation with three other poll workers, all white, older women, enacting the illegal Latino voter threat narrative. One poll worker observing Rodriguez bringing in groups of Latino voters said, "There he is again! Why is he bringing them in? Is he gonna win? Is he paying them to vote? How do we know they are not illegals?" When Maria Moreno answered that you cannot vote unless you are a U.S. citizen, the other ladies looked dissatisfied: "Yes, but how do we know?" The third poll worker suggested asking these Latino voters for ID to screen out "illegals." The fourth one said, "You cannot ask them for ID." Maria Moreno, assuaging, said, "Let's compare the signatures in registration book."

Magda Votante: U.S. Born, Treated as Illegal

Magda Votante, as I call her, is a young U.S.-born, Port Chester–raised Latina who tried to vote in 2014 and 2015. In 2014, she helped a naturalized citizen friend, translating for him as he showed an ID to vote. When she tried to vote, poll workers said they could not find her in the registry, asking whether it was her polling voting place. She withdrew without voting. When she tried to vote in 2015, she wanted to support Charlie Pino, who had personally asked for her vote. The first poll worker asked Magda her for ID. Magda replied, "I don't think I need to show you my ID." The poll worker insisted: "I just need to see it quickly." At this, Magda presented her ID. The poll worker then referred her to another poll worker to find Magda's name in the registry. The second poll worker said, "I don't think you're in here . . . Are you sure this is the right district?" She then, according to Magda, "flipped through the book" to find Magda's last name, but "she started like in the middle of the book" even though Magda's last name began with a letter at the end of the alphabet. When the poll worker got to the section beginning with that letter, Magda assumed she would look toward the beginning of the listings—the second letter in Magda's name is "a." The poll worker flipped all the way through the pages, not once, but three times, never making eye contact with Magda or asking how to spell the name. After the third time, Magda said, "Let me see the book." She had seen her signature as the poll worker had flipped through the pages. With the book turned around, Magda pointed to her signature. She was then allowed to vote.

Magda was upset that she was required to show ID. She also saw the two poll workers exchange "a look" when she said that she did not need to show her ID, and another look when she found her own signature. Magda said, "I feel like she thought I couldn't vote . . . they looked at each other while I was going through the book . . . I didn't know if they were trying to say something . . . if she thought I couldn't vote" because she was not a citizen. She felt stigmatized as an "illegal" trying to vote.

Magda both resisted and recognized that they were discriminating against her as a Latina. The encounter raised questions for her about discrimination, even as it prompted her to rationalize the poll workers' behavior as something other than discrimination. She did not want to think her neighbors would discriminate; she wanted to extend the presumption of moral competence and goodness she wanted them to extend to her. She wondered what the rules were—is it ok to ask for identification in Port Chester? She wondered whether the ladies had been told to ask Latinos for ID, whether it was a practice among poll workers. If so, she should not individually fault the two she had dealt with. "If you know that white people think that Latinos can't vote or that illegals are trying to vote—it's this already made-up idea— if your supervisor had told you . . . if other poll workers thought . . . that Latinos who couldn't vote were trying to vote . . . or other poll workers ask for ID—so she did it. [Then] She's not a racist."

Asking Latinos for IDs this way imposes a stigma: "But when Latinos come in to vote, they can't vote because you're [poll workers are] supposed to ask them for ID. . . . It was obvious that my name was there the entire time. It really *was* to give me a hard time—because my name was there the entire time!" When Magda pointed to her name in the book, she thought, "Really—you couldn't see this?!" In her account, she alternatively tried to explain the poll workers behavior as nondiscrimination, or at least as not motivated by their personal racism, and being angry she felt targeted by the "made-up idea" that "illegal" Latinos were voting. When I asked about this slippage, she said, "When I came in, I didn't think she's gonna give me a hard time. . . . I don't like to say people are racist—even Donald Trump. I don't want to believe this." This treatment conflicted with what she expected as an American who works hard and plays by the rules, and earned a merit scholarship in college. Her question was, why *would* someone discriminate against her?

These cases tell the same story. First, Maria Moreno's interaction takes place three years after, and Magda Votante's eight years after, the VRA trial, suggesting that discrimination continues. Second, white poll workers in each case enact the illegal Latino voter threat narrative. In Maria's story, the threat of Joe Mano's winning is linked to the threat of "illegals" voting, illegal vote buying, or Latino electoral power. By asking these questions in series, these poll workers linked Latinos with potential illegality, just as Ms. Valdes described. Third, Magda was treated as if she were "illegal." The apparent attempt to keep her from voting was only defeated by her seeing her signature and demanding they turn the book around. Finally, the white poll workers deny Magda the presumption of legitimacy they extend to other voters. She feels that they gave her a hard time because they thought she was "illegal"—stigma in action. Other Latinos, some voting for more than a decade, report being asked to present an ID to vote. I have confirmed with voting officials that none has *ID* next to their name in the registry, and therefore should not be asked for it.

These cases resonate with Eddie Lavoro's seeing a voter who needs translation as an "illegal." (I have observed Eddie with friends of other races, and recall he and his wife giving a friend from the senior center, an African American, a ride to a summer picnic. Their relaxed conversation showed mutual fondness and friendship. I report this to avoid caricaturing those who have trusted me by giving interviews.) In the polling place, Eddie silently objected when poll workers translated:

> In the last election . . . a guy in front of me was talking in Spanish to a girl, who showed him how to fill out the election sheet [ballot] . . . he has to know that *without* an assistant. . . . to be a citizen, you have to speak English . . . to read a paragraph. . . . My impression—he is not a citizen. They shoulda kicked his ass outta there. He shouldn't be allowed to vote.

Eddie did not report speaking to the man needing translation, nor does objection to this translation make him a bigot. But objecting to legally required language assistance for an apparently naturalized U.S. citizen voter *does* enact the illegal Latino voter threat narrative and white citizen gaze. Such quiet objections, in combination with poll workers openly discussing the threat of "illegals" voting, would create a hostile, discriminatory climate for Latino voters.

CONCLUSION AND ANALYSIS

This paper documents dangers to American democracy. Divisive voter ID laws are a cure worse than the declared illness: data point to virtually no voter imposter fraud, which voter ID laws fight, but show many older, poorer, minority and naturalized immigrant voters being prevented from voting. These facts, and others—gun permits, but not college IDs, can be used to vote in some states—suggest that such laws seek to limit voting to favor Republicans. In Port Chester, stronger voter ID laws were publicly urged to defend against the threat of "illegal" Latino voters. This narrative was enacted in conversation in polling places and in questionable requests for ID from Latino voters. Such stories set off my crazy meter: why *would* undocumented people hiding their lives from the government try to vote and risk arrest and deportation?

The illegal Latino voter narrative harms American democracy. This paper documents an election stolen by racial discrimination; a lawyer and local leader demanding protection from the effects of America's key voting rights law; another leader attacking a Latina leader as such for her political engagement; citizens and poll workers who look at and treat Latino citizen voters as potentially illegal voters; and a young U.S. citizen Latina who felt treated like an "illegal" by poll workers. The illegal Latino voter narrative is expressed through the white citizen gaze and tells a story wherein many white Americans see Latinos as dangerous if politically active, as unworthy of full membership in American society, and as causes of decline in American life. This narrative makes all Latino voters potential "illegals," depriving them of the presumed legitimacy extended to other voters (Goffman 1963; Gonzales 2016). The narrative also emerges in many white Port Chester residents' belief that an unknown but huge percentage of Latinos in Port Chester are

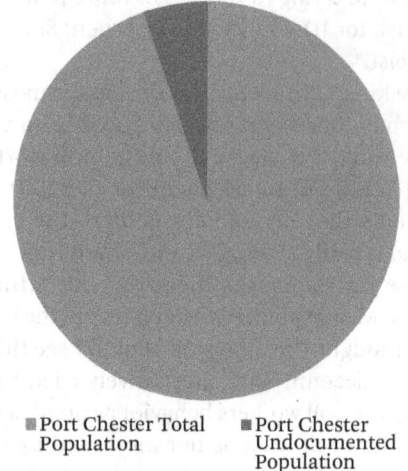

Figure 1. Port Chester Undocumented Population

■ Port Chester Total Population   ■ Port Chester Undocumented Population

Source: Author's compilation.
Note: I estimate that about 5.6 percent of Port Chester's population is undocumented Latino immigrants. I have no evidence of any noncitizen voting.

undocumented. Figure 1 shows that the undocumented Latino population in Port Chester is about 5.6 percent of the total population, a slim slice of the pie chart.[19] Figure 2 shows how the emotional perception of the percentage of "illegal" Latino voters changes when looking

---

19. I offer an estimate, drawing on my prior work for the Census Bureau (Smith 1996), ten years in the field in Port Chester, and review of other such estimations (Passel 2016), using the 2014 American Community Survey (ACS) data, the best, most recent data available. The 2014 ACS estimates Port Chester has 29,275 persons, including 11,534 born in Latin America. I will focus my estimation on those from Mexico and Central America, because I believe they account for a very large majority of the undocumented population in Port Chester, and that Colombians, Ecuadorians, and Peruvians have very low rates of undocumented status. The ACS shows 9,340 foreign born noncitizens, including 8,777 noncitizens born in Latin America. It reports 3,444 *persons* born in Mexico and 2,562 born in Central America, for a total of 6,006 persons born in those two regions. ACS data also show 2,945 and 2,029 *noncitizens* from Mexico and Central America, respectively, for a total noncitizen population from these two regions of 4,974. (The difference between persons and noncitizens is an estimate of naturalized citizens from those countries.) Estimating conservatively, we assume a 10 percent undercount of the foreign-born Mexican and Central American population in Port Chester, for a total estimated population of 5,527. Port Chester is likely to have a lower undercount than other places (for example, with migrant workers or mainly new immigrants) because it is an urban location with a mainly settled immigrant population, and it worked with the Census Bureau in 2010 to increase awareness of and trust in the census to get an accurate count. Also, I use the 10 percent rate usually used to estimate undocumented persons; but legally resident persons are usually missed at a lower rate, 2.5 percent, so my estimate should be high. Assuming a 30 percent rate of undocumented status among Mexican and Central American noncitizen immigrants (some undocumented people gain legal status over time) yields 1,658 undocumented Mexicans and Central Americans in Port Chester. Dividing 1,658 by the 29,275 total population suggests that 5.6 percent of the total population of Port Chester is undocumented. Interestingly, Port Chester had 3,050 naturalized citizens in 2000 (U.S. Census) and 3,906 in 2014 (ACS), an 856 citizen increase. The undocumented population is much less than the naturalized citizen population.

Figure 2. Illegal Latino Voter Threat Narrative

Source: Author's compilation.
Note: The circles represent how the illegal Latino voter threat narrative can alter the perception of some in Port Chester to see all Latino voters as potentially illegal Latino voters, especially if they have an accent, need translation, or "look Spanish."

through the white citizen gaze. The illegal and Latino sets can be nearly coterminous, because all Latinos are seen as *potential illegals*.

The stigma of illegality and the white citizen gaze can undermine intergroup relationships by introducing scorn and envy into social life (Fiske 2011). We envy those we see as our social betters, wanting what they have, but dehumanize those we scorn, even comparing them to animals. Using brain imaging, Fiske finds that when seeing pictures of the most scorned, stigmatized types of people—drug addicts, the homeless—the medial prefrontal cortex does not activate as it does when seeing images of all other groups, stigmatized or not. We can speculate that narratives aggressively stigmatizing Latinos as "illegals"—or comparing them to animals, as I have heard done in Port Chester—puts them in a social category where stigmatizers do not respond to them, biologically, as fellow humans (Hodson, Kteily, and Hoffarth 2014; Kteily, Watz, and Cotterhill 2015).

The longitudinal saturated case study is well suited to document how narratives circulate and foster discrimination. The survey shows widespread belief that "illegal" Latinos are voting in Port Chester. Ethnography and interviews document how people have experienced this narrative in voting. Using various data sources to study the same processes over time and in situ strengthens the analysis, contributing to research on implicit bias, voting rights, and how to better integrate immigrants and their children into American politics.

This analysis points to several policy recommendations (see Presidential Commission 2014). First, New York State voting law and practice should be changed to require poll workers to document every time someone is redirected to another polling place, asked for identification, or told they are not in the voting registry, and these records should be reviewed right after the election with the poll workers involved. Although state law currently requires a challenge report of anyone trying to vote but not in the registry, these measures do not address all the ways voters get turned away. Latino voters report being told they are not in the registry or are in the wrong polling place and sent to another one, where they may again not be listed, and give up. Currently, such redirections and dismissals are largely without cost. No one knows how many people are redirected, turned away or asked for ID, or why. Explicitly requiring poll workers to record, justify, and review every request could decrease discrimination by making them think it through in the moment and be accountable afterward. Such steps would also prevent or catch imposter voting, the goal of voter ID laws. Contact information for the voter should be kept for easy follow-up.

A hidden cost to being treated badly at the polls, or making voting difficult, is to discourage future voting. David Cruz supporters would not turn out for the rerun election because they did not believe their vote would be counted. Magda Votante fears she will be treated as an "illegal" again. There is an incentive in political systems to have opponent's supporters treated worse than your own, so they do not show up to vote next time. We must recognize this incentive and fight it.

Second, poll worker training in bias, including on implicit bias, should be mandatory. If we follow Magda Votante's and David Cruz's generous view, the issue could be that the poll workers asking Latinos for ID or saying "Don't let the illegals vote" do not realize that their actions can constitute discrimination. If there is intent to discriminate, training combined with the reporting requirements listed earlier could help limit it. In poll worker trainings I attended, bias and what would concretely constitute it have not been fully discussed. They told poll workers to not discriminate—a fair point, but not enough.

Third, Port Chester and America must reframe how they talk about immigrants and integration, especially in politics. Immigrants are revered in American history, but have been repeatedly vilified, especially during ethnic succession, when one ethnic group emerges in its own right in a place where another has continued to hold power despite declining numbers. I would adapt Laurence Fuchs's (1990) insight that America is first a civic community united by a commitment to a set of political beliefs and institutions, driven by the belief that hard work should create opportunity for one's children. When these conditions are met, it should be possible to accommodate racial, ethnic, and religious difference.

In its 2.3 square miles, Port Chester confronts key issues confronting America: immigrant integration in towns with older, white voters and younger, nonwhite immigrants and their children; the challenges of having good schools, affordable housing, and reasonable taxes; and more. A key question underpinning many issues is this: Whose town (or country) is it? Who truly belongs here, and is truly a member of the community, and who is not? And how do you know? Like America, Port Chester is schizophrenic on these questions and immigration. Many smart, dedicated people work to develop all of Port Chester, but others believe that immigration has ruined the town and America. They see the past as better, and blame the federal government for letting in too many Latino immigrants and giving away the country. In this view, Latinos—unlike Italian or Polish immigrants—do not know how to assimilate.

Such threat narratives undermine integration in Port Chester, as in Barry Deutche's racially divisive attacks on Bianca Ibanez. First vilified as a double *and* triple agent—whatever that means—for Latinos against Port Chester, Ibanez represents something great about Port Chester and America. That a young girl could come to Port Chester, attend its schools, get a graduate degree, and come back to serve her home town in her professional and political life embodies the American Dream. That she was treated—in a divisive electoral strategy—as a Latina who had gotten out of her place, constituting a threat to Port Chester—is shameful. Yet all is not lost in Port Chester, nor in America. Many people of goodwill seek to integrate immigrants and their children and to create a stronger community.

REFERENCES

Abbott, Andrew. 2001. *Time Matters*. Chicago: University of Chicago Press.

Alba, Richard. 2014. *Blurring the Color Line. The New Chance for a More Integrated America*. Cambridge, Mass.: Harvard University Press.

Alba, Richard, and Nancy Foner. 2009. "Entering the Precincts of Power: Do National Differences Matter for Immigrant Minority Political Representation?" In *Bringing Outsiders In: Transatlantic Perspectives on Immigrant Political Incorporation*, edited by Jennifer Hochschild and John Mollenkopf. Ithaca, N.Y.: Cornell University Press.

Alba, Richard, and Victor Nee. 2003. *Remaking Assimilation Theory*. Cambridge, Mass.: Harvard University Press.

Allport, Gordon. 1958. *The Nature of Prejudice*. New York: Doubleday.

Anderson, Kristi. 2008. "In Whose Interest? Political Parties, Context and the Incorporation of Immigrants." In *New Race Politics in America: Understanding Minority and Immigrant Politics*, edited by Jane Junn and Kerry L. Haynie. New York: Cambridge University Press.

Aptekar, Sofya. 2008. "Highly Skilled But Unwelcome in Politics: Asian Indians and Chinese in a New Jersey Suburb." In *Civic Hopes and Political Realities: Immigrants, Community Organizations and Political Engagement*, edited by Karthick Ramakrishnan and Irene Bloemraad. New York: Russell Sage Foundation.

Black, Tim. 2009. *When A Heart Turns Rock Solid: The Lives of Three Puerto Rican Brothers On and Off the Streets*. New York: Vintage.

Blair, George S. 1958. "Cumulative Voting: Patterns

of Party Alliance and Rational Choice in Illinois State Legislative Contests." *American Political Science Review* 52(1): 123–30.

Blalock, Hubert M., Jr. 1967. *Towards a Theory of Minority-Group Relations*. New York: John Wiley & Sons.

Blanton, Hart, and James Jaccard. 2008. "Unconscious Racism: A Concept in Pursuit of a Measure." *Annual Review of Sociology* 34: 277–97.

Bloemraad, Irene. 2006. *Becoming a Citizen*. Berkeley and Los Angeles: University of California Press.

———. 2013. "The Great Concern of Government: Public Policy as Material and Symbolic Resource." In *Outsiders No More: Models of Political Incorporation*, edited by Jennifer Hochschild, Michael Jones-Correa, Jacqueline Chattopadhyay, and Claudine Gay. Oxford: Oxford University Press.

Blumer, Herbert. 1958. "Race Prejudice as a Sense of Group Position." *Pacific Sociological Review* 1(1): 3–7.

Bobo, Lawrence, and Vincent L. Hutchings. 1996. "Perceptions of Racial Group Competition: Extending Blumer's Theory of Group Position to a Multiracial Context." *American Sociological Review* 61(6): 951–72.

Bobo, Lawrence, James R. Kluegel, and Ryan A. Smith. 1997. "Laissez-Faire Racism: The Crystallization of a Kinder, Gentler Antiblack Ideology." In *Racial Attitudes in the 1990s*, edited by Jack Martin and Steven A. Tuch. Westport, Conn.: Praeger.

Bonilla-Silva, Eduardo. 2006. *Racism Without Racists*. Lanham, Md.: Rowan and Littlefield.

Boyce, M. E. 1995. "Collective Centering and Collective Sense-Making in the Stories and Story-Telling of One Organization." *Organization Studies* 16(1): 107–37.

Brischetto, Robert, and Richard L. Engstrom. 1997. "Cumulative Voting and Latino Representation: Exit Surveys in Fifteen Texas Communities." *Social Science Quarterly* 78(4): 973–91.

Browning, Rufus, Dale Marshall, and David Tabb. 1984. *Protest Is Not Enough: The Struggle of Blacks and Hispanics for Equality in Urban Politics*. Berkeley: University of California Press.

Butler, John Sibley. 1978. "Institutional Racism." *Journal of Black Sociology* 7(1): 5–25.

Calogero, Rachel. 2004. "A Test of Objectification Theory: The Effect of the Male Gaze on Appearance Concerns in College Women." *Psychology of Women Quarterly* 28(1): 16–21.

Canon, David. 1999. *Race, Redistricting and Representation: The Unintended Consequences of Black Majority Districts*. Chicago: University of Chicago Press.

Chavez, Leo. 2008. *The Latino Threat Narrative*. Stanford, Calif.: Stanford University Press.

Cobb, Rachel, D., James Greiner, and Kevin Quinn. 2012. "Can Voter ID Laws Be Administered in a Race Neutral Manner? Evidence from Boston in 2008." *Quarterly Journal of Political Science* 7(1): 1–33.

Cohen, Stanley. 1972. *Folk Devils and Moral Panics* London: MacGibbon and Kee.

Cole, Richard L., Delbert A. Taebel, and Richard L. Engstrom. 1990. "Cumulative Voting in a Municipal Election: A Note on Voter Reactions and Electoral Consequences." *Western Political Quarterly* 43(1): 191–99.

Coontz, Stephanie. 2000. *The Way We Never Were*, 2nd ed. New York: Basic Books.

Costelloe, Michael. 2006. "Immigration as Moral Panic: Ideology and the Universalization of Threat." Paper presented at the annual meeting of the American Society of Criminology. Los Angeles (November 1).

Croom, Adam. 2008. "Racial Epithets: What We Say and Mean by Them." *Dialogue* 51(1): 34–45.

Crosby, Faye. 1984. "The Denial of Personal Discrimination." *American Behavioral Scientist* 27(3): 371–86.

De la Garza, Rodolfo O., and Louis DeSipio. 2006. "Reshaping the Tub: The Limits of the VRA for Latino Electoral Politics." In *The Future of the Voting Rights Act*, edited by David Epstein, Richard H. Pildes, Rodolfo O. de la Garza, and Sharyn O'Halloran. New York: Russell Sage Foundation.

De la Garza, Rodolfo O., Angelo Falcon, and F. Chris Garcia. 1996. "Will the Real Americans Please Stand Up?" *American Political Science Review* 40(2): 335–51

Delano, Alejandro. 2014. "Invisible Victims: Undocumented Migrants and the Aftermath of September 11th." *Politics and Society* 42(3): 399–421.

DeSipio, Louis. 2013. "From Naturalized Citizen to Voter: The Context of Naturalization and Electoral Participation in Latino Communities." In *Immigration and the Border: Politics and Policy in the New Latino Century*, edited by David Leal and

Jose Limon. Notre Dame, Ind.: University of Notre Dame.

DeSipio, Louis, and Rodolfo O. de la Garza. 2015. *U.S. Immigration in the Twenty-First Century: Making Americans, Remaking America*. Boulder, Colo.: Westview Press.

DiTomaso, Nancy. 2013. *The American Non-Dilemma: Racial Inequality Without Racism*. New York: Russell Sage Foundation.

Duneier, Mitchell. 1999. *Sidewalk*. New York: Farrar, Strauss and Giroux.

Engstrom, Richard L. 1992. "Modified Multi-Seat Election Systems as Remedies for Minority Vote Dilution." *Stetson Law Review* 21(3): 743–70.

Engstrom, Richard, and Robert Brischetto. 1997. "Cumulative Voting and Latino Representation: Exit Surveys from Fifteen Texas Communities." *Social Science Quarterly* 78 (December): 973–91.

Engstrom, Richard L., Delbert A. Taebel, Richard L. Cole. 1988. "Cumulative Voting as a Remedy for Minority Vote Dilution: The Case of Alamogordo, New Mexico." *Journal of Law and Politics* 5(3): 469–97.

Epstein, David L., Richard H. Pildes, Rodolfo O. de la Garza, and Sharon O'Halloran, eds. 2006. *The Future of the Voting Rights Act*. New York: Russell Sage Foundation.

Erie, Stephen. 1998. *Rainbow's End: Irish-Americans and the Dilemmas of Urban Machine Politics 1840–1984*. Berkeley: University of California Press.

Esposito, Luigi, and John Murphy. 1999. "Desensitizing Herbert Blumer's Work on Race Relations." *Sociological Quarterly* 40(3): 397–410.

Ewick, Patricia, and Susan Silbey. 1995. "Subversive Stories and Hegemonic Tales: Toward a Sociology of Narrative." *Law and Society Review* 29(2): 197–226.

Feagin, Joe. 2006. *Systemic Racism*. New York: Routledge.

Feagin, Joe R., and Douglas Lee Eckberg. 1980. "Discrimination: Motivation, Action, Effects and Context." *Annual Review of Sociology* 6: 1–20.

Ferrara, JoAnne, Janice Nath, and Irma Guadarrama. 2014. *Creating Visions for University-School Partnerships: Research in Professional Development Schools*. Charlotte, N.C.: Information Age Publishers.

Fiske, Susan. 2011. *Envy Up, Scorn Down: How Status Divides US*. New York: Russell Sage Foundation.

Flores, Rene D. 2014. "In the Eye of the Storm: How Did Hazelton's Restrictive Immigration Ordinance Affect Local Interethnic Relations?" *American Behavioral Scientist* 58(13): 1743–63.

———. 2015. "Taking the Law into Their Own Hands: Do Local Anti-Immigrant Ordinances Increase Gun Sales?" *Social Problems* 62(3): 363–90.

Foucault, Michel. 1977. *Discipline and Punish: The Birth of the Prison*. New York: Pantheon Books.

Fuchs, Laurence H. 1990. *The American Kaleidoscope*. Hanover, N.H.: University Press of New England.

Gamson, William A., and Andre Modigliani. 1989. "Media Discourse and Public Opinion on Nuclear Power: A Constructionist Approach." *American Journal of Sociology* 95(1): 1–37.

George, Alexander, and Alexander Bennett. 2005. *Case Studies and Theory Development in the Social Sciences*. Cambridge, Mass.: Harvard University Press.

Goffman, Erving. 1963. *Stigma: Notes on the Management of Spoiled Identity*. Upper Saddle River, N.J.: Prentice Hall.

Goldburg, Carol B. 1994. "The Accuracy of Game Theory Predictions for Political Behavior: Cumulative Voting in Illinois Revisited." *Journal of Politics* 56(4): 885–900.

Gonzales, Roberto. 2016. *Lives in Limbo*. Berkeley: University of California Press.

Gordon, Milton. 1964. *Assimilation in American Life*. New York: Oxford University Press.

Gronke, Paul, Eva Galanes-Rosenbaum, and Peter Miller. 2007. "Early Voting and Turnout." *PS: Political Science* 40(4): 639–45.

Gronke, Paul, and Daniel Krantz Toffey. 2008. "The Psychological and Institutional Determinants of Early Voting." *Journal of Social Issues* 64(3): 503–24.

Guinier, Lani. 1994. *The Tyranny of the Majority: Fundamental Fairness in Representative Democracy*. New York: The Free Press.

Hajer, Maarten A. 1995. *The Politics of Environmental Discourse: Ecological Modernization and the Policy Process*. Oxford: Oxford University Press.

Hajer, Maarten A., and David Laws. 2006. "Ordering Through Discourse." In *The Oxford Handbook of Public Policy*, edited by Robert Goodin, Michael Moran, and Martin Rein. New York: Oxford University Press.

Haynes, Chris, Jennifer Merolla, and S. Karthick Ramakrishnan. 2016. *Framing Immigrants: News*

Coverage, Public Opinion, and Policy. New York: Russell Sage Foundation.

Hochschild, Arlie Russell. 2016. *Strangers in Their Own Land: Anger and Mourning on the American Right*. New York: The New Press.

Hochschild, Jennifer, Jacqueline Chattopadhyay, Claudine Gay, and Michael Jones-Correa, eds. 2013. Introduction to *Outsiders No More? Models of Immigrant Incorporation*. New York: Oxford University Press.

Hochschild, Jennifer, and John Mollenkopf. 2009. *Bringing Outsiders In: Transatlantic Perspectives on Immigrant Political Incorporation*. Ithaca, N.Y.: Cornell University Press.

Hodson, Gordon, Nour Kteily, and Mark Hoffarth. 2014. "Of Filthy Pigs and Subhuman Mongrels: Dehumanization, Disgust and Intergroup Prejudice." *Testing, Psychometrics and Methodology in Applied Psychology* 21(3): 267–84.

Holmes, Seth. 2012. "The Clinical Gaze in the Practice of Migrant Health: Mexican Migrants in the United States." *Social Science and Medicine* 74(6): 873–81.

Johnson, James, Leslie Ashburn-Nardo, and Len Leccil. 2013. "Individual Differences in Discrimination Expectations Moderate the Impact of Target Stereotypically Black Physical Features on Racism-Related Responses in Blacks." *Journal of Black Psychology* 39(6): 560–84.

Jones-Correa, Michael. 1998. *Between Two Islands: The Political Predicament of Latinos in New York City*. Ithaca, N.Y.: Cornell University Press.

———. 2005. "Language Provisions Under the Voting Rights Act: How Effective Are They?" *Social Science Quarterly* 86(3): 549–64.

———. 2009. "Bringing Outsiders In: Questions of Immigrant Incorporation." In *The Politics of Democratic Inclusion*, edited by Christina Wolbrecht and Rodney E. Hero. Philadelphia, Pa.: Temple University Press.

———. 2013. "Thru-Ways, By-Ways and Cul-de-Sacs of Immigrant Political Incorporation." In *Outsiders No More? Models of Immigrant Incorporation*, edited by Jennifer Hochschild, Jacqueline Chattooadhyay, Claudine Gay, and Michael Jones-Correa. New York: Oxford University Press.

Junn, Jane, and Kerry Haynie. 2008. *New Race Politics in America: Understanding Minority and Immigrant Politics*. New York: Cambridge University Press.

Kasinitz, Phillip, John Mollenkopf, Mary Waters, and Sarah Holdaway. 2008. *Inheriting the City: The Second Generation Comes of Age*. New York: Russell Sage Foundation.

Katz, Jack. 1997. "Ethnography's Warrants." *Sociological Methods and Research* 25(4): 391–423.

———. 2001. "From How to Why: On Luminous Description and Causal Inference in Ethnography, Part 1." *Ethnography* 2(4): 443–73.

———. 2002. "From How to Why: On Luminous Description and Causal Inference in Ethnography, Part 2." *Ethnography* 3(1): 63–90.

Kteily, Nour, Emile Bruneau, Adam Watz, and Sarah Cotterhill. 2015. "The Ascent of Man: Theoretical and Empirical Evidence for Blatant Discrimination." *Journal of Personality and Social Psychology* 109(5): 901–31.

Levitt, Justin. 2007. *The Truth About Voter Fraud*. New York: Brennan Center for Justice.

Longazel, Jaime. 2016. *Undocumented Fears: Immigration and the Politics of Divide and Conquer in Hazleton, Pennsylvania*. Philadelphia, Pa.: Temple University Press.

Marrow, Helen B. 2011. *New Destination Dreaming: Immigration, Race, and Legal Status in the Rural American South*. Stanford, Ca.: Stanford University Press.

Massey, Douglas S., and Magaly Sanchez. 2008. *New Faces in New Places*. New York: Russell Sage Foundation.

Matsuda, Mari, Charles R. Lawrence III, Richard Delgado, and Kimberle Crenshaw. 1993. *Words That Wound: Critical Race Theory, Assaultive Speech, and the First Amendment*. Boulder, Colo.: Westview Press.

Maxwell, Rashaan. 2014. "Perceived Discrimination Across Institutional Fields: Racial Minorities in the United Kingdom." *European Sociological Review* 31(3): 342–53.

McCrary, Peyton, Christopher B. Seaman, and Richard Valelly. 2006. "The Law of Preclearance." In *The Future of the Voting Rights Act*, edited by Rodolfo de la Garza and Louis DeSipio. New York: Russell Sage Foundation.

Minnite, Lorraine C. 2009. "Lost in Translation? A Critical Reappraisal of the Concept of Immigrant Political Incorporation." In *Outsiders In: Transatlantic Perspectives on Immigrant Political Incorporation*, edited by Jennifer Hochschild and John Mollenkopf. Ithaca, N.Y.: Cornell University Press.

———. 2010. *The Myth of Voter Fraud*. Ithaca, N.Y.: Cornell University Press.

Mollenkopf, John. 2013. "Dimensions of Immigrant Political Incorporation." In *Outsiders No More? Models of Immigrant Incorporation*, edited by Jennifer Hochschild, Jacqueline Chattooadhyay, Claudine Gay, and Michael Jones-Correa. New York: Oxford University Press.

Myrdal, Gunnar. 1964. *An American Dilemma*. New York: McGraw Hill.

New York Times. 2016. "The Success of the Myth of Voter Fraud." Editorial, September 19.

Page, Antony, and Michael J. Pitts. 2009. "Poll Workers, Election Administration and the Problem of Implicit Bias." *Michigan Journal of Race and Law* 15(1): 1–56.

Parker, Christopher, and Matt Barreto. 2013. *Change They Can't Believe In: The Tea Party and Reactionary Politics in America*. Princeton, N.J.: Princeton University Press.

Parrett, William, and Kathleen Budge. 2012. *Turning High Poverty Schools into High Performing Schools*. Alexandria Va.: ACSD.

Patterson, Maurice, and Richard Elliott. 2002. "Negotiating Masculinities: Advertising and the Inversion of the Male Gaze." *Consumption, Markets and Culture* 5(3): 231–49.

Passel, Jeffrey. 2016. "Measuring Illegal Immigration: How Pew Research Center Counts Unauthorized Immigrants in the U.S." September 20. Washington, D.C.: Pew Research Center. Accessed February 28, 2017. http://www.pewresearch.org/fact-tank/2016/09/20/measuring-illegal-immigration-how-pew-research-center-counts-unauthorized-immigrants-in-the-u-s/.

Pease Chock, Phyllis. 1995. "Ambiguity in Policy Discourse: Congressional Talk About Immigration." *Policy Sciences* 28(2): 165–84.

Port Chester Comprehensive Plan. 2012. Village of Port Chester, Comprehensive Plan. Recommendation Draft. March 21, 2012.

Portes, Alejandro, and Rubén G. Rumbaut. 2001. *Legacies*. Berkeley: University of California Press.

Presidential Commission on Election Administration (Presidential Commission). 2014. *The American Voting Experience: Report and Recommendations of the Presidential Commission on Election Administration*. Washington: Government Printing Office. Accessed January 19, 2017. https://www.supportthevoter.gov/files/2014/01/Amer-Voting-Exper-final-draft-01-09-14-508.pdf.

Pritchard, Annette, and Nigel Morgan. 2000. "Privileging the Male Gaze: Gendered Tourism Landscapes." *Annals of Tourism Research* 27(4): 884–905.

Quillian, Lincoln. 1995. "Prejudice as a Response to Perceived Group Threat: Population Composition and Anti-Immigrant and Racial Prejudice in Europe." *American Sociological Review* 60(4): 586–611.

———. 2006. "New Approaches to Understanding Racial Prejudice and Discrimination." *Annual Review of Sociology* 32 (August): 299–328.

———. 2008. "Does Unconscious Racism Exist?" *Social Psychology Quarterly* 71(1): 6–11.

Ramakrishnan, S. Karthick, and Irene Bloemraad. 2008. *Civic Hopes and Political Realities: Immigrants, Community Organizations and Political Engagement*. New York: Russell Sage Foundation.

Rutenberg, Jim. 2015. "The Dream Denied: Disenfranchised." *New York Times Magazine*, August 2.

Sawyer, Jack, and Duncan McRae Jr. 1962. "Game Theory and Cumulative Voting in Illinois: 1902–1954." *American Political Science Review* 56(4): 936–46.

Skelton, Christine. 2010. "Constructing Dominant Masculinity and Negotiating the 'Male Gaze.'" *International Journal of Inclusive Education* 6(1): 17–31.

Skocpol, Theda, and Vanessa Williamson. 2013. *The Tea Party and the Remaking of Republican Conservatism*. New York: Oxford University Press.

Slatky, Alec. 2010. "Debunking Myths About Port Chester." *Fair Vote*, June 25. Accessed December 8, 2016. http://www.fairvote.org/debunking-the-myths-about-port-chester.

Smith, Robert Courtney. 1996. *Counting Migrant Farm Workers: Causes of the Undercount of Farmworkers in the Northeastern United States and Strategies for Improving the 2000 Census*. Final Report to the United States Census Bureau. Washington: Bureau of the Census.

———. 2006a. First Declaration, *U.S. v. Village of Port Chester*, U.S. District Court, S.D. N.Y.

———. 2006b. *Mexican New York*. Berkeley: University of California Press.

———. 2007. Second Declaration, *U.S. v. Village of Port Chester*, U.S. District Court, S.D. N.Y.

Snow, David A., and Robert D. Benford. 1992. "Master Frames and Cycles of Protest." In *Frontiers of Social Movement Theory*, edited by Aldon D. Morris and Carol McClurg Mueller. New Haven, Conn.: Yale University Press.

Somers, Margaret. 1994. "The Narrative Constitution of Identity." *Theory and Society* 23(3): 605–49.

Staats, Cheryl. 2014. *State of the Science: Implicit Bias Review*. Columbus: Ohio State University.

Stein, Robert M. 1988. "Introduction: Early Voting." *Public Opinion Quarterly* 62(1): 57–69.

Stone, Deborah A. 1989. "Causal Stories and the Formation of Policy Agendas." *Political Science Quarterly* 104(2): 281–300.

Thernstrom, Abigail. 1987. *Whose Votes Count? Affirmative Action and the Minority Voting Rights* Cambridge, Mass.: Harvard University Press.

Varsanyi, Monica, ed. 2010. *Taking Local Control: Immigration Policy Activism in U.S. Cities and States*. Stanford, Calif.: Stanford University Press.

Weiser, Wendy, and Vishal Agraharkar. 2012. *Ballot Security and Voter Suppression*. Brennan Center Report.

Winders, Jamie. 2013. *Nashville in the New Millennium*. New York: Russell Sage Foundation.

Wolbrecht, Cristina, and Rodney Hero. 2005. *The Politics of Democratic Inclusion*. Philadelphia, Pa.: Temple University Press.

Wong, Jannelle, S. Karthick Ramakrishnan, Taeku Lee, and Jane Junn, eds. 2011. *Asian American Political Participation*. New York: Russell Sage Foundation.

Zuniga, Victor, and Ruben Hernandez. 2005. *New Destinations: Mexican Immigration in the United States*. New York: Russell Sage Foundation.